This is the second of a set of three volu[...]
which provide a fresh appraisal of the [...]
important thinkers of the nineteenth c[...]
the West. Some essays centre on majo[...]
the period; others cover topics, trends [...]
schools of thought between the French
Revolution and the First World War. The
contributors are amongst the leading scholars in
their field in Europe and North America. They
seek to engage their subjects not only in order to
see what was said but also why it was said and to
explore what is of lasting value in it. Readers,
therefore, will find the essays not only highly
informative about their subject-matter, but also
distinctively personal contributions to the task
of re-evaluating the thought of the nineteenth
century. Contributions are sufficiently clear to
be of use to students in religious studies and
cognate disciplines, but have enough depth and
detail to appeal to scholars.

NINETEENTH CENTURY RELIGIOUS T
IN THE WEST

VOLUME II

NINETEENTH CENTURY RELIGIOUS THOUGHT

IN THE

WEST

VOLUME II

Edited by

NINIAN SMART, JOHN CLAYTON,
STEVEN T. KATZ *and* PATRICK SHERRY

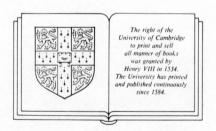

The right of the
University of Cambridge
to print and sell
all manner of books
was granted by
Henry VIII in 1534.
The University has printed
and published continuously
since 1584.

CAMBRIDGE UNIVERSITY PRESS

Cambridge

London   New York   New Rochelle
Melbourne   Sydney

Published by the Press Syndicate of the University of Cambridge
The Pitt Building, Trumpington Street, Cambridge CB2 1RP
32 East 57th Street, New York, NY 10022, USA
10 Stamford Road, Oakleigh, Melbourne 3166, Australia

First published 1985

Printed in Great Britain at the University Press, Cambridge

Library of Congress catalogue card number: 84-14207

British Library Cataloguing in Publication Data
Nineteenth century religious thought in the West.
Vol. 2:
1. Theology, Doctrinal – History – 19th
century
I. Smart, Ninian
230'.09182'1   BT21.2
ISBN 0 521 22832 8

CONTENTS

VOLUME II

I

Samuel Taylor Coleridge

CLAUDE WELCH

In the generation following Coleridge's death in 1834, he was widely recognized as a religious thinker of the greatest significance. True, in the early nineteenth century the apologetic evidence-theology, which had been spurred to renewal (though not reform) by David Hume's essay on miracles, still so preoccupied the English theological scene that Coleridge's *Aids to Reflection* (1825) at first received little notice in either the religious or the popular press. And not a few were then and later to complain of his lack of system and to accuse him variously of being confused, eclectic, muddle-headed, inconsistent, incoherent, a rationalist, a pusillanimous drug-addicted dreamer, and even a papist.

Yet in the much-quoted essays on Bentham and Coleridge (1838 and 1840), John Stuart Mill, certainly no Coleridgean himself, could say that 'there is hardly to be found in England an individual of any importance in the world of the mind, who . . . did not first learn to think from one of these two'; and again that 'every Englishman of the present day is by implication either a Benthamite or a Coleridgean; holds views of human affairs which can only be proved true on the principles either of Bentham or of Coleridge'.[1] And in 1860 Mark Pattison, in *Essays and Reviews*, could write that 'theology had almost died out when it received a new impulse and a new direction from Coleridge'.[2]

Among those most deeply influenced in the nineteenth century by Coleridge were F. D. Maurice (his most famous 'disciple'), Julius Hare, Thomas Arnold, Edward Irving, James Martineau, John Sterling, Thomas Carlyle, and later P. T. Forsyth. F. J. A. Hort, of the Cambridge triumvirate, said that *Aids to Reflection* was a book to be read again and again. And John Henry Newman was impressed. In America, where an edition of the *Aids* was published in 1829, with a long introductory essay by James Marsh, Coleridge affected the course of theology through the Transcendentalists, who read him enthusiastically, and notably through his impact on Horace Bushnell, sometimes called the 'liberalizer' of American theology. *The Friend* and *The Statesman's Manual* were also published (in 1831 and 1832) in the United States.

In the later nineteenth and early twentieth centuries, Coleridge was less widely attended to as a religious thinker. But a powerful resurgence of interest has appeared in recent decades, marked by an extensive literature, much of it drawing on the Notebooks, the Marginalia, etc., recently published for the first time (see the Bibliographical Note). Coleridge must again be seen as a real turning point into the new kinds of theologizing that mark the nineteenth century, a thinker as important for British and American thought as were Schleiermacher and Hegel.

The context of Coleridge's religious thinking

Our concern is with Coleridge as a religious thinker, and particularly with his principles and themes as they came to mature expression in the writings from 1817. Yet Coleridge was remarkably sensitive to the many movements of his time, and prior to his decisive meeting with Wordsworth (1795) and turn to poetry rather than politics, he had gone through an intellectual odyssey that included being an enthusiast for French Republicanism, a necessitarian of the school of Hartley (even to the insistence on the corporeality of thought), and a unitarian of the school of Priestley. The years from 1795 to 1802 were the great burst of his creative imagination, the time of his best-known poetry, joyous in nature, immanental and panentheistic in outlook.

A 'middle period' culminated in the composition in 1815 of the *Biographia Literaria: Or, Biographical Sketches of My Literary Life and Opinions* (pub. 1817), the climax of his literary criticism and theorizing. This was the period of his deepest plunges into Kant, Fichte, and Schelling, as well as new reading of Jakob Boehme, with whose work (along with Neo-Platonists, Scotus Erigena, and some Cabalistic writings) he had become acquainted earlier. And it was a time of intense personal struggle, not least with opium addiction, partly conquered in 1816.

In the prose writings after 1815 the religious and ethical reflections come strongly to the fore, and in the later poetry the concern with evil and with transcendence is strong. In addition to the *Biographia Literaria*, which concludes with Coleridge's identification of himself with the historic Christian faith, the principal writings in which his mature religious ideas were expressed were *The Friend* (1818, a revision of the periodical published 1809–10), *Aids to Reflection* (1825), *On the Constitution of Church and State*

(1830), and the posthumously published *Confessions of an Enquiring Spirit* and the *Essay on Faith*. In these works, above all in *Aids to Reflection*, are sounded the chief religious themes, which were also expanded and illustrated by Coleridge in his Notebooks, in the Opus Maximum, and in the Letters and the Marginalia.

Though the unpublished elaborations reflect Coleridge's desire to write a *Summa* for his age, it is more useful, both in Coleridge's religious ideas and in his thinking generally, to seek out themes and principles than to look for systematic completeness. Coleridge was much more interested in communicating a process of thinking than in the tidy ordering of thoughts. As he put it early in *The Friend*, his aim was to convey 'fundamental' instruction: 'not so much to show the reader this or that fact, as to kindle his own torch for him, . . . to refer men's opinions to their absolute principles, and thence their feelings to the appropriate objects, and in their due degrees; and finally, to apply the principles thus ascertained, to the formation of steadfast convictions concerning the most important questions of politics, morality, and religion – these are to be the objects and the contents of his work'.[3] Despite the sometimes fragmentary or tortuous or even haphazard articulation, the principles of Coleridge were coherent and consistent. His life may have been a muddle, but his thinking was not. The distinctively religious themes and principles, moreover, need to be set in the context of pervasive and life-long concerns, which gave his thought fundamental unity.

One of those was precisely a quest and sense for the whole as a living unity. As he wrote, 'My mind feels as if it ached to behold and know something *great*, something *one* and *indivisible*.'[4] Another was his deep sense of social need and his hope for the revitalization of the whole of morality and English society (including the church), a concern expressed from the time of the early political enthusiasms through the first 'Lay Sermon', *The Statesman's Manual* (1816), to *On the Constitution of the Church and State*.

In his writings on literature, grammar, biology, Baconian science, psychology, politics, philosophy and ethics, as well as theology, Coleridge was engaged in a great struggle for society and self, since he himself had to win the victory over the tradition of Locke and Hume (see esp. Chs. IX and X of *Biographia Literaria*). It was a war against the decayed rationalism of the dominant modes of thought. In theology, this eighteenth-century rationalism was supremely illustrated in the work of William Paley, notably his *Natural Theology, or Evidences of the Existence and Attributes of the Deity Collected from the Appearances of Nature* (1802; 20th ed., 1820) and his *Evidences of Christianity* (1794; 15th ed., 1811). It was Paley whom Coleridge again and again identified as the theological archenemy, who had to be

3

fought as both unphilosophical and irreligious. Coleridge wrote in the *Aids*: 'I believe myself bound in conscience to throw the whole force of my intellect in the way of this [Paley's] triumphal car, on which the tutelary genius of modern idolatry is borne, even at the risk of being crushed under the wheels.'[5] And he thought it a national disgrace that Paley's *Principles of Moral and Political Philosophy* (1785), in which it was affirmed that 'it is the utility of any moral rule which alone constitutes the obligation of it',[6] was adopted as a text at Cambridge.

But Paley's abstract and impersonal, cold and lifeless argumentation, his natural theology to which Christianity was finally an appendage, was only an epitome of the eighteenth-century rationalism that had to be rejected as bankrupt philosophy. Behind Paley was Locke's psychology and epistemology, which had made Hume's critique inevitable. And farther back was Descartes' absolute mental/material dualism, which for Coleridge had to be rejected in favour of a principle of polarity, of unity in variety. And alongside Paley was Jeremy Bentham (1748–1831), who, if Mill was right, was the real alternative to Coleridge, the symbol in his ethical utilitarianism of what the eighteenth century stood for.[7]

Against all this way of thinking, Coleridge posed a fundamentally contrary view. It was a view informed by Plato, Luther, the Cambridge Platonists, Boehme, Kant and Jacobi, Fichte and Schelling, among others. The extent of Coleridge's dependence on some of these sources, especially the German idealists, has been a matter of lively discussion. But the matter of extent need not concern us greatly. As Barfield puts it, 'there is not much doubt that, as the law now stands, Schelling could have sued Coleridge in respect of one or two pages in the *Biographia Literaria*'.[8] Much more important is the question how Coleridge used the ideas that he drew from many sources. That Coleridge was deeply influenced by Kant, whom he revered, cannot be doubted, but that Coleridge's philosophical orientation was provided by Kant – or by the Platonists or by Boehme – must be doubted. Too much has to be related to grounds of thought in his own existence and to many other thinkers whom he found serviceable. Coleridge's own genius and originality consisted in the power to assimilate and recreate for his purposes.

Against the dominant modes of rationalist thinking, then, which corrupted social thought and politics as much as ethics, philosophy, and religion, by limiting thought to the activities of the 'understanding', which can only distinguish, Coleridge wanted to offer another 'system', a Dynamic Philosophy. This philosophy is responsive to the hunger for unity, but a unity that is productive of differentiation. The key principle is polarity. Polarity is not to be confused with the simple opposition of contrariety, for *polar* opposites generate and interpenetrate each other, and are productive.

The importance of polarity is well put, for example, in the *Theory of Life*, Coleridge's sketch of a better science of nature. A proper theory of life does not rest on the commonplace 'mere assumption' of an arbitrary division of all into 'things with life and things without life'. Rather, he asks, 'what is *not* Life that really *is*?' If Life (= *natura naturans*) be preeminently defined as '*the principle of individuation*, or the power which unites a given *all* into a *whole* that is presupposed by all its parts'; if the 'link that combines the two, and acts throughout both' be defined by 'the *tendency* to *individuation*'; and if 'the one great end of Nature' be 'her ultimate production of the highest and most comprehensive individuality'; then the highest or most general law of that tendency must be '*polarity*, or the essential dualism of Nature, arising out of its productive unity, and still tending to reaffirm it, either as equilibrium, indifference, or identity'.[9]

Precisely in that productive power, by which polarity arises out of unity, do we encounter 'incompatibility with mathematical calculus'. But if the 'understanding' of eighteenth-century rationalism cannot apprehend this, the act of 'imagination' can (see below). Contrary to Descartes and his successors, intelligence and nature are a unity; or better, just as *natura naturans* and the sensibly apprehended *natura naturata*, while distinguishable, are an indivisible whole, so *natura naturans* and mind or intelligence form an indivisible whole. In the science of nature, in the perception of identity and contrariety in the arts, in the distinction of thinking and thoughts, in the relation of subjective and objective, of inner and outer, thus in a dynamic or constructive philosophy generally, the law of polarity is to be recognized.

The process of religious thinking

Coleridge was above all absorbed by the question of the nature of religious knowing, which was for him a problem of the rational character of faith and of the faithful character of true reason. Though he wrote a good deal concerning theological formulations, he was much more interested in the process or principles of religious thinking. Just this was his primary theme in *Aids to Reflection*

To understand Coleridge's view of that process, we need to take account of two further bases for his mature thinking, which were at least as important as the engagement with those philosophers whose thoughts he was able to employ. One was his own sense of the quality and character of personal religion, in which prayer and the struggle of sin and redemption were at the centre. For Coleridge (in contrast to Hegel) 'let us pray' represented a higher level of activity than 'let us think about God'; the relationship with the ultimate in prayer was too actual to be identified with mere meditation or reflection.

An hour of solitude passed in sincere and earnest prayer, or the conflict with, and conquest over a single passion or 'subtle bosom sin', will teach us more of thought, will more effectually awaken the faculty, and form the habit, of reflection, than a year's study in the Schools without them.[10]

Similarly, as this aphorism also suggests, moral experience was an irreducible datum. It was out of his own struggles that Coleridge understood the possibility that conscience can be killed in a man. He knew the reality of remorse, the originality of sin in the self as a conscientious being, and thus the great need and hunger in man that cries out for salvation.

Second, Coleridge's mature religious thinking was articulated from a position within the historic Christian faith. See his *Confessio Fidei* of 3 November 1816[11] and the conclusion of the *Biographia Literaria*. He had little interest in religion in general. Though his principles for religious thinking are of far more than Christian interest, his thought in *Aids to Reflection* moves from the beginning toward the 'Aphorisms on Spiritual Religion Indeed' (which for him meant Christianity). Coleridge's interest was in giving 'a reason of his faith' (first aphorism on Spiritual Religion). It is in the context of this life of Christianity in his own existence that the famous Aphorism 25 (of the 'Moral and Religious Aphorisms') needs to be understood: 'He who begins by loving Christianity better than truth, will proceed by loving his own sect or church better than Christianity, and end in loving himself better than all.' This Coleridge meant seriously, for Christianity cannot be so counterposed to truth; but for him the freedom for truth was grounded in faith rather than in uncertainty or disbelief. Thus his own aphorism was added to sayings drawn from Leighton in the preceding aphorism: 'He never truly believed, who was not first made sensible and convinced of unbelief. Never be afraid to doubt, if only you have the disposition to believe, and doubt in order that you may end in believing the Truth.'

In this connection another of J. S. Mill's comments on the difference between Bentham and Coleridge is relevant. For Bentham, said Mill, the question was always 'Is it true?' – and if it did not directly conform to his idea of truth, that was the end of inquiry. For Coleridge the great question was 'What is the meaning of it?' – since anything that had been so much believed by thoughtful men and generations had to be accounted for.[12]

On these bases, there were two opposing religious options that had to be rejected. One was the religious rationalism that had been revived most disastrously in Paley, and in other ways in unthinking orthodoxy and in the

6

Scottish common-sense philosophy. For Coleridge, Kant made clear that the metaphysical problems of God and the soul cannot be resolved by the categories of pure or scientific reason. But the opposition to theological rationalism was not based primarily on Kant. Kant made the weaknesses of religious rationalism evident, but more important were the demands of genuine *religious* knowing – and in general Coleridge's arguments for the 'idealism' drawn from the Cambridge Platonists and German philosophy were supports for his conviction of the shallowness and/or actual irreligion of rationalism, orthodoxy, and evangelicalism. 'Christianity is not a theory, or a speculation; but a life – not a philosophy of life, but a life and a living process.'[13]

On the other hand, Coleridge vigorously combated the nonrational idea of faith in both Schleiermacher and the evangelicals. It was not enough to assert 'I have felt' and to insist that the immediacy of religious experience refutes all doubters. The internal evidence of the spirit and the will and the sense of need and redemption are the starting point, but emotionalism is no answer to the questions of reason. No more than Pascal (who at more than one point must be recalled in connection with Coleridge) was Coleridge satisfied simply to say 'the heart has reasons which the reason does not know'. Faith must be a reasoning faith, and reason must be understood more deeply than by either rationalism or the religion of the heart. There are mysteries in Christianity, but these are 'reason in its highest form of self-affirmation'.[14]

In the concluding paragraph of the *Biographia Literaria*, Coleridge affirms his object of showing 'that the Scheme of Christianity, as taught in the Liturgy and Homilies of our Church, though not discoverable by human Reason [= Understanding?], is yet in accordance with it; that link follows link by necessary consequence; that Religion passes out of the ken of Reason only where the eye of Reason has reached its own Horizon; and that Faith is then but its continuation'.[15] The language of such a statement seems relatively traditional. That Coleridge's fundamental meaning was not can be made clear by identifying four levels of argument that are present in his own programme for reflection on religion, levels that seem to form an ascending spiral: (1) the crucial distinction between 'Reason' and 'Understanding', (2) the role of imagination, (3) the religious authority of conscience, and (4) fidelity in reason.

Reason and understanding

The distinction between reason and understanding was one that Coleridge returned to again and again. One main object of *The Friend*, he said in the

Biographia Literaria, had been 'to establish this distinction'.[16] Failure to make the distinction was the sleeping sickness of the age. It was as important for politics as for religion.

Reason and understanding are different in kind. Though he can speak of these as 'organs', Coleridge did not mean 'faculties' but powers, modes of being and thinking, different states of mind and ways of experiencing in the world. 'Reason is the power of universal and necessary convictions, the source and substance of truths above sense, and having their evidence in themselves . . . On the other hand, the judgments of the Understanding are binding only in relation to the objects of our senses, which we reflect under the forms of the understanding. It is, as Leighton rightly defines it, "the faculty judging according to sense".'[17] The distinction is obviously related to (and perhaps derived from) Kant's distinction, but Coleridge differed greatly from Kant in his view of reason's capacity to lay hold, in knowledge, of spiritual realities. He was closer to Jacobi, but even more he reached back to the realism of the Cambridge Platonists, though that also was fundamentally qualified in his conceptions.

There is, then, spiritual truth to be apprehended – laws and principles that exist outside the mind, and supremely the personal reality of God, in which Truth rests. To them are related Ideas, laws contemplated in the mind, intuitions that are not sensuous. These spiritual realities cannot be known by the understanding. Understanding is directed to the phenomenal world of sense-perception, in which it arranges and generalizes. It is the 'science of phenomena', it is (when it usurps the role of reason) the 'mind of the flesh', it is 'discursive', 'the faculty of reflection', and it 'refers to some other faculty as its ultimate authority'. Understanding is

the faculty of the finite . . . that which reduces the confused impressions of sense to their essential forms – quantity, quality, relation, and in these action and reaction, cause and effect, and the like; thus raises the materials furnished by the senses and sensations into objects of reflection, and so makes experience possible. Without it, man's representative powers would be a delirium, a chaos, a scudding cloudage of shapes.[18]

Understanding, simply, is the 'scientific' reasoning of the eighteenth century, of Bentham and Paley, the kind of thinking that separates, analyses, measures, classifies, knows in terms of cause and effect, is concerned with means rather than ends. It gives accuracy, it eliminates error. Within its proper limits this is an indispensable kind of thinking – for science, for much of the routine of life, for knowledge of the finite. Indeed, reason 'cannot exist without understanding; nor does it or can it manifest itself but in and through the understanding . . . or the discursive faculty', although 'understanding and experience may exist without reason'.[19]

But when only this sort of thinking is recognized, when it pretends to be all, then life, philosophy, and religion are denied. And that was the consequence of the eighteenth century: the philosophy of death, 'materialism, determinism, atheism, utilitarianism, the "godless revolution", "moral science exploded as mystic jargon", the "mysteries of religion cut and squared for the comprehension of the understanding," "imagination excluded from poesy"'.[20]

There is also, then, a knowledge of that with which the self as self is concerned, a 'conscious self-knowledge', an intuition of ourselves as related to the whole as a living reality, 'something one and indivisible', a knowing that is religious (and poetic), a seeing that goes beyond space and time, a power of acquainting the self with 'invisible realities or spiritual objects'. This is reason, whose proper objects 'do not appertain to the world of the senses inward or outward'. It is the 'organ of the supersensuous', the faculty of the infinite, the knowledge of 'the laws of the whole considered as one'. This power, which is found only within (and as the self is fully engaged in the search for truth), is alone capable of discernment of 'spiritual objects, the universal, the eternal, and the necessary'. And this organ is 'identical with its appropriate objects'.[21] Whereas understanding thinks 'about' things, reason is the thinking, it is being.

Imagination

The reason that is distinct from understanding also involves imagination. Imagination is a creative act of the self. It refers to the genuine activity of the mind in knowing (in contrast to the mind's supposed passivity, in the Lockean psychology). Imagination carries reason beyond understanding. In *The Statesman's Manual* (1816) Coleridge put it this way: 'The completing power which unites clearness with depth, the plenitude of the sense with the comprehensibility of the understanding, is the imagination.' By being impregnated with imagination, 'the understanding itself becomes intuitive, and a living power'. It is thus a constituent of reason, i.e., reason 'substantiated and vital'. 'This reason without being either the sense, the understanding, or the imagination, contains all three within itself, even as the mind contains its thoughts, and is present in and through them all.'[22]

Though Coleridge later drew back from the tendency, perhaps present here, to equate the higher reason with imagination,[23] and the direct discussion of imagination falls away in later treatments of reason and understanding (e.g., in the *Aids*), the imaginative process must be considered an enduring constituent of Coleridge's idea of reason's functioning. In the well-known passage on the primary and the secondary imagination at the end of chapter XIII of the *Biographia Literaria* (which Coleridge promised to explicate at length in the Constructive Philosophy), the creative function was specified:

The primary IMAGINATION I hold to be the living Power and prime Agent of all human Perception, and as a repetition in the finite mind of the eternal act of creation in the infinite I AM. The secondary Imagination I consider as an echo of the former, coexisting with the primary in the *kind* of its agency, and differing only in *degree*, and in the *mode* of its operation. It dissolves, diffuses, dissipates, in order to re-create; or where this process is rendered impossible, yet still at all events it struggles to idealize and to unify. It is essentially *vital*, even as all objects (*as* objects) are essentially fixed and dead.[24]

Hence imagination is contrasted to fancy in a way not unlike the contrast of reason and understanding. Imagination refers to the very power of growth and production, fancy does not. Fancy 'has no other counters to play with, but fixities and definites' and 'must receive all its materials ready made from the law of association'.[25] In a marginal note, Coleridge once set down the order of these 'mental powers' in the following way:

from the lowest:	*from the highest*:
Sense	Reason
Fancy	Imagination
Understanding	Understanding
Understanding	Understanding
Imagination	Fancy
Reason	Sense

In this scheme, which is also important for its portrayal of understanding in a double form, i.e., as active and as passive, imagination marks the movement from active understanding to reason, fancy the movement from passive understanding to sense. Imagination is a creative power, fancy only an aggregating power. The double column is also significant in indicating the nearness, in terms of polarity, of reason to sense. As Coleridge put it in the *Aids*, 'Reason indeed is much nearer to Sense than to Understanding: for Reason (says our great Hooker) is a direct aspect of truth, an inward beholding, having a similar relation to the intelligible or spiritual, as Sense has to the material or phenomenal.'[26]

Imagination, then, is thinking as creative act. It is, to use the word Coleridge coined in the *Biographia Literaria* to denote it, 'esemplastic' power, the power 'to shape into one'.[27] It is strictly *Einbildungskraft*. It is the apprehension of productive unity, that is to say, of polarity. It is the mind's approach to self-knowledge. It is the power of identification with reality beyond the self, of bringing together the opposites of subject and object. It is a dimension of reason in the special function of seeing the whole in the parts and comprehending the parts as a whole. In the way it makes things real to the self it allows objects to be living (does not kill them by dissection and analysis) and it embraces the interpenetration of the polarities of existence in man and nature. Thus it is also an act of creative interchange in the knowledge of other selves and of God.

Imagination can also be spoken of as a symbol-making power. In *The Statesman's Manual*, Coleridge wrote of the histories in Scripture (in contrast to the histories produced in the eighteenth century) as

living educts of the imagination; of that reconciling and mediatory power, which incorporating the reason in images of the sense, and organizing (as it were) the flux of the senses by the permanence and self-circling energies of the reason, gives birth to a system of symbols, harmonious in themselves, and consubstantial with the truths of which they are the conductors.[28]

A symbol, as Coleridge went on to say, in contrast to the literal and the metaphorical, or the dead letter and the allegory, 'is characterized by a translucence of the special in the individual, or of the general in the special, or of the universal in the general; above all by the translucence of the eternal through and in the temporal'. Symbol 'partakes of the reality which it renders intelligible'. Thus the symbols of Scripture are a living medium of interchange with the living God. And the book of nature, too, is to be read as symbolic. Granted that Coleridge did not write much explicitly on symbol, the concept seems integral to that functioning of reason to which the word imagination directs us.

Morality in reason

In his *Confessio Fidei* (1816) Coleridge began: 'I believe that I am a free agent, inasmuch as, and so far as, I have a will . . . Likewise that I possess reason, or a law of right and wrong, which, uniting with my sense of moral responsibility, constitutes the voice of conscience. Hence it becomes my absolute duty to believe, and I do believe, that there is a God.'[29] Thus reason is intrinsically moral. It includes conscience or the moral sense. It is a will for the good quite as much as it is cognition of being, though the will for the good *is* a knowledge of being. Conscience can be called the chief witness for spiritual realities.

At the outset of his treatment of the difference in kind between reason and the understanding in the *Aids*, Coleridge pointed to a distinction in reason itself, relative to whether we view it as the ground of formal principles, or as the source of ideas. 'Contemplated distinctively in reference to formal (or abstract) truth, it is the Speculative Reason; but in reference to actual (or moral) truth, as the fountain of ideas and the light of the conscience, we name it the Practical Reason.'[30] This of course is Kantian language, and as Coleridge was excited by Kant's argument that metaphysical knowledge of God, the self, freedom, and immortality could not be provided by 'pure reason', so he was also impressed by Kant's turn to the practical reason as the basis for religious affirmation. But even before he encountered Kant, Coleridge tells us in the *Biographia Literaria*, he had become persuaded of this point:

I became convinced, that religion, as both the cornerstone and the keystone of morality, must have a *moral* origin; so far at least, that the evidence of its doctrines could not, like the truths of abstract science, be wholly independent of the will. It were therefore to be expected, that its *fundamental* truth would be such as MIGHT be denied; though only by the fool, and even by the fool from the madness of the *heart* alone.[31]

Further, Coleridge made the practical reason be more than Kant was willing for it to be. In *The Friend*, after describing his metaphysics as 'merely the referring of the mind to its own consciousness for truths indispensable to its own happiness', he went on to assert that 'above all' God gave us conscience. The authority of conscience is direct and indisputable. Conscience 'unconditionally commands us to attribute reality, and actual existence, to those ideas and to those only, without which the conscience itself would be baseless and contradictory, to the ideas of soul, of free-will, of immortality, and of God'.[32] Postulates are not enough. The practical reason alone becomes reason in the full and substantial sense. And to the 'ideas' should be added, for Coleridge, original sin and redemption.

The commands of conscience are not necessary in the sense of the postulates of geometry, but to reject them is to narrow and debase reason. They can be denied, but no good man will deny the premises of moral science. The fundamental truth of religion, again, is such as might be denied, but only by the fool from the madness of his heart.

Faithful reason

This brings us again to the will, and even to the will (and right) to believe. The practical reason is, of course, inseparable from the will, and conscience can be described as the point of synthesis of reason and will. But it can also be said that 'faith subsists in the *synthesis* of the reason and the individual will'.

By virtue of the will, faith is an energy relating to the whole moral man. By virtue of reason, 'faith must be a light, a form of knowing, a beholding of truth'.[33] Here we encounter a fourth and highest level in Coleridge's view of religious thinking, a level at which reason and faith become one, where reason is fidelity.

Now faith is 'fidelity to our own being – so far as such being is not and cannot become an object of the senses, and hence . . . to being generally, as far as the same is not an object of the senses'. Also, faith can be described as 'the fealty of the finite will and understanding to the reason, *the light that lighteth every man that cometh into the world*, as one with, and representative of, the absolute will, and to the ideas or truths of the pure reason'.[34] But this means that reason itself, at the highest point, requires an act of will, a venturing forth, a throwing of oneself into the act of apprehension of spiritual truth. Just as faith must give a reasoned account of itself, so a reason that has no fidelity in it is unfaithful to reason. Only at this level do the deepest differences of Coleridge's thought from supernatural rationalism emerge – as do also his differences from Schleiermacher, Hegel, Kant, and Schelling, both in the idea of faith as fidelity (with Luther, against Schleiermacher and Hegel) and in the conception of the rationality of faith.

'Christianity is not a theory or a speculation . . . but a life and a living process.' Thus every theology of evidences (or a Hegelian proof) is both useless and a misunderstanding; it is irreligious. Or, if one were to try to speak of 'true evidences', the highest would be the experience of need in the soul of the believer for redemption and 'the actual *Trial* of the Faith in Christ, with its accompaniments and results, that must form the arched ROOF, and the Faith itself is the completing KEYSTONE'.[35] The life of faith cannot be 'intellectually more evident' than the law of conscience commands 'without becoming morally less effective; without counteracting its own end by sacrificing the *life* of faith to the cold mechanism of a worthless because compulsory assent'.[36] The faithful reason is characterized by a real venture. Here Pascal's wager must be recalled, and William James's 'will to believe' is anticipated.

In Coleridge's conception of religious thinking, there is a logical movement from the acknowledged wants or religious needs of men, through the demands of the moral sense, to the injunction: 'Try it!' The whole programme of the *Aids to Reflection*, from 'Prudential Aphorisms' to 'Moral and Religious Aphorisms' to 'Aphorisms on Spiritual Religion Indeed' is designed to elicit a kind of religious thinking which recognizes that the culminating test is of an experimental, even pragmatic, sort. As faith is properly the fidelity of man to God, so to the question 'How is Christianity to be proved?' Coleridge finally offered the answer 'Try it!' Courage is a necessary means of laying hold of the spiritual truth. This did not of course mean discarding everything else that had to be said about religious knowing; rather, it was a final integral element in the entire way in which one 'must give a reason of his faith'.

Scripture and the act of faith

The culminating step in the process of religious knowing, as set forth in the *Aids to Reflection*, was reemphasized in Coleridge's systematic account of the authority of Scripture. This took the form of seven letters which he had planned should comprise one of several disquisitions to supplement the *Aids*. That they were not published until after his death, under the title *Confessions of an Inquiring Spirit* (1840),[37] was due to Coleridge's desire that they not interfere with the impact of *Aids*. For by the time of Coleridge's death the storm of biblical criticism had not yet broken over England. Rumblings of the developments in Germany had been heard, and a translation of the fourth edition of Strauss's *Life of Jesus* was to be published in 1846 by the young Marian Evans (George Eliot). But it was not really until the publication of *Essays and Reviews* in 1860 that extensive and open debate took place in established theological circles. Until then, for the most part, the English divines retreated into insularity, almost a conspiracy of silence, or a rejection out of hand (as by Newman in 1837) of 'the connection of foreign Protestantism with infidelity'.

Coleridge knew that the *cordon sanitaire* could not be maintained. He was himself in close touch with biblical scholarship on the Continent; he had read Semler and Paulus, Eichhorn and Reimarus, Lessing and Schleiermacher – and he seems to have been particularly indebted to Lessing. He had no interest in publicly pursuing detailed biblical-critical investigations, though his notebooks were filled with commentary, notes on questions of biblical authorship and authenticity, historical background, literary form, and symbol, myth and allegory in the interpretation of the Scripture. But when the major changes in biblical studies in England did come, they were deeply under the influence of perspectives that Coleridge had earlier set forth, particularly in the *Confessions*. Those views were mediated especially by F. D. Maurice; they were operative in the work of B. F. Westcott, J. B. Lightfoot, and F. J. A. Hort; and they influenced the whole programme of the liberalization of theology in Britain and America at the end of the nineteenth century.

Coleridge's chief interest in the *Confessions* was restatement of the principle of biblical truth, which would exhibit its actual authority in the face of both rationalist challenge and orthodox misconstruction, especially the latter. He judged the Bible to be genuinely a book of revelation, its authors to be inspired. But just as he had to attack the theology of evidences as a fundamental violation of the nature of Christianity, in the interest of a different approach to the question of religious truth, so he had to reject with equal vigour what he called bibliolatry (possibly taking the term from Lessing). The great enemy, as Coleridge identified it in the *Confessions*, to be fought with the same kind of passion as Paley was to be fought, was in fact the 'orthodox' doctrine of infallibility. Thus at the beginning of the *Confessions*, he set forth the alternatives:

1. Is it necessary, or expedient, to insist on the belief of the divine origin and authority of all, and every part of the Canonical Books as the condition, or first principle, of Christian Faith? 2. Or, may not the due appreciation of the Scriptures collectively be more safely relied on as the result and consequence of the belief in Christ; the gradual increase – in respect of particular passages – of our spiritual discernment of their truth and authority supplying a test and measure of our own growth and progress as individual believers, without the servile fear that prevents or overclouds the free honour which cometh from love?[38]

The first part of the second question may bear comparison with Schleiermacher's statement in section 128 of *The Christian Faith*: 'The authority of Holy Scripture cannot be the foundation of faith in Christ; rather must the latter be presupposed before a peculiar authority can be granted to Holy Scripture' – though there is no reason to suppose that Coleridge had Schleiermacher's views particularly in mind.

The response to the first question is unequivocally negative. Christianity cannot be simply identified with the contents of the Bible, for though the Bible 'contains the religion of Christians', it is not the case that 'whatever is contained in the Bible is the Christian religion'.[39] Nor can anything be established by the claim of biblical inerrancy. This is not primarily because of the weakness of the attempts to defend such a view of Scripture – the weakness of 'the forced and fantastic interpretations', 'the literal rendering of Scripture in passages, which the number and variety of images employed in different places, to express one and the same verity, plainly mark out for figurative', of the strange and unparalleled 'practice of bringing together into logical dependency detached sentences from books composed at the distance of centuries, nay, sometimes a *millennium*, from each other, under different dispensations, and for different objects'.[40] Such matters are of lesser importance. Much more basically, the notion of the dictation of the Scriptures by an infallible intelligence violates the living character of revelation and faith:

The doctrine in question petrifies at once the whole body of Holy Writ, with all its harmonies and symmetrical gradations. This breathing organism, this glorious *panharmonicon*, which I had seen stand on its feet as a man, and with a man's voice given to it, the doctrine in question turns at once into a colossal Memnon's head, a hollow passage for a voice, a voice that mocks the voices of many men, and speaks in their names, and yet is but one voice and the same; and no man uttered it, and never in a human heart was it conceived.[41]

The authority of the Bible, which is indeed a conservatory, 'an indispensable criterion, and a continual source and support of true Belief', needs no such defence or prior establishment just because Scripture is its own sufficient evidence when it is approached in the right way, with a humble spirit that is hungering and thirsting after righteousness. One may take up the Bible tranquilly as one would any other collection of ancient writings and be impressed by its superiority. To the one who comes to the Bible with a sense of need and manifold imperfection it will be an organ of living truth; he will find in it copious sources of the bread of life. The Bible is not to be thought true and holy and unquestionable because we already believe it to be the Word of God; rather 'the Bible, considered in reference to its declared ends and purposes, is true and holy, and for all who seek truth with humble spirits an unquestionable guide, and therefore it is the Word of God'.[42]

That is to say, again, that no 'evidence' of authority or truth in religious matters is to be found apart from human need. The proof of the divine authority of the 'truth revealed through Christ' is in its 'fitness to our nature and needs; the clearness and cogency of this proof being proportionate to the degree of self-knowledge in each individual hearer'.[43] In that assertion, Coleridge seems to come close to identifying the criterion of religious truth simply with man's apprehension of his spiritual wants, and thus of opening the way to thorough subjectivism. But that he does not do. The subjective and the objective are both to be maintained, in the polarity in which all power manifests itself. What Coleridge was saying was, rather, an echo of a fundamental theme of the criticism of the theology of evidences in *Aids to Reflection*: 'Evidences of Christianity! I am weary of the word. Make a man feel the want of it; rouse him, if you can, to the self-knowledge of his need of it; and you may safely trust it to its own Evidence.'[44] This truth, in other words, is not to be proved or even apprehended or understood apart from self-knowledge. The pragmatic, existential character of the 'Try it!' is implicit. The right view of the authority of Scripture and the right idea of the nature of faith must here come together. In both respects Coleridge brought to vivid expression one of the most basic motifs that emerged in nineteenth-century religious thinking: the active role of the self in all genuinely religious knowing. What most distinguished his own account of the venture of faith was his effort to explicate the rationality of it, to show that this venture is neither against nor beyond nor apart from true reason, but is reason's own highest moment.

16

God – sin – redemption

While Coleridge's chief importance lies in his distinctive way of interpreting the process of religious thinking, certain other themes need to be noted. Much of the *Aids*, after all, consisted of commentary ranging over the staple elements of the received Christian tradition: God, election, sin and redemption, atonement, justification by faith, baptism and regeneration, belief in a future state. Such doctrines are reviewed as 'aids' to reflection (i.e., as symbols?) such that when their rationality is shown, and objections removed by the recovery of a scriptural view, the reader of the *Aids* may come to see that the mysteries of the distinctive doctrines of Christianity are 'reason in its highest form of self-affirmation'. Of these topics, it is most important to mention Coleridge's discussion of sin and redemption and his idea of God.

Ostensibly, Coleridge developed his interpretations in the *Aids* in relation to the earlier Anglican and Protestant controversies, and in particular in dialogue with Leighton and Taylor. The *Aids* can also be read, however, as a sustained argument with Kant's *Religion Within the Limits of Reason Alone*.[45] That is clear notably in Coleridge's treatment of original sin and redemption, 'the two great moments of the Christian Religion'. Original sin, of course, is to be related to Kant's notion of 'radical evil', and in his explication of individual guilt, of the problem of evil and the will, Coleridge follows Kant quite closely. The moral law is ingredient in human life and the acknowledgment of the moral law should in itself be sufficient to determine the will to free obedience of the law. Moral evil has its origin in the will and the will must be ultimately self-determined or else it is simply a nature under the mechanism of cause and effect. The will cannot be intrinsically evil, or made so by God, or any other principle than itself. The responsible will ought to be able to act in accord with the demands of the moral law, the voice of (practical) reason in the idea of humanity itself. Yet the universality of evil is a fact, a fact acknowledged in almost every religion. An evil common to all must have a ground common to all. This is what Christians call original sin. (The truth of original sin was thus, for Coleridge, not doctrine about the first human parents, but a doctrine about every person, so that here every person is an adequate representative of all persons.)[46]

For Kant, radical evil remains a surd, unintelligible to reason. Coleridge, however, seems to point to a way out of the dilemma, which is indicated by his assertion that while the doctrine of original sin concerns all men, it concerns Christians only in connection with the doctrine of redemption. This is the basis for his identification of the evil will as the finite will asserting itself *in independence and deviation from the absolute will*. The perfect law of freedom exists 'only by its unity with the will of God' and 'whatever seeks to separate itself from the divine principle, and proceeds from a false centre in the agent's particular will, is evil – a work of darkness and contradiction. It is sin and essential falsehood.'[47] The finite will indeed constitutes a true beginning, but only 'by coincidence with that Absolute Will, which is at the same time Infinite Power'. Thus, as Coleridge elaborated the discussion of evil in the Notebooks,[48] the true freedom of the will, its positive potency, is its harmony with the Absolute Will. The negative potency, to will itself in its individuality, in conflict with other wills and thus in destruction of itself, is the possibility of evil. Yet the will remains good and free in that fallen man remains potentially redeemable. And in consequence of the free gift of redemption, the power of the will to repent and to have faith in the Gospel sense of the word is provided; 'the guilt of its rejection, the refusing to avail ourselves of the power, being all that we can consider as exclusively attributable to our own act'.[49] This obviously does not eliminate the mystery of the origin of evil, or the mystery of actualization of the good will in faith. Nor did Coleridge suppose that it does. But it gives a quite different specificity from Kant's and it sets forth a lively possibility of the actualization of the good will in faith, by giving up the clinging of the finite will to itself.

The other side of the *Auseinandersetzung* with Kant in the *Aids* was Coleridge's enlargement of the concept of truth. 'Reflection' carries a richer and heavier freight than for Kant. Thus the 'doctrines' that Coleridge calls 'aids' are quite different sorts of aids than Kant was willing to allow to prayer, church-going, baptism, and communion. Baptism and communion were for Coleridge far more than rationalized moral allegories. Though Coleridge was not at all full in his interpretation of the sacraments, except for his discussion of infant baptism, his view of these as aids seems to express his understanding of symbol (see above). It was at the point of prayer, of course, that the sharpest conflict with Kant emerged. Prayer is the heart and soul of religion, the actual relation of a will to a will, the means of achieving the union of the finite will with the Absolute Will. It is the epitome of existential assent.

Coleridge's chief 'doctrinal' concern, however, was with the idea of God. Though he kept coming back again and again to the question of how God is known, his published and unpublished works are filled with reflection on the nature of God. On the one hand, he imbibed fully the idealist objection to orthodoxy's crude anthropomorphism and supernaturalism, and he was especially opposed to deism's mechanical and absentee God. He was for a time much attracted to the identity philosophy and its tendency to monism.

This reinforced the sense of striving that he says was in him from childhood, the sense of the whole and of unity, of 'God in all and all in God', his mind's feeling 'as if it ached to behold and know something *great*, something *one* and *indivisible*'. Thus Spinoza's 'intellectual love of God' and Schelling's 'intellectual vision' of God were truer than any deism or unitarianism. But he drew back from idealistic monism as finally involving gross materialism and an impersonal and abstract Absolute, incompatible with religion. 'For a very long time, indeed', Coleridge wrote in the *Biographia Literaria*, 'I could not reconcile personality with infinity; my head was with Spinoza, though my whole heart remained with Paul and John.'[50]

The God of a mature faith cannot be an unconditioned Absolute. Absolute Will must not be understood in a way that excludes the personality of God or identifies deity with the totality of nature. Pantheism and atheism come to the same thing. A less than personal God is religiously insufficient. God must be viewed as the superindividual self, the ground of all the vastness of existence. As the root of all, the eternal antecedent and coeternal being, he is 'superessential Will'. The personal relationship of distinction and nearness is essential to moral experience, to obedience and fidelity and the will in man. God must be conceived as personal (or superpersonal) because the focus of religion is prayer, a real 'religious inter-communion between man and his Maker'. The theological formulation must be accountable to the fact that religion is finally the relation of a will to a will (Will being finally deeper than Reason). To express both the personal reality of God and the 'diversity' of the Creator from the whole of his creation, Coleridge spoke of the 'personeity' of God.

Coleridge saw especially in the idea of the Trinity the way of preserving both the Absoluteness of God and the reality of personal relations. Though the Trinity would have been only a necessary idea of speculative reason, he said in both the *Confessio Fidei* and the *Aids*, it is a belief demanded in consequence of our redemption.[51] Coleridge remained persuaded that the doctrine of the Trinity is grounded in revealed religion (that is, in actual religion, since all religion is 'revealed'). But he also wanted to say that only in the trinitarian idea is a way provided of maintaining the unity of God without collapsing God and the world into bare monism. (Recall the 'productive unity' which the idea of polarity expresses.)

His own formula for Trinity, or better 'the one and triune God', involved a *tetractys* rather than mere threefoldness: The Identity, The Ipseity, The Alterity, and The Community.[52] The *Identity* is absolute subjectivity, the ground, the absolute will, '*theos* without an article, and yet not as an adjective'. Yet that which is essentially causative of all true being is causative of its own being. Hence the *Ipseity*, 'the eternally self-affirmant self af-firmed', the I am that I am, the Father, the Holy One. In the eternal act of self-affirmation, the *Alterity* is co-eternally begotten: the Son, the Word, the divine objectivity, the true. But the relatively subjective and the relatively objective require for completion a co-eternal: the *Community*, the eternal life which is love, the Spirit. Here, plainly, the ultimate ground or unity is prior to the threefoldness, and Coleridge was unhappy with the language of the Athanasian Creed on that account. His own view, elaborated extensively in the Notebooks and the Opus Maximum,[53] Coleridge thought made more clear how the idea of God itself implies the idea of triunity, and how a real functional diversity emerges from unity.

The National Church and the Church of Christ

The occasion for the publication of Coleridge's *Constitution of the Church and State According to the Idea of Each* (1830) was the Catholic Emancipation Act of 1829. More important, however, since the particular application to the reform bill itself need not concern us, is the way in which this work, though only a sketch, sums up Coleridge's life-long desire to serve the social whole. From the beginning, for him, religion and politics were essentially intertwined.

Most distinctive in the *Constitution of the Church and State* was the idea of the 'National Church' in contrast to the 'Christian Church'. By 'idea', in this connection, Coleridge meant something like an 'ideal type' – neither an abstraction nor a generalization from particular historical forms or modes, buċ an idea framed by the knowledge of the 'ultimate aim' of something, whether church or state or constitution. The truth of the idea lies in its comprehension of the final objective. Similarly, Coleridge suggests, the validity of the idea of the 'social contract' is not in the least dependent on there having been any historical original compact; the demands of such a contract arise out of the very constitution of humanity.[54]

The idea of a National Church is the idea of a 'third estate' in the nation, having a distinct 'end or national purpose'. The other estates are the agricultural, or the land-owners, and the mercantile or commercial (includ-ing the free artisans and the distributors). The former may also be designated as the Landed Interest; it provides for the permanency of the nation. The latter may be called the Personal Interest; it provides for progressiveness and personal freedom. Both these estates are represented in the constitution of the English nation. But what needs to be recognized is that 'third estate of the realm', which is in truth the ground of both the former, whose object is 'to secure and improve that civilization without which the nation could be neither permanent nor progressing'. This is something that belongs to the essential elements and proper ordering of any national life. It is distinct but not separate from the other estates.

This third estate is the National Church, or the 'Clerisy' as Coleridge also calls it. 'Clerisy' is not identical with the ecclesiastical in the common sense of that term, but draws rather on the 'original and proper sense' of 'clergy'. Clerisy comprehends 'the learned of all denominations, the sages and professors of the law and jurisprudence, of medicine and physiology, of music, of military and civil architecture, of the physical sciences . . . in short, of all the so-called liberal arts and sciences, the possession and application of which constitute the civilization of a country, as well as the theological'. The theological sciences have properly been placed at the head, because they contained 'the interpretation of languages . . . of ethical science, in relation to the rights and duties of men . . . and lastly, the ground-knowledge, the *prima scientia* . . . the doctrine and discipline of ideas'. The National Church is thus an inclusive guild of the learned professions, providing for the well-being of the whole community.[55]

The idea of the National Church is also to be related to the idea of the State – distinguished but not to be separated, for National Church and State are related in polarity, with the king as head of both. They are 'two poles of the same magnet', the magnet constituted by their being the constitution of the state.[56] The relation seems close to that of *natura naturans* and *natura naturata*. We need a right idea of National Church to balance the idea of the State in any full view of the constitution of the nation. And England is to be thankful for having had from the beginning such a church. This is a treasure to be retained.

But the idea of the National Church is not to be confused with the 'Christian Church' (which is also here distinct from 'Christianity', the latter referring to the whole redemptive process that begins with the first moment of creation). The Church of Christ has four essential distinguishing characteristics. (1) It is 'no state, kingdom or realm of this world', nor an 'estate' of such, but an opposite to them all – 'the sustaining, correcting, befriending opposite of the World'. It asks and demands of the state 'only protection and to be let alone, i.e., nothing that citizens cannot already demand as citizens'. (2) The Christian Church is no 'secret community'. It is not invisible, not a kingdom of God within, but quite visible, a city on a hill, 'an institution consisting of visible and public communities. In one sentence it is the Church visible and militant under Christ.' In view of the first characteristic, the Christian Church is thus, in contrast to the National Church, not the 'counterpole to any particular State', not the 'church' in 'church and state'. It has 'no Nationality entrusted to its charge'. Its contrast is the 'World'. In view of the second characteristic, it is to exist in every state and country. (3) But the first and second characteristics require effectuation by a third: 'namely, the absence of any visible head or sovereign, and by the nonexistence, nay the utter preclusion, of any local or personal centre of unity, of any single source of universal power'. (4) It follows from the first and third characteristics that the Christian Church is truly universal – 'neither Anglican, Gallican, nor Roman, neither Latin nor Greek'. Rather, 'through the presence of its only Head and Sovereign, entire in each and one in all, the Church Universal is spiritually perfect in every true Church'.[57]

Finally, however, it must be recognized that the Christian Church and the National Church intersect in the persons of individuals, who are both spiritual leaders in the Church of Christ and appointed functionaries in the National Church. Christianity (here Coleridge can use the term interchangeably with Christian Church) in fact supports and gives life to the National Church, though that can be called a 'blessed accident', in the sense that 'Christianity is an aid and instrument, which no State or realm could have produced out of its own elements, which no State had a right to expect. It was, most awfully, a GOD-SEND.'[58] Individuals should exercise these functions with a due sense of their distinctness and independent rights, as different trusts that are held. Yet the relation is also positive, for while there can be a National Church without Christianity, and the state for its own good needs to support the clerisy, Christianity does prove at the same time to be the greatest invigoration and nourishment of the National Church. Thus church establishment is to be supported, as in the case of England a bulwark of toleration and a support for the National Church. For if the Church of England were to be disestablished, the idea of a National Church would wither.

Postscript

Coleridge's death in 1834 was, for religious thought in the nineteenth century as a whole, one of the landmarks of transition to a new era. Schleiermacher died in the same year. Hegel had died in 1831, and Bentham and Goethe in 1832. Following their generation, altered impulses, moods, and problems were clearly emerging. In Britain, the Oxford Movement quickly occupied the centre of the stage – and with its quite different ideas about church reform (as well as doctrine) doubtless inhibited serious exploitation of Coleridge's intriguing idea of the National Church, though

22

Coleridge's religious passion for social well-being was to be powerfully reflected in F. D. Maurice. In Germany, David Friedrich Strauss's *Life of Jesus* (1835) began a new radicalization of the biblical-critical problem, and the idealist understanding of religion was dethroned by Feuerbach and Marx in the 1840s. In America, the novel impulses were to appear in Emerson and the Transcendentalists (again in the 1830s).

Yet in the originality and breadth of his thinking, Coleridge was by no means to be left behind. His conception of the process of religious thinking requires him to be set alongside Schleiermacher as an early impetus in the nineteenth century's new way of understanding that God and faith belong together. Here was a Socratic turn to the self, a new recognition of the role of the religious subject in anything that can properly be called religious knowing or believing: in the religious self's point of view, its cognitive act, its 'interest', its willing and choosing. Theology deals with God, but insofar as God is the object for religious reflection, the believing self is also always given in the concrete choosing and affirming and apprehending that is faith. God is available as an 'object' only from and with the point of view of a subject.

The contrary supposition might (and did) take two forms. It might be expressed in a natural theology which, excluding every appeal to the particularities of faith or revelation or encounter with God, seeks to derive and validate assertions about the divine reality simply from the experience of something other than God, i.e., which seeks to bring God into view as an object by inferences from the knowledge of the world as such. The contrary supposition might also take the form of an 'objectivized' view of revelation, i.e., one in which the divine disclosure is thought to be independent of the self's acknowledgment of it, in which revelation is something 'in itself' and 'out there' (e.g., in Scripture) rather than a relation between beings, in which there is a 'revealed truth' that can be 'objectively' specified and interpreted (or even attacked and defended by appeal to 'evidences' other than itself). In both forms of the supposition, it is assumed that theology can deal with its proper object, be it God or Word of God, as something available for analysis 'in itself' apart from faith's act of affirming or knowing.

Against such suppositions was to stand the main course of Protestant theology in the nineteenth century – though in many different specific formulations. The religious subject is that with which theological reflection has to begin. Consciousness of the truth of the religious object is peculiarly one with self-consciousness. This is an ineradicably 'subjective' (though not subjectivist) viewing of the religious 'object'. Significant talk about God is talk in which the self is concerned. The religious 'object', God, is present for reflection only in and with the religious subject in relation to God. Religious truth is not of a disinterested, neutral sort, but irreducibly involves the believer's being in the truth.

Naturally, one expects Kierkegaard to be cited as evidence of this shift in the understanding of religious thinking. And rightly so. For the point could hardly be put more sharply than in his insistence that, religiously speaking, 'truth is subjectivity', so that the question of religious truth is the question of my relation to the truth rather than any question of the 'objective' truth of that to which I am so related. At least at the level of Religiousness A (in the *Postscript*), the question is wholly one of the quality and intensity of passion in the relationship, or 'subjective' rather than 'objective' validity, even to the point of the contention that the highest subjective truth is compatible only with the greatest objective uncertainty.

But at the beginning of the century, Schleiermacher had also made a decisive turn to the self, in his locating of the religious in *Gefühl*, as a mode of self-consciousness, and in his new conception of a *Glaubenslehre*, in which theological assertions are throughout to be understood as grounded in and drawn from the present religious consciousness of the historical Christian community. Christian doctrines are precisely explications of the consciousness of sin and grace, 'accounts of the Christian religious affections'. Thus theological talk about God is never about God 'in Himself' or as an object of metaphysical speculation, but always as reflection on the 'immediate utterances of the religious self-consciousness'. Indeed, the direct reference of theological assertions is to the states of self-consciousness, and only out of those 'descriptions of the human states of life' is it permissible to develop statements about the divine attributes and modes of action and about the constitution of the world.

Coleridge's view was of course in many respects sharply opposed to that of Schleiermacher. Yet in his attack on Paley and the religious rationalism Paley stood for, and in his opposition to the bibliolatrist's idea of revelation in Scripture, as well as in his own idea of genuine religious thinking, Coleridge too was making the point that there is no possible theological beginning without the active involvement of the self. And in England and America, it was Coleridge as much as Schleiermacher who brought about this new way of looking at things.

The impact of Coleridge is especially to be found in F. D. Maurice (his greatest 'disciple'), with Maurice's insistence on the partiality of every Christian apprehension of the lordship of Christ. No one claim to the truth, whether of individual or sect or party, can rightfully assert that it is exclusively the whole truth; each may be a view of the truth, but it is a viewing that stands alongside (and should recognize) other viewings. And Horace Bushnell said he was more indebted to *Aids to Reflection* than to any other extra-scriptural authority. The idea of the 'subjectivity' of religious truth came to special expression in Bushnell's theory of language, according to which the language of religion is naturally akin to that of poetry, and religious dogmatism (or rationalism) is impossible because theological words are never unambiguous, all being necessarily understood in relation to the personal history of each individual; religious truth must always be expressed in the forms of our own life and experience.

Finally, though without suggesting any dependence on Coleridge, one may recall Albrecht Ritschl's insistence that religious knowledge consists simply in *Werturteile*, in judgments that involve personal commitment, assertions of worth 'for us', and that theology is to be based wholly on such judgments of the practical reason, in contrast to 'objective' or 'theoretical' or 'disinterested' (scientific or speculative) judgments. And in a still different mode, though far more in the spirit of Coleridge, there is William James's account of the will and right to believe, which teaches in another way that religious truth is preeminently practical truth, that in religious options it is necessary and right to venture forth in decision and risk in order to find truth, and that indeed one's believing plays a creative part in the making of religious truth.

The point is not that all these views are the same, or even that they are all consistent with one another, but rather that just in their varying ways (and others could be cited) they all testify to the essential place that the believing subject has come to occupy in the understanding of religious truth. There is no need to argue that this recognition was utterly new in the nineteenth century. It was not. It has its antecedents in Luther and Kant, in Pascal and pietism, and so on. But the convergence is striking and the fundamental shift in perspective is indisputable. And in that change, Coleridge's conception of religious thinking was of great moment.

Notes

1 *Mill on Bentham and Coleridge*, ed. F. R. Leavis (London, 1950), pp. 39, 102–3.
2 Leipzig edn (1862), p. 236.
3 W. G. T. Shedd (ed.), *The Complete Works of Samuel Taylor Coleridge* (7 vols., New York, 1853), vol. II, pp. 26–7.
4 Cited in Basil Willey, *Nineteenth Century Studies* (London, 1949), p. 4.
5 *Complete Works*, vol. I, p. 364.
6 Paley, *Works* (Boston, 1811), vol. III, p. 70.
7 For a brief discussion of Bentham as the major alternative to Coleridge, see my *Protestant Thought in the Nineteenth Century* (New Haven, Conn., 1972), vol. I, pp. 110–12.

8 Owen Barfield, *What Coleridge Thought* (Middletown, Conn., 1971), p. 6.
9 *Hints Towards the Formation of a More Comprehensive Theory of Life*, cited from Donald A. Stauffer (ed.), *Selected Poetry and Prose of Samuel Taylor Coleridge* (New York, 1951), pp. 573, 578–80. See *Complete Works*, vol. I, pp. 373–416.
10 *Aids to Reflection*, Introductory Aphorism 11; *Complete Works*, vol. I, p. 120.
11 *Complete Works*, vol. V, p. 15.
12 *Mill on Bentham and Coleridge*, pp. 99–100.
13 Cf. Aphorism 7 on Spiritual Religion Indeed; *Complete Works*, vol. I, p. 233.
14 Preface to *Aids*; *Complete Works*, vol. I, p. 115.
15 *Selected Poetry and Prose*, pp. 427–8.
16 *Ibid.*, p. 193.
17 *Aids*; *Complete Works*, vol. I, pp. 241, 242. See the whole of pp. 241–53, 'On the Difference in Kind of the Reason and the Understanding'.
18 *Essay on Faith*, in *Literary Remains*; *Complete Works*, vol. V, p. 562.
19 *The Friend*, in *Complete Works*, vol. II, p. 145.
20 Willey, *Nineteenth Century Studies*, p. 29.
21 Cf. *The Friend*, in *Complete Works*, vol. II, pp. 144–5, and *Essay on Faith*, in vol. V, pp. 561–2. In the last statement, Coleridge makes clear his divergence from Jacobi.
22 *Complete Works*, vol. I, p. 461.
23 Cf. Boulger, *Coleridge as Religious Thinker* (New Haven, Conn., 1961), pp. 105–8.
24 *Selected Poetry and Prose*, p. 263.
25 *Ibid.*
26 *Complete Works*, vol. I, p. 246. For a detailed discussion of this scheme of the mental powers, see Barfield, *What Coleridge Thought*, esp. pp. 96–103, 127–9, 219.
27 *Selected Poetry and Prose*, p. 191.
28 *Complete Works*, vol. I, p. 436.
29 *Complete Works*, vol. V, p. 15.
30 *Complete Works*, vol. I, pp. 241–2.
31 *Selected Poetry and Prose*, p. 212. Cf. also p. 211.
32 *Complete Works*, vol. II, pp. 103, 106.
33 *Essay on Faith*, in *Complete Works*, vol. V, p. 565.
34 *Complete Works*, vol. V, pp. 557, 591.
35 *Biographia Literaria*, in *Selected Poetry and Prose*, p. 426.
36 *Ibid.*, p. 212.
37 Ed. by H. N. Coleridge; 2nd edn, 1849, 3rd edn, 1853. See *Complete Works*, vol. V, pp. 569–623. See also the edition, with introductory note, by H. StJ. Hart (London, 1956).
38 *Confessions of an Inquiring Spirit*, ed. H. StJ. Hart (London, 1956), p. 38.
39 *Ibid.*, p. 61; see also p. 57.
40 *Ibid.*, pp. 58–9.
41 *Ibid.*, pp. 51–2.
42 *Ibid.*, p. 68.
43 *Ibid.*, p. 64.
44 *Complete Works*, vol. I, p. 363.
45 See the penetrating article by Elinor S. Shaffer, 'Metaphysics of culture: Kant and Coleridge's *Aids to Reflection*', *Journal of the History of Ideas*, 31 (1970), 199–218.
46 See *Aids*, in *Complete Works*, vol. I, 284–9.
47 *Complete Works*, vol. I, pp. 292, 274n.
48 See particularly Notebook 26, cited at length in Boulger, *Coleridge as Religious Thinker*, pp. 150–60.
49 *Complete Works*, vol. I, p. 307.
50 *Selected Poetry and Prose*, p. 211.

51 See *Literary Remains*, in *Complete Works*, vol. v, p. 17, and *Aids*, in vol. 1, pp. 216–20. For various statements on the scriptural bases, see also *Literary Remains*.
52 *Formula Fidei de Sanctissima Trinitate* (1830), in *Literary Remains*; *Complete Works*, vol. v, pp. 18–19.
53 Relevant sections are elaborately marshalled in Boulger, *Coleridge as Religious Thinker*, pp. 133–41.
54 See *Complete Works*, vol. VI, pp. 30–2.
55 *Ibid.*, pp. 52–4; cf. also p. 97.
56 *Ibid.*, p. 44.
57 *Ibid.*, pp. 98–105.
58 *Ibid.*, p. 60; cf. also p. 105.

Bibliographical essay

With the permission of the Yale University Press, I have in the preceding essay drawn extensively on material from my earlier and briefer chapter, 'Reasoning faith and faithful reason: Coleridge and the struggle against the eighteenth century', in *Protestant Thought in the Nineteenth Century* (New Haven, Conn., 1972), vol. 1, pp. 108–26.

The fullest source for Coleridge's published works is still W. G. T. Shedd (ed.), *The Complete Works of Samuel Taylor Coleridge* (7 vols., New York, 1853), though the *Collected Works* are now being published under the general editorship of Kathleen Coburn (Bollingen Series 75, London and Princeton, 1969–). Useful editions of individual works include the *Biographia Literaria*, ed. J. Shawcross (2 vols., Oxford, 1907); *The Complete Poetical Works of Samuel Taylor Coleridge*, ed. E. H. Coleridge (2 vols., Oxford, 1912); and *The Confessions of an Inquiring Spirit*, ed. H. StJ. Hart (London, 1956). A good selection is found in D. A. Stauffer (ed.), *Selected Poetry and Prose of Samuel Taylor Coleridge* (New York, 1951).

For the unpublished materials, see especially Kathleen Coburn's editions of *The Philosophical Lectures of Samuel Taylor Coleridge* (New York, 1949); *The Notebooks of Samuel Taylor Coleridge* (3 vols., New York, 1957–73); and her *Experience into Thought: Perspectives in the Coleridge Notebooks* (Toronto, 1979); also E. L. Griggs (ed.), *Collected Letters* (6 vols., Oxford, 1956–71). The 'standard' biography is J. D. Campbell, *Samuel Taylor Coleridge: A Narrative of the Events of His Life* (London, 1894); see also E. K. Chambers, *Samuel Taylor Coleridge: A Biographical Study* (Oxford, 1938).

An extensive history of the commentary on Coleridge's religious thought has been provided by Philip C. Rule, S. J., 'Coleridge's reputation as a religious thinker: 1816–1972', *Harvard Theological Review*, 67 (1974), 289–320. Of particular interest is the evidence of Coleridge's impact on the generation following his death, the relative paucity of significant studies after about 1860, and the renewal of serious interest in Coleridge as a religious thinker after 1930.

John J. Muirhead, who was the first to draw on the unpublished materials and who remains one of the few professional philosophers to have dealt seriously with Coleridge, included a chapter on the relation between philosophy and religion in his *Coleridge as Philosopher* (London, 1930), which helped to revitalize interest in Coleridge as an original thinker. Muirhead saw him as mainly influenced by the Cambridge Platonist tradition. In the following year, René Wellek, in *Immanuel Kant in England* (Princeton, 1931), launched his continuing campaign against both the viability and the originality of Coleridge's thought, attacking the latter's 'pernicious teaching of double truth', his 'plagiarisms', and his fundamental dependence on Kant and German idealism. Elisabeth Winkelmann, *Coleridge und die Kantische Philosophie* (Palaestra, 1933), offered a more balanced account of Coleridge's debt also to Schelling, Fichte, Jacobi, and Schleiermacher.

I. A. Richards, *Coleridge on Imagination* (London, 1934), gave important impetus to the general reconsideration of Coleridge, and C. R. Sanders, *Coleridge and the Broad Church Movement* (Durham, N.C., 1942), recalled anew and vigorously the influence of Coleridge on Maurice, Hare, Arnold, Carlyle, *et al.* Coleridge's religious position was treated significantly in H. N. Fairchild, *Romantic Faith* [vol. III of his Religious Trends in English Poetry] (New York, 1949), and in D. J. James, *The Romantic Comedy: An Essay on English Romanticism* (London, 1949), focusing on Coleridge and Newman. Basil Willey included a fine chapter on Coleridge in *Nineteenth Century Studies: Coleridge to Matthew Arnold* (London, 1949).

The real revival of Coleridge as religious thinker, however, has come since 1960, with a spate of books, some drawing extensively on the Notebooks, the Marginalia, etc. The first full-scale work was James D. Boulger, *Coleridge as Religious Thinker* (New Haven, Conn., 1961). This remains an important study, though it takes little account of Coleridge's profound concern with religion and society. David P. Calleo, *Coleridge and the Idea of the Modern State* (New Haven, Conn., 1966), offers a useful interpretation of Coleridge's political theory. J. Robert Barth, *Coleridge and Christian Doctrine* (Cambridge, Mass., 1969), attempts a systematic account of Coleridge's mature views on a broad range of doctrinal topics, setting these in relation to a variety of other Christian options. The interpretations are responsible, even though somewhat unColeridgean in systematization. Barth's *The Symbolic Imagination: Coleridge and the Romantic Tradition* (Princeton, 1977) is quite different, moving from a useful analysis of what Coleridge meant by symbol to the nature of Romanticism as a whole. Elinor S. Shaffer, *'Kubla Khan' and the Fall of Jerusalem: The Mythological School in Biblical Criticism and Secular Literature, 1770–1880* (New York, 1975), is helpful particularly in relating Coleridge to German higher criticism and to British exegesis. See also Laurence S. Lockridge, *Coleridge the Moralist* (Ithaca, 1977).

In G. N. G. Orsini, *Coleridge and German Idealism: A Study in the History of Philosophy with Unpublished Materials from Coleridge's Manuscripts* (Carbondale, Ill., 1969), Thomas McFarland, *Coleridge and the Pantheist Tradition* (Oxford, 1969), Gabriel Marcel, *Coleridge et Schelling* (Paris, 1971) – the publication of an essay originally written in 1909 – and Norman Fruman, *Coleridge, The Damaged Archangel* (New York, 1971), the questions of Coleridge's use of or dependence on German idealism are again reviewed. In Orsini, McFarland, and Marcel, the treatment is informed, sympathetic, and instructive. Fruman's work is largely antagonistic debunking, with little attention to the religious writings.

Attempts are made in Bernard M. G. Reardon, *From Coleridge to Gore: A Century of Religious Thought in Britain* (London, 1971), and in Claude Welch, *Protestant Thought in the Nineteenth Century*, vol. I: 1799–1870 (New Haven, Conn., 1972), to give full recognition to Coleridge's importance in the development of nineteenth-century theology.

Owen Barfield, *What Coleridge Thought* (Middletown, Conn., 1971), deals directly with the religious ideas only briefly, but sets these in the context of a penetrating discussion of the pattern of Coleridge's thinking, with particularly valuable analyses of the relations of Understanding and Reason and of Imagination and Fancy. Basil Willey, *Samuel Taylor Coleridge* (London, 1972), provides the best available account of the *development* of Coleridge's religious ideas.

Among recent articles on particular aspects of Coleridge's thought, the following are worthy of note: J. Robert Barth, S. J., 'Symbol as sacrament in Coleridge's thought', *Studies in Romanticism*, 11 (1972), 320–31; James D. Boulger, 'Coleridge: the Marginalia, myth-making, and the later poetry', *ibid.*, 304–19; L. O. Frappell, 'Coleridge and the "Coleridgeans" on Luther', *Journal of Religious History*, 7 (1973), 307–23; David R. Sanderson, 'Coleridge's political "sermons": discursive language and the voice of God', *Modern Philology*, 70, no. 4 (1973), 319–30; and Elinor S. Shaffer, Meta-physics of culture: Kant and Coleridge's *Aids to Reflection*', *Journal of the History of Ideas*, 31 (1970), 199–218.

2

Ralph Waldo Emerson
and
The American Transcendentalists

SYDNEY E. AHLSTROM†

Transcendentalism is the single most provocative spiritual movement in American history. In proportion to its size and duration it has stimulated a body of literature that is probably unequalled in detail, interest, and profundity. At its centre stands the serene, enigmatic and challenging figure of Emerson – the poet, prophet and seer who more than any other personified its central impulses, propounded its most troubling paradoxes, and stimulated the diverse reformers who constituted the movement.

From almost the outset Emerson has been the object of very contradictory interpretations. He has repeatedly been seen as at once an other-worldly mystic and a practical Yankee; as an uncritical celebrant of American culture and as one of its most penetrating critics. As early as 1907 George Woodberry spoke of 'the double image on the mind that has dwelt long upon his memory. He is a shining figure on some Mount of Transfiguration; and he is a parochial man.'[1] He has been seen as a child of the eight Puritan ministers in his ancestry, and as a blasphemous champion of Romantic extravagance. Emerson himself is at least partly to blame for the difficulty of interpreting his published work. There are very few writers who have indulged less in self-disclosure, whether in public or to friends. Not only did he refuse to explain himself, he constantly and deliberately deepened the mystery by planting misleading clues for the gullible to find. Crucial to our understanding of his thought, therefore, are the immensely voluminous notebooks which he maintained assiduously from his college days on. They constitute a vast *oeuvre* in themselves, a record of his activities, his reading and above all the multiple dimensions of his inner life. So rich and fascinating are these notebooks that many scholars have been seduced into doing less than justice to the published works.

† It is with great sorrow that we record the death of Professor Ahlstrom in the summer of 1984, whilst this volume was in press.

Emerson's literary method was shaped by his vocation as a lecturer. Wherever he was he continued to keep his notebooks. He referred to them as his savings bank, and drew from them as needed. They in turn provided many ideas and much illustrative detail for his lectures – which were, of course, constantly being borrowed from and revised as his lecture schedule required. The published works, in turn, stemmed in various ways and degrees from lectures, though they were carefully reworked and grouped before publication. So fascinating and time-specific are these various materials, which also include a vast collection of letters, that almost every student of his works (including myself!) is constantly tempted to seek out the time and circumstances pertaining to Emerson's reading of a book, forming of an idea, shaping a metaphor, or writing a poem. There exists, therefore, an inescapable controversy as to which layer of writing is primary and as to whether the craft of a literary artist is more important than the final statement of a thinker.

Emerson was determined above all that his words and positions would never be thoughtlessly adopted. For the same reason he avoided the kind of exposition that would suggest the existence in his mind of a finished system. Lapidary essays glancing off each other were far more appropriate to his purposes. Wishing above all not to shape new dogmas that would simply displace the orthodoxies he had so bitterly critized, Emerson shaped both his message and his semi-sermonic style to accentuate the self-reliance of all. To this end he, more effectively than any other American writer, perfected an aphoristic mode of discourse, rich in paradox and metaphor. The startling, sharply worded sentence was a distinguishing mark of his rhetoric. On many occasions he defended this dialectical emphasis. 'Speak what you think today in words as hard as cannon balls, and tomorrow speak what tomorrow thinks in hard words again, though it contradict everything you said today.' Despite all these highly purposive bafflements and hurdles, however, he produced a remarkably consistent body of thought, and the principal aim of this chapter will be to expound it.

Essential to the successful prosecution of this task, however, is a recognition of the larger social and intellectual context and historical background in which his life's endeavour was carried out. This requires some account of the rise of Transcendentalism (whether or not Emerson himself fully recognized his indebtedness to this larger fellowship) and some explanation for the tardiness with which Americans responded to European Romanticism.

In respect to the latter, the facts are not in dispute. At the turn of the nineteenth century, Western Europe was experiencing a surge of artistic and philosophical and literary innovation of unparalleled scope and depth. In America, on the other hand, the Romantic generation was at this time just being born! Two main factors account for American tardiness in responding to this trans-Atlantic innovativeness. First, the lively experientialism of the Puritan tradition had answered to human needs and sustained the religious life far more effectively than had been the case in the Old World. The other great factor was the exhilarating experience of the American Revolution and the emergence of a fervent patriotic tradition in which the traditional themes of civil religion were fused with the millennial expectations of the country's future glory. In this context even the Deism and the rationalistic theology of the Enlightenment, which were so central to the faith of the Revolutionary generation, continued for many years to supply a vital religious and moral dimension to the vast majority of the population of the 'first new nation'.

During the 1830s, Emerson and many others who would participate with him in the Transcendental movement were finding this patriotic celebrationism to be increasingly banal and inappropriate. He expresses this restiveness very perceptively in his impressive but little read 'Historical Discourse' of 1835 for the bicentennial observance of the founding of Concord, a work in which his own ancestors figure so prominently that it almost becomes a species of autobiography. He concludes with a strong reminder that circumstances beyond our control are now inaugurating a new age of hope and national self-consciousness. Even so, he could hardly have expected that a hundred years later 1836 would be hailed as the *Annus mirabilis* of Transcendentalism. The term may be somewhat hyperbolic, but it was a year marked by many strong and controversial publications, including his own. Most memorable was the series of events by which what had been a vague impulse shared by various fellow spirits now took on the habiliments of organization. For the first time there were some grounds for saying that a Transcendental *movement* had come into existence.

For a decade or more tensions had been growing in the Unitarian churches, especially among the younger clergy. Membership was declining and complacency was widespread. Conservatism in theology and unresponsiveness to the growing social problems provided other provocations. Finally a group of the most disaffected were brought to the point of collective action. On the evening of 19 September 1836, due to a proposal of Frederic Henry Hedge, who was then a minister in Bangor, Maine, the famous but loosely organized Transcendental (or Hedge) Club held its first meeting at the home of George Ripley, who was then minister of the Purchase Street Church in Boston. This group continued to meet at irregular intervals, but with declining vigour, for three or four years – the indefiniteness of its demise no doubt being an index of its ever-decreasing effectiveness. Twenty-six persons remained closely associated with its meetings. Four of these were women. All but four of the men were or had been Unitarian ministers. Beyond this group of friends, however, there was a larger group of thoughtful and articulate people, intellectuals of various types who by their writings, ministerial practice or their reform activities can be identified as more or less self-conscious participants in the movement.

Alexander Kern has shown that certain major tendencies of their thinking were almost unanimously shared: (1) dissatisfaction with the traditional forms of New England's ecclesiastical life and doctrine, (2) a shift from neo-classical norms and conventions to a greater emphasis on personal and symbolic forms of expression, (3) a turning from mechanistic to vitalistic and organic views of reality, (4) a movement away from the sensationalist epistemology of John Locke toward a stronger emphasis on intuition, (5) a pronounced preference for idealistic ways of thinking, whether Platonic or Kantian, (6) a tendency in ethics to stress the importance of individual fulfilment of one's potentialities, and (7) a growing dissatisfaction with what was perceived as the increasing commercialism of American life and as a consequence the deterioration of the human relationship to Nature. Summarizing nearly all these convictions was their general repudiation of the 'Enlightened' mentality and a turn toward the Romantic attitudes that had been gaining favour in Great Britain and the Continent since the later eighteenth century.[2] Accompanying this enthusiasm, and to a certain extent mitigating it, was a pervasive anxiety about America's place in the larger frame of world history. The problem was that America, which was socially and politically the *avant garde* of the whole world, was in many ways culturally retarded. Even Emerson admitted to a certain discomfiture, and at an early meeting of the Transcendental Club declared that 'it was a pity that in this titanic continent, where nature is so grand, genius should be so tame'. And a year later in his famous address on 'The American Scholar' he would forcefully return to this same theme.

It hardly needs saying that the group of Transcendentalists who participated in these meetings were by no means obedient followers of Emerson or anyone else. Theodore Parker did once refer to the 'young Emersonidae' who worshipped at the master's feet; but in general they were remarkably diverse in their interests and thinking. For this reason the most representative and important of them will be individually considered in the final section of this essay. In the interests of an orderly exposition of the movement, however, it is imperative that we give brief attention to the major phases of Emerson's long and productive life.

Ralph Waldo Emerson was born on Election Day, in the parsonage of Boston's First Church on 25 May 1803. At the time his father, William

Emerson, was visiting the Governor of Massachusetts, which gives some indication of the family's social status. The household in which he grew up, despite his father's liberal theology, was shaped by the piety and moral austerity of the long line of Puritan ministers in his lineage, and made even more pronounced by the presence of an aunt, Mary Moody, who was firmly committed to the older theology. The family routines were marked by prayers, Bible readings and sabbath-keeping that began on Saturday evening. Ralph Waldo from the first seems to have assumed that he would in due course enter the ministry. The way to this result, however, was made more difficult by the death of his father in 1811 and the resultant penury of his mother, which required her to become a keeper of boarding houses and her sons to earn as much as possible by teaching school or private tutoring. Despite premature deaths and much ill health in the family, Ralph Waldo was able to attend the venerable Boston Latin School, and achieve there an excellent academic record, which was in due course followed by admission to Harvard College with some financial aid. With settled family life a thing of the past, however, he was now presented by several deeply perturbing dilemmas that would only very slowly be resolved. Most obvious were the religious alternatives posed by the Unitarian rationalism of his father and the lively traditional faith of his learned and articulate aunt.

Only at the very end of his time at Harvard (1821) was he truly stirred. The occasion was an oration 'On Genius' delivered as part of the commencement proceedings by a young Swedenborgian, Sampson Reed. This exhilarating discovery was followed by conversations with Reed, readings in the *New Jerusalem Magazine*, and, most important by far, his study of the voluminous works of Emanuel Swedenborg (1688–1771). Further stimulation came in 1826 with the publication of Reed's *Reflections on the Growth of Mind*, which Emerson hailed, with characteristic lack of restraint, as 'the best thing since Plato'.

Two closely related facts about this course of events must be emphasized. Most importantly, he had confronted a body of thought that spoke directly to his own spiritual needs. This discovery was the closest he came to having a 'conversion experience'. In any case, it moved him toward a basic religious attitude that he never altered, and it gave a quality to his writing and thinking that set him apart from many of the prevailing tendencies of Western thought. The second fact is simply an extension of the first. This experience put him on the way to a body of writings and sources of inspiration which were far removed from his New England heritage, and most especially from biblical, Calvinistic, and Enlightened elements of his nurture. His powerful attraction to Swedenborgian modes of thought opened his mind to new realms of religious expression, a novel theory of language and symbolism, and a dynamic view of Platonism that would continue to shape his life long after his early passion for the Swedish seer had been modified.

Through Swedenborg Emerson had discovered that great alternative to the 'Orthodox' views of philosophy and biblical truth which is commonly referred to as the Hermetic or Secret tradition. Emerson's writings are hereafter filled with the allusions, tropes, and ideas which reveal his indebtedness to this great alternative to the biblical orthodoxies of the West. His most important testimony to the importance of this line of thought came in the 1845 lecture series on *Representative Men* in which Swedenborg is chosen as the representative mystic. In the same essay, he also gives a brief but very enthusiastic account of Jakob Boehme (1575–1642):

He is tremulous with emotion, and listens awestruck with the gentlest humanity to the Teacher whose lessons he conveys; and when he asserts that in some sort, love is greater than God, his heart beats so high that the thumping of his leathern coat is audible across the centuries.

Yet Emerson was not uncritical of these two great seers. He believed that both men had failed 'by attaching themselves to the Christian symbol instead of the moral sentiment'. He objected in particular to Swedenborg's dogmatic use of symbols and his unimaginative literary expression. Despite his reservations, however, he speaks of Swedenborg as 'the last great father in the Church', and as 'a thinker whose moral insights rank him out of comparison with any other modern writer . . .'. Emerson's entry into this vast and arcane world of thought was possibly the most important event in his personal spiritual history.

During the years of *Sturm und Drang* that followed his college graduation in 1821 Emerson gradually found himself, his essential message, and his vocation. First comes a period of interleaved school teaching, private tutoring, reading in divinity along with intermittent studies at the Harvard Divinity School. Despite persistent health problems, both personal and in the family, and great vocational uncertainty, it was a time of omnivorous reading, and concerted efforts to give meaning and direction to his life. The poet and the preacher, the old religion and the new one that is dawning strive in his soul. Then a tentative commitment is solemnized by his seeking and receiving a licence to preach in 1826. There follows a very active period of 'candidating' in many New England parishes. At this time he even shows an interest in a vacancy in the Cambridge Swedenborgian church. Outwardly he remains an apologist for liberal Christianity but his sermons reflect a declining interest in expounding biblical texts and a steady movement of his thought towards more generic moral and religious concerns. This trend becomes increasingly explicit after his ordination at the Second Church of

Boston on 11 March 1829. His interest in the history of philosophy becomes very marked, especially as he finds it in the works of two French thinkers, Degerando and Victor Cousin, both of whom are critical of the Enlightenment tradition and very favourably inclined to post-Kantian trends in Germany. They also deepen his knowledge of the Platonic tradition in all of its phases. Coleridge and then Wordsworth are also very positively entertained, and particularly the dual concepts of the Fancy and the Imagination, and the Understanding and the Reason. Beneath these famous distinctions, especially the latter, he is, of course, brought to further consideration of the Kantian turn in philosophy and the Romantic idealistic tradition that flows from it. Immediately attractive for Emerson in this context was Coleridge's strong doctrine of Reason and the Intuition, which also reflects both Swedenborg's and Schelling's emphasis on the unity of the real and the ideal. Of greatest impact on him personally was his discovery in October 1832 of Thomas Carlyle's anonymous deliverances in various British periodicals – and then most striking of all, his reading of Carlyle's serialized version of *Sartor Resartus* (1833–4). Prophetic, comic, existential and stylistically provocative, this work by Carlyle provided the young minister with an example of a non-ecclesiastical vocation and a powerfully stated point of view that seems to have become both immediately and permanently relevant. There are even signs that from this time forward Emerson's physical health is restored. Not surprisingly, he resolves to have this great work appear first in book form in America. And in 1836 it did appear, with a brief preface by Emerson.

In the midst of these promising developments, however, Emerson was brought to the point of deep personal crisis. He had married Ellen Tucker in September 1829 shortly after his ordination, but in February 1831 she died of consumption, leaving him in a state of desolation that his long contemplation of the question of immortality could not assuage. As in the similar instances of grief experienced by Novalis and Schelling, a change of outlook occurred. Emerson's commitment to his ministerial vocation became weaker and the link between the Scriptures and his preaching more attenuated. Before long he confessed to a 'positive dislike . . . for these great religious shows, congregations, temples, and sermons'. His notebooks, meanwhile, reveal a continuing movement away from the apologetical casuistry which he had come to hate. In this state of mind his long-standing objections to public prayer and the ordinance of the Lord's Supper led him to propose revisions of tradition that his parish could not accept. On 9 September 1832 he preached his farewell sermon, and in December he embarked on a long and strenuous voyage abroad. His primary objective in making that journey was fully achieved: it had enabled him to have extended conversations with Carlyle, Wordsworth, Coleridge and Walter Savage Landor. Having now seen and talked with the men he most admired, he vowed to be less timid in voicing his own thoughts.

The years between Emerson's move to Concord in 1834 and the publication of *Nature* (1836) was a time of accelerating movement in his thought and of growing confidence. He was discovering the meaning of his own experience. The fundamental elements of his view of reality were taking a form that he would never have to repudiate. The movement of his thought was gradual but its tendency was unmistakable. His repudiation of 'the pale negations' of Boston Unitarianism had involved a deep personal struggle. In 1833 when he characterized Jesus Christ as 'a minister of pure Reason' one sees a sign of his trouble. And still clearer evidence is suggested when in a journal entry of 27 December 1834, he says: 'I find the Christian religion to be profoundly true; true to an extent that they who are styled its most orthodox defenders have never, but in rarest glimpses, once or twice in a lifetime, reached.' Yet he goes on in the same passage to say that 'I, who seek to be a realist, do deny and put off everything that I do not heartily accept, do yet catch myself continually in practical unbelief of its deepest teachings.' There can be little doubt but that his decision to write a book on Nature arose from a need to state what he did 'heartily believe' and to lift from his conscience the personal deceits and theological conceits which for years he had been half-heartedly voicing.

The appearance in Boston on 9 or 10 September 1836 of a small anonymous book entitled *Nature* created no great stir or outbreak of controversy, though it was deemed by some to be a Swedenborgian publication. By Emerson's friends it was very favourably received. His fundamental doctrine of Correspondence – that Nature is a symbol of spirit – was unmistakably stated, but the book lacked the clarity and finesse and even the literary grace of a philosophical classic. Only after considerable elucidation, much controversy and years of scholarly discussion would the work be remembered as a major manifesto, and a challenge to the imagination.

It was a radical book that challenged the authority of the Bible and of the institutions that rested on its Word. It would replace the traditional faith with another. On this point the thirty-three year old teacher and poet minced no words. With inimitable orphic sentences he outlined his critique and proposed his alternative. 'Our age is retrospective. It builds on the sepulchers of the fathers. Why should not we enjoy an original relation to the universe? Why should we grope among the dry bones of the past? The sun shines today also. Let us inquire what end is Nature.' On the title page of the book stood a quotation from Plotinus which provided a valuable clue to a central thesis of this new teacher and to the sources of his teaching: 'Nature is but an image or imitation of wisdom, the last thing of the soul; nature being a thing which doth only do, but not know.'

The relationship of that which knows to that which knows not was, of course, the central concern of the little book, but not in a merely academic sense. He was delivering a summons, even a gospel, that reflected the remarkably serene and integrated life that Nietzsche would so much admire and which Emerson was already leading. There is, nevertheless a double irony that runs through this book and nearly everything that Emerson said. Relatively serious was the way in which the freedom and self-reliance that he sought for himself and for all who heard his voice was deeply indebted to a vast host of thinkers, prophets, seers, and lovers of wisdom. More profound and substantive was the closely related fact that his 'original relation to the universe' was based on a tradition as old as that which he was repudiating. He faced, in fact, the ancient alternative that Tertullian raised in the third century: Athens or Jerusalem. Emerson chose the former and compromised his position only very slightly, if at all, by his warm admiration of the Swedenborgians who contended that human-kind is now living in a dispensation that lies beyond the Grand Assize.

What Athens symbolizes in this formulation, however, is in no sense the classicism of the Athenian apogee nor that of the Roman Republic, but rather the religious philosophical tradition that had its centre in the Neo-Platonic School of Plotinus (A.D. 205–270). In Emerson's countless references to the Soul and to the Over-Soul, as well as in his mystical interpretation of Nature there are almost always strong overtones that are drawn from these ancient enthusiasms. This vast syncretistic conglomerate containing many Christian, Judaic and pagan elements had been perpetuated during the Middle Ages as a 'secret tradition' and widely rediscovered by many Romantic thinkers. The huge imaginative act by which Emerson translated this arcane tradition into a modern mode is perhaps his supreme achievement.

Except for a small group of initiates, readers of *Nature* often found many of its pronouncements mysterious and arcane, and one cannot deny that at many points it is needlessly unclear. But with the passage of time its epoch-making qualities were recognized, most forcefully by Carlyle. But Emerson had the good fortune to be invited to deliver the *Phi Beta Kappa* address at Harvard on 31 August 1837. In 'The American Scholar', which is surely one of his finest statements, he was forceful, clear and inspiring in ways that left his audience awed and exultant. It was seen by many as a declaration of

America's intellectual independence. More important for his own career, it left few grounds for doubt as to the substance of his central affirmations. His most controversial negations, however, were left unspoken. But very soon he was invited by the graduating seniors of the Harvard Divinity School to appear before them, and on 15 July 1838 delivered an address which unambiguously exposed the hard edges of his thought. This address was Emerson's *apologia pro vita sua*. It was by far the most profoundly existential of anything he had said so far. It was at once a harsh critique of the churches and of Christian theology, and an explanation of his resignation from the Christian ministry. It revealed all the pent-up fury that had been accumulating in his mind (and his notebooks) for several years. He accused the churches of preaching as if 'God were dead'. He perceived signs of a 'death of faith' and spoke of the churches' 'noxious exaggeration about the person of Jesus'. He spoke of the prevailing view of miracles as 'monster'.

In the more constructive part of his lecture he praised the institutions of the Sabbath and the Pulpit and bade each of the students before him to become a 'newborn bard of the Holy Ghost'. But there were also pantheistic overtones to his message that raised the spectre of heresy. All in all it was a bomb-shell. Almost immediately the 'Second Unitarian Controversy', which had been precipitated earlier in the year by George Ripley's attack on the traditional view of miracles, was blown to new levels of acrimony. Emerson, of course, was frequently and fervently defended by his friends, but he himself never entered the fray. In replying to the criticism of his former friends (in October 1838) he took a typical stance: 'I delight in telling what I think, but if you ask me how I dare say so or why it is so, I am the most helpless of mortal men.' It was clear, however, that he had clarified the substance of the apostolate to America which he began now to prosecute so vigorously.

The circle of Emerson's thought

The various elements of Emerson's message were ever more tightly interwoven as he explored their implications. In a manner not unlike Hegel, his thought tends towards circularity as his ideas reach out to the utmost extreme and then return, fulfilled, to their point of origin. In this restless movement can be seen the coherence of Emerson's thought. For the circle, he once wrote, 'is the highest emblem . . . the primal figure, the cipher of the world'. Possibly out of deference to Emerson's own wishes, few have measured the circle of his thought or attempted a systematic account of the thought of this man who throughout his life feared the emergence of an Emersonian system. And yet, despite his frequent resort to paradox and his characterization of consistency as the hobgoblin of small minds, his mature thought from the publication of *Nature* in 1836 to the end of his days forms a rounded whole.

I. The attack on materialism and the doctrine of 'Correspondence'

In his unusually lucid exposition of 'the Transcendentalist' in the address of that title delivered at the Masonic Hall in Boston (1842) Emerson observed that 'mankind have ever been divided into two sects, Materialists and Idealists'. He then went on to define and defend Idealism but his essay also serves a larger purpose by showing Transcendentalism as a movement that not only opposed materialism as a specific philosophical position, but also a movement for the reshaping of a culture and the reforming of a social order that was abandoning the principles of morality and justice. It was, moreover, also joined with other Romantics in America and in Europe in the hope of overturning the prevailing views and values of the Enlightenment in almost every realm of thought and practice. They envisioned a society that would not lay waste its powers in getting and spending. They would break from all forms of living and thinking that were spiritually inert. And since Boston Unitarianism was the only denomination in America that had committed itself to the Enlightenment position, the reformers were usually severe in their criticism of the attitudes and institutions of the tradition they had inherited. What they did locally, however, was deemed applicable to the condition of the entire American nation.

As one moves from the general aims of a movement to Emerson himself we face the vocational questions which troubled him for many years, but which he solved in a very distinctive way. 'I am born a poet', he assured himself on 1 February 1835, '. . . of low class without doubt, yet a poet . . . I am a poet in the sense of a perceiver of the harmonies that are in the soul and in matter, and especially of the correspondence between these and those.' In his later essay on this topic the form and content of the poet's role was far more developed – and magnified.

The poet is Representative, he stands among partial man for the complete man . . . He is isolated among his contemporaries by truth that will draw all men sooner or later . . . The poet is the sayer, the namer, and represents beauty. The sign and credentials of the poet are that he announces that which no man foretold. He is the true and only doctor . . . an utterer of the necessary and the causal . . . there is a great public power on which he may draw . . . he is caught up in the life of the universe . . . The poet knows that he speaks adequately only when he speaks somewhat wildly.

This resounding description is at once both general and self-referential. The Poet is the seer, Prophet, and teacher who speaks the truth from on high. The mere savant 'is chatty and vain. When hard questions are asked, they will come to Plato, Proclus, and Swedenborg.' Except by implication Emerson never places himself in the same exalted category, but everywhere in his writing the unspoken conclusion is assumed; and an essential aspect of Transcendentalism will be misunderstood if this element is ignored.

As one considers Emerson's delineation of the poet it becomes apparent that Nature and the doctrine of Correspondence are intrinsic elements of his thought. Like Jonathan Edwards before him he was in the most direct and crucial way fascinated and deeply moved by the natural world around him, whatever its mood. The starlight, the snow, the rocks by the seashore were his friends and comforters, a source of endless delight, a challenging mystery and also a stimulus to the poetic imagination. He was first led to this life-long interest by his friends in the New Church who lived in the awesome shadow of Emanuel Swedenborg, but his most sustained source of illumination stemmed from his reading of the Neo-Platonic writers of antiquity and other hermetic and gnostic thinkers in the Western tradition. From this viewpoint all of nature in its parts and as a whole is a symbol of spiritual reality. A further effect of this angle of vision was that it revived Emerson's interest in the Baconian ideal, which, in turn, lent new relevance to his collegiate study of Thomas Reid and Dugald Stewart who had strongly supported the inductive methods that led to the formulation of Nature's laws in ways that might ultimately explain every aspect of the physical world. From this point on Emerson's knowledge of these laws and his interest in the exploits of scientists is continually evidenced in nearly all of his works.

At the same time, however, Nature became for him a holy thing that shimmered before his gaze as an object of profound religious significance. With deep indebtedness to Bishop Joseph Butler's *Analogy* (1736) Emerson built his own theory of correspondence that freed him from the literalism and specificity of Swedenborg's system. It became for him a mode of expression of great literary and rhetorical power. Nature became the ground for an almost infinite extrapolation of moral and religious implications. Nature was a symbolic system which lent itself to the rich multiplications of metaphor that characterize all of his writing and almost make 'tropology' a name for his system of thought. All the 'compensations' visible in Nature could be given moral equivalents. Time after time in ways that remind one of Jonathan Edwards, 'images and shadows of divine things' and certainly with an awareness of the Puritan propensity to typological interpretations of Scripture, Emerson would open or illuminate his discourses with images that had for him the authority of scriptural texts. Whereas Swedenborg had developed an hermeneutical system that justified a spiritual interpretation of an ostensibly infallible Bible, Emerson moved directly from Nature in almost any of its manifestations and then, in a manner unique to him, developed a sermonic mode that invested his lectures and then his essays with a strength that was both edifying and normative in its effects.

In this same context it is important to recognize that Emerson's interest in symbols and correspondence was significantly informed by the alchemical tradition, in fact the instances are so numerous they are often not noticed. Some are veiled, as in the final paragraph of his essay on Nature where he sees the world as mind precipitated. 'Nature is the incarnation of thought, and turns to thought again as ice becomes water and gas.' More specific but too long for quotation here is the opening of his abstruse but central essay on Intellect where he develops the spiritual implications of the 'law' that 'every substance is negatively electric to that which stands above it on the chemical tables'.

How thoughts like these stimulated the imagination and made it a power unto itself is obvious, as is its significance in the rise of modern symbolism; but it also has a transforming impact on the relation of Nature to human being. In this sense it is appropriate to interpret Emerson's thought as a profound form of nature mysticism.

II. Mysticism and the 'Catholic' Emerson

The modulation from the topic of Nature in Emerson's thought to that of mysticism is not only inescapable but also difficult. Creating the largest problem is the cacophony of clashing definitions. The word 'mysticism', even in the usage of respectable scholars, leads us to a wild array of people whose only common trait is religious fervency. My solution to this problem is to limit the category to those whose thought and attitudes more or less approximate the classic and perennial tendencies associated with Meister Eckhardt, Teresa of Avila, John of the Cross, the anonymous author of *The Cloud of Unknowing*, and, above all, Plotinus, who is the fountainhead of the Western tradition in both its 'orthodox' and 'heretical' forms. The other great problem is that created by Emerson himself, in that his departures from the classic pattern are both obvious and important. On the other hand, his intellectual and spiritual commitments and, to a certain extent his personal comportment, keep him within the mystic circle. He qualifies, therefore, as a modernizing adept who shares the rapture of the ancient mystery religions and perceives their relationship to the more distant traditions of Persia and India. His interest, moreover, is subjective and existential and not primarily scholarly. When he sought inspiration, he turned to the *Timaeus*, the *Symposium* and the *Parmenides* – all works which had been most admired by Neo-Platonists, ancient and modern.

Emerson's own commitment to Platonic thought was unqualified and life-long: 'Plato is philosophy, and philosophy Plato . . . out of Plato all things come that are still written and debated. With him we have reached the mountain from which all these drift boulders were detached.' But Emerson's Platonism was suffused by the religious ethos of late Classical times and far removed from the more objective and 'scientific' translations of later decades. Inspired as he was by the ecstasies of ancient religion, Emerson (like Edwards before him) could lament the routinization of religion. In his own way he therefore called for a revival and even spoke of the divine gift and of inner experience. Early in his essay on the Over-Soul he says that

Our faith comes in moments; our vice is habitual . . . When I watch that flowing river which out of regions I see not pours for a season its stream into me, I see that I am a pensioner, not a cause, but a surprised spectator of this ethereal water . . . and I put myself in the attitude of reception. From some alien energy the visions come.

This sublime influx he was happy to call *revelation*, 'an ebb of the individual rivulet before the flowing surges of the sea of life'. It is received in joy and obedience, with awe and delight, as if from the Divine Mind, the Eternal One.

In the procession of topics from mysticism to Catholicism there is an obvious logic since the Western mystical tradition has been largely Catholic. One must recognize at the outset, nonetheless, that both Emerson and his Unitarian predecessors understood themselves to be carrying the Reformation impulse a large and important step beyond that of Luther and Calvin. Emerson bore to his life's end many marks of his Puritan legacy, even though he abhorred the doctrinal stance and dogmatic attitudes of the Reformed tradition. Among Protestants only the Quakers and the Swedenborgians received his favour, though he would always praise an authentic prophet like the Methodist Father Taylor, of the Boston seaman's mission, or at the other end of the spectrum, the irenic Dr Channing whom he regarded as the bishop of the Transcendentalists.

For the post-Tridentine Roman Catholic Church he had less good to speak. Its authoritarian structure, its dogmatic inflexibility, and its long record of heretic-hunting ran counter to his democratic sympathies, his educational theory, and his understanding of true self-hood. On the other hand, many aspects of Emerson's outlook during his most creative period were not only catholic but profoundly Catholic. First and most ironic was the simple fact that almost any movement away from Puritanism is unavoidably toward Catholicism, in that Puritanism can almost be defined as systematic anti-catholicism. He also took a more positive stance in many other respects. Most important was his sustained appreciation for the Neo-Platonic heritage which he shared with 'heretics' like Origen and pagans like

Plotinus, as well as Church Fathers like Clement and Augustine. In these writings he discovered an unfettered imagination in the use of symbols, metaphor, and allegory that not only awakened his own imagination but deepened his respect for contemplative piety, a philosophical approach to theology and lively appreciation for the numinous or mysterious dimensions of religion. Perhaps above all he shared its cosmic concern and its recognition that reality is a unified whole. In this latter respect, however, Emerson showed a clear preference for the more heterodox or esoteric forms of speculation that seemed to flourish more luxuriantly in Catholic than in Protestant contexts.

The primary stimulation for this general tendency in Emerson seems to have come first of all from the essentially Catholic mentality of Shakespeare – and the worlds bodied forth in his plays. Almost as incontinently did he admire the baroque imagery and daring heresies of Milton's cosmic dramas. Of lesser moment but also important were those Catholic worlds that live in the works of Chaucer, Dante, Spenser and Goethe's *Faust*. Finally, and perhaps as important as any, was the impact of Emerson's extensive – and always intensive – travels in Europe. He was not as enraptured as Longfellow or even Irving had been, but his travel diaries and retrospective writings reveal a steady modification of inherited attitudes. He discovers the values of Catholic worship and he admires Catholic attitudes towards the arts.

Odd as it may seem, a very significant aspect of Emerson's growing openness to Catholic thought and culture stems from his even greater enthusiasm for the paganism of antiquity – Greek, Roman and Egyptian. Emerson reversed the characteristic views of the Protestant Reformers. He was grateful for the syncretistic tendencies of the Roman Church. Catholicism appealed to him *because* many aspects of the ancient pagan world lived on in its thought, piety, ceremony and religious culture. Like Schleiermacher he came to appreciate the difference between worship that concentrated on the word and that which stressed symbolic action. As he distanced himself from his parish experience he also recognized the values of ceremony and pageantry. In his essay on the subject he acknowledged that 'worship is in some commanding relationship with the health of man'. He also knew that people of every type and clime will have their days, their festivals and their shrines, 'we are born believing. A man bears beliefs as a tree bears apples . . . You say there is no religion now? It is like saying in rainy weather that there is no sun.'

We must recognize, moreover, that a rising interest in Catholicism was not only present in the larger sphere of European Romanticism but also in the Transcendental movement itself. Orestes Brownson, Sophia Ripley, and

Isaac Hecker became Roman Catholics as did several others who were more remotely related to the movement. Still others took positions on various issues in ways that suggest a similar rationale. Acute dissatisfaction with those forms of the religious life engendered by the Puritan tradition turned them in varying degrees towards the most imposing alternative, at least to the extent of adopting more charitable attitudes. It would thus appear that the main tenets of Transcendentalism encouraged this tendency in several positive ways.

III. Fate and organic form

Robert C. Pollock in his penetrating study of Emerson from a professedly Roman Catholic point of view reserves some of his strongest approbation for Emerson's 'unwearying effort' to 'free men from the delusion of a split universe', and returning them to a view of 'the eternal One'.[3] The point is justly made. Aside from the intrinsically related problem of self-reliance and the question of human freedom, Emerson asserts no doctrine with greater frequency and force than his *monism*. And it is nowhere stated more clearly than in the 'sublime creed' which he set forth in his Divinity School Address:

The world is not the product of manifold power, but of one will, of one mind; and that one mind is everywhere active, in each ray of the star, in each wavelet of the pool; and whatever opposes that will is everywhere balked and baffled, because things are made so, and not otherwise.

That Emerson remained steadfast in this creed is documented by explicit statement or innuendo in nearly everything he wrote after 1836; but it is important that these statements always entailed certain corollaries: that Nature was always 'and everywhere active, and that reality must be understood as a living organic whole in which spirit and nature are not separated'. These corollaries are in fact clearly stated on the two or three pages that follow the creed, but it was in the opening paragraphs of 'The American Scholar' of 1837 that he most successfully summarized his idea of organic form, and then linked it to the larger question of the religious life. As usual Nature was his starting point:

There is never a beginning, there is never an end to the inexplicable continuity of this web of God, but always circular power returning to itself. Therein it resembles his own spirit, whose beginning and ending he can never find – so entire, so boundless. Far too as her splendors shine, system on system, shooting like rays upward, downward, without centre, without circumference – in the mass and in the particle, Nature hastens to render account of herself to the mind.

This dynamic process, moreover, portended much more than remorseless and meaningless change; it was an evolutionary process of development. At least by 1844 Emerson had read and thought his way to a theory of evolution not unlike that which Goethe for similar reasons had been moving toward for two decades. When Darwin's *Origin of Species* and *Descent of Man* were published, Emerson was unperturbed. Having no positivistic inclinations, however, he was not drawn toward hastily conceived doctrines of social Darwinism. On the other hand, his notion of inexorable laws and his conception of organic form did bring the question of freedom prominently to the fore.

It was in his famous essays on 'Self-Reliance' and 'Fate' that he came to terms most directly with the two poles of his thinking. As one would expect, his position on fate and freedom is dialectical. He remains steadfast to the optimistic conclusions of his pivotal essay on 'Compensation'. 'The soul refuses limits and always affirms a progress, not a station.' He asserts the doctrine of Nemesis which lets no offence go unchastised. Speaking from personal experience, he says that even the death of a wife or brother which at first seemed to be nothing but privation, 'somewhat later assumes the aspect of a guide or genius'. The universe is never malignant. Nature is compensatory. Evil is privative. The perception of the law of laws is divine and deifying. 'It is the beatitude of man.' If rightly perceived, it has all the force of Nature behind it. Each person's duty, therefore, is to participate in the purposes of the Almighty. 'Trust thyself' he says at the outset of 'Self-Reliance', 'every heart vibrates to that iron string. Accept the place the Divine Providence has found for you . . . who would be a man must be a non-conformist. Nothing is at last sacred but the integrity of your own mind. Absolve you to yourself.'

During the decade that separated 'Self-Reliance' and 'Fate' Emerson became more sombre but there is no change in his viewpoint: 'Fate is unpenetrated causes.' At another point he hazarded a contradiction: 'Freedom is necessary.' In explaining the processes of life, however, he gives large attention to the historical, hereditary and social factors that shape the course of human affairs. Yet he knew that 'Nature is no Sentimentalist . . . At Naples three years ago ten thousand persons were crushed in a few minutes . . . Providence has a wild rough road to its end.'

For him history is the interaction of Nature and thought – two boys pushing each other on the kerbstone of the pavement. Everything is pusher or pushed.

Therefore let us build altars to the Blessed Unity which holds nature and souls in perfect solution and compels every atom to serve a universal end . . . Let us build altars to the Beautiful Necessity, which secures that all is made of one piece. Why should we be afraid of nature, which is no more than philosophy and theology embodied?

We cannot shun a danger that is appointed or incur one that is not. 'There are no contingencies: the law which rules throughout existence . . . solicits the pure in heart to draw on all its omnipotence.' It is clear in any case that Emerson, in his own way was moving, as many a Romantic before him, toward a form of dynamic pantheism. The Swedenborgian doctrine of Providence provided an early impetus, and it was soon strengthened by his reading Coleridge's more daring early writings, though he found the later works too conservative, and still later judged Coleridge as 'tarnished' by his plagiarisms. By and large, however, his indebtedness is beyond tracing, though it is clear that Goethe's serene stance was an inspiration to him and he seems to have at least heard about Herder's *Conversations on God and the Spinozan System* (1787) which was a milestone in the revival of Spinoza's reputation and the rise of Romantic pantheism. For the most part he worked out his own way to an 'Identity-Philosophy'. 'Do not teach me of Schelling', he expostulated, 'I shall find it all out for myself.' How this view of things went far beyond the satisfactions of working out a philosophical idea is suggested at least in the reflections occasioned by the death of his wife in 1831: 'I loved Ellen and love her with an affection that would ask nothing but its indulgence to make me blessed. Yet when she was taken from me . . . I still felt that it was particular, that the universe remained to us both.'

IV. Romantic idealism

Emerson once confessed that his 'first lesson in idealism' had come to him as a child, musing in the church pew about the arbitrary linkage of words and things. It was a disposition he never lost. Almost all of his subsequent reading and thinking seemed to deepen his commitment to an idealistic view of reality. 'There are degrees in idealism', said Emerson in 'Circles'. 'We learn first to play with it academically as the magnet was once a toy', but later 'its countenance waxes stern and grand, and we see that it must be true.' Perhaps most decisive in deepening his own commitment were those primal mystical experiences that came to him as revelation. They gave substance to the Coleridgean distinction between the Understanding and the Reason as well as his life-long commitment to Plato and the Neo-Platonists; his disdain for Locke and his dissatisfaction with the Scottish realists turned him to a very serious study of Kant and his Romantic successors. The resultant tensions became a major element in the inner dialogue of his mind. By the time *Nature* was being written the Fichtean distinction between the Me and the Not Me was anchored in his mind. Even more revealing was the distinction he made in Chapter Four between 'the sensual man [who] conforms thoughts to things and the Poet [who] conforms things to thought'. Here too, he insists that 'the imagination may be defined as the use which Reason makes of the material world'. By 1842, as we have seen, he explicitly makes idealism the central mark of the Transcendentalist.

Emerson by no means recapitulated in his own mind the argument of Kant's critiques of the Pure and Practical Reason nor did he try to penetrate the famous set of modulations that led to Fichte's *Theory* of *Knowledge* (*Wissenschaftslehre*, 1794) or the subsequent developments of Schelling and Hegel.

From very early in his career, however, the phenomenal nature of our knowledge of the world was an intrinsic element of Emerson's thought. His view of the moral life and his notion of 'Character' likewise bear the marks of a strong Kantian influence. There also came to be a very close affinity between Emerson's thought and the almost mystical way in which Fichte in his *Theory of Religion* (*Religionslehre*, 1806) affirmed the unity of the finite consciousness and the infinite ego. He strove to develop a point of view that would satisfy his own inner needs and give philosophical shape to his vision of a unitary and dynamic cosmos. These views had been taking shape in his mind since his earliest reading of Sampson Reed, Swedenborg, and Plotinus. Taken together, these influences virtually required him to formulate a philosophy of identity. To a degree he had been aided in this search by Coleridge, Spinoza and Schleiermacher. He also knew of Schelling's tendencies but insisted on using his own compass. And this he did during the years after his announcement of the idea in the 1830s. Probably unaware that Schelling was deeply inspired by similar influences, Emerson turned to the esoteric doctrines of the Neo-Platonists and Jakob Boehme and their concept of the World-Soul, the *Anima Mundi*, the intermediating principle between mind and matter. He sees the primordial atom as a micro-example of the soul in which there is a kind of potential omniscience. 'Every natural fact is an emanation from which other emanations will follow.' But beneath all differentiations of thought and things, as he declares in his great essay on the Over-Soul, there is the eternal ONE, 'and in this deep power . . . the act of seeing and the thing seen, the seer and the spectacle, the subject and the object are one'. According to the same logic, as he said over and over in many ways, the worshipper is one with the object of adoration.

If Emerson in his own way adopts the critical outlook of Kant, the idealism of Fichte, and a movement toward the Identity-Philosophy of Schelling, it is appropriate and tantalizing to ask the question: Did he in any ways approximate to the philosophy of Hegel? The answer, despite the widely held view to the contrary, must be affirmative. In fact he established his interest in the subject very early by delivering a twelve-part lecture series on the Philosophy of History in 1837. He returned to it frequently as he became more interested in the nature of organic process in both the human realm and the natural world. One may thus speak of his entire oeuvre as a 'phenomenology of spirit'. A constantly deepening historical consciousness is apparent. Both thinkers quite independently were fascinated and deeply affected by the phenomenon of Napoleon – the *Weltsehle* and the Representative man. 'Napoleon is Europe', writes Emerson, 'it is because the peoples he sways are little Napoleons.' With Hegel, too, he shares an awareness that history is the great slaughter-bench of the people, just as they both felt that 'history is the judgement of the world' (*Weltgeschichte ist Weltgericht*) and saw in the turbulent events of the years of 1789 to 1815 the dawn of a new age.

Because he has been so widely misread Emerson, unlike Hegel, is almost never seen as formulating an historical view of reality; but evolutionism is intrinsic to his very thought – from the self-kindling atom to the great social processes by which 'each nation grows after its own genius'. The first sentence of Emerson's essay on 'History' opens the door to this misunderstanding with the assertion that 'there is one mind common to all individual men'. He gives the impression that human historicity is an illusion, when, in fact, he is providing his own equivalent to Hegel's notion of the *Selbstbewustsein Überhaupt* (the general self-consciousness). But he quickly corrects this impression by insisting that 'man is explicable by nothing less than all of his history'. In 'Circles', despite another confusing essay title, he sketches out the view of time's remorseless out-dating of all our changing grounds of interpretation that dramatically anticipates the *Weltanschauungslehre* which Hegel adumbrated and which Wilhelm Dilthey developed in the early twentieth century. Emerson even goes on to the view of Dilthey and Croce that historicism of this sort is in fact a work of human liberation – a break from the bondage of tradition.

Every ultimate fact is only the first of a new series . . . In the thought of tomorrow there is a power to upheave all thy creed . . . and marshall thee to a heaven that no epic dream has yet depicted. There is not a piece of science but its flank may be turned tomorrow; there is not any literary reputation . . . that may not be revised and condemned . . . Life is full of surprises.

When Emerson is empathically read – as he was by Walt Whitman – he awakens the spirit of Hegel.

V. Reform and social order

'The country is full of rebellion', says Emerson in the opening gambit of his essay on 'New England Reformers'. But in comparing the country's myriad reformers to 'a congress of kings', he had already disclosed his strategy. In an oft-quoted letter to Carlyle his lack of sympathy was made explicit: 'We are all a little wild here with numberless projects of reform. Not a reading man but has a draft of a new community in his waistcoat pocket.' Emerson was not a reformer. In the first place he was temperamentally almost incapable of joining a group or participating in a collective enterprise. He also perceived the essential superficiality of many of the campaigns being launched and the unworthiness of others. Yet neither was he a revolutionary with hopes for deep structural change. He understood better than most that from a world perspective the very continued existence of the United States constituted a permanent revolution. He realized, too, that even aside from the horror of constitutionalized chattel slavery, that injustice, materialism and corruption were rife in the land. Everywhere people were laying waste the land, and losing themselves in a search for wealth and power. In the face of this moral crisis, however, he regarded the ameliorative efforts of revivalists and reformers as trivial.

Emerson's direct and purposive efforts to effect objective changes in the world were almost non-existent. He did, while a pastor, get the Second Church to adopt a new and more liberal hymnal and construct a new vestry hall; but he had small confidence in institutions other than secular forms of the Sabbath and the Pulpit. He expected very little from the American political order. 'The State must follow and not lead the character and progress of the citizen.' His essay on 'Politics' tends toward a minimal view of laws. 'The less government we have, the better.' 'Every actual state is corrupt.' He was noncommittal on the two major parties: 'One has the best cause, and the other contains the best men.' Having more confidence in persons than in platforms, he leaned toward conservative men – the Whigs, until the rising anti-slavery movement slowly drew him into the abolitionist ranks; but it was only after John Brown's raid that he was aroused, and even then he admitted that the only thing worse than his anti-slavery lectures was slavery itself. The only despot he would listen to was Nature: 'We must trust finitely to the benificent necessity which shines through all the laws.' Compared to the stern rule of this powerful goddess, reform movements seemed futile, even if directed by his dearest friends at Brook Farm.

As a critic of society, on the other hand, he could be extremely severe, and not only with regard to the immemorial venality of office holders. To him the traditional American understanding of 'equality no longer looked so self-evident as it appeared in former times, because our laws and usages allowed the rich to encroach on the poor, and keep them poor'. Referring to the 'popular' Jacksonian party, he believed that 'our American radicalism is destructive and aimless; it is not loving. It has no ulterior and divine ends.'

With regard to the economic system he foreshadows Karl Marx's prediction of the dehumanization of work. 'Piracy and war gave way to trade, politics and letters; the war lord to law-lord; the law-lord to the merchant and the mill owner . . . capitalists have the same power over the workers that the feudal lords had over churls.'

It must never be said, therefore, that Emerson was oblivious to the social and political realities of his time. He recognized the significance of techno-logical change and the awful impact of machine production. But he saw his own mission as that of altering the only thing that could alter the system. He sought a redirection of the moral sentiment. The Emerson revolution called for a *bouleversement* of values and a more profound understanding of the ultimate. In this respect too, he shows a certain affinity to Marx. Yet in politics as in every other realm of concern Emerson championed a radical individualism that verged on anarchism. Freedom of thought and individual development were the primary goods. He hated authoritarian institutions of all sorts – and intolerant persons as well. He was disgusted by the crass and materialistic attitudes engendered by capitalism, and was appalled by the injustice it created but could not amend. At times, therefore, he exposed a certain nostalgia for the less depersonalized life of earlier ages. But his love of intellectual liberty and self-development, together with his distrust of government and his fear of collective enterprises of all sorts brought him back to his central theme – that only the moral transformation of individuals could lead the people to a new and better social order. 'The antidote to the abuse of power was the influence of character.' He conceded that 'in our barbarous society the influence of character is in its infancy', but its potential for growth modified his despair for the country's future. We cannot embark here into the complex history of the concept of 'character' in the nineteenth century, but for Emerson it was 'Nature in its highest form'. In his essay on the topic, he equates it with 'selfsufficingness'. Basically, however, this issue becomes the occasion for issuing yet another moral summons.

Emerson was thus a revolutionary reformer, but only in the radical spiritual sense of the term. What was to become for him a settled conviction was revealed on 5 March 1834 in an afterthought recorded in his journal.

I regret one thing omitted in my late course of lectures: that I did not state with distinctness and conspicuously, the great error of modern society in respect to religion, and say you can never come to any peace or power until you put your whole reliance in the moral constitution of man, and not at all in a historical Christianity. The belief in Christianity that now prevails is the Unbelief of men. They will have Christ for a Lord and not for a brother. Christ preaches the greatness of man, but we hear only the greatness of Christ.

In July 1835 (undated) he made the same point in another way: "tis curious that Christianity . . . is sturdily defended by the brokers, and steadily attacked by the idealists'. And from this time on through his entire active career, despite chilling rebuffs and hostile criticism, he made his unique nature-rooted message of deliverance the central element of his social gospel. He calls for that identification of human being and natural being on which all morals and all religion depend. To have character in its highest form is to align one's self with those spiritual laws which are transparent in nature. One who makes those laws the ground of a stern imperative will love justice and become incorruptible. The sentiment of virtue or the religious sentiment, as Emerson declares in the Divinity School Address, is 'divine and deifying' and for that reason 'it is the foundation of society'. He insists, however, that this state of beatitude is an intuition of the Reason and not a thing of the Understanding or a matter of mere intellectual assent. It comes only by provocation: 'it is a primary faith which I must find true in me, or reject'. Politics and existential religion are one.

Representative American Transcendentalists

Ralph Waldo Emerson – body, soul and *oeuvre* – constitutes a single entity, complex and enigmatic to be sure, but a concrete object of historical interest. Transcendentalism, however, presents more difficult conceptual problems, chief among which is the question of boundaries. Whom do we include? The answer is not easily given, and even at the time there were sceptics and critics who saw the 'movement' as a miscellaneous gathering of malcontents and radicals. One cannot doubt however that a network of friends defended each other and participated in a bitter controversy that continued for at least four decades. During that long period the group institutionalized its ideals through the Transcendental Club, the famous communal experiments (one led by the Ripleys, the other by the Alcotts) and two periodicals, *The Dial* and *The Harbinger*. In an ideal sense, as we shall see, it still has its votaries.

The most thoughtfully inclusive roster of the Transcendental fellowship is that compiled by Alexander Kern, who named no fewer than thirty-nine participants.[4] It is clear that here we can attend to only the leading voices of the movement. Nine stand out from the others: Henry David Thoreau (1817–1862), Orestes Brownson (1803–1876), Theodore Parker (1810–1860), Frederic Henry Hedge (1805–1890), James Freeman Clarke (1810–1888), Margaret Fuller (1810–1850), George Ripley (1802–1880), Sophia Ripley (*c.* 1807–1861) and Bronson Alcott (1799–1888). And, of these, only five can be singled out for extended treatment: Thoreau, Brownson, Parker, Fuller and Alcott.

Born fourteen years after Emerson and dying a decade before him, *Henry David Thoreau* was often taken as no more than an acolyte of the master, in whose house he lived for a time. Thoreau's importance was only slowly acknowledged. Octavius Brooks Frothingham in his important history of the movement (1876) ignored him almost entirely. By the time of the centennial observances of 1961–2, however, a drastic revision of his reputation had taken place. A controversial postage stamp was issued depicting him with a beard. He had become the most widely read of the Transcendentalists. *Walden* had been published in more than 130 editions, his works had been collected in a twenty-volume edition, forty-one book-length biographies and monographs and at least thirty-two doctoral dissertations had been written. Even more consequential was the way in which his 'Civil Disobedience' became the bible of that decade's protest movements, whether for peace, racial justice, or the environment. As the technocratic evisceration of American life and culture continued, there were strong grounds for expecting his reputation to continue its growth.

Thoreau was born in Concord in 1817 and except for the first six years lived there with his family until his death in 1862. At Harvard he received an education much like that of Emerson, even to the detail of hearing a commencement speaker of unusual rhetorical power. The day was made memorable for him by Emerson's delivery of his address on 'The American Scholar'. In that very year Thoreau opened his private journal and began his long but not always easy friendship with Emerson. His interests and enjoyments were extremely diverse. He taught school, delivered occasional lectures, worked as a surveyor, assisted at his father's lead-pencil factory and developed valuable technological improvements. He was also a very skilled craftsman and woodworker. For a time he assisted Emerson in the editing of the short-lived Transcendentalist magazine, *The Dial*. He was an insatiable reader with an extremely wide range of interests, and a very gifted linguist in the classical and major European languages. In the field of natural history his interests were intense, continuous and productive. His studies of Walden Pond give him a place in the history of limnology; he was also a pioneer ecologist before the term was current, and even more ahead of the times as a conservationist. It is very important, therefore, that he not be categorized as a sentimental nature-lover or as a wilderness-loving recluse. After one of his visits to the Maine woods he indicated a preference for Concord rather than the wilderness; and it was in that town, as he also said, that he did most of his travelling.

In the most direct and simple sense Thoreau is an essayist and minor poet in the Emersonian tradition. Nearly all of his best-known works, as well as the minor ones, bring the reader and the writer alike into a direct confrontation with Nature in its detail and with the cosmos as a whole. The basic subject matter of his discourse, however, is fundamentally religious and ethical, though these two interlocking concerns are woven together in a mode and idiom that is also autobiographical and uniquely his own.

His decision to become a writer, and even the self-knowledge that dictated his approach seems to have come very early; and his first great step in fulfilling that aim came only two years after his graduation when he and his brother, John, spent their now famous week on the Concord and Merrimack rivers. The book of that title, however, was not written until he made his even more famous two-year stay at Walden Pond (1845–7), and it would not be published until 1849. But in that year he laid the groundwork for yet another work, by making a walking-tour of Cape Cod. *Walden*, or *Life in the Woods* would appear in 1854, but *Cape Cod* and *The Maine Woods* were published posthumously in 1864 by his sister, Sophia, and the younger William Ellery Channing. Though he wrote many other essays in this same mode, these are the works that above all reveal his capacity for combing and illuminating detail and meditative study of his own life that would at the same time be existentially relevant to his readers. Crucial to the substance of Thoreau's thought is his concern for the inner landscape. It was more important to him than all the wondrous things he beheld in the outer world. Sherman Paul in his fine introduction to *Walden* refers to Thoreau as the 'pre-eminent self-surpasser'. He asks us to consider the rewards and costs of a personally formed life. He asks us not to consider our roles, but our vocations, and to find vocations that in the old religious sense are justifiable. And no aspect of his life and thought is more universally conceded than that he most nearly achieved his own purposes in the book *Walden*, which was published in 1854 at his own expense. It is at that place by Walden Pond where he built his hut on Emerson's wood lot that the pilgrims come, year after year, and reverently pause as if they stood on holy ground.

Exactly why he took this ascetic venture can only be guessed, since his own words on the subject are cryptic. 'My purpose', he says, 'was not to live cheaply or dearly there, but to transact some private business with the fewest obstacles.' But in his conclusion he is more explicit about what he learned.

I learned this at least, by my experiment; that if one advances confidently in the direction of his dreams, and endeavors to live the life which he had imagined, he will meet with a success unexpected in common hours. He will put some things behind, will pass an invisible boundary; new, universal, and more liberal laws will begin to establish themselves around and within him; or the old laws be expanded and interpreted in his favor in a more liberal sense, and he will live with the licence of a higher order of beings. In proportion as he simplifies his life, the laws of the universe will appear less complex and solitude will not be solitude, nor poverty poverty, nor weakness weakness.[5]

In any general assessment of Thoreau's work as a whole it must be said that his most famous and influential utterance was his essay on 'Civil Disobedience' which figured prominently in the thought of both Gandhi and Martin Luther King. It was published in 1849 to justify his refusal to pay the town poll tax and to dramatize his opposition to slavery. But he was not either a social reformer or a persistent abolitionist. As has already been suggested, his primary interests were moral and religious; and their basic thrust has a threefold character.

The first matter to clarify is Thoreau's large and continuing indebtedness to Emerson. It may be seen in the passage quoted above, and many of the leading Emersonian concepts constantly recur, most often in his statements on Nature and its immutable laws, and on fate, as well as on his general religious views. This tendency continues, moreover, despite his unsatisfactory intellectual relationship with the older man. At the same time Emerson learned much from Thoreau and showed his deep respect in his memorial essay though he was somewhat churlish in his suggestion that Thoreau 'seldom thanked colleagues for their service to him, whilst yet his debt to them was important'. Yet Emerson's tribute was both admiring and perceptive. Never, he said, were soul and body so well fitted. He also stood in awe of Thoreau's skills, his strong hands, his powers of mensuration, and his extraordinary knowledge of natural history.

Equally important to an understanding of Thoreau is his almost total alienation from Christianity and the biblical tradition. Emerson to a degree may have contributed to this attitude, but Thoreau is far more vehement, persistent and compulsive in his denunciation of theology, the clergy, and the churches. Contrary to the views of nearly all visitors to New England, he deems the church buildings to be 'the ugliest structure in any town'. In 1841 he withdrew his membership from the First Parish in Concord.

In the final analysis, however, Thoreau's tiresome negations are far less important than his remarkable commitment to the study of mysticism and the world's great religions, for it was in this sphere that his life-shaping affirmations become manifest. 'I am a mystic' he once declared and in that realm even the edifying works of the Christian, Francis Quarles, inspired him. But it was the religions of the East that became the centre of his interest. Independently and in collaboration with Emerson on translations published in *The Dial*, and through intensive reading of European scholarship he became one of the country's foremost authorities. After receiving a gift of forty-four major works in the field from the admiring Englishman, Thomas Cholmondeley, Thoreau may have owned the best private library on the subject in the country. It is only with the publication of his classic, *Walden*, however, that readers could benefit from the depth and insight that had come to him.

Orestes Augustus Brownson was a stormy spiritual wanderer who moved into the Transcendental ambiance with *élan*, positivity and unusual philosophical talent and then with equal decisiveness made a sudden exit as a Catholic, denouncing his erstwhile colleagues as so many lost sheep. He was born in rural Vermont into an orthodox family and after a considerable time of religious drift had entered the Presbyterian church in 1822, but after two years in a context that he found cramped and dogmatic, he shifted his allegiance to the Universalists in whose company he became, between 1824 and 1829, an effective preacher and the editor of a denominational journal, until his increasing liberalism led to dissatisfaction in the constituency. He then became, as he confessed, a free-thinker in association with the British reformer Fanny Wright. In this period he also became active in the Working Men's Party. Then in 1831 his life was drastically changed: deeply moved by the writings of William Ellery Channing, he became a Unitarian, and after some short ministries elsewhere he entered the Boston scene in 1836, where he soon became an enthusiastic Transcendentalist. Always energetic, he founded a reform journal and organized the Society for Christian Union and Progress with the hope of reaching the labouring class of Boston. Though widely read, he was especially attracted to various French thinkers, particularly Benjamin Constant, Victor Cousin and a group of Saint-Simonian thinkers; and out of these studies came his important little book, *New Views of Christianity, Society, and the Church*. What above all characterized his thinking was a thoroughgoing doctrine of the divine immanence and an idealistic view of reality: 'God can only manifest what is in Himself. Consequently there is in creation nothing but thought and intelligence.'

Brownson was particularly interested, however, by a line of thought developed by the Saint-Simonian, Pierre Leroux. It awakened Brownson's interest in the social aspect of human life. This, in turn, led him to think of the church as an ideal community. Thus the Jacksonian champion of the working class became dissatisfied with the extreme individualism of Emerson and others. In due course, therefore, in an open letter to Dr Channing in which great thankfulness was expressed, he now accused his former mentor of an insufficiently strong doctrine of the Christian community, the Church. To the astonishment of his friends, the ideas of Leroux were leading him to a conception of the ideal society that to his mind only the Catholic Church could supply. On 20 October 1844, after receiving catechetical instruction from Bishop John Bernard Fitzpatrick, Brownson entered the Roman Church. In doing so, moreover, he raised the question of Catholicism and Transcendentalism in a very important way – especially because he was not alone. His friend Isaac Hecker, a sometime New York Methodist who had participated in the life of both Brook Farm and Fruitlands, had preceded him in his decision. Among Romantics in Germany, England and France there were many earlier instances of the same trend. After the collapse of the social effort at Brook Farm, Sophia Ripley, who had been one of its most dedicated leaders, also entered the Catholic Church, as did Hawthorne's daughter and a number of others who were more distantly related to the movement. This is not the place to develop a general theory of the Catholicizing tendency, but it certainly did bear some relation to human needs for corporate religious expression which had disappeared from the religious institutions of New England except for the fervent evangelical denominations who, during these very years, were thanking God for the greatest outpouring of revivalistic success in American history. Perhaps more pertinent here is the way in which Brownson carried his Transcendental outlook into his new career as one of the church's most impressive religious thinkers. His emphasis on the corporate aspects of a nation's life remained a central element in his great work, *The American Republic* (1886) and in his theology, apologetics and epistemology despite accusations of heresy. The influence he carried into the Catholic Church, therefore, reflects his long-standing respect for the indexed thought of the Turinese theologian, Vicenzo Gioberti (1801–1852), whose radical ontologism is often compared to that of Fichte. All knowledge emanates from the Divine Mind: God is apprehended in all cognition. What intellectual influence Brownson had in the Catholic Church, therefore, bore the marks of his years in Boston.

Theodore Parker was as stormy and controversial as Brownson but far more consistent in his position and steady in his objectives. No Transcendentalist had so great an effect on the course of Unitarian history. He was born on a farm near Boston and received very little formal schooling; but by dint of his own efforts he gained admission to Harvard College classes (but not a degree) and then went on to the Harvard Divinity School. After being certified there he entered the Unitarian ministry in 1836 at the church in West Roxbury not far from Boston. By this time he was recognized as a linguistic prodigy and the chief authority in the Transcendental Club on the subject of modern biblical studies. In the year of his ordination he also began his translation of DeWette's radical *Introduction to the Old Testament* which he would publish (largely at his own expense) in 1843 after greatly expanding the original work. By that time, however, he had become famous and notorious on other grounds: for his forceful defence of Emerson in the controversies that followed the Divinity School Address, for a radical ordination sermon delivered in South Boston in 1841 on 'The Transient and the Permanent in Christianity', and finally for a lecture at Boston's First Church in January 1844 on 'The Relation of Jesus to His Age and the Ages'. Due to the further series of bitter attacks and outright exclusions he finally decided to found a new and independent public ministry in Boston. As a result the Twenty-eighth Congregational Society was organized with Parker as its minister. In due course the vast and stately Boston Music Hall became the locus of his preaching ministry. Unlike Emerson, Ripley and many other Transcendentalists, Parker would not leave the church. Nor did he need to, for the Twenty-eighth consistently drew the largest Sunday audiences in the city. Indeed his influence increased with his radicalism, especially after he turned to the great social issues before the nation, especially the antislavery movement. His ministry ended only when his failing health required a period of rest. He died and was buried in Florence in 1860. Some idea of the feelings he had aroused was indicated when the Harvard Divinity School alumni voted down a note of sympathy to the dying man. The Civil War would for a time quiet these antagonisms, but in the first year of peace they were renewed in New York in 1865 where the national Unitarian conference was being organized. Because the radicals felt that they were being excluded from Unitarian fellowship, they founded the Free Religious Association and elected Octavius Brooks Frothingham as its first president. The radicals uniformly regarded Emerson and Parker as their heroes and progenitors despite the great differences between the two thinkers. Parker's relationship to Emerson was complex and somewhat ambiguous, but at the outset his respect was unbounded. After hearing the Divinity School Address he declared that 'Emerson surpassed himself much as he surpasses others in the general way . . . so just, so true, so beautiful and terribly sublime. My soul was roused.'

On the question of reason and the religious intuition Parker, if anything, goes beyond the claims of Emerson and Coleridge; it is an unimpunable source of certainty and a 'Guarantee of the Christianity of the ages', and the truth of absolute religion. Yet the two men diverge; Emerson becomes an idealistic identity philosopher, a mystic and a pantheist, whereas Parker shows none of these inclinations.

Though a serious student of Gnosticism, he shows no positive interest in the esoteric tradition and has grave misgivings with regard to the visions and spiritual exegesis of Swedenborg. The difference between the two is the fact that Parker is primarily a biblical scholar in the German tradition that runs from Semler and DeWette to Baur and Strauss. He is probably the first American to write a critical review of Strauss's *Leben Jesu*. Though he learned much from Strauss, he insisted that only an historical Jesus could give rise to a powerful mythic tradition. Strauss's scholarship, however, probably did intensify Parker's naturalistic tendency, his inability to understand Emerson's spirituality and his social complacency. He also had a low estimate of neo-Spinozism, seeing it as a degenerate form of monotheism. In his historical sketch of religion in the life of the world he finds pantheism as at best penultimate. Finally one must observe that though Parker was the most erudite scholar in the movement and though he was deeply informed by the European Romantics, he never shared the dominant spirit of the Transcendentalists. He was basically a child of the Enlightenment, and even a forerunner of positivism. He was, nevertheless, from his days at the Harvard Divinity School to his death, the great *provocateur* of the Transcendentalist Controversy. Had he not been on the scene the movement would surely have had a different and calmer history.

Margaret Fuller (Marchese Ossoli) was the complete Transcendentalist. No other participant in the movement so fully embodied all of its aspirations or experienced so many of its implications. She alone participated in an actual revolution. She spoke of herself on one occasion as 'a citizen of the world', and indeed her interests were boundless and constantly widening. Perhaps for these very reasons she was perceived by others in diverse and contradictory ways: affectionate and condescending, fascinating and preposterous, beautiful and homely, compassionate and cruel. It was only after her tragic death that her gifts and contributions were fairly assessed. In the two-volume *Memoir* lovingly written and edited by three of her dearest friends, James Freeman Clarke, William Henry Channing, and Ralph Waldo Emerson, a fair measure of her gifts and character is given. But during the century of critical scholarship which followed, her stature as a person and a cultural critic has not waned but grown.

Margaret was born in Cambridgeport, Massachusetts, the oldest daughter of a lawyer and congressman, and from her earliest years received an intensive education, not unlike that of John Stuart Mill. As a result there were few, if any, comparably learned women in the country. She is alleged to have said that she had never confronted an intellect superior to her own – and as Perry Miller remarked, 'the sad fact is that she spoke the truth'. Despite the limited opportunities open to women, she was ambitious. She knew of the great Romantic women, Madame de Staël, Dorothea von Schlegel and

Bettina von Arnim, and hoped to equal their attainments. Her capacity to hold the interest of her Transcendental colleagues was remarkable, and she seems to have established a more than ordinarily meaningful relationship with Emerson, especially when they were collaborating on *The Dial*. As a writer, translator and critic she had an important public career. Everyone who knew her seemed to agree that it was her personal presence, her style and manner, the direct force of her mind that made her a major factor in the shaping of the Transcendental movement.

It may be that in the force of her personality, which profoundly influenced her friends, lay the essence of Fuller's importance. But she also produced a body of literary criticism that went far beyond the prevailing moralism. Through her translations from Goethe, Eckermann, and Bettina von Arnim she provided invaluable clarifications of German Romanticism. In the 'Conversations' that she organized for the women of Boston, partly as means for her support, she developed a salon-like atmosphere for the discussion of literary, philosophical and feminist issues which provided a means for cultural development that was unique in her time, and in her book, *Women in the Nineteenth Century* she provided a distinctive intellectual dimension to the women's rights movement in America. It was the first full philosophical and historical statement of feminism by an American. As editor for two years and a contributor during the four years of its existence she was a major force behind *The Dial*, a quarterly journal devoted to literature, the arts and cultural criticism which opened a new field in American journalism. As a dear friend and collaborator with Emerson during these years she also helped him become a bolder and more challenging exponent of the Transcendental idea.

Her greatest opportunity opened in August 1846, when she departed for an extended stay in Europe as a correspondent of the New York *Tribune*, where she had been employed for two years. In England and Scotland, she visited the cities, shrines, and persons that every romantic American hoped to see, even to a retracing of John Gilpin's ride. But her most portentous meeting was with Giuseppe Mazzini, the exiled Italian nationalist whom she deemed 'by far the most beauteous person I have ever seen'. Next on her itinerary was a busy two months in France during which she visited Chopin and the tomb of Petrarch's Laura in Avignon. From Marseilles, she and her party sailed to Genoa, made their way to Naples and finally to Rome, the city of her dreams, in April 1847. It was in St Peter's during Holy Week that she accidentally met the Marchese Giovanni Angelo Ossoli who became her friend, then her lover, and finally the father of her son, and her husband. The background of these personal events was the revolution in 1848 in Italy and throughout

Europe. As a partisan of the Republican cause she thus experienced the early triumph and then the collapse of the revolution in Rome. In May 1850, soon after this blow to their aspirations she, and her husband and their son, Angelo Eugene Philip, embarked for America; but on 19 July, after a long and troubled passage, they were drowned when their ship foundered on a sandbar off Fire Island, New York.

Amos Bronson Alcott is an appropriate choice for a concluding biographical account. His lifespan, reaching from 1799 to 1888, brackets the liveliest years and the most influential participants of the American Transcendentalist movement. Intellectually he probably stood in a closer relationship to Emerson than any other. He was also at the centre of the movement by reason of the vast journals that he kept. This great undertaking was begun in 1832. According to his biographer, Odell Shepard, the work as a whole runs to nearly five million words, and was not drawn to a close until 1882. In one respect this work deserves comparison with the great Romantic journals of Senoncoeur and Amiel. From another perspective it provides an invaluable running commentary on the thoughts and deeds of the movement from the first gathering of the Transcendental Club to the autumnal days of the movement. In this way too, Alcott occupies a central place in Transcendental history. He was, as it were, its Boswell or its Eckermann. A random opening of almost any page in his journal usually yields a glimpse of the times, an interesting exchange of ideas, or a subjective note, as when in 1869 he rejoices in the applause that his daughter, Louisa May, is receiving after her publication of *Little Women*.

Alcott was born in Wolcott, Connecticut, into an orthodox background, and was for a time a Yankee pedlar in the South, but his career proper begins with his move to Boston and his marriage in 1830 to Abigail May, who throughout her life shared his aspirations and counter-balanced his excesses. Like so many Transcendentalists he was an educational reformer, but the radicalism of the experimental school which he founded in Boston soon evaporated his clientele. He did, nevertheless, publish his two-volume *Conversations with Children on the Gospels* (1837). Off and on, all through his life, he remained a teacher in one or another arrangement. After 1859 he was superintendent of schools in the public schools of Concord. The Alcotts had moved to Concord in 1840, in large part to be near Emerson; and except for Emerson's resistance to communitarian activism and Alcott's tendency to carry almost all of his ideas to extremes, the two men consistently deepened each other's thought on almost every major issue.

Given these congenial circumstances it is ironic, or humorous, that Emerson indirectly contributed to the founding of the most radical experi-

Ralph Waldo Emerson

ment in the annals of nineteenth-century communalism. Because admiration for Alcott's educational theories had led a group of progressive educators in Richmond, England, to name a school in his honour, Emerson offered to pay for his trans-Atlantic passage. In the midst of many exhilarating experiences, it was Alcott's fate to come under the influence of Charles Lane, a utopian dreamer who regarded America as the promised land and who committed all of his earthly resources to the purchase of a ninety-acre farm in the town of Harvard, Massachusetts. On this site in June 1843 Fruitlands was duly founded on the principles of individual cooperation, wherein neither human beings nor animals were to be coerced and where life would be unsullied by the corrupting practices of capitalism. When Lane insisted on the abolition of the family, however, Alcott was adamant, whereupon Lane departed, first for a brief sojourn with the celibate Shakers nearby, and then for a permanent return to England. Before the end of the year Fruitlands entered history, and as several observers noted, Abigail Alcott was freed from her slavery.

The extravagances and failure of Fruitlands, however, must not be allowed to veil the larger and more sustained concerns of Alcott. He was deeply perturbed by the rising inequalities in American life, and well before Thoreau he demonstrated his opposition to the slave-power by refusing to pay the Concord poll tax. He also showed a life-long interest for the humane treatment of children. The primary concern of his life was indubitably the spiritual life. More even than Emerson he lived in the world of the Neo-Platonic and esoteric tradition, searching out its most delicate nuances and applying them to the problems of life and to his understanding of the cosmos. No Transcendentalist was more insistent on the primacy of the spirit. 'Orphic Sayings', written in the epigrammatic manner of Friedrich Schlegel's *Fragmenten* were his favoured literary form, and many of them were published in *The Dial*: 'Man is a rudiment and embryon of God: Eternity shall develop in him the divine image . . . Believe, Youth, that your heart is an oracle; trust her instinctive auguries, obey her divine leadings . . . Know, O man, that your soul is the Prometheus who receiving the divine fires, builds up this majestic statue of clay, molds it in the deific image, the pride of the Gods, the model and analagon of all forms.' Given these philosophical convictions, it is not surprising that in 1876 Alcott probably became the first major American intellectual to praise the 'sacred truths' of Christian Science in the years before Mary Baker Eddy became famous. The degree to which he also contributed to the growth of Platonic religion can only be surmised, but it was considerable.

In 1872 Alcott published his last important book, *Concord Days*. It was a distinctly personal production, a literary curiosity shop, sentimental and nostalgic, arranged in six chapters named for the months from April to September. Something of its mood is suggested by the epigraph on the title page: 'Cheerful and various thoughts not always bound to counsel, nor in deep ideas bound.'

The detailed table of contents suggests an orderly series of topics, but the actual contents are often extensions of his diaries, comments on passing events, references to the history of Concord and seemingly random reminiscences about the many Transcendentalist associates that had figured strongly in his life. Free association provides such logic as runs through its alternating snatches of poetry and recollected incidents. Yet it has a seductive charm, and when read to the end, it provides a fascinating survey of an exciting episode in American thought. His final contribution to the Transcendental impulse was his founding and directing of the Concord School of Philosophy (1879–88) which contributed significantly to the rising interest of American thinkers in philosophical idealism.

A brief retrospect

In order to understand the Transcendentalists, one must bear in mind James Freeman Clarke's quip that the only grounds for seeing them as a club of the like-minded was that none of them thought alike. Every person named on Kern's long honour roll was unique and deserves long and thoughtful study. These unique individuals can nonetheless be variously grouped for different purposes. They can be divided, for instance, according to their response to the issue of social activism. Some were rather quietistic; others, like George Ripley, were more militant in their demands for social change. Parker, Brownson and Alcott were of a similar disposition to that of Ripley, who kept his distance from those who exhibited in their thought and action a 'profound indifference to the great humanitarian movements . . .'. Whether or not fairly, he included among them Emerson himself.

Far less recognized and much more important is the presence within the movement of two distinctly different tendencies in the religious and philosophical realms. There is one group that with the usual individual reservations, implicitly recognizes Emerson as the normative exponent of Transcendentalism. They share his radical dissatisfaction with the Church and the orthodox Christian tradition, and they are inspired by Emerson's correspondential vision. They accept his view of Nature, and his distinctive doctrines resonate in their thinking. Even his strong gnostic tendencies and his pantheism gain their favour. Most pronounced in this allegiance was

Emerson's neighbour and close friend, Bronson Alcott, though Margaret Fuller shocked even Emerson with her paganism. Thoreau, in his way, was similarly unconventional. On the other hand, there is a considerably larger group who avoided the anti-biblical stance as well as Emerson's esoteric modes of thought. This dissenting group should probably be referred to as Radical Unitarians since they did not discontinue their concern for the churches. Theodore Parker was the most outstanding member of this group, but there were also men like Frederic Hedge and James Freeman Clarke who continued to express and to defend conservative positions in theology.

Finally, and quite aside from its almost ineffable difficulties, it is imperative that the question of the influence of the Transcendentalist movement be considered. Despite much controversy on the subject there is at least one fact that can be asserted: that the truth lies somewhere between Henry Steele Commager's reference to the controversy as a tempest in a Boston tea cup and George Hochfield's claim that 'Emerson made a lasting impression on the American Character.'[6] More modestly we can certainly say that the Transcendentalists did with great literary power and philosophical force present Americans with a drastic alternative to the conventional, moral and religious attitudes that had held sway since the founding of the Puritan commonwealths of the seventeenth century. Due to the dialectical restlessness of these liberal New Englanders and a few outsiders drawn to their midst, the nation was confronted with a wide range of Romantic ideas that had been growing in strength since the late eighteenth century. With radical communal experiments and other forms of agitation, they not only took up the cause of anti-slavery but questioned the basic structures of the social order as a whole. The movement made no large dent in the prevailing consensus, but it did announce the advent of the modern with sufficient force to precipitate many controversies and to create ever-widening circles of influence.

The inner circle may have been no more than a cluster of fellow spirits who gathered for conversations in Elizabeth Peabody's bookshop in Boston; but there were ever-widening circles of influence, and considerable evidences of this wider community of thought have been discerned both in time and in space; some as remote as Nietzsche, others as near as the elder Henry Adams. Scholars, moreover, are constantly discovering diaries and letters that reveal a more covert following that was hitherto unknown. Ernest Fenallosa who awakened many Americans to the beauty of Japanese art is a good example. The modernist composer, Charles Ives, is another. Still more recent is the express admiration of the poet, Wallace Stevens. Perhaps more important than any of these is the way in which the participants in the cultural and social upheavals of the 1960s discovered the testimonies of Thoreau and Alcott on racial justice and civil disobedience. At almost the same time other young Americans were being attracted by Emerson's strong interest in the Eastern religions. In the years that followed, the dramatic rise of interest in so-called 'new religions' became so strong that the churches and the American people generally were becoming deeply concerned. Even in the 1980s there continues to be a strong and rising interest in Emerson's ethical doctrine of self-realization. During all the years since his death, moreover, his persistent emphasis on the gnostic and esoteric aspects of religion has always strengthened theosophical movements such as those of Madame Blavatsky, and for similar reasons also those of Christian Science and the 'New Thought' movements concerned with health, happiness and human composure. Among the many who looked to him in this regard the most enthusiastic champion of Emerson as well as the most prolific and popular exponent of the cause was Ralph Waldo Trine, whose magnum opus, *In Tune With the Infinite* (1879) is still for many a favourite book. Whatever else can be said of Emerson, therefore, it must be realized that his thought does to a degree place him in the tradition of Positive Thinking that leads to Norman Vincent Peale and his competitors.

In the literary realm which Emerson addressed so fervently in 1837, his hopes were extravagantly realized. It seems to be fully recognized that what is now conventionally referred to as the American Renaissance is a movement that he to a significant degree inspired. Charles N. Feidelson has shown in his profound study *Symbolism in American Literature* that 'the unified phase of American Literature that begins with the tales of Hawthorne and Poe and ended with Whitman and Melville' can now be seen as a symbolist movement, and that 'the Representative Man of the era was Emerson himself'.

Since this praise and vindication was very late in coming, it is all the more remarkable that in the later nineteenth century despite his many heresies Emerson came to be regarded as the great American sage whose works were bound in gilt-edged editions and placed on Victorian parlour tables. Along with Longfellow and the other New England poets his works were scriptures of a sort. Down to the 1920s he was a classic, studied in the schools and colleges. His poems were memorized, and more than his popular rivals, Emerson is still seriously read and studied. There are also signs of a widespread revival of Romanticism that may further enhance his reputation. The future, of course, is very dimly lit but there are also grounds for thinking that various forms of alienation and disaffection are so deeply rooted in the American social order that Emerson's view of religion, and of reality in general, is becoming increasingly relevant and attractive. In that case one could observe the irony of the world's 'first new nation', drawing spiritual sustenance from the crumbling Roman world in which Plotinus propounded his Platonic interpretations of life and reality.

Notes

1 George Woodberry, *Ralph Waldo Emerson* (Macmillan, 1907), p. 1.
2 Alexander Kern, 'The rise of Transcendentalism', in Harry Hayden (ed.), *American Literary History* (Duke University Press, 1954), pp. 247–313; William R. Hutchison, *The Transcendentalist Ministers* (Yale University Press, 1959), *passim*.
3 Robert C. Pollock, 'The single vision', in *American Classics*, ed. Harold C. Gardner, S. J. (New York, 1958), p. 19.
4 Kern, 'The rise of Transcendentalism', p. 98.
5 Henry David Thoreau, *Walden*, ed. Sherman Paul (Boston, 1957), pp. 220–1.
6 Henry Steele Commager, *Theodore Parker, Yankee Crusader* (Boston, 1947), p. 80; George Hochfield (ed.), *Selected Writings of the American Transcendentalists* (New York, 1966), p. ix.

Bibliographical essay

The Transcendentalists were most of them prolific writers, and their importance to American religious history has ensured the later collection and publication of much of their output. One must begin with Emerson, whose works and other papers are widely available. Start with *The Complete Works of Ralph Waldo Emerson* (12 vols., Boston, 1903–4), edited by Edward Waldo Emerson. A new edition, *The Collected Works*, edited by Joseph Slater *et al.*, is in progress (2 vols. to date, Cambridge, Mass., 1979–). In the meanwhile, useful supplements to the *Works* include: Clarence Gohdes (ed.), *Uncollected Lectures of Ralph Waldo Emerson* (New York, 1933), *The Uncollected Writings*, edited by Charles C. Bigelow (New York, 1912), and Arthur Cushman McGiffert (ed.), *Young Emerson Speaks: Unpublished Discourses on Many Subjects* (Boston, 1938). Stephen E. Whicher *et al.* have produced an edition of *The Early Lectures of Ralph Waldo Emerson* (3 vols., Cambridge, Mass., 1959–72). Emerson's *Journals* are available in two editions, the first (10 vols., Boston, 1909–14) edited by Edward Waldo Emerson and Waldo Emerson Forbes; the second, still in progress, includes *The Journals and the Miscellaneous Notebooks of Ralph Waldo Emerson*, and is edited by William H. Gilman *et al.* (14 vols., Cambridge, Mass., 1960–). Ralph L. Rusk edited *The Letters of Ralph Waldo Emerson* (6 vols., New York, 1939), while letters of special interest can be found in C. E. Norton (ed.), *The Correspondence of Thomas Carlyle and Ralph Waldo Emerson* (2 vols., Boston, 1883). Emerson has also been anthologized, of course. Stephen E. Whicher provides well-chosen *Selections from Ralph Waldo Emerson* (Boston, 1957), including *Nature* and the Divinity School Address.

Of the other five Transcendentalists given major attention here, three have been honoured by major collections of their papers. See *The Works of Orestes A. Brownson*, edited by Henry F. Brownson (20 vols., Detroit, 1882–1902); *The Writings of Henry David Thoreau* (20 vols., Boston, 1906), with a modern edition in progress out of Princeton, edited by William Howarth *et al.*; and *The Works of Theodore Parker* (15 vols., Boston, 1907–13). Parker's *Works* is available in a reprint edition, as is his important *Discourse on Matters Pertaining to*

Religion (1842, repr. New York, 1972). As for Margaret Fuller, her editorship (with Emerson) of *The Dial* (Boston, 1840–4) offers some insight; see also Mason Wade (ed.), *The Writings of Margaret Fuller* (New York, 1941) and Perry Miller (ed.), *Margaret Fuller, American Romantic: A Selection* . . . (New York, 1963). Amos Bronson Alcott, to give him his full name, is also more difficult to track down. His important *Conversations with Children on the Gospels* (2 vols., Boston, 1836–7) has recently been reprinted (New York, 1972). See also Richard L. Herrnstadt (ed.), *The Letters of Bronson Alcott* (Ames, Iowa, 1969) and Odell Shepard, *The Journals of Bronson Alcott* (Boston, 1938). For Alcott, one might also consult Elizabeth Peabody, *Record of a School, Exemplifying the General Principles of Spiritual Character* (Boston, 1835). It should be said, here, that many of Thoreau's individual works have been widely reprinted; perhaps he has occasionally seemed more timely than many of his friends and mentors. Publishers have found *Walden* and the essay *On Civil Disobedience* especially tempting.

In this essay I have on principle dealt chiefly with the works which Emerson prepared carefully for publication. To encourage the reading of complete essays, which are available in the above sources and elsewhere, I have not provided detailed annotations to the vast editions of his journals, lectures, and letters despite their fascinating qualities and biographical value. I have instead indicated the location of the more important essay passages. In my short sketches of other Transcendentalists, I have followed the same policy. The intention throughout has been to accent their religious thought. The sources listed above, however, also offer the keen reader an introduction into biography and general history.

Interest in biography, historical context, and religious thought can of course be pursued through a mountain of scholarly secondary literature. The output has been so vast as to make a survey pointless; here I aim chiefly to provide points of departure. The route, one may say, is well marked.

The primary biographies are Ralph L. Rusk, *Ralph Waldo Emerson* (New York, 1949) and Stephen Whicher, *Freedom and Fate: The Inner Life of Ralph Waldo Emerson* (Philadelphia, 1953). Also valuable is Frederick I. Carpenter's *Emerson Handbook* (New York, 1953) which provides a wide range of information, including an account of previous biographies. The most recent major work to appear is Joel Porte's *The Representative Man: Ralph Waldo Emerson and his Time* (New York, 1979). Other useful biographies include Arthur M. Schlesinger, Jr., *Orestes A. Brownson: A Pilgrim's Progress* (Boston, 1939); Henry Steele Commager, *Theodore Parker, Yankee Crusader* (Boston, 1947); Odell Shepard, *Pedlar's Progress: The Life of Bronson Alcott* (Boston, 1937). F. B. Sanborn, *Henry D. Thoreau* (Boston, 1917); and, in a somewhat different category, William Henry Channing, James Freeman Clarke, and Ralph Waldo Emerson, *Memoirs of Margaret Fuller Ossoli* (2 vols., Boston, 1852).

More general reading might begin with Octavius Brooks Frothingham, *Transcendentalism in New England: A History* (1876, reprinted, with an Introduction by Sydney E. Ahlstrom), Perry Miller's artfully arranged *The Transcendentalists: An Anthology* (Cambridge, 1950) and George Hochfield's excellent *Selected Writings of the American Transcendentalists* (New York, 1966). Also of large significance are William R. Hutchison's *The Transcendentalist Ministers: Church Reform in the New England Renaissance* (New Haven, Conn., 1959) and Paul Boller's more recent *American Transcendentalism: An Intellectual Inquiry* (New York, 1974), an insightful survey with a very useful bibliography. Brian M. Barbour's *American Transcendentalism: An Anthology of Criticism* (University of Notre Dame Press, 1973) contains both valuable articles and a very thoughtful guide to the literature. Especially pertinent to the present essay is Catherine Albanese's *Corresponding Motion: Transcendental Religion in the New America* (Temple University Press, 1977). Anne C. Rose studies *Transcendentalism as a Social Movement 1830–1850* (New Haven, Conn., 1981). Useful context on American antebellum religion is offered by Jerry W. Brown, *The Rise of Biblical Criticism in America* (Middletown, Conn., 1969); Perry Miller, *The Life of the Mind in America: From the Revolution to the Civil War* (New York, 1965); and Timothy Smith, *Revivalism and Social Reform: American*

Protestantism on the Eve of the Civil War (New York, 1965). Finally, it may not be inappropriate to say that my *A Religious History of the American People* (New Haven, 1972) contains several chapters dealing with the social background and the continuing significance of Emerson, the Transcendentalists, and the Swedenborgian impulse.

Students wishing further bibliographical guidance should turn to the *Emerson Society Quarterly*, founded in 1955, which is now published with enlarged scope as *ESQ: A Journal of the American Renaissance*. See also the many publications of the Society's founder, Kenneth W. Cameron.

3
John Henry Newman and the Tractarian Movement

J. M. CAMERON

I

What is the Church of England? To ask that question was to ask a hundred others. Creeds, dogmas, ordinances, hierarchy, parliamentary institution, judicial tribunals, historical tradition, the prayer-book, the Bible – all these enormous topics sacred and profane, with all their countless ramifications, were swiftly swept into a tornado of such controversy as had not been seen in England since the Revolution [of 1688].[1]

Thus John Morley, describing the ecclesiastical situation following the years marked by the repeal of the Test and Corporation Acts in 1828 and the passage of the first Reform Bill in 1832.

It is at first curious to be driven to note that the effect of the rage for reform should have been to stimulate Anglicans into a revival of the controversies that had divided Englishmen under Elizabeth, James and Charles, that had precipitated the Puritan rebellion, and that had gone to sleep in the eighteenth century. Men asked questions about church, prayer, grace, sacraments, priesthood, the authority of the Scriptures, that had been posed in the crisis of the Reformation, that had indeed been life-and-death matters down to the Civil War; now in the age of improvement, with gentler manners and more polished society and more prudish literature, the same questions were asked. But the resonance of the questions and their import for daily life were necessarily different. Indeed, the only place in England where one could almost think that the same debate was continued from the seventeenth century into the nineteenth was Oxford. There was to be found a place and an institution not unlike a Greek *polis* or a medieval city-state: the University of Oxford.[2] The University itself was a shadowy institution; power and prestige belonged to the colleges; but it was unified by a common ethos and a common devotion. The ethos was that of the Church by law established; and the devotion was to the historical past of this institution and especially to the monarchy, and here and there, though this was by now the purest sentimentality, to the extinct Stuart dynasty rather than to the lumpish Hanoverians brought over after the death of Queen Anne.³ Oxford, as Matthew Arnold was later to note, was, with its ravishing beauty of building and scene and with the quaint and on the whole unexacting dialectic that represented its intellectual life, out of its own time; the bells of the college chapels summoned to daily prayer, the dons, except for the heads of houses, were clerical celibates, a large proportion of the undergraduates went on to become clergymen; it was as though Laud had been not long dead and that the fury of the Puritan iconoclasts was still to come.

What the Oxford Movement was in its origins, how it developed by the inferences of many from its original premises, how these premises were formed, how far the logic of events determined its great climax and catastrophe, the conversion of John Henry Newman to the Church of Rome, what problems of permanent theological interest were raised by the Tractarians and their successors, in what respects Anglicanism and Catholicism have been radically affected by the thought of the movement, what have been the permanent effects of the Tractarian generation on English religion, these are complex questions. Again, how we are to situate this sign of life in an institution thought then to have the signs of decrepitude upon it in relation to the other spiritual movements of the period, especially to romanticism, this is a further question and one that has been variously answered. Some of these questions, though not all, turn out to be relatively manageable if they are centred upon the thought of Newman, for, as J. A. Froude put it many years after the events of the 1830s and forties, 'compared with [Newman], they [i.e. Keble, Pusey, and the other Tractarians] were all but as ciphers, and he the indicating number'.⁴ Of course, Newman's thought goes beyond the concerns of nineteenth-century Anglicanism; as one of the best students of the Oxford Movement has put it, 'there was always something in him which strove to get out of the narrow ring-fence of Tractarianism, and could not be confined within it for any length of time';⁵ but he represents the thought of the movement at its most original.

Newman in the *Apologia* and Dean Church in *The Oxford Movement 1833–1845* have defined the period in which Tractarianism sprang up and came to its maturity; it began with Keble's Assize Sermon, on 'National Apostasy', of 14 July 1833, and ended on 9 October 1845, when Newman was received into the Church of Rome. Never had the question as to what the Church of England is been more strenuously investigated. It would be a mistake to suppose that the nation was convulsed by religious controversy. Religion was no longer what it had been in the seventeenth century, a shaping and governing power able to pull down kings and mould social institutions. But it was of passionate concern to the pious, of whom there were many, among the middle and upper classes. It was even in worldly circles intimately connected with veneration for the English past and with sentiments of affection for the monarchy. Anglicans conceived themselves to be under the pressures of Protestant Dissent and unbelief, the two of them united in the campaign for political and ecclesiastical reform. The ogre of Popery was perhaps less dreadful than it had been thought to be,[6] though the campaign for Catholic Emancipation had been opposed by old-fashioned High churchmen, and there were always the Irish, so incomprehensibly ungrateful for the blessings of British rule, to provide a ready example of the poverty and vice that were thought to be the natural consequences of belief in Catholicism. The vice, if not the poverty, was no doubt for the most part in the eye of the beholder.

To take Keble's sermon as the beginning of a serious religious movement seems ludicrous, at first sight. Keble was attacking the decision of the Government to suppress ten Irish bishoprics. Now, the Church of Ireland was the church of a small Protestant minority, and its wealth and social importance in a predominantly Catholic society seemed in the new liberal atmosphere of English politics without justification. Indeed, the suppression of the ten bishoprics was thought a small, inadequate instalment of reform. But the theory Keble maintained was that the established Church in England and Ireland (not, of course, in Scotland, where the establishment was Presbyterian) was, whatever its entanglements with political institutions, the Church of the Apostles, in succession of hierarchy and doctrine identical with the churches established by Augustine and Patrick. They did not owe their existence to the State; but the State, in principle a Christian state, owed them its protection and encouragement. To touch the dioceses of the Church of Ireland and to divert their incomes to other purposes was sacrilege. To throw open the universities to Protestant and Roman Catholic dissenters and to unbelievers, was to depart from a sacred duty.

This seemed to most Englishmen who thought about it at the time a strange doctrine. It contradicted the generally received account of the Reformation and the Elizabethan ecclesiastical settlement. It was commonly supposed that those doctrines about the priesthood, the sacraments, and church order characteristic of the Roman and Byzantine systems had been put aside with decision in the sixteenth century. The Church of England was a Protestant church closely resembling the established Lutheran churches in Germany and Scandinavia; and by the nineteenth century it had become possible to inquire, as did Thomas Arnold and other members of the Broad Church, inheritors of the Latitudinarian traditions of the seventeenth and eighteenth centuries, if the time had not come to bring within the national Church all Protestant bodies willing to subscribe to a frugal statement of belief. In the year of Keble's sermon Arnold wrote to a friend:

I have been . . . urging an union with the Dissenters as the only thing that can procure to us the blessing of an established Christianity; for the Dissenters are strong enough to turn the scale either for an establishment or against one; and at present they are leagued with the antichristian party against one, and will destroy it utterly if they are not taken into the camp in defence of it. And if we sacrifice that phantom Uniformity, which has been our curse ever since the Reformation, I am fully persuaded that an union might be effected without difficulty.[7]

Arnold here shares with Keble a concern to preserve the Church establishment from a hungry State, but his motives are moral and political, and he thinks it time to purge the Church of some of the credal formularies so prominent in the Book of Common Prayer. He is acute and historically correct in suggesting that since the Civil War the Church of England has in effect been a sectarian body given its commanding political position by an accident of history. It had always excluded a great many Englishmen from its membership, for its distinctive credal position had been a cause of theological controversy since its foundation, and Puritans had always seen it clad in the rags of Rome. But under the influences of moral passion and political anxiety Arnold then, as always, failed to understand the theological position presented by Keble and the other Tractarians.

The impulse that brought about the publication of the early Tracts was a desire to emphasize, as uniquely authentic, a tradition in the Church of England which comes from the Anglican counter-reformation of the seventeenth century. This attempt by Laud, Andrewes, Cosin, and others to impose liturgical uniformity and comeliness in the forms of worship and moral oversight of the population necessarily took the form of a counter-reformation in a society that had been deeply moved by the impulses of the continental Reformation. It was an important element, indeed, the most prominent element, in the composite of royal policies that brought about the conflict with Parliament and the subsequent civil war. With the Restoration and the publication in 1662 of the final revision of the Book of Common Prayer it seemed as though Laud had been vindicated. But post-Restoration society was secular in spirit. Anglicanism of the Laudian sort took refuge with the Non-Jurors and the unestablished Scottish Episcopalians, and was served almost as a private cult in a few rectories, in particular families, and in dark corners of the ancient universities. But living religion in England was for the most part to be found among the Methodists and those known as Evangelicals. Without a transfusion of life from the Evangelical movement the Anglican revival brought about by the Tracts would not have been nationally significant. This transfusion was the work of John Henry Newman.[8]

The early Tracts are the best guide to the initial concerns of the movement. The first (by Newman) is often quoted, and it is an arresting document. It is an example of Newman's superb use of the educated vernacular, a conversational style touched lightly by scholarship. The tone of self-confidence was such that even bishops asked themselves if the doctrine of the apostolical succession, commonly thought to have gone out with the Non-Jurors, could after all be the doctrine of the Church of England.

I am but one of yourselves, – a Prestbyter; and therefore I conceal my name, lest I should take too much on myself by speaking in my own person. Yet speak I must; for the times are very evil, yet no one speaks against them . . . We encroach not upon the rights of the SUCCESSORS OF THE APOSTLES: we touch not their sword and crosier . . . Should the Government and Country so far forget their GOD as to cast off the Church, to deprive it of its temporal honors and substance, *on what* will you rest the claim of respect and attention which you make upon your flocks? Hitherto you have been upheld by your birth, your education, your wealth, your connexions; should these secular advantages cease, on what must CHRIST'S Ministers depend?[9]

Newman then goes on to cite the Book of Common Prayer, always the most effective weapon in the Tractarian armoury. He quotes from the formula for the ordination of priests, with its strong language about the giving of the Holy Ghost through the imposition of episcopal hands and the implication that the ordinand is by this rite empowered to administer the sacraments and to absolve men from their sins. He continues:

Keep [the priestly character conferred in ordination] before your minds as an honorable badge, far higher than that secular respectability, or cultivation, or polish, or learning, or rank, which gives you a hearing with the many . . . A notion has gone abroad, that they can take away your power . . . They think it lies in the Church property, and they know that they have politically the power to confiscate that property . . . Enlighten them in this matter. Exalt our Holy Fathers the Bishops, as the Representatives of the Apostles, and the Angels of the Churches; and magnify your office, as being ordained by them to take part in their Ministry.

But, if you will not adopt my view of the subject, which I offer to you, not doubtingly, yet (I hope) respectfully, at all events, CHOOSE YOUR SIDE.[10]

It has often been remarked that the Church of England came out of the turmoil of the sixteenth and seventeenth centuries with Protestant Articles of Religion and a Catholic Prayer Book. This rough characterization of the Church of England applied to more than its formal title-deeds. The *institutional* continuity with the medieval Church was, except for the break with the Papacy, plain. The *institution* that emerged from profound religious changes was as a structure and a legal entity plainly an unreformed medieval institution, unique in Christendom. Church courts with jurisdiction over the laity, tithes, lay presentation to benefices, pluralism and non-residence, prelates who lived in palaces and relatives and hangers-on of the great who gathered to themselves rectories, deaneries and cathedral stalls, such were the plainest features of the landscape down to the nineteenth century. What had in the rest of Europe been modified or destroyed by reformers, kings, and the Council of Trent still flourished in England. It was this that excited the rage of the reformers, this, and the concentration of immense wealth in the hands of the clergy and those who appointed them. The Tractarians reminded the reformers that the paradox of the Church was not only constituted by the co-existence of a Protestant establishment of religion with a medieval institution; it was also constituted by the presence, within a religious system that was popularly believed to have abandoned priestcraft and the sacramental system for ever, of a liturgical book, the Book of Common Prayer, out of which a clever and industrious man might dig the doctrines of Catholicism.

'It is evident unto all men diligently reading the Holy Scriptures and ancient Authors, that from the Apostles' time there have been these Orders of Ministers in Christ's Church; Bishops, Priests, and Deacons . . .' Thus the Preface to the ordination services. Other doctrines that might be extracted from the Book are: baptismal regeneration (this was a rejection of the entire Protestant attack upon the Catholic doctrine that sacramental grace is conveyed *ex opere operato*), a doctrine of the Real Presence in the Eucharist that seemed to be taught in the Catechism, a formula for Absolution as commanding as the Roman. And from the demonstration that what they had to say was strongly supported in the aboriginal documents of Anglicanism and in the tradition of the Anglicans of the second and third generation, those who reflected upon and expressed the tradition once the storms of the Reformation were quiet (at least for the time), the Tractarians went on to expound a positive theory of the Church. (It ought to be said that Newman's position was different from that of the other Tractarians. He encountered the Anglican divines *after* reading the Fathers. See T. M. Parker, in John Coulson and A. M. Allchin (editors), *The Rediscovery of Newman*, 1967 pp. 31–49.)

It may be idle to look for a single coherent theory shared by all the leaders of the Oxford Movement. Some of those who went along with the Tracts with growing reluctance but in the crises of the movement kept their loyalty – men such as William Palmer of Worcester and W. F. Hook – believed the Church of England was, substantially and in fact, what the Tracts claimed it to be; whereas Newman argued that high-church Anglicanism was a paper theory, realized only at particular moments and in particular places, the great question being whether or not it could become the theory and practice of the main body of Anglicans.[11] Others (Isaac Williams is a good example) thought the existing body of the Church in a state of captivity, of exile, justly punished for the sacrilege of the Reformation period and for subservience to the State. It seemed a necessary part of the theory that the bishops were, as successors of the apostles and witnesses to the deposit of faith, the divinely appointed rulers of the Church. Newman was perhaps the only Tractarian to take this seriously and was, after 1845, chided by Pusey for having relied upon the bishops.[12] What, retrospectively, seems to be the most prominent feature of Anglo-Catholic apologetics, the branch theory of the Church, only became a theory common to most members of the party under the pressures of the period after 1845. The attitude to the Church of Rome moved with extraordinary speed from the view that Rome was a hopelessly corrupt Church, and perhaps the Antichrist, at best a fallen sister prostituted to the world, to the view that it was, along with the Orthodoxy of eastern Europe, a living part of the one Catholic Church. The view that the Church was tripartite, with each of the parts reprobating the other two, had some amusing corollaries. It was seriously held that Roman Catholics were schismatics in England but not in France. It seems unclear what the status might be of Anglican communities in Mediterranean watering places or the Swiss resorts. At any rate, the theory unchurched not only English dissenters but also the Protestants of Europe, and this was certainly an immense departure from the Anglicanism of the seventeenth century.

It is hard to set out a definitive Tractarian position in ecclesiology. The Oxford thinkers knew they were, despite their appeals to antiquity and to the seventeenth century, attempting a new enterprise, and that simply to draw attention to Jeremy Taylor, or Pearson on the Creed, to Bishop Bull's Defence of the Nicene faith, to Beveridge, to Waterland, could scarcely be satisfactory to men in the middle of the nineteenth century. In some sense, no doubt, it could be agreed that Christianity, as the definitive and final self-revelation of God in Christ, was no mere historical phenomenon, as Hinduism, or the cult of the Druids, might be supposed to be. But this thought was then common to all the Christian bodies in England; what was, as Newman emphasized, a *problem* common to them all was that they were all of them, not simply Anglicans and Roman Catholics, remarkably different from any ecclesiastical body that could be discerned in the obscurity of the apostolic age. Questions of dogma, of church order, even questions having to do with the relations between the documents that made up the canon of Scripture, all raised the problem of *development*. What to the Protestant observer was so evidently true of Catholicism, that it had many beliefs that were not present on the surface of the New Testament, was in fact true of all ecclesiastical bodies in the nineteenth century. That the tenets of Anabaptism or of Presbyterianism, that the practices of Quakers or the theology of Unitarians, were to be found in the New Testament, was a prejudice, an interpretation of the sparse evidence for the character of the apostolic age. What could (the Tractarians argued) be relied upon was the witness, historically ascertainable and less, so they believed, ambiguous than the witness of the New Testament, of the age of the Fathers, the three or four or five hundred years that followed the first preaching of the apostles. And so we find in the Tracts much material from the sub-apostolic and patristic periods: the letters of Ignatius, the early accounts of the martyrdoms of Ignatius and Polycarp, Irenaeus and Tertullian on the rule of faith, Clement of Alexandria's addresses to the pagans, Cyprian on unity, Vincent of Lerins on catholicity and how it could be determined. Such writings were believed to be authoritative on the simple ground that the nearer one got in time to the apostolic preaching the more plausible were the accounts of the form and content of belief. The alternative view, pressed with some eagerness upon Protestant critics (i.e. as a *reductio ad absurdum* argument), was that Catholicism, as thought and cult, begins in the sub-apostolic age, that is, from the Protestant standpoint, the corruption of the Church is something primitive.

The collective witness of the Fathers, then, was for the Tractarians the Lydian-stone with which they could distinguish the gold of orthodoxy from the pinchbeck of heresy. This, it was believed, was the classic Anglican position, largely forgotten in the age of reason ('when love was cold').[13] That it presented difficulties Newman began to see very early. What was a witness for Catholicism might turn out to be a witness against Anglicanism.

The appeal to the first four or five centuries and to the early ecumenical councils is of the essence of the Tractarian dogmatic standpoint. It carried with it a number of corollaries, or what were taken to be such. First, it seemed evident that the Fathers took a 'high' view of the sacraments, especially the Eucharist. Secondly, they regarded sin after baptism as a grave matter and this led to the development of the private administration of the sacrament of penance, the practice of auricular confession. Thirdly, episcopacy and the succession of the episcopate from the apostles was thought to be the essence of the Church. Fourthly, the Church asserted itself, as having sovereign authority over the interpretation of the Gospel against kings and emperors; some common Anglican views of the doctrine of the Royal Supremacy were thus implicitly condemned. Fifthly, the principles of asceticism (morbid, unhealthy, unmanly, as Samuel Wilberforce and Charles Kingsley would come to think them), fasting, other physical austerities, the belief that the state of virginity is if consecrated a higher state than that of marriage, are commonplaces in the writings of the Fathers. Sixthly, the modes of worship the Fathers take as normal are more evident signs of the worship of the angels in the heavenly courts, than the humdrum, perfunctory, often slovenly liturgical practices of pre-Tractarian Anglicanism. Finally, ecclesiastical tradition is exalted as that aid without which the Bible is an enigmatic book; that there *is* a Bible, that is, that certain books are included in the canon of Scripture and others excluded from it, is the work of the Church, and it seems therefore to follow that it is one of the Church's prerogatives to say what the correct interpretation of the words of Scripture is.

Now, all of these positions could be justified individually by pointing to this or that Anglican writer. What seemed new was the holding of all these positions together. How far the system is internally coherent and how far it is compatible with the facts of Anglicanism, these are matters over which later generations of Anglo-Catholics (to use the terminology that in the end overcame 'Tractarian' and 'Puseyite') were to differ.[14] But we may take this particular composite of thought as what is distinctive of the Anglo-Catholicism that survived the debacle of Tractarianism in 1845. It is what Pusey believed all his life and what underlies his fine letter of 1851 to Bishop Blomfield.

It was out of Holy Scripture and the Formularies of the Church that Tractarianism arose. It was cherished by our English divines. It was deepened by the Fathers. It was ripened while most of the writers scarcely knew a Roman book, and only controversially. Tractarianism was entirely the birth of the English Church . . . Tractarianism was not beheaded with Laud, nor trampled under foot in the Great Rebellion, nor corrupted by Charles II, not expelled with the Non-Jurors, nor burnt, together with the Common Prayer-book, in Scotland, nor extinguished by the degradation of the Church through Walpole, nor in America by the long-denied Episcopate . . . Tractarianism, as it is called, or, as I believe it to be, the Catholic Faith, will survive in the Church of England while the Scriptures are reverenced, and the Ecumenical Councils received, and the Creeds recited, and the Episcopal Succession continues, and union with Christ her Head is cherished, and she acquiesce not, God forbid! in the denial of any article of the Faith.[15]

Anglo-Catholicism was a living movement and it would be a mistake to measure the contribution of Tractarianism, through this movement, to English religion simply as a strengthening of a particular dogmatic tradition. The unity of Tractarianism, in so far as it can be said to have had a single spirit, was that of a shared ethos, a characteristic style of feeling and devotion. It did not, of course, exist independently of particular dogmatic positions. The ethos was intimately connected with a view of Christian history, with a distinctive approach to liturgical worship and to individual piety, and with a high view of the sacramental system. This ethos was not always cherished by some of the later generations of Anglo-Catholics and was, paradoxically, an element inserted into the English Roman Catholic tradition by John Henry Newman. Among the Tractarian converts to Rome some, such as Faber, abandoned all that was distinctive of the Tractarian ethos. This ethos survived in the little Oratorian community at Birmingham and its persistence there may have been a factor, if a small one, in maintaining an irritated state of feeling between Newman and Manning. I propose, then, to take the term *ethos* to be a leading clue to the religious temper of Tractarianism.

Both in informal correspondence and in formal treatises the authors and friends of the Tracts use the term *ethos* a good deal. In Tract No. 86 ('Indications of a Superintending Providence in the Preservation of the Prayer Book and in the Changes which it has undergone') the author (Isaac Williams) twice uses it, in each case to suggest that the Book of Common Prayer reflects and expresses the 'peculiar and distinguishing ἦθος in our Church [which] we may expect to find . . . realized in the peculiar temper of her sons, if in churches, as in nations, there prevail certain characteristic qualities, which are shown by a predominant influence of the same in her members. Something of a quiet resignation and temper of repose is remarkable in those holy persons who have most closely adhered to the guiding hand, and drunk most deeply the spirit of our own Church.'[16] Again, Pusey, in a letter to Newman of 9 August 1841, writes: 'Our Reformation [i.e. as distinct from the Lutheran and Calvinist movements] has had a steady tendency to develop itself into Catholicism; and therefore I think we have a right to infer that there was a difference in their original ἦθος . . .'[17] Again, Pusey writes, after Newman's conversion to Rome (he is writing to T. E. Morris, whose brother J. B. Morris had just joined the Church of Rome): 'I could not imagine dear N [ewman] writing, as the French R.C. writers do, of the Blessed Virgin, and exciting the feelings by descriptions of her love and tenderness. It would be an entirely different ἦθος from his sermons.'[18] We may take *ethos* here as signifying 'disposition', 'temper', 'moral nature', 'character', even 'sensibility', all of them belonging to a particular circle of friends and fellow-labourers.

The sharing of a common ethos is a precarious, mutable thing. The common ethos will be felt more sharply by some than by others, and there will be instances where we can perceive another ethos separating itself out from the one in which a man thinks himself to dwell. We can now see that Newman and Hurrell Froude from the beginning had a more detached view of the Anglican ethos than had Keble and Pusey. Nevertheless, Newman, with Pusey, Keble, Isaac Williams, Charles Marriott, Copeland, Bloxam,

Church, and many others constituted what a modern student might call a sub-culture manifested by a common style of thinking and feeling.

One aspect of the ethos, an attitude likely to be misinterpreted today, is the habit of affection between members of the Tractarian circle. There was still no severe ban upon the expression of intense feeling in public; the educated Englishman had not yet come under the petrifying influence of the later public school spirit. When Newman preached his final sermon as an Anglican everyone wept. 'Dr Pusey, Morris of Exeter and some others sobbed aloud, and the sound of their weeping resounded throughout the church.'[19] As we shall see, the ethos of the Tractarians has a note of sobriety and restraint; but the restraint is not cold, the sobriety is not arid.

A further characteristic of the Tractarian ethos is that it is on the whole tied in its formative period to a particular region and to the rural areas within that region: to England south of the Trent and to the country parishes and the ancient universities. The background of *The Christian Year*, Keble's most distinctive contribution to the movement and the expression of a style of Anglican piety taken for granted as normal by those who wrote the Tracts, is wholly rural. The manner is that of a minor Wordsworth. The world of nature is viewed by the country gentleman, the secluded scholar, living in a village or a small country town. There is no concern for the new industrial towns with their novel styles of middle-class life and their great concentrations of the urban proletariat. In the poem for All Saints, the saints are pictured as *rural* hermits.

> Think ye the spires that glow so bright
> In front of yonder setting sun,
> Stand by their own unshaken might?
> No – where th'upholding grace is won,
> We dare not ask, nor Heaven would tell,
> But sure from many a hidden dell,
> From many a rural nook unthought of there,
> Rises for that proud world the saints' prevailing prayer.[20]

The soft southern landscape of villages, rivers, woods, meadows, ancient churches, small towns with a long history, is also in the main the background of Charlotte M. Yonge's novels. This has some importance, for it is as much through Miss Yonge's novels as through *The Christian Year* and *Lyra Innocentium* that something of the flavour of Tractarianism crept into the genteel consciousness, far from Oxford and from theological controversy. It is a pleasant, gentle landscape, one that seems almost bathed in grace; but it is the landscape as squire and parson, the gentry and the professional classes, would see it, not the landscape of the farmer or the agricultural labourer or the village craftsman or the new type of industrial entrepreneur. It is not the landscape of Cobbett's *Rural Rides*; for Cobbett knows about the detail of agriculture and how church rates and tithes look from below and he knows that the labourer in his smock frock may have secret ideas about the distribution of power and wealth in this rural world; what the ideas are may at times come out with the firing of ricks and the smashing of machines.

Charlotte Yonge knows about human misery in the countryside and it enters as a principal theme in *The Daisy Chain* (with *The Heir of Redclyffe* perhaps the most readable today of the novels). Let us note how it is handled. The members of the May family set out for Cocksmoor, where there are slate quarries. They look back from a height on their own town of Market Stoneborough. They see

the great old Minster, raising its twin towers and long roof, close to the river, where rich green meadows spread over the valley, and the town rising irregularly on the slope above, plentifully interspersed with trees and gardens.[21]

The cart track over the moor to Cocksmoor ends

in a broad open moor, stony and full of damp boggy hollows, forlorn and desolate under the autumn sky. Here . . . they walked along a very rough and dirty road . . . till they found themselves before a small, but very steep hillock, one side of which was cut away into a slate quarry. Round this stood a colony of roughly-built huts, of mud, turf, or large blocks of the slate. Many workmen were engaged in splitting up the slates, or loading waggons with them, rude wild-looking men, at the sight of whom the ladies shrank up to their protectors, but who seemed too busy even to spare the time for staring at them.[22]

The solution to the problem of Cocksmoor is the building of a school and, in fulfilment of the vow of the heroine, Ethel May, the erection of a church. There is some assumption that religion will have a civilizing influence and that the inhabitants of Cocksmoor will be cleaner, more industrious and more tractable through the influence of church and school; but the great end is spiritual. Miss Yonge's attractive heroine is censured by the worldly ladies of Stoneborough because she thinks it more important that babies be baptized than that they be clean and tidy. But we never forget our initial impression of the ladies' fear, as of a band of robbers or a savage tribe, at the spectacle of their fellow countrymen engaged in unfamiliar work.

The ethos of *The Christian Year* and of Miss Yonge's novels is given a distinctive theological expression by Isaac Williams. Williams is a minor figure, much loved by Newman when he was his curate at St Mary's, never tempted so far as we know to follow his leader in the crisis of 1845. In Tract 86 he comments on the general custom founded, he believes, on prescription rather than on the rubrics, that the priest in the sanctuary should face the congregation rather than the table, that is, that he should look to the West rather than the East.

What does this imply but that even in our religious worship we are to turn not to the East, the place where GOD has shown His countenance, but to the West; not to the light of the ancient Church, but to the eyes of the world; not to Angels assembled round the altar, but to the great men of our congregation . . . It is agreeable to this, that if there is anything unbecoming or negligent in the conduct of a chief or inferior Pastor, the remedy is at hand in an appeal to the public. This is considered the great corrector of abuses. And doubtless it is, and a very extensive and powerful one; but still it implies a very inferior condition that such should be requisite, not our singular advantage and happiness, but the sign of our captivity.[23]

'The sign of our captivity': here is a note sounded very strongly by all the Tractarians, at least until the coming of ritualism, a movement that developed a quite different ethos. It went with habits of piety that considered the verbal and visible consequences of the Reformation as bitter necessities and also opportunities for spiritual growth. This is far indeed from that spirit of Anglican triumphalism[24] that never ceased to speak of 'our incomparable liturgy' and to characterize the Church of England as 'the purest church in Christendom'. Some fellow-travellers of the movement, such as Palmer of Worcester and Hook, voiced their satisfaction with the Church of England in such terms; not so Williams, Hurrell Froude, Newman, Pusey.

What I have so far urged as to the character of Tractarianism seems not to support what is often taken to be a commonplace, namely, that Tractarianism is an expression in the religious sphere of the Romantic movement. I have already said that Keble's verse is that of a minor Wordsworth. But in so far as it is romantic, it is so as being touched with the sensibility of the precursors of romanticism, Collins, Gray, Cowper, as much of Wordsworth's minor work is. The problem is well discussed in Newman's 1839 article in *The British Critic*, 'The State of Religious Parties'. He gives an adequate account of the article's content in the *Apologia*.[25]

He is trying to account for a religious phenomenon, the rapidity with which theories conceived in Oxford colleges and country parsonages came to be the centre of popular excitements, the speed with which a theological position was transformed into a religious movement. He lists the influences of Scott and Coleridge, Southey and Wordsworth, as predisposing men to search in Anglicanism for what did not seem to lie on its surface. He speaks of Scott as 'stimulating [in his readers] their mental thirst, feeding their hopes, setting before them visions, which, when once seen, are not easily forgotten, and silently indoctrinating them with nobler ideas, which might afterwards be appealed to as first principles'. Coleridge 'instilled a higher philosophy into inquiring minds, than they had hitherto been accustomed to accept'. As Newman puts it, 'there was a spirit afloat'.[26]

All the same, Scott, or Coleridge, is no more than a remote predisposing cause of the movement out of which the Tracts came. Scott, considered in abstraction, we should have thought likely to encourage a taste for medievalism, whereas the Tractarians had their gaze firmly fixed on the first five centuries of Christianity; even the much loved seventeenth century was admired for its supposed patristic spirit. Medievalism came later. And one doesn't need to argue that the living influence of Coleridge is rather to be found in the thought of the Latitudinarians and in the obscure, original theology of F. D. Maurice. As to Newman's own thought, the affinities with the thought of Coleridge are evident, but it would probably be a mistake to see here a direct influence. Certainly, Anglo-Catholicism after the departure of Newman is syncretistic and draws much from medieval and post-Tridentine Catholicism, the latter, sometimes, almost to the point of caricature; but these are tendencies foreign to the thought and sensibility of the first generation of Anglo-Catholicism. Pusey went along with such tendencies but never much liked them.

Two questions can be raised about the ethos of Tractarianism. How far did it make for life and growth in English religion, within and outside the Church of England? What are the principal features of its 'myth' (it seems no longer necessary to protest that 'myth' is not a pejorative term and that it does not mean a false story), that is, the ensemble of ideas and attitudes round which the activities of the Anglo-Catholic party were arranged? And, since it was a movement that stood or fell by a particular interpretation of history, of Christianity in general and of England in particular, how far is the myth internally consistent and faithful to the evidence it appeals to?

It seems evident that Tractarianism was in many ways an enlarging influence upon English Christianity. The change in the externals of religious worship is very marked, so that wherever Anglicanism is now to be found there are many churches furnished with external aids to devotion of a kind unknown to (and on the whole undesired by) the men of the 1830s and forties. The style of worship – the use of incense and lights and rich vestments and ancient modes of music – characteristic of traditional Roman Catholic worship is now common in Anglican churches. It might be argued that a preoccupation with externals, a fussy concern with ecclesiastical millinery, has sometimes overlaid 'all that was best in Tractarianism . . . its reality, its depth, its low estimate of externals, its keen sense of the importance of religion to the individual soul'.[27] But the effect of the movement has often gone deeper: this shows itself in the use of the confessional, in the spiritual depth of many of those who are children of the movement, in the growth of a sense of mission to the poorest in our society – those who were largely untouched by the preaching of traditional middle-class Protestantism but who found the ministrations of the ritualist parsons (and the Salvation Army soldiers) warmed their hearts – above all in the astonishing growth of the religious life for men and women. This last, the growth within Anglicanism of communities dedicated to teaching, the care of the sick and dying, and contemplative prayer, is the finest and most enduring consequence of this Oxford Movement. Visual splendours may be sought from the shallowest of motives; but the life of the religious brother or sister, monk or nun, where it is persisted in, is necessarily a serious business.[28]

Tractarianism, then, refreshed a dry and formal, if not notoriously corrupt, religious establishment and gave Anglicans a sense of a religious body with a life transcending that of the State. In placing its foundation on the Fathers and on the Bible as understood in the patristic age it freed the Church of England from the Deism touched with Christian sentiment that was so strong a feature of Anglican piety after 1688 and it emancipated the Anglican mind from the preoccupation of Paley with questions of proof and evidence. Where the movement was not equal to the challenges of its period was in its inability to meet the difficulties, real or merely apparent, raised by the development of biblical criticism and the growth of the natural sciences. The Tractarians (Newman and Hurrell Froude were the exceptions, Church, too, though he was a younger man and came later into the movement) were perhaps deficient in irony – Pusey was monumentally deficient – and their examination of ancient sources was often a search for proof-texts rather than a genuinely historical investigation. A sense of irony and the historical sense seem equally required if we are to consider the dimensions of the Ark or the eloquence of Balaam's ass, the age of the rocks or the hypothesis of Natural Selection. At any rate, early Anglo-Catholicism declined the necessary task and was scandalized when it was taken up by the less devout but intellectually more agile authors of *Essays and Reviews* (1860).[29]

Despite the undoubted wish of the Tractarians to speak to the entire people of England, Stoneborough and Cocksmoor, to take Miss Yonge's two centres of interest as emblematic, did not often come together. Early Tractarianism, like Anglicanism as whole, was an affair of the gentry and the professional classes, and of the poor only in so far as they took these classes as exemplary. The difficulty was at bottom one of communication. The difficulties of the gentlemanly parson are affectingly set out by Dean Church.

I wish I could send you the medicine you ask about [he writes to Frederick Rogers in 1857] for an anti-talking-to-poor-people diathesis. After four years' trial I find it as strong in myself as ever, *i.e.* I know as little how to go about it satisfactorily, and still read with wonder and admiration any small book which describes the easy-going, glib, persuasive way in which the typical parson is painted talking to the members of his flock. To me they seem to live in impenetrable shells of their own; now and then you seem to pinch them or please them, but I can never find out the rule that either goes by. I think sometimes whether one ought not to give up reading, and all communication with the world one has been accustomed to, in order to try and get accustomed to theirs . . .[30]

Church is aware of the problems but even he takes for granted without much *ressentiment* the class structure that so securely imprisoned the higher clergy. When Gladstone wrote to him about a difficulty in the way of nominating Stubbs to the See of Chester, the difficulty in question being Mrs Stubbs, his reply was not a rebuke, but: '. . . the lady is not, I believe, of gentle birth: I think she was a school-mistress, but always of high character.'[31]

The whole of Tractarianism, in its depth as a religious movement, in its limitations as a social movement, is represented by an account of a sermon preached by Pusey on the last Sunday of 1847. One who was present wrote 'in all the fervour of his Protestantism':

[The sermon] was listened to throughout by that little crowded church-full with fixed and rapt attention, though it was neither declamatory, noisy, nor eccentric; but plaintive, solemn, and subdued, breathing throughout, I may say, a beauty of holiness and a Christian spirit so broad and catholic, so deep and devotional, that while the most zealous Protestant could find nothing in it he might not approve, the most bigoted Roman Catholic could not enter an exception to a single expression that it contained . . . He seemed . . . to love to dwell upon the sad and melancholy; and his voice, though clear and distinct, had something mournful, and at times almost wailing, about it . . . There he stood, a plain, and to all appearance, an humble and lowly man, preaching to a simple people, and speaking with the melancholy meekness as of one stricken and tried, yet uncomplaining . . .

'Who be he that preached?' said one young rustic maiden to another as we left the church; 'a monstrous nice man, but dreadful long.'

'Don't you know?' replied the other; 'it is that Mr Pewdsey, who is such a friend to the Pope; but come along, or we'll be late for tea'; and away they trotted.[32]

We have seen that what at first looked, with Keble's Assize Sermon, like a defence of the *status quo*, turned into an attack upon the generally received account of the Church of England. Tractarianism offered a radically new account of English history, a new interpretation of the English Reformation, a new rationale of the history of Christendom. Out of these things the myth of Anglo-Catholicism arose.

In his Anglican period Newman always thought the Protestant account of Anglican history plausible and the Tractarian arguments designed to weaken this account dangerous in that they could be thought to count in favour of Rome. The stance of the writers of the Tracts was thus polemical; and warlike on two fronts – against the popular English tradition and against the claims of Rome. In Newman's *Lectures on the Prophetical Office of the*

Church, viewed relatively to Romanism and Popular Protestantism it is argued that it is of the essence of the *via media* of Anglicanism to think the Church of Rome gravely corrupt. In *The Christian Year* we are urged to 'speak gently of our sister's fall'[33] – this phrase speaks, as they say, volumes – but 'Rome is our enemy and will do us a mischief when she can'; the decrees of the Council of Trent are 'the ruins and perversions of Primitive Tradition'; the distinctive error of Rome is its replacing of the appeal to Scripture interpreted by the united testimony of antiquity by the appeal to the present judgment of the Church. And

> however the mind may be entangled theoretically, yet surely it will fall upon certain marks in Rome which seem intended to convey to the simple and honest inquirer a solemn warning to keep clear of her, while she carried them about her. Such are her denying the cup to the laity, her idolatrous worship of the Blessed Virgin, her Image-worship, her recklessness in anathematizing, and her schismatical and overbearing spirit . . . I conceive . . . that while Rome confirms by her accordant witness our own teaching in all greater things, she does not tend by her novelties, and violence, and threats, to disturb the practical certainty of Catholic doctrine, or to seduce from us any sober and conscientious inquirer.[34]

Seventeenth-century Anglicanism, then, is a purged Catholicism without the abuses and superstitions of Rome but in full agreement with what was believed by the 'undivided' Chuch of the early centuries. Such was the Tractarian claim in the 1830s and 1840s. By the justice of this claim Newman was prepared to stand, or to fall.

How far is the appeal to early Anglican writers of one particular school justified? Are the doctrines cherished by the Tractarians to be found in them, not as individual doctrines held by this or that individual but substantially, as the doctrine of a dominant school? The writers of the Tracts had no doubt themselves that their hypothesis was borne out by the evidence of history. Were they mistaken?

Many of the writers of the Tracts were wary about appealing to the Anglican reformers, to Cranmer and Latimer and Ridley, and they practised a certain reserve in their discussion of them. The ecclesiastical role given by these reformers to the godly Prince was not welcome to them, and they knew that in sacramental doctrine the reformers had much in common with Luther, Calvin, and even Zwingli. In Tract No. 15 (by Newman) we find: 'The Church [at the Reformation] by its proper rulers and officers reformed itself. There was no new Church founded among us, but the rights and the true doctrines of the Ancient existing Church were asserted and established.'[35] This note was quickly muted, most of all perhaps under the influence of Hurrell Froude who thought the reformers a set of ruffians and chided Newman for his fervent disparagements of Rome. Nevertheless, it is clear that even when the strong anti-Roman polemic became gentler, the theological case against Rome was still stressed; this was historically the Anglican position, as much the position of the Caroline divines as of the first reformers.

Were, then, the Tractarians right in finding in those they held to be the classic Anglican theologians just those doctrines the Tractarians held to be fundamental? This is a question not altogether easy to answer, for on a variety of matters the writers appealed to are discordant among themselves, and the Tractarians sometimes appear to have picked out the bits they liked. But if we ask what is the fundamental doctrine of the Tracts, it is surely the one first to be advanced: that episcopacy founded upon the apostolical succession is of the essence of a true part of the Church; and it is this which constitutes an abyss between Anglicanism and Protestant dissent at home and the Lutheran, Calvinist, and other reformed churches in Europe.

It seems to me that in this matter the Tractarians were mistaken, in some degree wilfully. They knew, for example, that Hooker hesitated to assert that episcopacy was an absolutely primitive institution. He justifies Canterbury against Geneva on the ground of prescription, on the general witness of antiquity, on utility. Keble, who edited *Ecclesiastical Polity*, certainly knew this.[36] The matter is not much different if we examine the work of the Caroline divines. There are certainly some striking passages that seem to support the Tractarian interpretation. In Andrewes's controversy with Cardinal Perron he writes: '. . . there is no *interruption* in the *Succession of our Church*'; and 'Our Church doth hold, there is a *distinction* between *Bishop* and *Priest*, and that, *de jure divino*'.[37] And it is very common to find these divines holding that episcopacy is of *apostolical* institution, though they do this in such a way as not to commit themselves on the question of *Dominical* institution. This is why they always hesitate to call Holy Order 'a sacrament of the Gospel'. Even if we grant that there is a concurrence of opinions among the members of this school, we have to ask just what weight they put upon the doctrines of episcopacy and succession, what weight and what interpretation. The crucial issue is what view they take of the Protestant churches of Europe. These, except perhaps for the Scandinavians, lacked both succession and episcopacy; this was why the Tractarians shunned them and unchurched them. But even Andrewes, the strongest prototype the Tractarians could discover, thought of the non-episcopal reformed churches of Europe as sister churches and excused the non-episcopal character of (for example) the French reformed church on the ground that 'your France did not have kings so favourable to the reformation of the church as did our England', and argued that they should give their superintendents the title of

86

'bishop'.[38] Indeed, there may be some doubt as to whether the concept of 'succession' may not have become firmer and clearer in the hands of the Tractarians than it was in the period they looked back to. The general claim of the reformers was that they followed the apostles in purity of doctrine, and there is an echo of this in the Privy Council's instruction to Matthew Parker, who had been asked by Calvin to use his position as Archbishop of Canterbury to summon a general assembly to carry out a more thorough reformation in England and to abolish episcopacy and substitute for it a presbyterian order; the Privy Council told him to reply 'that the Church of England would still retain her Episcopacy, but not as from Pope Gregory . . . but from Joseph of Arimathea',[39] no doubt an allusion to the Glastonbury legend.

Much more historical material could be cited. But the conclusion seems plain: the Tractarians were right in finding in the writers of the old high-church tradition many doctrines and practices, and an ethos, very different from the humdrum Protestantism of the nineteenth century; but they were wrong in supposing that a well-organized system, centred upon episcopacy and the apostolical succession as being of the *esse* of the Church, was shared by the theologians they looked back to. Even for Andrewes, as for Hooker, episcopacy was highly desirable when it could be had; but it was not essential. This is not of course to assert the Tractarians were mistaken in their ecclesiology. It would still be possible to maintain, as we may take it Pusey and Keble did, that there was a providential overruling of the history of the Anglican communion, so that whatever defects and errors there might have been in its concrete existence and history, the episcopal succession and the doctrines contained in or implied by the Book of Common Prayer were simply facts.

The Tractarian account of English history has been influential, challenging but never overcoming the Whig interpretation, and has nourished the Anglo-Catholic myth that has tried to face down the two other myths that have striven to colour and order Anglican feelings, ideas, and loyalties. One is the Low Church myth, that makes Cranmer, Ridley and Latimer the martyr-saints of Foxe's *Book*, the Caroline divines an aberration, the Tractarians conscious or unconscious tools of Rome. The third myth, by far more influential than the other two, rests upon a kind of pragmatism, something its proponents believe, reasonably enough, guided the Elizabethan settlement. By the account of this myth, the Church of England has always been implicitly Latitudinarian, concerned with good citizenship and sound morality rather than with the rigidities of dogma. The Tractarians were always divisive, anxious to unchurch the Latitudinarians and some-

87

times the Evangelicals; their spiritual descendants have not always taken this line; the few Anglo-Catholics who became bishops often seemed converted to belief in comprehensiveness as the peculiar note of the Church of England and were irritated by the intransigence of the Anglo-Catholic clergy.[40] Comprehensiveness as the distinctive Anglican spirit is often traced back to Hooker, for whom Church and Nation were in principle identical. But Hooker, like almost all men of his time, thought it proper for the State to impose credal requirements and attendance at public worship by law, to put down disapproved rituals by law, to fine, imprison, and kill for religious offences. Comprehensiveness was asserted by him on terms that would have startled the nineteenth century had it really looked at him historically. Few nineteenth-century Anglicans wished to imprison nonconformists and take away their goods. If they repeated the catchwords of the seventeenth century, it was with a deafness to the tone of the old language and an unwillingness to draw from it the old political consequences.

II

We have already noticed that in the judgment of James Anthony Froude, as in the judgment of most later historians of the Oxford Movement, Newman was a special case. He was not the most learned of the Oxford leaders; simply as a scholar he was never in the same class as Pusey. But he was the greatest mind the movement had, the most fascinating person, and a writer of genius. He is, with Maurice and perhaps Dean Church, the only theological writer of the period who can today be read with interest by those not specialized students. His life was a dark comedy, as *The Winter's Tale* or *Measure for Measure* is. His influence after his death has been greater than it was during his life. Books and articles in every language are continually appearing, devoted to his theology, his intellectual strategies, his style and rhetoric, his personality. He has an assured place in the history of English thought and letters; one would no more leave him out of an account of thought in the nineteenth century than one would leave out Darwin or George Eliot or Matthew Arnold or Carlyle. As a Christian writer and thinker his place is with Pascal and Fénelon, with Kierkegaard and Solovyev. He pierces us, and turns us upside down. He did not, like Kierkegaard, play with the thought of martyrdom; but he narrowly escaped the martyrdom Kierkegaard feared, that of being trampled to death by geese.

His long life has been studied in immense detail, first by himself, for all his work, even the *Essay on Development*, is intensely personal and proceeds by way of reflection upon the incidents and experiences of his life, as schoolboy, as undergraduate at Trinity College, Oxford, as Fellow of Oriel, as Vicar of St Mary's, the University Church, as a Catholic convert at Oscott and in Rome, as the Superior of the Birmingham Oratory, as Rector of the Catholic University in Dublin, as, for the last ten years of his life, Cardinal of the Holy Roman Church. What the springs and impulses of this life were, how we are to understand the resolutions of its successive crises, these continue to be matters of dispute, and in such matters the later biographers (Miss Trevor, for example, and Sean O'Faolain), for all their access to a great mass of material not available to their predecessors, do not have a decisive advantage over such of the earlier as Wilfrid Ward and Bremond. In the mass of material that has appeared in the many volumes of the *Letters and Diaries* and has been used in Miss Trevor's monumental study there are no 'revelations' of a kind that would lead us greatly to alter our estimate of the mind and character. The new material simply gives confirmatory detail to a portrait the lines of which are already known; and where there are difficulties of interpretation, over, for example, his supposed egoism or morbid sensitivity, these difficulties remain. His thought, too, is undoubtedly well known in its main outlines and has, from *The Arians of the Fourth Century*, the *Parochial and Plain Sermons*, and the *University Sermons* (the works of his Anglican period) to his last substantial work, the *Grammar of Assent*, an astonishing continuity of theme and treatment. After he became a Catholic he never felt obliged to repudiate anything he had written, apart from isolated passages abusive of the Roman Church and crude fragments of polemic. Newman had little architectonic power; his writings are always 'occasional' (except the *Grammar* which was the fulfilment, at least in intention, of a long-cherished ambition); but the whole work strikes one as having a unity of, as it were, organic structure, a unity that comes, perhaps, from persisting inner compulsions of a kind that he did not himself fully understand. (He was often a puzzle to himself. During his illness in Sicily in 1833 he cried out in his delirium: 'I shall not die, for I have not sinned against the light.' In the *Apologia* he comments: 'I never have been able quite to make out what I meant.')[41]

Newman is historian, poet, philosopher, an independent thinker in religious matters – this is true of both his Anglican and his Catholic periods – a man of extraordinary charm and power over others, a man of great inwardness and yet one who was always prepared to turn outwards if there was some clear call for him to do so, whether this was a cry for help or advice by some quite obscure inquirer or an apparent duty imposed by some public controversy, as in the genesis of the *Apologia* or the dispute over the sense of the decrees of the first Vatican Council that caused him to write his *Letter to the Duke of Norfolk*. We cannot say he was a fine poet, or a distinguished historian, or a first-rate theologian; but it was the one man who was in all these things and who was great in the ensemble of these roles; and if we ask what, humanly speaking, was the source and character of this greatness, the answer may be (so far as anything adequate can be said) that it was the peculiar, arresting character of his vision of man, of the world, of man in the world, of human history, of the connections between the brightness of sacred history and the darkness of human history considered as an independent process, of the relations of man with God, the social relation in and with Christ that is the Church, and the ineffable relation of the one with the One. The essential note of his character is reflexivity, as it was for Augustine and Pascal and Kierkegaard. Self-judgment, self-explication, it is through the succession of such acts that he contributes to our efforts to define our fundamental problems. What looks to an idle or unsympathetic observer like egoism and even vanity is obedience to his vocation.[42] He seems to have sensed, without fully adverting to the complexity of the matter, that devotion to pure scholarship, to the pursuit of intellectual excellence purely conceived, would have been a betrayal of his vocation.

The *Parochial Sermons*, *The Arians of the Fourth Century*, and the *University Sermons*, are the signs of his maturing as a thinker. The last work, indeed, contains the themes that are to be treated in more detail in the *Essay on Development* and, twenty-seven years later, the *Essay in Aid of a Grammar of Assent*. His reflections upon Oxford and upon university education are set out in *The Idea of a University*, made up of lectures given during his rectorship of the Catholic University in Dublin. There is a great mass of writing, historical, polemical, devotional, in such collections as the *Historical Sketches* and *Discussions and Arguments* (this last contains 'The Tamworth Reading Room', one of his most brilliant comments on social questions). Finally, there is the *Letter to the Duke of Norfolk*, a measured but deeply felt expression of his tenaciously held view that the Ultramontane policies and doctrines of Manning in England and Louis Veuillot in France misrepresented the central tradition of Catholicism, a tradition compatible with (as Ultramontanism was not) freedom of speech, the rule of law, and the primacy of conscience. As to the *Apologia*, this is so much a key-document of the nineteenth century, with *Sartor Resartus*, Mill's *Autobiography*, Arnold's *Culture and Anarchy*, and Ruskin's *Praeterita*, that it is a necessary and not an optional item of the educated man's mental furniture.

We find almost all Newman's later preoccupations in *The Arians*. There is the connection upon which he always insisted between a right moral disposition and orthodoxy in faith ('coldness in faith is the sure consequence of relaxation of morals');[43] the sadness before the necessity, coming from the pressures of heresy, to hedge the mysteries of faith with dogmatic formulas ('freedom from symbols and articles is abstractedly the highest state of Christian communion, and the peculiar privilege of the primitive Church');[44] and there is the intense interest in the theory of belief and the nature of religious language.

When the mind is occupied by some vast and awful subject of contemplation, it is prompted to give utterance to its feelings in a figurative style; for ordinary words will not convey the admiration, nor literal words the reverence which possesses it; and when, dazzled at length with the great sight, it turns away for relief, it still catches in every new object which it encounters, glimpses of its former vision, and colours its whole range of thought with this one abiding association . . . the matter of Revelation suggests some such hypothetical explanation of the structure of the books which are its vehicle; in which the divinely-instructed imagination of the writers is ever glancing to and fro, connecting past things with future, illuminating God's lower providences and man's humblest services by allusions to the relations of the evangelical covenant . . .[45]

We find, too, that quasi-sceptical attitude to the physical world which is not so much a consequence of argument as a necessity of his temperament, so persistent is it, from his youth to his old age.

What are the phenomena of the external world, but a divine mode of conveying to the mind the realities of existence, individuality, and the influence of being on being, the best possible, though beguiling the imagination of most men with a harmless but unfounded belief in matter as distinct from the impressions on their senses?[46]

But scepticism is used with immense dexterity – this, too, goes on throughout his life – to press us into faith. We seem

to be floated off upon the ocean of interminable scepticism; yet a true sense of [the mind's] own weakness brings it back, the instinctive persuasion that it must be intended to rely on something, and therefore that the information given, though philosophically inaccurate, must be practically certain; and a sure confidence in the love of Him who cannot deceive, and who has impressed the image and thought of Himself and of His will upon our original nature.[47]

There seems no doubt that Newman derived this way of thinking about questions of knowledge and belief from the British empirical school, and his terminology of 'impressions' and 'ideas', with the schematic representation of man the perceiver and actor *vis-à-vis* a confused and almost inaccessible world of nature, comes from Locke and Hume.[48] It cannot be said to be a satisfactory or, at bottom, coherent way of talking. Newman's virtuosity lies in his use of the language of empiricism to persuade us to turn away from the world of nature and even, sometimes, from the world of history, so that we may face, alone, the awful claims of conscience and the implication of the existence of conscience, namely, the existence of God, not Paley's celestial watchmaker but the giver of the moral law.

In this Newman is the bearer of the Evangelical tradition as well as the child of empiricism. Not 1845, but his conversion when a schoolboy, was the great moment and turning-point of his life.[49] In this, as in his continual preoccupation with the visions and experiences of childhood and youth, he belongs to the romantic tradition of his time;[50] the *Apologia*, an autopsychography rather than an autobiography, is in some ways very like *The Prelude* of Wordsworth. It is from his own individual being, as from a luminous centre, that he looks out upon the spectacle of human history, an appalling and confused spectacle; this is for him a nightmare experience – 'If I looked into a mirror, and did not see my face, I should have the sort of feeling which actually comes upon me, when I look into this living busy world and see no reflection of its Creator';[51] the spectacle of the orderly processes of nature is for him beautiful and moving only from the standpoint of faith;[52] in the crisis of illness it was Pascal's fragment, 'Je mourrai seul', that he uttered;[53] it is as though God blinds him or dazzles him, so that whatever is not God is flickering, ambiguous, open to doubt.

But this is only one side of Newman. He impressed his friends as one who was interested in everything – science, politics, warfare, strange countries, curious anecdotes – and his bodily sensibility was keen. James Stephen described him as 'a sort of Benjamin Franklin graft upon a Fénelon stem',[54] and this, though more limiting than is just, seems acute. 'The Tamworth Reading Room', 'Who's to Blame?'[55] (a shrewd discussion of British politics in connection with the Crimean War), and the *Apologia* itself, all show an interest in the detail of social life and an ability to grasp the interplay of actions and institutions and ideas. The period of his Rectorship of the Catholic University in Dublin displays first-rate administrative ability. During the dark years between the secret delation[56] of his 'On Consulting the Faithful in Matters of Doctrine' to Rome and the apparent triumph of Ultramontanism at the first Vatican Council, he was ceaselessly concerned with examining the ecclesiastical scene and tracing the fortunes of men and policies in the Catholic world. His straightforwardness, almost John Bullishness, is given in the tone of voice in which he expresses his deep convictions about the nature of authority in Church and State. 'I give an absolute obedience to neither [Queen nor Pope]'; and:

conscience is the aboriginal Vicar of Christ, a prophet in its informations, a monarch in its peremptoriness, a priest in its blessings and anathemas, and, even though the eternal priesthood throughout the Church could cease to be, in it the sacerdotal principle would remain and would have a sway.[57]

And yet this is the same man who in describing the farewell to Oxford of the hero of *Loss and Gain* is surely telling us about his own feelings when in 1845 he chose a course of life that he knew would exile him from all that humanly speaking he had to love in this world.

The trees of the Water Walk were variegated, as beseemed the time of the year, with a thousand hues, arching over his head . . . He reached Addison's Walk; there he had been for the first time with his father, when he was coming into residence, just six years before to a day. He pursued it . . . till he came round in sight of the beautiful tower, which at length rose close over his head. The morning was frosty, and there was a mist; the leaves flitted about; all was in unison with the state of his feelings. He re-entered the monastic buildings, meeting with nothing but scouts with boxes of cinders, and old women carrying off the remains of the kitchen. He crossed to the Meadow, and walked steadily down to the junction of the Cherwell with the Isis; he then turned back. What thoughts came upon him! for the last time! There was no one to see him; he threw his arms round the willows so dear to him, and kissed them; he tore off some of their black leaves, and put them in his bosom. 'I am like Undine,' he said, 'killing with a kiss. No one cares for me; scarce a person knows me.'[58]

This is neither Fénelon nor Benjamin Franklin; it is certainly not John Bull.

If we ask what, apart from the gift of his own mind and sensibility, Newman has left to the world of religious thought, the common answer is bound to be: the theory of development, as it is expressed in the last of the *University Sermons* and in the *Essay on Development*, the product of Newman's bridge-period, the work he began as an Anglican and broke off on 9 October 1845 when he became a Catholic. Mark Pattison saw the book as a discovery that chimed in with the deep underlying theme of mind in the nineteenth century; Newman 'first started the idea – and the word – *Development*, as the key to the history of church doctrine, and since then it has gradually become the dominant idea of all history, biology, physics, and in short has metamorphosed our view of every science, and of all knowledge'.[59] I think there are two other possible answers to our question: he is the theologian of Grace, as this is expressed through all his sermons of the Anglican period, and systematically discussed in the *Lectures on Justification* (1838); and he is the man who attempted to construct, out of the difficult materials inherited through the British philosophical tradition, a theory of belief.

Enough has already been said on the elaboration and defence of the Anglican position in the *Prophetical Office* and the Tracts. One might be misled by Newman himself into thinking that the *Lectures on Justification* come under the general heading of Anglican apologetic. He tells us in the *Apologia* that it represented his 'desire to build up a system of theology out of the Anglican divines'.[60] It is arguable that the polemics that gathered round the *sola fide* of Luther and the whole question of Grace, polemics that echo in the Thirty-Nine Articles (in particular XI–XVII), express the most important questions that were at issue in the Reformation. If this is so, then plainly

Newman had to say something on this set of topics, more especially because the distinctive outlook of the Evangelical party was in this respect Lutheran, at least as Luther was then understood. Nevertheless, the *Lectures* are of more than merely historical or polemical interest; indeed, Küng calls them 'one of the best treatments of the Catholic theology of justification'.[61] The issues discussed are intricate and no adequate analysis is here possible. Crudely but accurately we may ask if God's acceptance of the sinner, who in the act of Divine acceptance is justified, rests upon as it were a legal fiction – God *imputes* justice to the sinner but this is a declaration of how God views the sinner and does not represent a real change in the nature of the sinner who remains a sinner even when he is justified (*simul iustus et peccator*) – or upon a real change in the nature of the sinner who is now sanctified, in Grace, a new creature, even (this was what irked the Protestant tradition) *meritorious*. Newman attempts to find a middle way (his slogan is: Not Luther but Melancthon!) between these two positions. He dislikes what he thinks to be at least the popular and practical Catholic position, with its quantitative view of merit and its quasi-materialistic view of Grace, but he finds himself unable to square the Evangelical view with the Anglican tradition, especially as this is expressed in the *Homilies*[62] and the Prayer Book. In particular, the doctrine of baptismal regeneration seemed to offer a formidable difficulty to the Evangelicals as it had to the Anglican Puritans of the sixteenth and seventeenth centuries.

Newman's argument on the point of principle – in what sense are we to see man as *simul iustus et peccator?* – is simple and decisive. 'Justification, being an act of Divine Mercy exerted towards the soul, does not leave it as it found it, – cannot but make it what it was not before . . .'[63] It follows from the fact that the declaration of justification is God's word that it is efficacious and that the analogy of a legal fiction is misplaced.

As to the *sola fide*, justification by faith alone, Newman argues that the doctrine originally designed to meet the difficulties of those troubled (as the young Luther was) with a multitude of scruples has itself become a source of anxiety. Luther 'found Christians in bondage to their works and observances; he released them by his doctrine of faith; and he left them in bondage to their feelings'.[64] We can easily become anxious over whether or not we have the feelings requisite in a justified man as over whether or not we have repented of our sins and made proper satisfaction for them. Above all, Newman grows impatient with the remoteness, the abstract character of much of the discussion and characteristically stresses the individual and concrete:

each existing man exists to himself, is an individual, complete in himself, independent of all others, differing from all others, in that he is he, and not they or one with them, except in name. No one thing can be another thing; faith in this man is not faith in that . . .[65]

The *University Sermons* cover a long period of time, from 1826, when the Tracts still lay in the future, to 1843, only two years before the end of his Anglican career. They contain lightly sketched positions on all the matters Newman will treat later in a variety of works (though with very little change in his own fundamental views). For instance, he anticipates his development in the *Grammar of Assent* of his concept of the Illative Sense in the sermon on faith as implicit reasoning (no. XIII). He also gives us his views on language (no. V), he advances a doctrine of the imagination close to that of Pascal, he shows us that he is aware of the decisive logical objections to the argument for the existence of God from the presence of 'design' in the universe, and argues that what divides him from Hume in this matter is a question of antecedent presumptions and not of logical analysis; and he expresses his despair over the efficacy of controversy: 'when men understand each other's meaning, they see, for the most part, that controversy is either superfluous or hopeless' (*Sermon* X).[66]

The main concern of the sermons is with what one can only call questions of religious epistemology: nature and revelation, the role of reason in relation to faith, the nature of conscience and its implications, and the problem of development in religious doctrine. They resemble in their scope and in their scrutiny of questions that lie on the borders of theology and philosophy the *Fifteen Sermons* preached by Bishop Butler at the Rolls Chapel a century before;[67] and the influence of Butler is, as almost everywhere in Newman's work, very marked, especially in what is said about conscience. The title of the first sermon, 'The Philosophical Temper, first enjoined by the Gospel', seems almost to belong to the eighteenth century; the last, 'The Theory of Developments in Religious Doctrine' plunges into problems of which the Newman of the first sermon was quite unaware and is a preliminary sketch for the *Essay on Development*.

It would not be misleading to view the sermons as so many attempts to come to terms with the immediate past of Anglicanism – the age which relied on 'evidences' and on the coercive force of arguments in natural theology, notably the argument to God's existence from the presence of 'design' in the universe – and to vindicate the dogmatic principle while, at the same time, meeting the difficulties (principally historical) adherence to the dogmatic principle necessarily raised for the believer. Of course, they are always *sermons* and thus kerygmatic, an attempt to preach the apostolic preaching and to commend it, not – at least, not viewed by Newman as – instances of private intellectual enterprise. They are strong against 'evidences' and against the view that the contemplation of the world of nature as exhibited to us by the natural sciences directly moves the mind from nature to God. They are also strong against the view that religion is a matter of inner feeling accompanied by moralizing. Equally, they bring out Newman's desire to give a faithful description of the act of faith and the inwardness of the life of faith and to show the shallowness of rationalism in religion. He is not afraid to say things that must have been found scandalous by the respectable religious people of his day. For instance:

The system of physical causes is so much more tangible and satisfying than that of final, that unless there be a pre-existent and independent interest in the inquirer's mind, leading him to dwell on the phenomena which betoken an Intelligent Creator, he will certainly follow out those which terminate in the hypothesis of a settled order of nature and self-sustained laws. *It is indeed a great question whether Atheism is not as philosophically consistent with the phenomena of the physical world, taken by themselves, as the doctrine of a creative and governing Power.*[68]

The last of the *University Sermons* leads us into the central theme of the *Essay on Development*.

It had been an indictment of the Church of Rome that it had *added* to the religious system to be discerned in the writings of the Fathers; and it had been, for the Tractarians, a decisive criticism of Protestantism that it took away or undervalued what was evidently a part of the same system. Newman began to see that the question what is to count as an addition was more difficult than he had thought it. He was faced with the historical difficulty once urged by the Jesuit Petavius in a famous work published in 1644. Petavius showed that, verbally at least, many of the ante-Nicene Fathers look like heretics. He had simply used this demonstration to show men that there was no intermediate position between a reliance on private judgment and acceptance of the Church's present authority. This is really an evasion of the historical difficulty and Newman began to see that the problem of development is more pervasive, raising questions about the relation of the earliest Fathers to the New Testament, and even raising questions about relations between different parts of the Bible itself.

Newman's polemical position in relation to Protestantism is: You have difficulties over the Eucharistic Sacrifice, the Real Presence in the Sacrament of the Altar, baptismal regeneration, priestly absolution, and so on, and the ground on which you declaim against them is that they are not primitive, not contained in the only authentic record of primitive Christianity, the New Testament. But what of other things you assume without hesitation to be primitive – the doctrine of the Trinity, of the Atonement, of the Godhead of the Holy Spirit? Is it really so plain that these doctrines are present on the surface of the New Testament record? Of course, it is not. You must believe more, or less; you cannot stay where you are. Newman used arguments of this kind (the most trenchant example is in Tract No. 85) with some reluctance, for they have a kill-or-cure character and may thrust a man into unbelief.

All Christians, then, not simply Roman Catholics, are faced with the historical difficulty that what they now believe and how they now organize their affairs does not plainly resemble what the Christians of the apostolic age believed and how they ordered themselves. Even Hooker had urged this difficulty upon the Puritans of his day in defending episcopacy against the Presbyterian model of church government. But it was the force of the *tu quoque* argument in the mouths of high Anglicans speaking to Evangelicals and nonconformists, and of Roman Catholics speaking to Anglicans, both parties speaking in defence of beliefs and practices that their opponents thought not to be 'primitive' or 'apostolic', that Newman stressed. He saw that what had been urged by Protestant controversialists as an argument against Rome, that Rome had 'added' to the original deposit of faith, was not so decisive as had been thought. The great question was: how can one distinguish between a true development and one that purports to be a development but is in effect an addition? In the early centuries the great questions had concerned the doctrine of the Trinity and the nature of the co-existence of Divinity and humanity in Jesus; in the post-Reformation period the central questions seem to centre upon the nature of the sacraments, the position of the Blessed Virgin Mary in the economy of salvation, and the authority of the Roman See.

Newman had always thought it plain that Protestantism could not appeal to antiquity. 'Whatever history teaches, whatever it omits, whatever it exaggerates or extenuates, whatever it says and unsays, at least the Christianity of history is not Protestantism. If ever there was a safe truth, it is this.'[69] He had thought it equally plain that Rome had added to what was held in the earliest centuries. He now had to ask himself if the distinctively Roman doctrines could be thought to be genuine developments from the primitive deposit. The problem was formidable, more so than perhaps Newman thought, for to work out by purely historical methods the content of the primitive deposit may be impossible. Certainly, the Christianity of history is not Protestantism. One might even say that Catholicism in the sense of a sacramental cultus is already present in the New Testament (e.g. in I Corinthians 11:23–32); but the connection between the papacy of Pius IX and the promises to Peter in Matthew 16:13–20 is not so evident; the passage becomes a defence of the papal claims only if we already see the emerging role of the papacy in the early centuries as a providential dispensation. Of course, Newman was aware that the argument for a given belief or practice could be circular, in that the starting-point only had the required meaning if the later development is taken to be authoritative, but this did not greatly trouble him, for he thought this was the necessary character of the problem. Nuclear events or utterances only have significance for posterity in the light of their presumed historical consequences. When *Mein Kampf* first appeared it might have been argued that the antisemitism was mere demagogic froth not to be taken seriously; the attempted organization of the Final Solution seems to set aside such an interpretation.

If there is a central Christian 'idea' (Newman often uses this term in something like the Coleridgean sense) the signs of it are too faint and broken for its character to be established by historical research. And yet, in no matter how fragmentary a form, the facts of history are there, setting a question mark against all later views as to what constitutes orthodoxy. The only way, so Newman thought, to answer the question lay in trying to determine how far the clue to the character of what is earlier is to be found in what is later and better known.

Development. . . How are we to understand this concept? And given that we know how to use the concept, how are we to sort out the genuine developments from what appear to be developments but are either pure additions or monstrous growths of what once was sound?

Newman seems to have two models of development in mind. First, there is the model of mental growth, the way in which an idea will grow in the mind of a reflective person. The text of the last of the *University Sermons* is: 'But Mary kept all these things, and pondered them in her heart'; and he takes Mary as a type of the mind of the Church. Then, lest we should take development too easily, seeing in it no more than a case of the deduction of truths hidden in a set of premises but all the same contained in them, he uses all the resources of his rhetoric to bring out what is superficially implausible about both the original apostolic preaching and its later developments. First, 'the pride of [ancient] science is seen prostrated before the foolishness of the preaching'.[70] He then takes the luxuriant development of Christian theology, how

a large fabric of divinity was reared, irregular in its structure, and diverse in its style, as beseemed the slow growth of centuries; nay, anomalous in its details . . . but still, on the whole, the development of an idea, and like itself, and unlike anything else, its most widely-separated parts having relations with each other, and betokening a common origin.

'And this world of thought', he goes on to say, 'is the expansion of a few words, uttered, as if casually, by the fishermen of Galilee.'[71]

The other model of development we find in Newman, and especially in the *Essay on Development*, is that of organic growth. This seems inevitable, almost a built-in feature of the language we use to handle the concept, though it often calls for ironical treatment. In describing, in the *Essay*, the tests (seven in all) that enable one to distinguish between a development and a corruption, Newman relies greatly upon the analogy of organic growth, though he has a sense of its limitations. But the tests are not used to construct would-be coercive proofs; they are rather apt illustrations of the growth of doctrines and dogmas, reminders for the devout soul rather than arguments against the sceptics and the minimizers.

What the arguments of his various 'tests' do is to exhibit the 'idea' of Catholic Christianity under various aspects and in connection with a great deal of historical data until, given it is a thing agreed upon that there is a Church dating from the time of the Apostles and having a continuous historical existence, we are moved to affirm that the Roman Church of the year 1845 is the legitimate historical development of that Church, its development being such as we should expect or at least not find incredible.[72]

It is tempting to consider the *Essay* as a particular application of the evolutionary hypothesis. This is, in my view, a temptation to be put aside. Of course, the *Essay* was an important agent in bringing about a different attitude to Christian development and its problems from that which had prevailed before Newman. But his intellectual formation was too purely English – the empiricists, Butler, the Fathers, the seventeenth-century divines, are the great influences – his ignorance of German work in history and biblical criticism was too great for him to be thought a child (as distinct from a maker) of the *Zeitgeist*.

The *Grammar of Assent* is Newman's final effort to come to close quarters with and to overcome what seemed to him formidable arguments standing in the way of Christian belief. He had been preoccupied with the problem almost since he began to think; even as a boy sceptical arguments seemed to him to have a dreadful plausibility. Enormously influenced by Butler's *Analogy*, he saw revelation as presenting us with difficulties like those we encounter in trying to gain from the world of nature some notion of God's achievements and purposes. We have already seen that he queries the clarity and certainty of what we encounter in ordinary sense-perception. And there seem to have echoed throughout his life the words he uses to record a memory of his earliest childhood: 'I thought life might be a dream . . . and all this world a deception . . .'[73]

The *Grammar* seems at first a very defective book. Its views on such matters as the status of propositions, truth, images, are confused and indefensible. But it has claimed readers since its first publication and it is still read. It has, in my view, certain peculiar merits. It represents an attempt by Newman to fight his way through and out of the tangle of philosophical problems he receives from Locke and Hume.

Men's claim to be sure, to believe with confidence, to *know*, at any rate in certain fields, has often seemed problematic to philosophers, in ancient Greece and in modern Europe. The special form in which Newman feels the difficulty probably derives (in his case) from Hume. If we ask what statements are certainly true we are inclined to pick out the conclusions of short pieces of deductive reasoning (as in Euclid's demonstrations) or what are sometimes called analytic statements ('All bachelors are unmarried men'). Some statements seem incorrigible, e.g. 'I have toothache'; if I say this I may be lying, but if I am not what I say could not be corrected. But most of the saving truths we need to find our way about in the world and to act effectively do not fall under such headings. That Britain is an island, that fire burns, that man is mortal, that events have causes to be searched for, such statements are doubtable. Any statement asserting *any* matter of fact may (it is argued) be doubted without absurdity; the sign of this is that if it is denied what is said is not self-contradictory, as the denial of an analytic statement or of the conclusion of a short piece of deduction is.

Such considerations often seem to point to the conclusion that even the best-attested statements about matters of fact are merely probable, no doubt with a probability in some cases so great that it would be absurd to doubt, but probable, and therefore doubtable, all the same. Newman sometimes, in moments of weakness, evades this difficulty, as Hume does, by saying that nature will not allow us to be sceptical; that is, the argument is turned aside, not by another argument, but by feeling. He even, on occasion, seems to think with Pascal that *il faut parier* – it is necessary to lay a bet.[74] But the interest of the *Grammar* lies in his refusing these ways out of his dilemma.

If the empiricists are right, then the certainty that we plainly do have about the truth of a great many statements that are about matters of fact or depend upon statements about matters of fact is a psychological feature of our life. If this were true, then we should have to say that we owe our confidence in the statement that all men are mortal to 'nature' or 'instinct', and, as we have seen, Newman does sometimes take this way out. But there is strong evidence that there is a better course of argument than this. He notes that Locke seems to have thought that the number of empirical propositions (that is, propositions about matters of fact) we have in practice to take as being as certain as those propositions that are true in virtue of their being analytic or in virtue of their being demonstrable in the strict sense is small in number 'and will be without any trouble recognized at once by common-sense', whereas

unless I am mistaken, they are to be found throughout the range of concrete matter, and that supra-logical judgment, which is the warrant for our certitude about them, is not mere commonsense, but the true healthy action of our ratiocinative powers, an action more subtle and more comprehensive than the mere appreciation of a syllogistic argument.[75]

Here is the justification of the Illative Sense. This way of putting things is not satisfactory, for to locate our certitudes in the exercise of yet another faculty cannot, plainly, enable us to break out of the circle of scepticism. But what Newman is here insisting upon is the pervasiveness of an immense variety of certainly true empirical statements and the suggestion that they have an indispensable logical role in the whole of discourse. He is moving in the right direction; and in his feeling for the right direction he is superior even to so acute a contemporary as John Stuart Mill. He is close to the Wittgenstein of *On Certainty*.[76]

Wittgenstein's main point is not obscure. The raising of doubts that are philosophical in the pejorative sense – How can I know there is a more or less spherical object to be identified as the planet Earth? Can I be sure that the world, with myself and my present memories all complete, was not created five minutes ago? How, since I sometimes dream, can I ever be absolutely certain I have a body? – destroys the language in which the doubts are expressed; the concept of doubt appealed to is not our ordinary concept of doubt, for where there is a doubt there exists the possibility of resolving it; whereas the doubts of philosophy have built into them the impossibility of their ever being resolved, and this 'doubt' is, then, a pseudo-concept. It is a refusal to share in the activity of language, though it draws its fascination from our pushing round and round the board linguistic counters that seem to have their ordinary value. In such speculations we are seized with vertigo. We seem to doubt; but this doubt cannot in principle be resolved; so perhaps this is how it is with all doubting. For there to be a procedure of doubting there must be a mass of empirical propositions, not a determinate number, that lie beyond doubt. It is the existence of such propositions that gives the concepts of wonder, of discovery, of doubt, their purchase and their point.

What the empiricists did, and Newman with them, was to stress the distinction between those propositions that in one way or another *cannot* be doubted, since to contradict them lands one in self-contradiction, and those propositions that are doubtable since their denials are not self-contradictory. Where they went wrong was to suppose that this committed them to thinking that all doubtable propositions are in some way doubtful; and we are then reduced to saying that some among them are *highly* probable, *practically* certain. Newman is still caught in the webs of empiricism; but even to have half-seen, as in the *Grammar*, that his central problem is that of the nature of those empirical propositions we should be mad to doubt is to have gone beyond most thinkers in this particular tradition. And to this particular intimation of a better way of handling traditional problems we must join his early thought, so close to that of Kierkegaard and the existential school, that the problems of faith are not solved at the level of speculation, but through decision and commitment.

If we are asked, how Faith differs from opinion, we reply, in its considering [God's] being, governance, and will as a matter of personal interest and importance to us, not in the degree of light and darkness under which it conceives the truth concerning them. When we are not personally concerned, even the highest evidence does not move us; when we are concerned, the very slightest is enough. Though we knew for certain that the planet Jupiter were in flames, we should go on as usual; whereas even the confused cry of fire at night rouses us from our beds. Action is the criterion of true faith, as determining accurately whether we connect the thought of God with the thought of ourselves, whether we love Him, or regard Him otherwise than we regard the solar system.[77]

Confidence in the judgments of common sense, despite the arguments for scepticism of which he feels the full force; a strong belief that good moral dispositions and a willingness to risk much are ordinary conditions for a firm faith in what God has revealed: these are constant features of Newman's apologetic position. He adds to these historical imagination. When he came to write the *Essay on Development* he found the chief difficulties in the way of Catholic belief to be historical; but he also in the end finds the coincidence of primitive Christianity with the contemporary Church of Rome decisive for him, simply because the picture of the Church as it is established by the historical imagination may be identified with the present Church of Rome, as we may see in the photograph of a young man the same features we now behold in the furrowed and wrinkled countenance of an old man physically before us.[78] 'Whatever be historical Christianity it is not Protestantism. If ever there were a safe truth, it is this.' There is no unity of feature. And:

Did St Athanasius or St Ambrose come suddenly to life, it cannot be doubted what communion they would mistake for their own. All will surely agree that these Fathers, with whatever differences of opinion, whatever protests, if we will, would find themselves more at home with such men as St Bernard or St Ignatius Loyola, or with the lonely priest in his lodgings, or the holy sisterhood of mercy, or the unlettered crowd before the altar, than with the rulers or the members of any other religious community. And may we not add, that were the two Saints, who once sojourned, in exile or on embassage, at Treves, to come more northward still, and to travel until they reached another fair city, seated among groves, green meadows, and calm streams, the holy brothers would turn from many a high aisle and solemn cloister which they found there, and ask the way to some small chapel where mass was said in the populous alley or forlorn suburb?[79]

This well-known passage illustrates what some have thought to be Newman's egoism. The picture of Athanasius and Ambrose turning away from high aisle and solemn cloister and making their way to the populous alley or forlorn suburb is, plainly, a representation of Newman's own turning away from the fair city of Oxford, set among groves, meadows and streams, taking with him only the black willow-leaves hidden in his bosom. But the egoism is a fruitful one, without vanity, and the intense self-scrutiny is for the sake of others. If Newman himself sought the 'Blessed Vision of Peace', it was that he might show it to the world lying beyond the *polis* that was Oxford. Oxford was still in his heart, and was never to leave it; but henceforth his seat was to be in Birmingham, the great capital of the Philistines.

Notes

(The place of publication is London unless otherwise stated.)

1 John Morley, *The Life of William Ewart Gladstone*, 1905 (1903), vol. 1 p. 157.
2 R. W. Church, *The Oxford Movement: Twelve Years 1833–1845*, 1922 (1891), pp. 159–61.
3 'Our own, our royal Saint', Keble writes of Charles I, in 'King Charles the Martyr', in *The Christian Year* (1827), John Keble, *The Christian Year, Lyra Innocentium, and other poems* (1914), p. 204. (This, the 'Oxford Edition', is useful in that it contains the text of the 1833 sermon on 'National Apostasy'.)
4 James Anthony Froude, *Short Studies on Great Subjects*, 1894 (1883), vol. IV, 'The Oxford Counter-Reformation', p. 270.
5 Yngve Brilioth, *The Anglican Revival*, 1933 (1925), p. 108.
6 Of course, there was still intense feeling of horror and repulsion before the Church of Rome, and anti-Catholic feeling within the Church of England remained a powerful influence down to the debates over the Revised Prayer Book in 1926–7. See E. R. Norman, *Anti-Catholicism in Victorian England* (1968). The anti-Catholic feeling provoked by Anglo-Catholicism is to be found in its most extravagant form in W. H. Walsh, *The Secret History of the Oxford Movement* (1893).
7 A. P. Stanley, *The Life and Correspondence of Thomas Arnold*, 1877 (1844), vol. I, p. 297.
8 On the complex question of the connection between Newman's thought and that of the Evangelicals, see David Newsome, 'Justification and sanctification: Newman and the Evangelicals', *Journal of Theological Studies*, XV (1964).
9 Tract No. 1, 'Thoughts on the Ministerial Commission' (1833), pp. 1, 2.
10 *Ibid.*, p. 4.
11 John Henry Newman, *Lectures on the Prophetical Office of the Church viewed relatively to Romanism and Popular Protestantism*, 1838 (1837), pp. 20–2.
12 '. . . I never attached any weight to the Bishops. It was perhaps the difference between Newman and me: he threw himself upon the Bishops and they failed him; I threw myself on the English Church and the Fathers as, under God, her support . . .' Letter of 2 January 1848, to Charles Marriott, Henry Parry Liddon, *Life of Edward Bouverie Pusey*, fourth edition (1898), vol. III, p. 163. (Liddon's four-volume *Life* was edited for publication after Liddon's death by J. O. Johnston and Robert J. Wilson and first appeared 1893–7.)
13 John Henry Newman, *Fifteen Sermons Preached before the University of Oxford*, 1918 (1843), p. 197.
14 There is an excellent note on 'The nomenclature of the [Oxford] Movement', in Raymond Chapman, *Faith and Revolt: Studies in the literary influence of the Oxford Movement* (1970), pp. 280–9.
15 Liddon, *Life of Pusey*, vol. III, p. 300.
16 Tract No. 86, 'Indications of a Superintending Providence in the Preservation of the Prayer Book and in the Changes which it has undergone', second edition (1840), p. 87.

17 Liddon, *Life of Pusey*, vol. II, p. 225.
18 *Ibid.*, p. 504.
19 Cited from *Autobiography of Robert Gregory*, ed. W. H. Hutton (1912), in R. D. Middleton, *Newman at Oxford* (1950), p. 215.
20 Keble, Oxford Edition, p. 186.
21 Charlotte M. Yonge, *The Daisy Chain* (1856), ch. III. (My quotations are from a more recent edition which has no date.)
22 *Ibid.*
23 Tract No. 86, pp. 76,77.
24 This spirit has persisted into the twentieth century and perhaps owes something to the Tractarian myth. An author cites Basire (Cosin's archdeacon) and (curiously) finds him 'ecumenically minded': 'I have surveyed most Christian Churches, both eastern and western, and I dare pronounce of the Church of England what David said of Goliath's sword, 'There is none like it, both for primitive doctrine, worship, discipline, and government', Beatrice M. Hamilton Thompson, in *The Apostolic Ministry*, prepared under the direction of Kenneth E. Kirk (1946), p. 416.
25 John Henry Newman, *Apologia pro Vita Sua*, edited, with an Introduction and Notes, by Martin J. Svaglic (Oxford, 1967), pp. 93,94.
26 On the whole question of the Oxford Movement and Romanticism, and on the question of Newman's affinity with Coleridge, see e.g. John Coulson, *Newman and the Common Tradition* (Oxford, 1970); D. G. James, *The Romantic Comedy* (1948); Stephen Prickett, *Romanticism and Religion* (Cambridge, 1976). In Newman there seems always to be some tension between his taste, which in architecture prefers the neo-classical to the Gothic, and in literature admires Dryden and Crabbe, and the persistent impulses of his nature, which draw him to the Romantics. A characteristic illustration: '. . . there is more to carry one away in Wordsworth's famous ode on the Reminiscences of Childhood or in the Happy Warrior than in all that Gray has written . . . the long majestic march of Dryden . . . has always delighted me more than the style of any English poet . . . as regards the power of words I prefer him even to Shakespeare', Letter of 22 November 1870, in Charles Stephen Dessain (ed.), *The Letters and Diaries of John Henry Newman* (1969–), vol. XXV, p. 234. In a letter to Hope-Scott he expresses his love for Sir Walter Scott and deplores his neglect, a neglect he shares with Johnson, Addison, Pope, and Shakespeare. 'Perhaps the competitive examinations [for the Civil Service] may come to the aid. You should get Gladstone to bring about a list of classics, and force them upon candidates', *ibid.*, p. 329.
27 Newman's obituary in *The Guardian*, 13 August 1890, cited in Middleton, *Newman at Oxford*, p. 240.
28 On the revival of the religious life, see Peter F. Anson, *The Call of the Cloister* (1955; revised edition edited by A. W. Campbell, 1964).
29 A generation later, under the editorship of Charles Gore, the liberal wing of the Anglo-Catholic party produced their own version of *Essays and Reviews – Lux Mundi* (1889). The survivors of the earlier Tractarian Movement were shocked. Liddon, Pusey's pupil and biographer, was especially disturbed.
30 *The Life and Letters of Dean Church*, edited by his daughter Mary C. Church (1894), p. 150.
31 B. A. Smith, *Dean Church: the Anglican Response to Newman* (1958), p. 208
32 Liddon, *Life of Pusey*, vol.III, p. 140.
33 Keble, Oxford Edition, p. 204.
34 *Prophetical Office*, pp. 324,325.
35 Tract No. 15, 'On the Apostolical Succession in the English Church', third edition, 1837, p. 4.
36 Keble admits that Hooker is ambiguous, but he considers that on balance, with certain

passages set aside and others interpreted benevolently, Hooker's authority can be claimed for the doctrine of the succession. In *The Works of Mr Richard Hooker*, arranged by John Keble and revised by R. W. Church and F. Paget, seventh edition (1888), vol. I, pp. lx–lxxxv.

37 Lancelot Andrewes, *Two Answers to Cardinal Perron and other Miscellaneous Works*, Library of Anglo-Catholic Theology (Oxford, 1854), p. 29.
38 Norman Sykes, *Old Priest and New Presbyter* (Cambridge, 1956) p. 74.
39 *Ibid.*, p. 86.
40 Gore, for example, became more establishment-minded when he became a bishop. See G. L. Prestige, *The Life of Charles Gore* (1935).
41 *Apologia.* p. 43.
42 'Newman is . . . the most autobiographical of men. The least of his books tells us about himself. The "I" . . . invades and even, in a certain sense, absorbs everything', Henri Bremond, *The Mystery of Newman*, translated by H. C. Corrance with an Introduction by George Tyrrell (1907), p. 6.
43 John Henry Cardinal Newman, *The Arians of the Fourth Century*, 1883 (1833), p. 9.
44 *Ibid.*, p. 36.
45 *Ibid.*, pp. 57,58.
46 *Ibid.*, p. 75. Newman later became more cautious in his expression of this view, but never altogether abandoned it. In a letter of 1865 he writes: 'I have not meant in my recent volume [the *Apologia*] to deny the existence of matter . . . But I am not prepared to say that the phenomena which present themselves to us are more than a particular mode in which the existence of matter is brought home to us . . . all I mean to say is that to distinguish between phenomena, and matter, is not to deny the existence of matter.' *Letters and Diaries*, vol. XXI, p. 474.
47 *Arians*, p. 76.
48 This seems now to be commonly accepted. See J. M. Cameron, 'Newman and empiricism', *Victorian Studies*, IV, no. 2, Indiana, 1960, 99–117, reprinted in J. M. Cameron, *The Night Battle* (1962), pp. 219–43; and J. M. Cameron, 'Newman and the empiricist tradition', in John Coulson and A. M. Allchin (eds.), *The Rediscovery of Newman: an Oxford Symposium* (1967).
49 *Apologia*, p. 17.
50 Eighty years after he left his childhood home at Ham, near Richmond, he wrote: 'I dreamed about it when a schoolboy as if it were paradise. It would be here where the angel faces appeared "loved long since but lost awhile".' In Wilfrid Ward, *The Life of John Henry Cardinal Newman*, 1913 (1912), vol. I, p. 29; see also *Letters and Diaries*, vol. XXXI, p. 119. In a sermon on 'The Mind of Little Children' he speaks of childhood as a time when 'he came out of the hands of God with all lessons and thoughts of Heaven freshly marked upon him'. *Parochial and Plain Sermons*, edited by W. J. Copeland, 8 vols. (1868–9), vol. II (new edition, 1896), p. 64.
51 *Apologia*, p. 216.
52 '. . . such works on Natural Theology as treat of the marks of design in the creation . . . are beautiful and interesting to the believer in a God; but when men have not already recognized God's voice within them, ineffective, and this moreover possibly from some unsoundness in the intellectual basis of the argument' (this last remark suggests Newman had profited from Hume's criticism of the argument from design). *University Sermons*, p. 70.
53 *Apologia*, p. 197.
54 David Newsome, *The Parting of Friends* (in the United States *The Wilberforces and Henry Manning*), 1966, p. 186.
55 Both in *Discussions and Arguments on Various Subjects* (1872).
56 In 1859.

57 *Newman and Gladstone*. The Vatican Decrees, with an Introduction by Alvan S. Ryan (Notre Dame, 1962), p. 129. *Newman and Gladstone* contains W. E. Gladstone, 'The Vatican Decrees in their Bearing on Civil Allegiance' (1874) and J. H. Newman, 'Letter to His Grace the Duke of Norfolk' (1875).

58 John Henry Newman, *Loss and Gain* (1848), ch. VI. (I cite the text from the convenient edition contained in *Newman Prose and Poetry*, selected with an Introduction by Geoffrey Tillotson (1957), p. 319. Tillotson's selection contains the second edition of the *Apologia*, the *Discourses on the Scope and Nature of University Education* (Dublin, 1852), 'The Tamworth Reading Room', and a few letters, sermons, and verses, as well as *Loss and Gain*.)

59 Cited in Owen Chadwick, *From Bossuet to Newman: The Idea of Doctrinal Development* (Cambridge, 1957), p. x. This is the best general study of the topic of the development of doctrine. A searching recent study of Newman's *Essay* is Nicholas Lash, *Newman on Development* (1975).

60 *Apologia*, p. 74.

61 Hans Küng, *Justification*, with a letter by Karl Barth, translated by Thomas Collins, Edmund E. Tolk, and David Granskou (New York, 1964), p. 212.

62 *Certain Sermons or Homilies appointed to be read in Churches in the Time of the Late Queen Elizabeth of Famous Memory* (Oxford, 1822).

63 John Henry Newman, *Lectures on Justification*, 1840 (1838), p. 144.

64 *Ibid.*, p. 386.

65 *Ibid.*, p. 290.

66 I have discussed some of these themes in more detail in my *The Night Battle* (1962), 'The logic of the heart', pp. 203–18. For detailed treatment of such themes see, for example, A. J. Boekraad, *The Personal Conquest of Truth according to J. H. Newman* (Louvain, 1955), and Thomas Vargish, *Newman: The Contemplation of Mind* (Oxford, 1970).

67 In *The Works of Joseph Butler sometime Lord Bishop of Durham*, edited by W. E. Gladstone (Oxford, 1897), vol. II.

68 *University Sermons*, p. 194.

69 John Henry Newman, *An Essay on the Development of Christian Doctrine*, 1890 (1878), p. 7.

70 *University Sermons*, p. 314.

71 *Ibid.*, pp. 316,317.

72 John Henry Newman, *An Essay on the Development of Christian Doctrine*, the edition of 1845, edited with an Introduction by J. M. Cameron (Harmondsworth, 1974), p. 41.

73 *Apologia*, p. 16.

74 'If it is but fairly probable that rejection of the Gospel will involve [a man's] eternal ruin, it is safest and wisest to act as if it were certain.' *Parochial and Plain Sermons*, vol. II, p. 21. On the relation between the thought of Pascal and that of Newman see my 'Pascal and Newman', *University of Leeds Review*, XII, no. 2 (1969).

75 John Henry Newman, *An Essay in aid of a Grammar of Assent*, 1906 (1870), p. 317.

76 Ludwig Wittgenstein, *On Certainty (Über Gewissheit)*, edited by G. E. M. Anscombe and G. H. von Wright, translated by Denis Paul and G. E. M. Anscombe (Oxford, 1969).

77 *Prophetical Office*, p. 106.

78 '. . . the very reason I became a Catholic was because the present Roman Catholic Church is *the only Church* which is like . . . the primitive Church, the Church of Athanasius . . . It is almost like a photograph of the primitive Church; or at least it does not differ from the primitive Church near so much as the photograph of a man of 40 differs from his photograph when 20. *You know that it is the same man.*' Letter of 30 August 1869, *Letters and Diaries*, vol. XXIV, p. 325.

79 John Henry Newman, *An Essay on the Development of Christian Doctrine* (Harmondsworth, 1974), p. 185.

John Henry Newman

Bibliographical essay

(Full titles, dates and places of publication are not given for works fully described in the notes.)

Extensive bibliographies are to be found in *Victorian Prose: A Guide to Research*, edited by David J. DeLaura (New York: The Modern Language Association of American, 1973); in the bibliographies published as supplements to the quarterly *Victorian Studies*, Indiana; in Owen Chadwick, *The Victorian Church* (2 vols., 1966 and 1970); in J. M. Cameron, *John Henry Newman*, Bibliographical Series on Writers and their Work No. 72 (1956); and in J. R. Griffin, *Newman: a Bibliography of Secondary Studies* (Front Royal: Virginia, 1981).

The often large volumes of lives and letters published in the nineteenth and early twentieth centuries, such as Liddon's *Pusey*, Stanley's *Arnold*, Mary Church's *Life and Letters of Dean Church*, J. T. Coleridge's *A Memoir of the Rev. John Keble* (Oxford, 1869), Mark Pattison's *Memoirs* (1885), Wilfrid Ward's *W. G. Ward and the Oxford Movement* (1889), Morley's *Life of Gladstone*, Wilfrid Ward's two-volume life of Newman, and his *Life of Cardinal Wiseman* (1897), are valuable sources of material. There are some outstanding volumes of reminiscence by men of the Tractarian generation: William Palmer's *A Narrative of Events connected with the Publication of the Tracts for the Times* (1843) – a second edition, revised and with additional material was published in 1883; F. Oakley's *Personal Reminiscences of the Oxford Movement* (1855); J. A. Froude's *The Nemesis of Faith* (1849) is, though in the form of fiction, a record of Froude's own reactions to the period; T. Mozley's *Reminiscences chiefly of Oriel College and the Oxford Movement* (1882) is entertaining, though not always accurate; *The Autobiography of Isaac Williams* (1892).

The classic work on the Movement is Dean Church's *The Oxford Movement*. It is well written, beautifully constructed, and full of generous feeling. Nothing published since has substantially changed the detail and the balance of Church's account. As well there is J. H. Overton, *The Anglican Revival* (1897) and S. L. Ollard, *A Short History of the Oxford Movement* (1915); both these works continue the story beyond the fateful year 1845. The centenary of Keble's sermon on 'National Apostasy' produced two very different works: Christopher Dawson's *The Spirit of the Oxford Movement* (1933) and Geoffrey Faber's *Oxford Apostles* (1933); the latter is a piece of psycho-history, using Freudian-style techniques to analyse relations within the Tractarian circle. Useful modern studies of the history of the Movement are Marvin R. O'Connell, *The Oxford Conspirators: a History of the Oxford Movement, 1833–45* (London, 1969) and John R. Griffin, *The Oxford Movement: A Revision* (Front Royal, Virginia, 1980). A fine study of the Movement's theology is Brilioth's *The Anglican Revival*, though the judgments are often unsympathetic. There are two collections of documents with valuable commentaries: *The Mind of the Oxford Movement*, edited with an Introduction by Owen Chadwick (1960) and *The Oxford Movement*, edited with an Introduction by E. R. Fairweather (New York, 1964). A fine collection of extracts from the Anglican divines to whose work the Tractarians appealed is *Anglicanism*, compiled and edited by Paul Elmer More and Frank Leslie Cross (1935).

The literature on Newman is vast. An excellent beginning is John Coulson, A. M. Allchin, and Meriol Trevor, *Newman: A Portrait Restored* (1965); this contains a list of works, with an analysis of some, and a biographical sketch. There is a complete list of Newman's published works at the beginning of each volume of the *Letters and Diaries of John Henry Newman*, ed. S. Dessain *et al.* (1969–); these volumes are an indispensable source for students of Newman. Joyce Sugg, *A Packet of Letters* (Oxford, 1983) is a useful selection from the letters. J. Rickaby's *Index to All the Works of John Henry Cardinal Newman* (1914) is useful but hard to find. There is now an up-to-date catalogue of Newman's writings: *John Henry Newman: Bibliographical Catalogue of his Writings* (Charlottesville: Bibliographical Society of the University of Virginia, compiled by Vincent Ferrer Blehl S. J., 1978). For the letters of the

Anglican period, we still depend upon *Letters and Correspondence of John Henry Newman during his life in the English Church*, edited by Anne Mozley (2 vols., 1891) and *Correspondence of John Henry Newman with John Keble and others*, edited at the Birmingham Oratory (1917), though some of the earlier volumes, which cover the Anglican period, of the *Letters and Diaries* have now been published. The autobiography included in Anne Mozley's collection has now been superseded by a full and unbowdlerized version, with added material: *John Henry Newman: Autobiographical Writings*, edited with introductions by Henry Tristram (1956). Of the many studies of Newman's life and thought Ward's large *Life* is outstanding, both for its details and for its analyses and interpretations. Also worth consulting are F. L. Cross's *John Henry Newman* (1933), and C. F. Harrold's *John Henry Newman* (New York, 1945), R. D. Middleton's *Newman at Oxford* and his *Newman and Bloxam* (1947), Maisie Ward's *Young Mr Newman* (1948), Sean O'Faolain's *Newman's Way* (1952), Louis Bouyer's *Newman: His Life and Spirituality*, translated by J. Lewis May (1958). Meriol Trevor's two-volume biography, *Newman: The Pillar of the Cloud* and *Newman: Light in Winter* (1962) is compulsively readable and based on all the material in the archives at the Birmingham Oratory. It has two deficiencies: there are no references to the material used; and the book is pervaded by the spirit of advocacy; Newman is invariably right; the relations of Newman with Faber and Manning, strongly dramatic in any case, are reduced to melodrama. But the two volumes are indispensable and gripping, valuable for the life but not for the work – accounts of the work are sketchy. See David Newsome's review in *Journal of Theological Studies*, vol. XIV, pt. 2, 1963.

Among modern editions of individual works by Newman the following may be mentioned: Svaglic's edition of the *Apologia*; Alvan S. Ryan's edition of *Letter to the Duke of Norfolk*; I. T. Ker's edition, with Introduction and Notes, of *The Idea of a University*; John Coulson's edition, with Introduction, of *On Consulting the Faithful in Matters of Doctrine*; D. M. MacKinnon and G. D. Holmes' edition of the *University Sermons*; N. Lash's edition of the *Grammar of Assent*; my own of the *Essay on Development*. Among selections and anthologies there are: E. Przywara, *A Newman Synthesis* (1930); C. F. Harrold, *A Newman Treasury* (1943); Geoffrey Tillotson's *Newman Prose and Poetry*; *A Newman Companion to the Gospels: Sermons of John Henry Newman*, edited by Armel J. Coupet (1966).

For specialized studies of the thought of Newman there are: J. H. Walgrave O.P., *Newman the Theologian* (1960); Thomas Vargish, *Newman: The Contemplation of Mind* (Oxford, 1970); the Oxford Symposium on *The Rediscovery of Newman* (the papers by David Newsome, T. M. Parker, C. S. Dessain, and John Coulson are especially interesting); A. J. Boekraad, *The Personal Conquest of Truth* (Louvain, 1955); A. J. Boekraad and Henry Tristram, *The Argument from Conscience to the Existence of God* (Louvain, 1961); David A. Pailin, *The Way to Faith: an Examination of Newman's Grammar of Assent* (London, 1969); and M. Jamie Ferreira, *Doubt and Religious Commitment: the Role of the Will in Newman's Thought* (Oxford, 1980). *The Philosophical Notebook of John Henry Newman*, edited with an Introduction by Edward Sillem and revised by A. J. Boekraad (2 vols., Louvain, 1970), contains unpublished philosophical fragments, of extraordinary interest, by Newman; the first volume is a general introduction by the late Edward Sillem to Newman's philosophical ideas and their diverse origins. *The Theological Papers of John Henry Newman on Faith and Certainty* and *The Theological Papers of John Henry Newman on Biblical Inspiration and on Infallibility* have both been collected and edited by J. Derek Holmes (1975 and 1979, respectively). On politics there is Terence Kenny's *The Political Thought of John Henry Newman* (1957). There has been much recent interest in Newman's style and rhetoric: a pioneer study is Walter E. Houghton, *The Art of Newman's Apologia* (New Haven, Conn., 1945); John Holloway's *The Victorian Sage* (1953) contains a study of the rhetoric; George Levine, *The Boundaries of Fiction* (Princeton, N.J., 1968), is an illuminating discussion and comparative study of Carlyle, Macaulay, and Newman. On Newman, Coleridge, and the Romantics, there are the books by Coulson (*Newman and the Common Tradition*), James (*The Romantic Comedy*), and Prickett

(*Romanticism and Religion*). An outstanding study of Newman's thought on education is A. Dwight Culler, *The Imperial Intellect* (New Haven, Conn., 1955).

On the question of church and society in the period, see R. A. Soloway, *Prelates and People 1783–1852* (1969) and E. R. Norman, *Church and Society in England 1770–1970* (Oxford, 1976). On Tractarians who fought hard to make a connection between church and people, see e.g. W. R. W. Stephen's *Life and Letters of Walter Farquhar Hook* (1878) and Brian Heeney, 'Tractarian pastor: Edward Monro of Harrow Weald', in *Canadian Journal of Theology*, XIII, no. 4 (1967), and XIV, no. 1 (1968).

There is a comprehensive account of recent work on socio-religious history in 'Recent studies in Victorian religious history', by Hugh McLeod, *Victorian Studies*, Indiana, XXI, no. 2 (1978), 245–55.

4
Drey, Möhler and the Catholic School of Tübingen

JAMES TUNSTEAD BURTCHAELL, C.S.C.

At the very south of the lands of Germany, standing directly against the Swiss frontier, enclosed to the west by the Black Forest of Baden and open on the east to the rolling plains of Bavaria, lies Württemberg. This countryside, formed mostly of the gentle hill slopes of old Swabia, sheds the waters that fall on it in two directions: some into the valleys feeding the Rhine, which is picking up momentum here for its mighty wash into the North Sea; the rest into the Danube, which has its small start here and then proceeds to drain the entire old Austro-Hungarian Empire on its ponderous way to the Black Sea. It was from Württemberg, and from its ancient university city of Tübingen, that fared forth a formidable school of Catholic theology which would, through the first half of the nineteenth century, have no better in Europe. Theologically, Württemberg was watershed of the Catholic world, with its headwaters in Tübingen.

Duke Eberhard had founded the University in 1477. Half a century later both duchy and university were given over to the Reformation. In years to come the institution would remember among its students Melanchthon, Kepler, Hegel, and Schelling. That this relatively small academy, settled in a largely Lutheran region, came to be the seat of a sturdy Catholic theological revival, is due to Napoleon Bonaparte as much as to anyone. His energetic efforts to subdue, incapacitate, and despoil the Catholic Church succeeded in freeing the Church's wits to explore the faith it had late been distracted from. In the Treaty of Lunéville, 1801, he arranged to attach the left bank of the Rhineland to France. The disadvantaged German princes were indemnified with the lands of the German prince-bishops. Thus in 1803 the duke of Württemberg found himself a king, and now the ruler of a large batch of Catholic subjects. In 1806 he awarded the Catholics religious freedom and in 1812 they established in the town of Ellwangen a small seminary to train students for the priesthood. When King Wilhelm was re-organizing the

University at Tübingen in 1817, he transferred the seminary there to serve as the nucleus of a Catholic theology faculty alongside the existing Protestant one, setting a pattern other major German universities would eventually follow.

The Tübingen faculty

The major scholars leading this Catholic faculty at Tübingen in subsequent decades included:

	Lived	Taught in Tübingen
Johann Sebastian von Drey	(1777–1853)	1817–46
Johann Baptist von Hirscher	(1788–1865)	1817–37
Johann Georg Herbst	(1787–1836)	1817–36
Johann Adam Möhler	(1796–1838)	1822–35
Franz Anton Staudenmaier[1]	(1800–1856)	
Johann Evangelist von Kuhn	(1806–1887)	1837–82
Karl Joseph Hefele	(1810–1893)	1840–69

Every one of these men came from simple parentage in small villages of Württemberg. Possibly no theological faculty of the time drew its professors from more homogeneous local stock, and kept them aside from the to-and-fro of the larger cities. How is it that these country boys from the Swabian farms managed to initiate a theological revival among Catholics of the nineteenth century? This may bear telling as much as does the theology they articulated.

To begin with, each of these men had training and interests in history, with special emphasis upon the history of the earlier Christian centuries and the more quarrelsome times surrounding the Reformation. Drey, for instance, had done research on Justin Martyr, the emergence of private confession in the patristic period, the Constitutions and Canon of the Twelve Apostles, and the controversy over the dating of Easter. Hirscher had published studies on the history of the Eucharist, church–state relations, and the life of Jesus. Herbst had done voluminous work on the Pentateuch, the earliest church councils, archaeological evidence regarding the presence of Peter in Rome, the history of the Church in Utrecht, the work of the Maurist Benedictines, and the literary achievements of the French Oratorians. Möhler, student of the previous three, worked on Athanasius and the Arians, the disputes between Peter and Paul and Augustine and Jerome, the Letter to Diognetus, Anselm of Canterbury, Islam and Christianity, the origins of Gnosticism, and the history of simony. Staudenmaier's published research touched on the history of the election of bishops, Gnosticism, and John Scotus Erigena. Kuhn's interests led him to investigate Pelagianism before Augustine, and the four Gospels. Hefele left behind him a monumental record of the early church councils that is still a classic source of documentation, and books on Cardinal Ximenes and the Inquisition, Bonaventure, the Letter of Barnabas, and John Chrysostom. Despite this welter of historical research through the past, the group was not just cinder-sifting. Their chief interest was theorizing. Yet they trained themselves for the task well by studying the muddled past, and by understanding that it would not so easily justify some of the simplified reports and conclusions of their colleagues at other universities.

Familiarity with the past made the Tübingen scholars free-spirited. Drey, for example, put out a book which argued that confession of sins to a priest had been unknown in the earliest centuries, and derived from no apostolic origins. For that he was reported to Rome, and blocked from appointment when later nominated as bishop. Hirscher's publications on the history of the Mass suggested a number of reforms then out of favour, such as worship in one's own tongue; he even offered several formularies in German. The book was promptly put on the *Index*. Hefele, who was in 1869 consecrated bishop of Rottenburg (the local diocese), one year later was at the Vatican Council offering vigorous historical arguments why the pope should not claim infallibility. Möhler was vetoed from a professorship in Bonn because the cardinal archbishop of Cologne thought his first book was heterodox. The Tübingen group was never popular in Rome, but at that time Rome was much distracted by the political turmoil in Europe, and had no resident theologians of sufficient capability to take sufficient notice of the Swabians. Later, as we shall see, when the Jesuits restored to Rome the teaching of scholastic theology following the tradition of Thomas Aquinas, they would look upon Tübingen with distinct misgivings. By and large, though, with no bishop in town, Rome looking elsewhere, and a Lutheran king in Stuttgart unconcerned with their theology, these divines had a free hand not enjoyed by their peers in other, more exposed, locales.

Another of the principal reasons for their eminence was their presence at a university. It was probably all the more stimulating in that it was a secularized, though predominantly Protestant university. Invariably, theological revival in Catholic Europe during the last century came through association with university life: in Germany (at Tübingen and later at Munich) during the early years, in England starting in the 1840s with the advent of the converts from Oxford, and in France with the establishment of the free faculties in the 1870s. The theology emanating from the seminaries, founded at the behest of the Council of Trent, was more narrowly drawn by men whose familiarity with contemporary learning was often minimal, as was their truly scholarly knowledge of the distant past. Yet the Tübingen theologians preserved themselves from the sterility that perverted much of the intellectual milieu in the universities of their time, because they were pastorally concerned. They were teaching candidates for the priesthood while they addressed problems of popular concern. Many of them, for instance, published catechisms.

Because they were scholars themselves, they moved familiarly among the works of their most influential contemporaries. They had read and criticized Kant, Hegel, Fichte, and Schelling. They learned from and argued with the leading Protestants, including Schleiermacher, Neander, Marheinecke, and Baur. They were conversant with the intellectuals who had repudiated the Enlightenment and had been converted to Catholicism – Baader, Müller, Novalis, Görres, Schlegel – and were even better critics than they of the intellectual vogue that had dominated Germany. In a word, they were the only Catholic group in Germany that maintained the highest standards of scholarship, refusing to sustain any received view of their faith if it allowed of no respectable academic defence. At the same time they turned their efforts to elaborating a serious account of the traditional faith of their fathers.

One further factor that contributed to Tübingen's wide influence was the *Theologische Quartalschrift*, a journal they founded in 1819, and which now survives as the oldest continuously published journal of German Catholic scholarship. It carried their pollen across the fields of all Europe.

They were, then, honest intellectuals and concerned priests. This need not have elevated them into a 'school'. A further advantage was that quality which German universities possess and Italian armies lack: a willingness to follow a leader. One man – Drey – received the respect of his early colleagues throughout their two decades together until the group broke up. Then in 1835 Möhler moved to Munich; Herbst died in 1836; and in 1837 Hirscher moved to Freiburg. Immediately a second generation sprang up, peopled by Kuhn, Staudenmaier, and Hefele. These also looked to Drey for the leadership and intellectual continuity that gave their years of work a momentum and an impetus that isolated scholars cannot enjoy.

Johann Sebastian von Drey

Let, us, then, examine the accomplishments of Johann Sebastian von Drey, founder and idea-giver of the *Katholische Tübinger Schule*. His beginnings were impoverished. Born a shepherd's son in 1777 in the village of Killingen,

Johann Drey had to work constantly to earn his way during years of study after he had enrolled for the priesthood in his then home diocese of Augsburg. Perhaps this onerous and worrisome path towards his career had something to do with the hypochrondria he developed during his student years and which plagued him throughout his life, though that life was strong enough to reach its 76th year. After ordination in 1801 he served a spell as *Vikar* (parish assistant) in his home village before receiving an appointment to teach at the Catholic school in Rottweil, with responsibilities for mathematics, physics, and the philosophy of religion (this was when he acquired his lifelong fascination with meteorology; for years he kept tables of weather observations). When the theological school was founded at Ellwangen he became a charter member of the staff, charged with teaching dogmatics, history of doctrine, apologetics, and *theologische Enzyklopädie* (theological method). Five years later he went with the entire faculty to Tübingen when the king grafted them on the university there, and then he quickly hit his stride. In 1821 the more established university at Freiburg offered him a chair which he declined. Two years later the king conferred knighthood on him and he became henceforth 'von' Drey. He was, as already mentioned, put forward to be first bishop of the new local diocese of Rottenburg but was set aside because of his venturesome theological manner. Eventually in 1837 he reduced his teaching commitments, and nine years later he retired completely. He had founded and led through the first half of the century a most ebullient and creative theological team.

For his students he prescribed a rigorous academic training. A future priest, he insisted, should begin by studying all the usual disciplines in a liberal education. He would also need to know the basic ancient and foreign languages, and should be familiar with philosophy, particularly those branches treating of knowledge and ideas. The seminarian should know about other religious traditions, their histories and beliefs. And, of course, there should be a thorough grounding in all history, both of the world and of the church. He was emphatically insistent on historical competence: the essential yet rare prerequisite for scientific theological work, he said, was the ability to understand each component of the faith against the historical background of its formulation. Only then might one be trusted to compose the various elements into an intelligible system. Besides all this, von Drey's students were advised that they would need psychology, the history of art, and supervised training in the techniques of teaching. One did not, evidently, loaf one's way through Tübingen.

Some measure of the man himself may be taken by comparing some of his presentations with the work of one of his most celebrated and successful contemporaries, Franz Leopold Bruno Liebermann, rector of the seminary at Mainz, whose *Institutiones Theologicae*, first published in five thick volumes, 1818–22, ran to ten editions in the next fifty years. It was possibly the most widely used seminary textbook in Europe. When dealing with the reliability of Scripture, Liebermann offers an elaborate defence of its total and literal veracity. He endorses the calculation that 3,000 years intervened between the creation of the world and the building of the temple by Solomon. He labours intricately to harmonize discrepancies between the different Gospels, such as the divergent genealogies of Jesus, the different dates for the last supper, etc. In a word, he is innocent of scholarly understanding of the biblical literature. Von Drey, at the very same time, was writing that the Bible should be studied as ancient literature and not misused as a catalogue of 'proof-texts'. Noting the poor state of biblical criticism, he complains: how long has it been since Richard Simon, and there is still no reliable theory of biblical criticism?

The four traditional 'marks' of recognition of the Church were that it was one, holy, catholic, and apostolic. Expounding upon the note of holiness, the Mainz scholar incorporates pages of Latin translations of earlier lyricism by Bossuet and Erasmus, arguing that the Catholic Church was to be acknowledged as the one true church because its members, and especially its hierarchical leaders, were so much more devout than were their competitors in other Churches. He notes with lengthy contempt the rather explicit lack of holiness in the lives of Luther, Calvin, and Zwingli. The Tübingen approach to the subject is different. The moral character of the Church's membership, writes Drey, will always reflect the dual nature of the enterprise. The Church is divine by virtue of its founding by God's Son and the constant activity of his Spirit who purifies and spreads Christ's teaching and brings it to harvest in the lives of believers. The human feature derives from the members themselves, called to be Christ's servants and instruments of the Spirit, yet by nature both free and corruptible. The Church is the ground of a struggle wherein the human proclivity to sin and confusion is opposed by God's gratuitous gifts of love and truth. The evil that is so obviously present does not gainsay or thwart the church's mission to be holy; but it does alert us to our fragility.

A view of the Church

Drey is sober when assessing the performance of his own Church's leadership. Church officers, he says, have a double function of government and of service. In their first role they preside over the Church as a group; in their latter, they care for individual people. The Protestants, he argues, only acknowledge this latter function.

How is it that Catholic theology still lacks counsel for those in church government, despite the fact that in our system this is an essential concern? Either because the theologians, who rank in the lowest order of the clergy, are not bold enough, because of some sort of hesitancy, to offer direction to their superiors on how they should exercise their responsibilities; or because these officials, reliant upon God's Spirit or their own wits, do not get around to asking for it.[2]

A chief task of Church leaders, in Drey's view, was that of moderating change and development. In matters of faith, leaders must have enough scholarly familiarity with its historical sources to recognize what is their authentic outgrowth and what is deviation. With respect to liturgical usage they must be supple. No single format of worship can long serve one people, or ever serve all peoples. The forms must always be changing, though not in a thoughtless or ungoverned fashion. He advocated considerable freedom of public expression within the Church, even though this always entails some disorder and awkwardness. Orthodoxy should be preserved in some other way than by suppressing the free expression of religious opinion. By the nature of things, teachers and writers in the Church, in their pursuit of knowledge, will have interests distinct from the dominantly practical concerns of the hierarchy. Church authority must simply find a way to keep scholars from weakening the faith of the people without stifling the virtuoso scholarship of the academics.

Church authority is inherently conservative. Its proclivity is towards what is customary; its tendency, to value what is from the past. The principle of continuity governs its outlook and leads it to avoid any break with the old ways in favor of the new. The new must always be viewed simply as another form of the old; even error is construed as an incomplete conception of the one, reliable truth. There must be, then, a sagacious way of governing which does not frustrate new development and the church's proper investment: maintaining continuity, yet neither uprooting truth along with error nor confusing what is fundamental to the church with what is merely conventional. All teaching in the church has its legitimate territory wherein it can serve well and be understood. A sensible rule for church government would, then, be for it to beware of intruding its teaching authority into regions where it will be unhelpful or even harmful. The more clearly church authorities, the organs of public understanding, are conscious of their proper role and their limited function in making public declarations, the more harmoniously and peacefully will developments unfold within the church.[3]

A healthy orthodoxy, Drey argues, should be able to differentiate what has been finally determined from what is arguable. Heterodoxy confuses the two, while hyperorthodoxy denies all freedom to argue by denying that doctrine can change, and then peddling its own opinion as dogma.

In the area of liturgy his views are always interesting. Reviewing a new book of rituals, he observes that all of the rites, including the sacraments, have been translated by the editor into German. The central portions of the sacraments are permitted only in Latin, but Drey supposes that pastoral need and custom will cause the clergy to wink at this rule and use German throughout. (At this time Liebermann in Mainz, by contrast, was explaining how wise the Church had been to withhold the communion cup from the laity.) He notices with displeasure, however, that the texts with which the clergy are supposed to explain the ceremonies are in stiff and formal language, riddled with rationalist philosophical jargon. Ritual is ritual, he says, not abstract reflection. Texts in worship should be warm, simple, and pastorally direct.

Preaching too had fallen on bad times. Christians expected to hear the faith from their pulpit.

But instead of that, what must we listen to from the pulpits these days? A shallow morality provided by trendy philosophy, a hodge-podge of naive yet crafty wisdom, trite commonplaces and a high but empty-sounding vocabulary, which may provide the preacher, his listeners, and his critics with large satisfaction, but afford the people little advantage save that they have been preached out of the church.[4]

One innovation he frowned upon was the practice of general confession being introduced by some priests round the country. These clergymen were failing to distinguish between an acknowledgement of sinfulness and the admission of specific sins. The practice of the ancient Church which they fancied themselves to be reviving had not, in fact, been general public confession, but public penance for specific crimes that were already publicly known. Private, or auricular confession emerged later than public penance, in the historical order of things. For centuries, he observed, the monks had had to replace the uninterested secular clergy as confessors to the people, just as the Dominicans stepped into their place as preachers in the twelfth century and the Jesuits as teachers in the sixteenth. Now, just at the time when the people were looking for confessors who would be more familiar with them and their problems in the world, the parish clergy were about to shrug off this important work.

Drey on Church–state relations

The relations between Church and state were a constant interest of his, and his general preference was for the two great institutions to go their own separate ways. Possibly the memory of Napoleon had been a bitter instruction, but even so Drey takes a more liberal stand in this matter than do many of his contemporaries. Church and state should be independent of one another, he says. The state should neither prefer nor persecute any Church, and the Church for its part should not call on the state to fight ecclesiastical battles. The record shows that it often has been otherwise. Churchmen tempted by power and statesmen drawn by church wealth have been tempted to reach into one another's affairs, and it has been this urge for self-aggrandizement that has inevitably brought the two authorities into contest.

At history's beginnings, explains Drey, religion and civil society were in harmony because civil laws were religiously sanctioned. All ancient religions were national religions. The Hebrew people began also with a religious state, though with the eventual weakening of the priestly caste they emerged with a state religion. Christianity was novel in being the first religion independent of a land, a country, or an ethnic people. It first provoked a clash with the Roman state by recruiting people into an elective Church, in defiance of a religion that automatically included all nationals. After an initial experience of persecution Christianity itself became a state church, at first dominated by the state, and later dominating it. After the Church split into factions, some of these enjoyed state recognition and protection while others were merely tolerated. Which, asks Drey, of all these many relationships, is the desirable one? In the United States of America, he points out, there is a new yet beguiling arrangement. For the state, the Church simply does not exist. Though strange to those used to European ways, so accustomed to patronage and control and exploitation of the Church by the state, the American way deserves attention as a formula for giving each institution its rightful autonomy. The first amendment to the American Constitution provides that 'Congress shall make no Law respecting the Establishment of Religion, or prohibiting the free exercise thereof.' Since 1789 millions of immigrants from the most diverse confessional origins have crowded into America, he writes, and new sects have also arisen there, with strident religious controversy, yet the Congress still stands by this amendment. The welfare, population, and power of the United States are, despite the sometimes fanatical excesses of some religionists, increasingly vigorous. All this, he concludes, is the accomplishment of freedom.

A renewal of theology

One of Drey's repeated themes was the expression of a dislike for the scholastic theology which had flourished in the Middle Ages and was preserved – indeed, had been quite fashionable – in virtually all seminaries and Catholic faculties of times recently past. It must be remembered that the scholasticism he was criticizing was not the work of Aquinas and the Schoolmen, which was to enjoy a healthy revival later in the nineteenth century, but the burden of stylized and artificial textbooks of the intervening centuries. Says he:

Now that theology has been freed from the fruitless bickering and frivolous wordplay of the era dominated by Aristotelian scholasticism, we have seen a rigorous development of the historical and exegetical disciplines . . . At that earlier time when theology was first purged of scholasticism, it succeeded in purifying itself of useless, niggling speculation, ineffectual haggling and squabbling, and a barbaric vocabulary, so as to create a science that was more Christian and theologians that were more devout.[5]

No wonder that, after the Neo-Thomist movement which swept the Catholic establishment a half-century later, Drey would not loom large in remembrances of the nineteenth century or of its scholars.

The truly singular characteristic of Drey's theology is that he is *thinking*. He is a loyal and devout churchman, yet he does not enter into controversy simply to score a point for his team. Much of his writing constitutes a persistent critique of Protestantism, yet he draws heavily and effectively on Protestant scholars in his work, and is as ready to criticize Catholic misadventure. His orthodoxy is fed by a profound reverence for the tradition, while it is kept healthy by an astute eye for necessary progress. Of all divines, he is perhaps the best in his time to argue for theological reform without pique or immoderate puffery. There is a sobriety and a sense about his erudition. He turns his attention to practical matters like concordats and confession, while his abiding interest turns to more theoretical issues such as faith and tradition. The balance becomes him well.

Drey's most persistent interest

Having said all this, one must now turn to the abiding theological interest which occupied Johann Sebastian von Drey throughout his career. Christianity, he asserted, is composed of an inner essence and an outer form. Inwardly the Spirit gives life to the Church, while the Church gives outward embodiment to the Spirit's work. The belief, discipline, and worship of the Church are expressions and objectifications of her inner life and spirit. Each constituent offers something essential. The Church's claim to teach the truth derives from the Spirit, her constant guide. As the Spirit and the Son are one, so it is only in the true Church that true teaching will be preserved.

What is this differentiating quality, inner essence, or formative idea which, distinguishable from its historical embodiments, gives the Church sense, coherence, and identity? It is God's mysterious plan to reconcile all mankind to himself in a kingdom. At the invitation of Christ, reconciler and intermediary, each human is called, taught, and prepared

(a) to recognize his true relationship in the universe to God, the increasing lordship of God over him, and the emptiness of all his own selfish efforts to build, in separated isolation, a world of his own that would be independent of and opposed to God's;

(b) to submit himself freely to God's rule;

(c) and thus to release himself from endless struggle with himself and the world, as well as from the consequences of that struggle, and to draw near once more, in the spirit of a child, to God – to be received by him in fatherly love, in the midst of a general celebration of reunion.[6]

To the extent that the Church might fail to serve these purposes and might stray from its inner spirit, it needs to be hailed back into conformity with duty. The Church is, in fact, always well served by those whose mystical sense preserves the organization from being a lifeless mechanism. Mysticism fastens its attention directly on the internal vision of religion, of which it sees only the symbol, appearance, and disclosure in Church institutions. Drey reminisces that this mystical spirit was in the ascendant in the earliest centuries of the Church, and that it moved into the desert and the cloister when churchmen began to be more occupied with organization and authority and ritual. The Reformation might have been a timely revindication of this mystical spirit, for its first generation of leaders was inspired by a commitment to rediscover and redisclose the inner spirit and task of Christianity. Theirs was, however, a mysticism *manqué*, for they thought it possible to preserve the Spirit while they broke with the historically continuous outward tradition within the one Church of Jesus.

Here Drey turns to what is perhaps the central theological concern he had, and surely the most significant contribution he would make to future discussion. His first extensive research had led him to the discovery that the sacrament of penance, involving the private confession of sins to a priest, had evidently not existed in the first centuries of the Church. It was a later outgrowth of the old discipline of ecclesiastical penance, administered publicly by the bishops to those who confessed certain crimes of a public nature. Rather than repudiating the subsequent practice as inauthentic and novel, he reflected that not all valuable practices and beliefs in the Church need have been there in full form at the beginning. The same Spirit which was in Jesus to found the Church remained in the Church to lead it through appropriate development. The test of later variations was not whether they had been there at the start, but whether they were faithful to and congruent with the developing tradition. Already in the New Testament, he noticed, there can really be no telling difference drawn between the texts which represent Christ's teaching (the Gospels) and those which present the teaching of the apostles (the Epistles), since we have in any case the former on the word of the latter. God's word uttered to mankind is not limited to the sayings of Jesus, nor indeed to the short years when he walked the earth, nor even to that obviously formative period when the apostles worked in his absence. The fact is that the Lord is never absent as long as the Spirit which lived in him lives in the community that believes in him. Authentic faith is preserved, not simply by referring back to those privileged beginnings, but by reflecting on them in the present. The Church, then, lives on both memory and consciousness. Her memory is in her written tradition; the consciousness is her living tradition.

Speech and writing, the two strategies of tradition, complement one another. Oral communication is simplest, lies at the base of all social life and intercourse, and is the medium to which we resort when others fail. It is most vividly able to convey conviction and to persuade. It can better avoid misunderstanding and confusion. Yet it enjoys these advantages only when one is speaking from one's own experience. When the word must be passed on orally through a series of persons over a long time, it is easily distorted and loses its original force and focus. Writing can capture more firmly and objectively the message of tradition, preserve it if temporarily forgotten, and spread it more swiftly and more widely. Yet it can obsolesce too, and because it is clothed in the forms of the past it can give rise to misunderstanding in the present. The farther back written tradition takes us, the fewer persons are adequately familiarized with the terms and assumptions of long ago and far away.

The development of revelation in a living tradition

Drey's point is not simply that the Church has access to a tradition which is in some respects fuller and better preserved than what written documents bring us from the founding days. That had been an assertion of the early Gnostic sects, and the Gnostics were much studied and much repudiated in Tübingen. It had, so Drey thought, been an old arrow in the quiver of the Counter-Reformation: that the Bible was incomplete, and needed to be put together with supplemental teaching preserved through the same period of time by oral transmission. Drey is arguing that if we believe in the abiding presence of the Spirit, then new revelation is truly telescoping out of the old as the Church develops. Our understanding of God is that he is unlimited and ceaselessly active. Congruent with such a God is a revelation that is not briefly displayed in a single place and time, but unfolds endlessly, through successive stages in developmental sequence, with the same Spirit providing a living continuity.

Plato and Aristotle had more disciples – and apparently cleverer ones – when they departed from this life and world, than would Christ have had under the same conditions. But their wisdom and their school ceased to exist, for neither the power of their spirits nor that of their disciples survived, and they were unable to bequeath or hand them on to others. Christ's new creation would have met with this same fate if his Spirit had not remained at his task and if the divine power that had visibly emerged through him had not invisibly continued in the same fashion after his disappearance, and thus provided his work with endurance and increase.[7]

The purpose of Christ's revelation is to unite, or to reunite, all mankind within God's kingdom. Just as God's powerful grace was needed to allow Christ's ministry to touch his hearers' hearts and convert them, so the same powerful grace is needed to enliven every other believer. The outward rallying of all believers into one kingdom/Church requires the same unending expenditure of divine power. The same force which set in motion the long process of faith still draws it forward to completion. The Christian revelation is not handed on: it hands itself on. In fact, it will authenticate itself more truly by its development than by its beginning; more by the miracles of its increase and preservation than by the more limited miracles of its founding. It is a most important task for the theologians, says Drey, to produce criteria and evidence for the soundness of relationship and congruence between the beginnings of revelation and its progress.

Scripture, then, is neither the only, nor the first, nor even the most effective conveyance of the original Christian revelation. If that revelation is to be handed on and preserved in the world, then it must be done through the most pervasive medium possible. How does the inspiration of the sacred authors serve future ages? Just as we believe that in scripture we still have a word of God, so it follows that what we call its inspiration must be something continuing still, not simply in the writings of Christianity but in its entire enterprise.[8]

In defence of his outlook Drey opposes what he takes to be the classical Protestant view: that God's revealing activity was a transitory, momentary power which was quickly spent and is not available to us through other human intermediaries. No, he insists. It is a permanent, continuing activity and is accessible to us, not only at the time of origin, but in ages to follow, in a living tradition.

Unfortunately, both philosophy and theology were dominated by a Catholic faith so unintellectual in its manner during the High Middle Ages that an inward, irresponsible mysticism suppressed the objectivity proper to philosophy. All of human nature became an allegory for the divine, rather than being studied in its own right. When Aristotle's philosophy was brought to Europe by the Arabs, philosophy released itself from this bondage and, in the Renaissance, turned quite profane and hostile towards degenerate scholasticism. The new thought rejected all authority (wrongly, since no individual by himself can master more than a small sector of knowledge), and in reply the scholastics thoughtlessly ascribed to a single human person the authority which rightly belongs to an entire community. The reformers, seeking some objective mainstay for their system of thought that was essentially subjective (for Drey, any doctrine not living within the true Church is subjective), found it in the books of Scripture, which for them now became the sole authoritative source for faith. Instead of drawing on the

organism of the believing Church, theology turned to the fragmentary
writings of dead men written in languages that are now dead and even then
were not native to them. They were episodic statements, not utterances of
large perspective. And they were being interpreted 1,500 years later in an
alien culture. The living Spirit of the Church, on the Protestant view, now
had no living body, but only a dead letter. How could one bring that letter to
life?

All those strong, miraculous powers which had once animated it and procured for it victory
over the world, when God's Spirit had first uttered it through the mouths of simple men – all
these powers were now dormant, for human wisdom had it in mind to outstrip them. Now that
help was no longer received from above, man had to fend for himself. Knowledge of the ancient
languages, the art of exegesis, research into and interpretation of ancient and foreign customs
and expressions, venturesome hypotheses, the careful adaptation of modern ways of thinking
to ancient models, the collection of manuscripts, fragments, and variant readings – in a word,
the entire *apparatus eruditionis* – as disjointed and incoherent as anything in the world: all of
this now became the *sine qua non* of authentic theology. Out of these ashes the rejuvenated
Phoenix was supposed to arise. Anyone who could master a single one of these tools, even a
grammarian, could now get the upper hand on the most speculative of theologians.[9]

The reformers, sincerely intent upon restoring their mystical vision of
Jesus and his call, made the mistake of departing from the community where
that vision, although often blurred and confused, is alone restorable. And by
attributing sole authority to the Bible, they ensured that the living tradition
of the Church would no longer be enabled to correct and enliven their
attempts to construe that Bible. Freed from such lifegiving subordination,
they and their successors would stray from the truth they had so sincerely
sought. Their hearts, says von Drey, were better than their advice.

Lest he be seen as merely complaining about his Protestant neighbours, he
should also be heard out on what his coreligionists had done by way of
response to the Reformation. That mystical spirit which had offered initial
hope to the reforms withered among the Catholics. Pascal and Fénelon
sought after it but they were suppressed. The dominant party, like the
Protestants, chose to rely upon a dead letter, only to the Bible they added the
writings of the Fathers and councils and popes. They too were victimized by
the spirit of the age. They engaged in artless, mindless arguments that relied
upon exegesis, with no sense of living in an organic continuation of that
which was being studied. They were not even aware that it was their
continued work within the Church which preserved their faith from their
exegesis.

It is curious that Sebastian von Drey managed to be so able in his use of
others' work, yet was so little considered by the theological schools of the
time as an ally. His familiarity with and indebtedness to many scholars, both

Catholic and Protestant, was prodigious: Kant, Fichte, and Schelling; Schlegel, Lessing, and Novalis; Baader, Müller, Jacobi, and Sailer. With all of these he held much in common. Yet he was so very much his own man. His free-spirited ideas on liturgical reform, authority in the Church, and the degeneracy of scholastic theology ensured him against popularity in Rome and caused some critics in this century to blame him for the start of Modernism. Yet he was accused of ultramontane sympathies towards Rome by the younger liberals of his day. He was a trenchant critic of contemporary Protestant theology, but a discriminating one, never carping.

The most beguiling paradox of this shepherd's son become theological leader is his attitude towards scholarship. What he most regularly berated his own Catholic colleagues and bishops for was their lack of historical erudition, their naive inability to know the background of rules, rites, and beliefs so as to judge better wherein they might well be changed without forfeiture of substance. The faith, he scolded, was ill-served except by patient, scientific study. Yet at the very same time he avowed that what kept all this erudition from going rotten was a simple, submissive subordination to the Church.

For Drey, no amount of dedication to Christian ideals could save a man if he be unwilling to join in with the realistic comradeship and realistic faults of the Christian flock. The Church, after all, must be the basis, source, and context of all theology: for Drey, it is to the theologians what the state is to the political scientist and the animal organism to the medical scientist. It presents itself to the scholar, not as the theoretical ideal of what Christ knew, but as the sometimes disappointing and sinful embodiment of what he saved. What made Johann Sebastian von Drey so effective a mentor and *paterfamilias* to his colleagues at Tübingen and to his students who carried their loyalty to him throughout Germany was his dedication to fearless scholarship and fearless public expression, combined with devout concern for the Church and a constant commitment to the training of good churchmen.

Johann Adam Möhler

In 1815, when Drey was teaching at the seminary in Ellwangen, a 19-year-old arrived to pursue his studies: Johann Adam Möhler. Master and pupil spent two years together there, and one more at Tübingen when the entire programme was transferred there. Möhler, who had been raised as the son of a relatively prosperous innkeeper in the village of Igersheim, seems from the start to have looked down his nose at the then rather unambitious academic standards of the country seminary, and to have relished the move to the university more for its intellectual opportunities than for the faster city life his fellow-students hankered after. He did not suffer his fellow-students gladly, especially the less serious among them. But Drey and he got on well. After ordination, and then only a single year in a parish assignment, he was back at the university preparing to be a teacher of classics. In 1822, when it came time to find him an appointment, there was a vacancy instead in church history. Drey and his colleagues, desirous of having young Möhler in their faculty, arranged for him to be chosen. As a gesture towards professional preparation he was given his *congé* throughout the next year so as to be able to tour selected universities and observe at first hand some of the major historically grounded theologians working at their craft. The better devotees of Clio in Germany at that time were Protestant, and Möhler was most impressed and influenced by those he listened to in Berlin: Schleiermacher, Neander, and Marheinecke. Like them he would ground his work in historical study but then proceed to reflect the past in a systematic, theological way. In 1823 he arrived back in Tübingen ready to begin his teaching career.

It was an extraordinary career. For one thing, it was brief. Möhler really had only twelve productive years as a scholar, from 1823 until 1835. Two years after he began to teach church history, canon law, and patristics and to handle most of the book reviews in these fields for the *Quartalschrift*, he published his first book, the *Einheit: The Unity of the Church, or the Principle of Catholicism, Expounded in the Spirit of the Fathers of the Church of the First Three Centuries*. Two years later he produced another on Athanasius and the Arians, and in 1832 he brought out what would be his best-known work, the *Symbolik: Creed-Study, or an Explanation of the Doctrinal Differences between Catholics and Protestants Displayed in their Official Professions of Faith*. This initiated a peppery controversy with Ferdinand Christian Baur, leading scholar and personality in the Protestant faculty of theology. Baur was only four years older than Möhler, but much his theological senior and, after all, a Protestant in a Protestant university, city, and principality. The next year Baur published a critique of the *Symbolik*, which had its reply in book form from Möhler in 1834. By 1835 Tübingen had become an unwelcoming place for Möhler, and he accepted a chair in Munich, at the centre of Catholic Bavaria. But his health there frustrated both teaching and research, and in 1838, at the age of 42, he was dead. His *Symbolik* was just about to emerge in its fifth edition in seven years, somewhat symbolic of the author who had put forth such an energetic burst of theology in so short a career.

Far more than his faculty comrades, Möhler embroiled himself in controversy. Like Drey he was denied preferment by churchmen who doubted his orthodoxy. A professorship for him at Bonn was vetoed by Count von Spiegel, archbishop of Cologne, who was persuaded that the *Einheit* was perverse and wanted Möhler to repudiate what he had written. It was not in Möhler to recant. His relations with the state were not without strain. In Stuttgart, where the government was not yet that adept at forging civil unity between Protestants and Catholics, he was told he was a disturber of the peace. As a student he had known difficulties with his peers (one roommate had to be moved to other quarters), and at the very threshold of his entry into the teaching guild he publicly rebuked a senior faculty member at Tübingen for what he considered anti-Catholic bias. After he had rebutted Baur's criticisms he admitted to a friend that he had taken a nasty tone of which he was not proud: polemics had, he confessed, brought out a dark side in his character. Yet Möhler's quarrels were rarely just a matter of personal pique. Generally there was a point of truth he saw being dishonoured.

He was, it seemed, alike at his best and his worst in polemics. They energized him. Controversy brought him most eagerly to his work. But argument also had a way of luring him too quickly into brilliant assertions that were difficult to integrate into the panorama of his theology, and of compelling him to yield the agenda, not to what was interesting or enlightening, but simply to what was under dispute. For example, he introduced his study of the Reformation by first determining which expressions of faith should be used to display the range of faith of the two parties, Catholic and Protestant. He set aside all of the more ancient creeds and council statements as having no bearing on the matter, since they had been accepted by both sides. He even eliminated contemporary documents of the Reformation if they were not written *against* the other side. At the end he selected only the statements that were clearly polemical in tone and substance. His study, then, could not encompass the full spread of belief in the two camps, but forced itself to define each one exclusively in terms of opposition to the other. Good debate; poor diagnosis.

Möhler on Church and state

Some of these characteristics of Möhler might be seen in his views on a subject that he approached often, and from different directions: Church–state relations. He wrote, as did Drey, at a time when the depredations of Napoleon were fresh remembered, and when one was not yet assured how the churches would fare now that the old confessional states, into which the German lands had been divided since the sixteenth century, were regrouped into secular states with mostly mixed populations. It was a time when church leaders, both Protestant and Catholic, were anxious about a new kind of vulnerability to civil rulers.

Möhler, somewhat askew of the thinking of his fellow-churchmen, saw merit in dissolving the old church–state bonds. In an 1830 essay on Islam, he noted that it was a religion founded for the practice of a single people, and that it had always been sustained and spread by the agency of a civil power. This sanctioning of the state by the authority of religion catches the political enterprise within a double jeopardy, Möhler argued. In one phase, the whole of the state's constitution, and even its individual enactments, are characterized as sacred. Hence they are unassailable. In another phase, when politicians move to carry out any radical reforms, they risk the loss of their religious legitimacy. Religion may seem to offer stability to the state, but more often it exercises a stifling, conservative influence. As for religion itself, it is most often discredited by this task of blessing the state, both when it absolutizes institutions that need frequent change and adaptation, and when it stands in the way of that change. 'A religion that has the misfortune to be identified with the State, is on this very account brought into trouble by [it].'[10] While Möhler is directing his remarks to the distant world of the caliphs, there is here surely some oblique reference to that more familiar world of the cardinals. Since much of the savagery so recently visited upon the churches had been wrought in the name of reform, these words of Möhler must have been hard sayings.

Four years earlier he had offered comment closer to home which had aroused fits in his coreligionists. The Netherlands had lately been reconstituted, with the Protestant Dutch and Catholic Belgians now subject to a Protestant king. The government had just decreed that a college of philosophy would be established in Louvain, staffed by state-appointed professors; that all candidates for the Catholic priesthood would have to complete the course of studies there; and that no one could be admitted to the college (and hence to ordination) who had taken his preliminary studies in the liberal arts in a foreign country. The Belgians, especially the Walloons, were irate at the obvious intent to exclude French influence from their education, culture and church. The Catholics, all the way to Rome, were inflamed because a hostile state was moving to assume control over the selection and training of their clergy. Möhler came out in favour of King Willem. What the clergy of the Netherlands needed was rigorous education, particularly in philosophy. They were hardly going to get it from France where, in Möhler's estimation, nothing but empiricists had been seen since the time of Descartes. It little mattered that the state, for motives of its own that were suspect, and in a high-handed manner that was galling to churchmen, was forcing young clerics to undergo a training not of their choice. What mattered most was that a first-class education was being made available at state expense, and it behoved the church to take it.

He then accused Rome of having made matters worse by intervening. Local bishops, he argued, are quite able to see to these matters, much as the bishops around Alexandria had, without papal intrusion, founded there a famous academy for the clergy.

People in Rome are totally uninstructed about the needs of our churches. They evaluate everything by the situation in Italy. And that is held in the sleep of death. There is no visible literary activity, and apparently no religious interest . . . From Rome, nevertheless, come attitudes, judgments, and decrees which seem to emanate from another world, and an ancient one at that.[11]

Rome, complains Möhler, is not ready to rely upon the Church's proper tactics to promote the truth. Instead of publishing what is true, it tries to lobby for civil laws and penalties. The leaders of the ancient Church, he observes, strove to remove error from men's hearts and minds; these people want to keep it out of the newspapers. What had the Church to fear from the world of ideas and knowledge? It should enter that field with enthusiasm rather than naysaying.

The laws on publishing and censorship stifle every stirring of the spirit, the good along with the bad. By this unnatural restraint, all life is stultified and stagnated. The occasional movement that stirs the surface of this enterprise is often only a sign of the decomposition underneath. In France, Germany, and the Netherlands wrong has the freedom of the streets along with right; only the inner strength of the latter, and the nerve and the versatility of its partisans, will allow it to emerge as victor in the struggle.[12]

So much for the Roman curia. Two years later, however, in 1828, he had quite other things to say. A number of scholars at the University of Freiburg in nearby Baden had petitioned for the abolition of required celibacy for priests. In his observations on this, after an elaborate historical treatise on the development of clerical celibacy, he noted that a celibate clergy gives the Church a certain independence from the state. Some were arguing for a change because, by making the Church more subservient to the state, it would oblige the pope to yield some of his influence over it.

The pope, then, should recede ever farther into the background than he is? Possibly because we Catholics are now pretty powerful? Because he has just acquired for us some helpful concordats? Try and let the bishops enter into negotiations with the government, say, to secure funding for a cathedral chapter or a seminary, and see what comes of it! Bishops are dealt with as subjects, while the pope is considered a recognized power, independent of every state. In him we ourselves are still free . . . The pope is the hub and nub of the church;

whoever weakens him destroys it . . . The common spirit of the church is first incorporated in him, and finds in him its expression, its veracity, and its security.[13]

In between this Guelph Möhler and that Ghibelline Möhler was the historian, who during these same years was putting another interpretation on an activist papacy. It was, he argued, during the rambunctious years when the faith was spreading through Europe that development of belief had to be suspended. There were countries to be civilized first, and coarse ways had to yield to cultured ones. People had to submit to the Church with a resolute and uninquisitive belief in its authority, and to be held in unity by a firmer, sterner central power than would otherwise be needed. Yet this centralization of power in the papacy, though timely and necessary, opened the way to abuses which were constant. The normal and healthy desire for freedom, Möhler hopes, which misfired in the Reformation, still strives to finds its satisfaction, and an internal cohesion of faith will eventually bind the community more truly together than has the disciplinary jurisdiction of Rome.

Möhler knows what clout is, and he is happy to see it used in defence of the rights and freedom of religion. But he is loath to see it used by obscurantist churchmen to stifle the mind's search. Some years later, when he was near death, the determination of the Prussian government to subdue the Catholics led them to imprison the uncompliant archbishop of Cologne, Clemens August Cardinal von Droste-Vischering. Möhler hailed the stubborn cardinal for defying the state. Yet one sees here, not just a theologian who knows how to wield a complex principle in differing situations, but a controversialist who is better at replying to weak arguments than he is at elaborating a consistent position that can be stated fully at any one time and survive the different uses to which it must be put. Unfortunately some of Möhler's most engaging writing is in the form of critique, rather than constructive presentation. But that may also be why people still read him.

Möhler and the true Church

Möhler shared with his mentor Drey an abiding preoccupation with the Church as a central theological issue. His views on the matter, like Drey's, grew forth from historical inquiry; in fact, he displays an erudition which goes well beyond that of the older man. Unlike Drey, however, he shaped his statements to conflict. How, asked Möhler, did the rightful Church differ from other Christian undertakings?

The spirit of Christ lives in all believers. Since by nature it is a spirit of love as well as of truth, it gives off love as a native characteristic and so it binds all believers into concord. The spirit creates community. Möhler speaks repeatedly of this spirit in an ambiguous way. Since in German every noun is capitalized, there is no clear way to distinguish between the personal *Geist*, or 'Spirit' of God who dwells in human and the characteristic *Geist*, or 'spirit' of the Christian community, somewhat like the 'spirit' of the German people. Möhler does not desire to make this distinction, and he purposely draws his bow across both strings. The spirit of Christ dwells in the Church corporately as well as in believers singly. If anything, it resides primarily in the community, not the individual. It is from the loving life of the Church that the Christian must appropriate for himself what he needs, drawing on its corporate experience to provide himself with his own values and convictions.

The intellectual features of this Christian life are especially derivative of the Church. There is a living tradition, an unbroken community consciousness which the spirit breathes into the group, and in which the individual finds his own understanding of the mystery. Christianity, as Möhler presents it, does not consist in formulae or teachings or creeds. It is an interior life, a holy power, and all dogmas are valuable only insofar as they give expression to this inner consciousness which was there in the Church long before dogmas were put into words. As I have summarized Möhler elsewhere on this same point:

Christianity was never a religion propagated by writing. A book-religion is a fundamentally individualistic, private affair: each man reads by himself and draws his own conclusions. Christ and the Church have always approached men through preaching, a communal activity. The message was never given and received as something immediately understood, but rather as something to be pondered and fathomed gradually. This was never, even in apostolic times, the task of the individual; it was the community concern of the entire Church. It is this community, spread horizontally across the world and vertically across the ages, that is possessed of the Spirit, and is protected – the individual is not – from distorting or losing any part of Christ's teaching.[14]

Möhler's theology of an indwelling 'spirit' is matched by his theology of the Church as a continuation of God's enfleshment in Jesus. Since God's word took on human flesh, in a visible, historical, human individual, and spoke as man to man, and suffered in order to win men, it is not incongruent that God's mysterious and saving activity should continue in this same manner.

The Deity having manifested its action in Christ according to an *ordinary human fashion*, the form also in which His work was to be continued, was thereby traced out. The preaching of his doctrine needed now a *visible, human* medium, and must be entrusted to visible envoys, teaching and instructing after the wonted method; men must speak to men, and hold intercourse with them, in order to convey to them the word of God. And as in the world nothing can attain to greatness but in society; so Christ established a community; and his divine word, his living will, and the love emanating from him exerted an internal, binding power upon his followers; so that an inclination implanted by him in the hearts of believers, corresponded to his outward institution.[15]

There is, he argues, within the Church as within Christ, a divine and a human element, although in the Church there is sin and unworthiness. Christ's teaching is embodied in his community of believers, somewhat as the Word was in Jesus, and simply by remaining within this flesh-and-blood community, the believer can be provided with a sure yet unfolding sense of what the true tradition is, a common 'inclination' to God's mind.

It is otherwise with heretics. As Möhler sees it, they typically tend to argue that although the faith was well kept during some classic period at the beginning, it has gone awry since then and the individual seeker needs to look at the mass of evidence and sort things out personally. The Church of the present time is not quite to be trusted. Instead, appeal is made to some special tradition, whether a secret revelation handed down among a select cadre of initiates, or a written tradition which rests on the authority of the very first believers. Möhler has in mind the dissenters of the first three centuries and the Protestants of the sixteenth century, who seemed to him to share the same principles. The earliest heretics did not appeal to Scripture against the Church in quite the same way as had the reformers. Either they wrote their own additional books, or they rejected some of the Gospels, or they manhandled the text of certain passages, or they construed the texts in ways that did violence to grammar, context, or editorial purpose. The defenders of the faith did meet their critics on these fine matters of text and interpretation; indeed, that is how the lore of biblical interpretation began to be assembled. But they never imagined that the integrity of Christian teaching depended on their scholarship, nor that it could be menaced by the elaboration of outsiders. The faith came primarily from the community and its common mind. The Gospels do not legitimate the Church; they are accepted by the Church because they harmonize with what it believes, as they harmonized from the first with the faith of the earliest Christians.

Möhler agrees with the judgment of the ancient church that heresy was evil, that it was bred of an egoism and a virtuoso sort of stubbornness that disliked submitting one's mind to the rather mixed band of folk who inhabit the real Church, in favour of some ideal gathering recruited according to a prior set of principles. He explains that he is speaking here of the spirit of heresy. There are surely some folk who derive their basic dispositions of faith from the Church but have not managed to bring their minds into full harmony with what is commonly received. This is not full-blown heresy. In fact, he avers, heresy, like orthodoxy, is never quite so homogeneous in the real as it is in the ideal. It is (unlike the Church), ironically, an institution whose reality is better precisely to the extent that it does not measure up to its ideals. Heterodoxy is not simply a matter of holding deviant notions about some matter of faith. Against that standard no one would survive close scrutiny. No, it is the wilful, isolationist dissent that stems from departure more than from disagreement.

Unity yet individuality in the Church

After the long contrapuntal fugue on unity and concord, Möhler fills out his statement by maintaining that the Church, assured of a close cohesion among its members, indulges them in extensive individuality. As long as they are loyal to the spirit, there is no possibility of independent style leading Christianity into chaos.

The theologian does not come to his task prepared to scrutinize the Church with a philosophy or with other criteria which he has learned elsewhere. It is after all by being given faith that his intellectual powers have been roused to full strength. Thus the theologian brings philosophy and other normative disciplines into dialectic with faith, that they might themselves be subjected to a corrective. This leads, he admits, to something of a circle. Christians see in Christ the unique fulfiller of human reason; and yet it is within the precincts of faith that they develop their criteria for what is reliable and what ersatz. There is no appeal to independent reason to affirm Christianity; *au contraire*, it is Christianity that sits in judgment on the accomplishments of reason.

The Church has the task of refining its belief but, to tell the truth, it addresses this duty hesitantly. During the second to the sixth centuries, for instance, when controversy about the status of Jesus was unremitting, the Church always preferred to state exactly what was *not* true, postponing as long as possible the onus of making a positive affirmation that could at last be written into one of the creeds. This is probably due to the influence of the mystically minded in the Church, who have little readiness to define these deeper matters, yet are instinctively drawn to those components of the mystery that are most positively crucial. They dampen the enthusiasm of the speculative or dialectical types, who are always restless to analyse and expound.

The area of moral behaviour is one wherein Möhler tries to display the characteristically different approaches of the Church and its competitors. Many early heretics rejected all need for moral preaching, since they were sure that their religious rebirth guaranteed their virtue. This usually was the prelude to some remarkably dissolute living. Others, however, imposed on themselves and their followers a fearful discipline. The Church, in those days when there were many areas left up to individual judgment that later came under common judgment, proposed to its members abstinence from marriage, or from sex, or from second marriage after widowhood, or from plentiful food and drink. These were never imposed, but they were gestures against a world given over to sensuality. To right and to left, however, these human values were either spoilt by over-indulgence or forbidden by rule. In the Church there grew up a commonly received discipline of repentance for sin. In the sects, either there was no possible reconciliation after sin or whole classes of people were consigned to penitential status as an everyday thing.

Protestantism parted ways with the Church most distinctively in this matter of moral behaviour. Möhler claimed that Luther, followed closely by Zwingli and Calvin, had insisted morality did not pertain to religion. It was a matter of law, and Christ had freed believers from the law. At best the state should be heeded in its moral requirements. The Catholic line was that faith and works were bound to each other, in an organic unity.

It is undeniable, and no arts can long conceal the fact, that Christ proposed, in the most emphatic manner, to his followers, the highest ethical ideal, corresponding to the new theoretical religious knowledge, and further developing the Old Testament precepts. It is likewise equally certain, that in his name are announced to all, who believe in him, grace and forgiveness of sins; that is to say, pardon for every moral transgression. These are two phenomena, which, as they stand in direct opposition one to the other, require, in consequence, some third principle which may mediate their union. The third conciliating principle, as it is to unite the two, must be akin alike to law and to grace, to the rigid exaction and to the merciful remission. This is the sanctifying power which emanates from the living union with Christ; the *gratuitous grace* of holy love, which, in justification, he pours out upon his followers. In this grace all law is abolished, because no outward claim is enforced; and, at the same time, the law is confirmed, because love is the fulfilment of the law; in love, law and grace are become one.[16]

The worm in the wood, as Möhler read his Luther, was not a variant theological explanation of sin or freedom or grace or rescue by the Lord. It was plainly that Luther, at a certain point, no longer chose to undergo the discipline of accounting for his view of things to the old community. There was a break, first of the spirit, then of the mind.

The Church, in Möhler's perspective, is a motley group of unworthy believers that is somehow haunted by a commonly shared sense of belief. That group is little likely at any given moment to be ready or even able to give a nicely articulated statement of its faith on any point that you may wish to pursue much beyond the point where discussion last left off. But the vision remains a possession of the group, and the group uncannily manages to preserve and treasure it. There are grounds for impatience and controversy and rebuke to the face of the most highly placed. But leave the group, and the life is somehow withered and the theology goes stale.

In the hands of slothful believers this is a line of discourse that convinces few and excuses much. In the hands of Möhler, surely one of the most recondite young theological savants of his era, it was a tenacious way of saying that the intellectual task in theology is not quite the same as that of the other disciplines.

The vision of Church drawn by Drey and Möhler was distinctive. To begin with, they both draw it from Scripture and from the early Church Fathers, with very little sense of obligation to the more juridical and polemical views that had been dominant since Bellarmine and the Counter-Reformation. Despite Möhler's investigation of the polemical literature, he owed his basic theology to older, more normative sources. Their joint discovery in these sources was that the Church's authenticity comes from the mystical presence within the community of the Spirit of God, bringing Christ continuously into human embodiment. They also taught that no churchman or intellectual could appeal to a private hold on the Spirit to defy and abandon the institutional Church, for that Church is where the Spirit dwells. It is a sinful group, and sometimes confused, and never quite worthy. It will always be so.

Actually, though the two theologians appeared to be framing a controversial Catholic argument, they were formulating a position that was ecumenical and balanced, the beginning of a fresh understanding that would eventuate in *Lumen Gentium*, the dogmatic constitution of Vatican II on the Church. After a long lapse of interest in Drey and Möhler, the latter especially caught the eye of a cadre of French patristic scholars, notably Henri de Lubac, a Jesuit, and Yves Congar, a Dominican, whose writings were most instrumental in giving highest acceptance to the view of a church incarnate, with equal emphasis on both mystical spirit and institutional loyalty. Drawing also on another work that had seemed polemical but was in fact ecumenical – John Henry Newman's 1845 *Essay on the Development of Christian Doctrine* – theologians of the *aggiornamento* re-stated Drey's early teaching that Christian belief must develop, unfold, renew, innovate: its surety and vouching being not a verbal repetition of what had been stated at the beginning, but the presence of one same Spirit that speaks one message differently through different mouths.

There are other Tübingen divines about whom this essay has too little scope to offer extended comment. Kuhn and Staudenmaier carried on the work of Drey and Möhler, and in our own day this little university town in Württemberg is, on both Catholic and Protestant sides, theologically energetic. The writings of the men who created the 'school' in those early days are much read today in Germany, but unfortunately have not yet reached their full span of influence in other language zones, particularly that of English, for want of adequate translations. Probably no comparably influential group of theologians is so little accessible to those who know not the *Umlaut*.

There is no characteristic 'teaching' left behind by these men. Some have thought there was, but in any case it would be no necessary compliment to say it was so. What they bequeathed to those who follow was a reverence for two things: for the Church, and for the hard and sober scholarship her service deserves. They were loyal to the Church. Despite the fact that they were willing and devastatingly able to criticize their fellow churchmen, there seems to have been no mental detachment from its welfare such as to allow them to appreciate in all instances the criticisms outsiders were making. What is so admirable about them is that the Church they attacked was the Church everyone knew, the band of Germans and Scots and Indians and Syrians with rank faults and muddled thinking. The Church they defended was not quite so realistic; it was the Church *de jure* which has, partly from their nagging, become at least somewhat more *de facto* since Johann Sebastian von Drey packed his books in Ellwangen. He set out with the belief that Hirscher and Herbst and Möhler and Kuhn and Hefele and the rest came to share: that neither faith nor theology had anything but advancement to expect from honest learning, and that there was too little of these in the university and Church of their time.

Notes

1 Staudenmaier, though a Tübingen pupil, taught elsewhere. His intellectual resonance with the faculty in Tübingen has often led to recognition as an effective colleague, albeit from a distance.
2 *Kurze Einleitung in das Studium der Theologie* (Tübingen, 1819), p. 220.
3 *Ibid.*, pp. 231–2.
4 'Ueber öffentliche oder liturgische Beichten', *Theologische Quartalschrift*, 17 (1835), 513.
5 Quoted in Joseph Rupert Geiselmann (ed.), *Geist des Christentums und des Katholizismus* (Mainz, 1940), p. 89.
6 *Kurze Einleitung*, p. 17.
7 *Die Apologetik als wissenschaftliche Nachweisung der Göttlichkeit des Christenthums*, vol. 1 (Mainz, 1838), p. 401.
8 *Kurze Einleitung*, pp. 156–7.
9 In Geiselmann, *Geist*, p. 93.
10 *On the Relation of Islam to the Gospel*, transl. J. P. Menge (Calcutta, 1847), pp. 49–50.
11 'Ein Wort in der Sache des philosophischen Collegiums zu Löwen', *Theologische Quartalschrift*, 8 (1826), 91–2.
12 *Ibid.*, p. 91.
13 'Beleuchtung der Denkschrift für die Aufhebung des den katholischen Geistlichen vorgeschriebenen Cölibates', *Der Katholik*, 30 (1828), 293–4.
14 *Catholic Theories of Biblical Inspiration since 1810* (Cambridge, 1969), p. 19.

Drey, Möhler and the Tübingen School

15 *Symbolism, or, Exposition of the Doctrinal Differences between Catholics and Protestants as evidenced by their Symbolical Writings*, transl. James Burton Robertson (6th ed.; London, 1906), sec. 36, p. 258.
16 *Ibid.*, sec. 24, p. 183.

Bibliographical essay

Those wishing to walk first in a wide circle around the Tübingen School, to view it against the wider panorama of its time, might begin with Alexander Dru, *The Church in the Nineteenth Century: Germany 1800–1918* (London, 1963) and with Thomas F. O'Meara, *Romantic Idealism and Roman Catholicism* (Notre Dame, 1982). A dependable though early survey of religious doctrine is offered in Karl Werner, *Geschichte der apologetischen und polemischen Literatur* (Schaffhausen, 1861–7; reprint Osnabrück, 1966), and his *Geschichte der katholischen Theologie seit dem Trienter Concil bis zur Gegenwart* (Munich, 1866; reprint New York, 1966). A very helpful source – really an annotated bibliography – is Edgar Hocedez, *Histoire de la Théologie au XIXe siècle* (Brussels and Paris, 1947–52). Also to be consulted is Georges Goyau, *L'Allemagne religieuse: Le catholicisme (1800–1848)* (Paris, 1905). On German romanticism one ought to read Albert Béguin, *L'âme romantique et le rêve* (Marseille, 1937). A very attractive study of a subject paramount in Tübingen thought is by Owen Chadwick: *From Bossuet to Newman: The Idea of Doctrinal Development* (Cambridge, 1957). Another presentation of a general theological discussion with special contributions from Tübingen is by James Tunstead Burtchaell, C.S.C.: *Catholic Theories of Biblical Inspiration since 1810* (Cambridge, 1969).

Moving closer to Tübingen itself, one has available a variety of studies. Not all are sympathetic. Those would include Edmond Vermeil, *Jean-Adam Möhler et l'école catholique de Tubingue* (Paris, 1913); Léonce de Grandmaison, 'L'école catholique de Tubingue et les origines du Modernisme', *Recherches de Science Religieuse*, 9 (1919), 387ff; Hermann Joseph Brosch, *Das Uebernatürliche in der katholischen Tübinger Schule* (Essen, 1962). An early, favourable review by a descendant in the same faculty was published by Paul Schanz: 'Die katholische Tübinger Schule', *Theologische Quartalschrift*, 80 (1898), 1–49. A sesquicentennial issue of this journal which was founded by Drey and his associates gives short biographies of all professors in the Catholic theological faculty at Tübingen since its inception, as well as a brief history of the journal itself: *Theologische Quartalschrift*, 150 (1970), no. 2. Most of the criticism of the Tübingen School from Catholic writers derives from the scholasticism developed by the Roman Jesuits in the later nineteenth century. A review of these Roman misgivings about Tübingen, sympathetic to the latter, has recently been published by Gerald A. McCool, S.J.: *Catholic Theology in the Nineteenth Century: The Quest for a Unitary Method* (New York, 1977). To acquaint oneself with the Protestant counterparts at Tübingen one must refer to chapters 7 and 8 of Volume 1 of this present publication.

Rising up amid all this evaluative literature, however, stands the lifetime work of a recent Tübingen scholar who since 1930 made it his great endeavour to render his predecessors familiar to and esteemed by his contemporaries: Josef Rupert Geiselmann. So uniquely has he dominated this field of research that what Wolfgang Ruf wrote of him concerning studies on Drey could be said with reference to the entire Tübingen School. Under the heading, 'The Position of Research', Ruf writes: 'The position of research is wherever Prof. Geiselmann happens to be standing.'

Geiselmann's first service was to publish critical editions of important texts that had become virtually unavailable. First he produced *Geist des Christentums und des Katholizismus* (Mainz, 1940), a catena of articles by Sailer, Drey, Möhler and others. Due to the unfortunate political circumstances of the year when it appeared, this book is scarcely to be found in American or British libraries. Later Geiselmann published editions of Möhler's two principal

JAMES TUNSTEAD BURTCHAELL

works: *Die Einheit in der Kirche, oder das Prinzip des Katholizismus dargestellt im Geiste der Kirchenväter der drei ersten Jahrhunderte* (Cologne, 1957); and *Symbolik, order Darstellung der dogmatischen Gegensätze der Katholiken und Protestanten nach ihren öffentlichen Bekenntnisschriften* (Cologne, 1958–61).

To these editions he added five compendious monographs which analyse the work of the Tübingen divines: *Johann Adam Möhler: Die Einheit der Kirche und die Wiedervereinigung der Konfessionen* (Vienna, 1940); *Lebendiger Glaube aus geheiligter Ueberlieferung: Der Grundgedanke der Theologie Johann Adam Möhlers und der katholischen Tübinger Schule* (Mainz, 1942); *Die theologische Anthropologie Johann Adam Möhlers: Ihr geschichtlicher Wandel* (Frieburg, 1955); *Die lebendige Ueberlieferung als Norm des christlichen Glaubens: Die Apostolische Tradition in der Form der kirchlichen Verkündigung – das Formalprinzip des Katholizismus dargestellt im Geiste der Traditionslehre von Johannes Ev. Kuhn* (Freiburg, 1959); and *Die Katholische Tübinger Schule: Ihre theologische Eigenart* (Freiburg, 1964). None of these books is available in English. A full list of Geiselmann's publications up to 1960 is included in a presentation volume honouring his 70th birthday: *Kirche und Ueberlieferung*, ed. Johannes Betz and Heinrich Fries (Freiburg, 1960). Leo Scheffczyk, shortly after Geiselmann's death, published a retrospective piece on his career: 'Josef Rupert Geiselmann – Weg und Werk', *Theologische Quartalschrift*, 150 (1970), 385–95. A recent work which may challenge the position of Geiselmann as ultimate interpreter is Rudolf Reinhart's *Tübingen Theologen und ihre Theologie* (Tübingen, 1978).

A complete and annotated bibliography of Johann Sebastian von Drey's works is printed by Wolfgang Ruf in his *Johann Sebastian von Dreys System der Theologie als Begründung der Moraltheologie* (Göttingen, 1974). Major publications include his *Kurze Einleitung in das Studium der Theologie* (Tübingen, 1819; reprint Frankfurt, 1966); *Die Apologetik als wissenschaftliche Nachweisung der Göttlichkeit des Christenthums* (Mainz, 1838–47; reprint Frankfurt, 1967). Several shorter essays have been edited and reprinted by Franz Schupp in *Revision von Kirche und Theologie: Drei Aufsätze* (Darmstadt, 1971) and numerous other Drey materials are published by Geiselmann in his *Geist*. Drey's scores of articles and book reviews in the *Theologische Quartalschrift* are listed by Ruf. His copious manuscripts are much used by Geiselmann, especially in his *Die Katholische Tübinger Schule*. Unfortunately Drey has not nearly elicited the secondary literature that has been given his disciple, Möhler. See, though, Franz Schupp, *Die Evidenz der Geschichte: Theologie als Wissenschaft bei J. S. Drey* (Innsbruck, 1970), and *Reich Gottes und Gesellschaft nach Johann Sebastian Drey und Johann Baptist Hirscher*, by Josef Rief (Paderborn, 1965).

For a basic bibliography of Möhler, consult Rudolf Reinhart et al., *Verzeichnis der gedruckten Arbeiten Johann Adam Möhlers (1796–1838)* (Göttingen, 1975); and Stephen Lösch (ed.), *Johann Adam Möhler: Gesammelte Aktenstücke und Briefe* (Munich, 1928). A first posthumous publication of his works was put out by Johann Josef Ignaz Döllinger: *Gesammelte Schriften und Aufsätze* (Regensburg, 1839–40). As noted above, Möhler's two best-known works, the *Einheit* and the *Symbolik*, originally published in 1825 and 1832, have enjoyed critical editions by Geiselmann. Other Möhler books include *Athanasius der Grosse und die Kirche seiner Zeit, besonders im Kampfe mit dem Arianismus* (Mainz, 1827; reprint Frankfurt, 1972), and his reply to Baur: *Neue Untersuchungen der Lehrgegensätze zwischen Katholiken und Protestanten* (Mainz, 1834; reprint Frankfurt, 1969). In English one may find, translated by James Burton Robinson, *Symbolism, or, Exposition of the Doctrinal Differences between Catholics and Protestants as evidenced by their Symbolical Writings* (London, 1843). Also in translation are two of his articles, put out in book form: *On the Relation of Islam to the Gospel*, transl. J. P. Menge (Calcutta, 1847); and *The Life of St. Anselm, Archbishop of Canterbury*, transl. H. Rymer (London, 1842).

The best introductory book on Möhler in English is *Johann Adam Möhler: The Father of Modern Theology*, by Hervé Savon, transl. Charles McGrath (Glen Rock, N.J., 1966). On the debate with Baur read *Moehler and Baur in Controversy, 1832–38: Romantic-Idealist Assess-*

138

ment of the *Reformation and Counter-Reformation*, by Joseph Fitzer (Tallahassee, 1974). See also Henry R. Nienaltowski, *Johann Adam Möhler's Theory of Doctrinal Development* (Washington, 1959); George B. Gilmore, 'J. A. Möhler on doctrinal development', *Heythrop Journal*, 19 (1978), 383–404; G. Voss, 'Johann Adam Möhler and the development of dogma', *Theological Studies*, 4 (1943), 420–44; and Philip J. Rosato, S. J., 'Between Christocentrism and Pneumatocentrism: an interpretation of Johann Adam Möhler's ecclesiology', *Heythrop Journal*, 19 (1978), 46–70; Karl Bihlmeyer, 'J. A. Möhler als Kirchenhistoriker, seine Leistungen und seine Methode', *Theologische Quartalschrift*, 100 (1919), 134–98; M. J. Congar, 'Sur l'évolution et l'interprétation de la pensée de Möhler', *Revue des Sciences Philosophiques et Théologiques*, 27 (1938), 205–12; Paul-Werner Scheele, *Einheit und Glaube: J. A. Möhlers Lehre von der Einheit der Kirche und ihre Bedeutung für die Glaubensbegründung* (Munich, 1964); a collection of essays edited by Pierre Chaillet, *L'Eglise est une: Hommage à Möhler* (Paris, 1939), which later appeared in German as *Die Eine Kirche, zum Gedenken J. A. Möhlers: 1838–1938*, ed. Hermann Tüchle (Paderborn, 1939); and Joachim Köhler, 'War Johann Adam Möhler (1796–1838) ein Plagiator?' *Zeitschrift für Kirchengeschichte*, 86 (1975), 186–207.

Heinrich Fries and Johann Finsterholzl are general editors of a series of biographies of German theologians of this period: *Wegbereiter heutiger Theologie* (published by Styria, in Graz). See *Johann Adam Möhler*, by Paul-Werner Scheele (1969); *Johann Baptist Hirscher*, by Erwin Keller (1969); *Johannes von Kuhn*, by Heinrich Fries (1973); and *Franz Anton Staudenmaier*, by Peter Hünermann (1975).

In the early days of the *Theologische Quartalschrift* the authors, following widespread custom, were not identified. All scholars are indebted to Stephen Lösch for having disclosed which names belong to which articles: see *Die Anfänge der Tübinger Theologische Quartalschrift (1819–1831)* (Rottenburg, 1938). Also, the Minerva Verlag in Frankfurt is publishing a set of very helpful reprints of the early Tübingen books.

5

Roman Catholic Modernism

BERNARD M. G. REARDON

Identifying the Movement

The term 'Catholic Modernism' is referred to a movement within the Roman Catholic Church at the turn of the present century the aim of which was to bring traditional Catholic teaching into closer relations with current thought, especially in philosophy, history and social theory. Although the actual word *modernism* did not come into use until about 1905, and at first only among the movement's opponents, the tendencies so designated may be said to have emerged about 1890 and to have been brought to an end some twenty years later by the imposition of the anti-Modernist oath not only upon teachers in Catholic seminaries and universities but upon all ordinands to the priesthood. Yet if its dating presents little difficulty, many scholars would regard it as misleading if not false to describe it in a way that suggests a clear consistency of interests and purposes and even a measure of organization. To the student of the period it may seem to have possessed no real unity and indeed to be more aptly characterized as a complex of movements, each very largely determined by the personality and pursuits of its leading figure or figures, as also to some extent by its geographical provenance. In any case it was at least twofold, in the sense that although its concern was chiefly theological it was also not without a politico-social aspect, while those who could be regarded as 'progressives' in one field were by no means necessarily so in another. But it has to be admitted that with all its internal diversity the Modernist enterprise acquired an historical identity which many had no hesitation in ascribing to it at the time and which the much lengthened perspective of our own viewpoint has done nothing to destroy. Fr Tyrrell in a moment of anger may have declared the thing to have been an invention of Pius X's, but whatever judgment be passed on the papal encyclical, *Pascendi dominici gregis*, by which it was finally condemned, there can be little doubt that in the eyes of the Vatican a trend of opinion was then clearly discernible in the Church which, on the pretext of 'modernizing', was insidiously hostile to the faith as officially understood and taught.

All the same, *Pascendi* does not present a readily acceptable account of what Modernism was. The work, evidently, of a skilled theologian trained in the scholastic method, the encyclical classifies and schematizes the often disparate views with which it deals into a clearly articulated system in which, nevertheless, those who felt their orthodoxy to be impugned failed to discover any genuine reflection of their attitudes. They did not see themselves as a homogeneous and united group, a 'school', still less as an organized body of writers and teachers, lay as well as clerical, working on the basis of shared principles and by co-ordinated means towards an agreed end. In particualar the charge that their conclusions sprang from a common philosophy, identified by the encyclical as '[Kantian] agnosticism' – the doctrine that 'human reason is confined entirely within the field of *phenomena*' – or a metaphysic of 'vital immanence', according to which any explanation of religion 'must be looked for in the life of man', was unhesitatingly repudiated by them. Certainly Loisy, the most prominent of all the Modernists, had little knowledge of philosophy and on his own admission was not interested in it – his concerns lay elsewhere – and in commenting on the encyclical (along with the decree *Lamentabili* which preceded it by a couple of months) he dismissed the pope's whole exposition of the 'modernist' doctrines as 'practically a fantasy of the theological imagination'.[1] In England Fr Tyrrell, in a letter to *The Times* newspaper,[2] denounced the papal utterance as a travesty of the Modernists' real aims and ideas, an act which drew upon him the minor excommunication.

The object of the encyclical was as much polemical as judicial: not only was Modernism to be censured without qualification, the errors with which it was equated called for specification in detail. To do this it was necessary to present a kind of *modernisme schématique* to which indeed the opinions of no single thinker might be completely assimilated but in which, by means of a comprehensive arrangement of ideas culled from a variety of sources, all of them could in one way or another be implicated. It thus would be seen for what it in fact was, 'a compendium of all the heresies', to use the papal phrase. To this, however, Loisy's rejoinder was simply that if those now accused happened to find themselves in agreement on certain points, it was because they had entered by different routes into the current of contemporary thought and through their differing experiences had reached the same conclusions – a situation, he thought, 'misconceived from the beginning to the end' of the Holy See's pronouncement.[3] Or as Tyrrell more bluntly put it: 'With due respect to the encyclical *Pascendi*, Modernists wear no uniform nor are they sworn to the defence of any system; still less of that which His Holiness has fabricated for them.'[4]

Yet in its attempt to characterize Modernism as a whole the encyclical was not altogether wide of the mark. There was among the Modernists some community of outlook and purpose, as Loisy himself admitted. All of them were dissatisfied with traditionalist positions: biblical fundamentalism, intellectual dogmatism, neo-scholasticism, an out-dated apologetic, ecclesiastical authoritarianism and political reaction. Individual thinkers may each have had his own particular target, but all were moved by the conviction that the Catholic Church needed an infusion of new intellectual life and that the intransigence expressed in the *Syllabus errorum* of 1864 would have to be abandoned if Catholicism were to succeed in making any appeal to the educated public of their day. The relatively liberal pontificate of Leo XIII, spanning as it did the transition from the nineteenth century to the twentieth, encouraged them to believe that the Vatican had undergone a change of heart and that opportunity had arrived for initiating the wide-ranging intellectual renewal which they desired.

Who then were the Modernists? Those whose names came to be well known were not numerous, and some who have frequently been classed as Modernists – for example, Blondel – repudiated the connection. Again, not all to whom the term was applied were formally condemned, while others made their submission, if not to the extent of actually recanting their views, then, as in the instance of Laberthonnière, by suspending all further publication. The central figure was of course that of Alfred Firmin Loisy (1857–1940), a biblical scholar of international repute who in the eyes of many characterized the entire movement. Yet in spite of his voluminous *Mémoires* – and he was always acutely conscious of his own place in the unfolding pattern of events – he remains in some respects enigmatic. Was his sincerity, as has been suggested, open to doubt? At any rate did he not throughout his career both within the Church and outside it convey the impression of only half believing the views which he so provocatively expounded? On the other hand George Tyrrell (1861–1909), the Anglo-Irish Jesuit converted to Roman Catholicism while still a youth, presents a wholly different image. Less a theologian *de métier* – although for two or three years he taught philosophy at Stonyhurst – than a preacher, spiritual director and ecclesiastical journalist, he was by nature outspoken and impulsive, at times to the point of recklessness, as in his bitter attack on Cardinal Mercier in 1908. But he, more probably than anyone else, stands out as the typical Modernist. Also his intimate friend Friedrich von Hügel (1852–1925) is usually considered to qualify easily for the designation, though as to this opinions may still vary: certainly he never adopted the immanentist philosophy which *Pascendi* attributed to the Modernists generally and with which Tyrrell himself, and still more conspicuously some of the Italian group, were clearly in sympathy. Yet Paul Sabatier, a close contemporary observer of Modernism on the Protestant side, dubbed him 'the pope of Modernism' – the patron of all its activities and an unfailing spring of personal encouragement to all who sought to promote its ends. Even if in after years he seemed to wish to dissociate himself from the past, or at least to look back on it only as a phase of his life by then definitely over, he was unquestionably in the very thick of things during the crisis itself. The position of Maurice Blondel (1861–1949), whom as a thinker von Hügel greatly admired, is more equivocal. His metaphysic of 'action' was held by many at the time to constitute a full and explicit statement of the voluntarism with which the philosophy of the movement has been commonly associated, a view strengthened by the writings of his avowed disciple, Lucien Laberthonnière (1860–1932), of the Oratorian College at Juilly, whose works, unlike Blondel's, which were never censured, were placed on the Index. But Blondel himself, a devoted churchman ever respectful of authority, rejected the description of Modernist as applying to himself and was firmly opposed to Loisy's standpoint on certain issues of biblical theology. Even Laberthonnière, to whom the Modernist label did become attached, was in a number of respects critical of Modernism and had no wish to be classed as an adherent, and indeed the enforced demise in 1913 of his periodical *Annales de philosophie chrétienne* was attributable as much to his hostility to *Action française* as to his unwelcome theological views. Nevertheless he remained an unrelenting critic of Thomism, the presuppositions of which he judged to be more pagan than Christian. By contrast, of the Modernism of Edouard Le Roy (1870–1954), a disciple of Bergson, there can be no dispute. His religious pragmatism, as set out in *Dogme et critique* (1907), was considered emblematic of the 'subjectivism' and 'psychologism' with which Modernist thinking was generally deemed to be infected.

Turning to the Italian scene one finds a similar situation. In a very few instances the designation Modernist appears well merited, in a few more only questionably so. Although under Ernesto Buonaiuti's leadership some attempt at concerted action is evident, little has come to light to suggest the existence of a widely influential school of radical thought and nothing to justify the charge of a conspiracy. Again, whether Modernism had its representatives in Germany is still a matter of some dispute. Thus Loisy admitted the existence of isolated individuals holding Modernist opinions, but denied that they had any considerable following among the clergy, while the German Catholic bishops were emphatic that *Pascendi* had no bearing on the situation in their country, where 'extreme' views had not taken root. The

Reformkatholizismus movement, associated with the names of F.X. Kraus (1840–1901) and Hermann Schell (1850–1906), had more affinity with the liberal Catholic movements of the nineteenth century than with the Modernism in evidence elsewhere.

The line between Modernist and 'progressive' is not, then, easily drawn. Jean Rivière, whose *Le Modernisme dans l'Eglise* (1929) still offers the most comprehensive survey of the movement yet undertaken, believed otherwise; but it is common knowledge that he was motivated by his concern to exculpate Pierre Batiffol (1861–1929) and his circle – he was himself Batiffol's pupil and loyal friend – from any imputation of heresy, notwithstanding the fact that the first edition of Batiffol's book on the eucharist had been placed on the Index and its author forced to resign his rectorship of the Catholic Institute at Toulouse. An interesting figure, in view of his ecclesiastical rank, was Eudoxe-Irénée Mignot (1842–1918), archbishop of Albi. 'The Erasmus of Modernism', as he has been called, he was well aware of the difficulties which critical biblical study had created for the traditional Catholic teaching, and indeed was the personal friend and ready supporter of Loisy. But in this respect he stood virtually alone in the French hierarchy. Von Hügel's attitude was in some ways similar to that of Mignot, but as a layman he had less to lose. Two other names that may be cited here are those of the historian Louis Duchesne (1843–1922), director of the French School in Rome, and Henri Bremond (1865–1933), author of a monumental history of seventeenth-century French spirituality. Both of them men of letters and members of the Académie Française, the former is said by those who knew him well to have been a sceptic who prudently concealed his real opinions, and although he had been one of the first to encourage Loisy's critical research he himself played no active part in the Modernist movement. Bremond, as the friend of Blondel, von Hügel, Tyrrell and Loisy, was markedly in sympathy with the movement's objectives, but he published nothing to which the Modernist stigma could fairly be attached, although his study of Newman involved him in difficulties with the ecclesiastical authorities and his *Life* of Mme de Chantal was consigned to the Index. Moreover, for officiating at Tyrrell's funeral he was suspended *a divinis* for a year.

Modernity and the Catholic Church

Modernism in the doctrinal sense was born, as we have said, of dissatisfaction with what were felt to be the inadequacies of the Church's intellectual response to the needs of the age, particularly in the realms of philosophy, apologetics and biblical exegesis. This in part could be attributed, in Acton's phrase, to that 'zeal for the prevention of error which represses the intellectual freedom necessary to the progress of truth'.[5] 'Modernity' in thought and learning was suspect, the unhallowed offspring of Protestantism and eighteenth-century rationalism, and as such had already been denounced by an earlier pontiff. But it was attributable in part also to the inertia and unimaginative conservatism in seminary teaching which had long before been deplored by, among others, Joseph de Maistre and Lamennais. Indeed the conviction that in the post-revolutionary era the Church was under obligation to seek new and improved methods of presenting and defending its faith had given rise to a variety of liberalizing tendencies, signally in France and Germany but also in England and Italy. In this respect Liberal Catholicism – though its manifestations were diverse – was less concerned with the problems of adapting Catholic dogmatic teaching to the cultural outlook of a world in which science had achieved an undisputed autonomy than in those arising from the Church's position in a society increasingly secularized and democratized. Montalembert's ideal of 'a free Church in a free state' was fundamentally an expression of belief in the rights of conscience and the essential justice of an educated public opinion. Thus in the Liberal Catholic view political democracy and ecclesiastical reform went hand in hand. Even so there were men like Döllinger and Acton who were anxious also for the rights of historical scholarship and deeply resentful of any attempt on the part of the Church to inhibit it or suppress its results; although in the field of biblical study Catholicism, as compared with Protestantism, continued to make only a poor showing. The one area in which it can perhaps be demonstrated that Modernism was consciously perpetuating an earlier trend is that of philosophy, where in contrast with scholastic rationalism the voluntarism traceable back to Maine de Biran had already found clear utterance in the work of Bautain and Gratry.

The wider intellectual background of the Modernist movement must be sought therefore over the entire course of the nineteenth century rather than in any specific tradition in Catholic thought. Ecclesiastical authority had largely forbidden to Catholic scholarship the freedom enjoyed in the Protestant world. What Catholics felt had now to be reckoned with was, in particular, the vast growth in historical knowledge resulting from the use of new methods of research. It was inevitable that the implications of such knowledge for a proper understanding of the Church's own historical existence, and more especially of the sacred scriptures to which it made authoritative appeal, would sooner or later pose questions to which the more searching intelligences would demand a convincing reply. Here in truth was the issue to which Modernism was in the main the response. Further, it was one which extended the age-old controversy between Catholic and Protestant into a new sphere. Protestantism itself had had to confront the biblical question, and in Germany, ever the pioneer in biblical studies, the answer had taken a radical form, such that Catholicism, if it were to continue to meet the Protestant challenge, would be unable to ignore. The entire debate on scripture and tradition thus acquired a fresh aspect and urgency. Moreover a key-idea in nineteeth-century thought was that of development: to comprehend the nature of a thing one needs to study its genesis and morphology; what it is cannot be determined apart from what it has been. This concept, applied first to the phenomena of human history, had also been validated, thanks chiefly to Darwin, in the field of biological science. But Catholics could remind themselves that the principle had been utilized in theology by both J. A. Möhler in his *Symbolik* (1832) and J. H. Newman in his *Essay on the Development of Christian Doctrine* (1845; 3rd ed. 1878). Neither work when it first appeared had made much impression on the prevailing scholasticism, but when the problems raised by the conditions of historical change came at last to be taken seriously Catholic thinkers had before them a precedent which might be usefully followed. Newman's example could be thought especially profitable. That Catholic Christianity had not remained the same over the ages did not imply corruption of the 'purity' of the original deposit but rather the natural expression of a vital spiritual impulse. In Newman's own words, 'a power of development is a proof of life, not only in its essay, but in its success . . . A living idea becomes many, but remains one.' To Loisy the English divine seemed 'the most open-minded theologian the Church had had since Origen'.[6]

Modernism, as the final phase of the nineteenth-century liberal movement in Catholicism, occurred when it did thanks largely to the encouragement – illusory as in the event it proved – of a new and seemingly liberal pontificate. Leo XIII, who succeeded Pius IX in 1878, outlined in his first encyclical letter, *Inscrutabile Deo consilio*, a programme for the reconciliation of the Catholic Church with modern civilization, thus evidently reversing the policy of his predecessor. Other weighty pronouncements followed, notably the encyclicals *Aeterni Patris* (1879), enjoining the renewed study of the philosophy of St Thomas Aquinas, *Rerum novarum* (1891), on Catholic social theory, and *Providentissimus Deus* (1893), on the study of Scripture, especially in view of recent work in archaeology and literary criticism, although it alluded incidentally to certain 'disquieting tendencies' which, were they to prevail, 'would not fail to destroy the inspired supernatural character of the Bible'. Leo also opened the Vatican library to students regardless of their religious allegiance. The not unreasonable impression that the pope was exhorting the Church to adopt a more favourable attitude to modern knowledge and ideas gained ground therefore. The establishment of the Biblical Commission in 1902 with the object of furthering biblical studies in the light of modern scholarship was also welcomed by not a few as a genuine advance in a hitherto neglected area: Baron von Hügel, for example, who was himself offered a place on it, was optimistic as to future possibilities, and the actual membership of the Commission, when publicly announced, gave some grounds for liberal hopes – although Loisy, with the reception given to his own exegetical work in mind, was decidedly less so:[7] were the earlier ruling of the Holy Office in the matter of the Comma Johanneum (I John v.8) a portent of what was to come then his doubt would be amply confirmed.

Leo was in truth much less a liberal intellectual than a *politique*, more solicitous than was his predecessor for the enlightened image which the Catholic Church should now present to the world. The substance of Vatican policy continued, that is to say, as before; it was only that the means of effecting it were altered. And that such was the case was soon apparent with the accession, on Leo's death, of Cardinal Sarto, the Patriarch of Venice, as Pius X. At the very outset of his reign, in his encyclical *E supremi Apostolatus* of 4 October 1903, he warned the clergy against the 'insidious manoeuvre of a certain new science which adorns itself with the mask of truth'; a 'false science, which, by means of fallacious and perfidious arguments', pointed the way to the errors of rationalism and its like. In the following December five of Loisy's exegetical writings were placed on the Index, although his final condemnation was delayed until some four years later, when first the decree of the Holy Office *Lamentabili sane exitu* (3 July 1907) was published – a collection of sixty-five 'objectionable' propositions culled mainly from his own works – and then, as a definitive pronouncement, *Pascendi*. The former, presented schematically and in Latin, was designed to convey the impression of an articulated body of heretical doctrine. The latter, unusually lengthy for a papal document, went further and offered, as we have seen, what purported to be a systematic indictment of the whole 'Modernist' programme, the term itself thus receiving official recognition. In addition, by the 'motu proprio' *Praestentia sacrae scripturae*, the decrees of the Biblical Commission, both past and future (whatever they might be) were declared binding upon the conscience in exactly the same way as were the doctrinal decrees of the Sacred Congregations, issued with papal approval. The crisis was ended by the imposition of the anti-Modernist oath in the autumn of 1910. Meanwhile Tyrrell had been deprived of the sacraments (22 October

1907) and Loisy excommunicated *vitandus* (8 March 1908), while practically all the identifiable Modernist publications were formally condemned.

A new apologetic: Alfred Loisy

If the impulse behind Modernism was essentially apologetic – to render Catholic doctrine intelligible to the modern world – this in turn could not but involve a searching reappraisal of the traditional positions. In other words, scholasticism and biblical fundamentalism alike would have to give way to a theology more in accord with the modern outlook. But, as *Pascendi* demonstrated, it was for precisely this reason that the Vatican found itself unable to come to terms with the movement. Throughout the nineteenth century its policy had been to maintain traditional views of the Bible and dogma intact, and it reaffirmed the scholastic rationalism as the only permissible basis for the apologist to work on. The Modernist plea was for a reversal of this, to the extent of welcoming new knowledge and at least the toleration of a fresh enterprise in speculative thought. The movement's brusque condemnation was thus the clearest possible demonstration that no such changes would or could be contemplated. The root cause of Modernist errors was, in the Vatican's judgment, a false philosophy resting on the twin principles of 'agnosticism' and 'vital immanence'. From these, it was alleged, the Modernist account of the biblical history and Christian origins and of the nature and development of dogma was said to proceed naturally and inevitably. To this the Modernists' reply was that – in the words of an anonymous Italian *apologia* for the movement, *Il Programma dei modernisti* – 'so far from our philosophy dictating our critical method, it is the critical method that has, of its own accord, forced us to a very tentative and uncertain formulation of various philosophical conclusions, or better still, to a clearer exposition of certain ways of thinking to which Catholic apologetic has never been wholly a stranger'.[8] This assuredly was the opinion of Loisy. Christianity as an historical religion – one, that is, whose truth hinges on the authenticity of specific historical events – could not be insensitive to modern critical methods of study; the scope and limits of which are not to be prescribed by ecclesiastical authority. Theology was one thing, scientific historiography another.

Loisy was indeed well aware that the application of such methods to the study of the Bible would have implications to which the dogmatic theologian could not be indifferent. What made him a Modernist – the most remarkable and, in many respects, typical of all the writers to whom the designation came to be affixed – was the fact that he was prepared to pursue his critical investigations to the point where theological reassessment became a patent necessity; a task moreover which he himself, exegete though he primarily was, appeared not at all unwilling to attempt. It is Loisy's work therefore that we must now look at in some detail if the historical (and most significant) side of the Modernist apologetic is to be appreciated, since in him it received its most audacious expression. The question is whether in presenting it he could ever genuinely have supposed it would win official countenance; though the doubt so raised prompts further query as to his own motives and even – because the point has been mooted – his personal integrity as a priest.

Loisy's reputation as a biblical scholar was acquired from the time of his appointment as professor of Holy Scripture at the Paris Institut Catholique, where he had already taught for some years as a lecturer in Hebrew and had come under the strong personal influence of Duchesne. He immediately drew up a comprehensive programme of instruction extending over the entire field of biblical study and making use of the sort of critical approaches necessarily involved in serious biblical research. He also founded a bimonthly review, *L'Enseignement biblique*, in which to give the substance of his courses a wider publicity. But his tenure of office was not to last for long; critics of his efforts were numerous and influential, and an article of his on the subject of biblical inspiration[9] led to his dismissal in November 1893. The chaplaincy to a girls' convent school in a Paris suburb which he thereupon took up afforded him, if not academic standing, at any rate abundant leisure to pursue his scholarly interests. These furthermore were taking him outside purely historical and exegetical work: his apologetic concern was growing. As far back as 1883 he had composed an imaginary dialogue between an enquiring young scholar and a personification of the Church, in which the latter concedes that 'my teaching, immutable in its principles and its end, can and should be modified in its form and perfected in its exposition, in order that it may the better respond to the needs of the generations which it must bring to God'. During 1897 he drafted an ambitious apologetic treatise to which he gave the unassuming title of 'Essais d'histoire et de philosophie religieuses'. This in its original shape was never published,[10] but it provided the material used later in, among other things, the famous *L'Evangile et l'Eglise* (1902).

Loisy's apologetic (or Modernist) writings thus stand apart from his critical work, although they presuppose it. Besides *L'Evangile et l'Eglise* and its sequel *Autour d'un petit livre* (1903) he contributed a series of articles to the *Revue du clergé français* under the not very opaque pseudonym of 'A. Firmin'. In these he dwells in turn on the nature of religious truth, the meaning of revelation and the idea of doctrinal development, the last more particularly with reference to the views of J. H. Newman, whose writings he had for some time been studying 'with enthusiasm'.[11] The article on development was in fact the first to appear.[12] Newman's treatment of this theme had seemed to him fruitful, and suggested an answer to some of the problems with which he himself was grappling. He in fact considered the theory as elaborated by the English thinker to be superior to any other form of it, in that it clearly envisaged the Christian religion as a living entity, changing continually but always maintaining its essential identity. Regrettably the notion of development was still foreign to the traditional theology, but whether recognized or not the phenomenon of development was something to which the entire history of the Church bore witness. Loisy's own conception of it was, however, at this stage generalized rather than precise and could hardly be characterized as 'evolutionist' on the biological analogy.[13] All that he sought was a principle which would legitimize the transformations historic Christianity has obviously undergone on the grounds that its intrinsic nature has nonetheless been preserved. A detailed application of the theory in regard to both the Catholic Church's dogma and worship, as well as its hierarchical structure, was to be demonstrated a few years later, in *L'Evangile et l'Eglise*.

In discussing the nature of religion and the idea of revelation Loisy had in his sights the recently published volume of Auguste Sabatier, *Esquisse d'une philosophie de la Religion* (1897),[14] although it soon becomes clear to the reader that there is also common ground between them, especially the conviction that in the last analysis religion springs from man's sense of 'absolute dependence upon God'. At the same time Loisy thinks it wrong to equate religion with feeling, irrespective of its intellectual and social concomitants, since in all its higher forms it claims to be a *total* response to man's moral and spiritual needs. But although religion contains an intellectual element it is not to be confused with theology and dogma, the role of which as an interpretative expression of religion is secondary and subordinate to the fundamental experience itself. Man's sense of God is inward or immanent before it is externalized in articulated forms. Sabatier's mistake lay in confining religion to a predominantly individual type of experience.[15] To discount the social embodiment of Christianity is to negate its history and thus to misconceive the nature of religion as a projection of the 'whole man'. Yet the necessary externalization of the religious impulse implies that its forms inevitably change. Church doctrine would simply petrify were it to be identified with particular theological formulations regarded as immutable. The risk ever to be run is in equating faithfulness to tradition with immobility within it; and – Loisy adds – of supposing that the interests of religion coincide also with the advantages of the hierarchy.[16]

The problems posed by Christianity's record can be explained only by reference to the necessities of its continuing life. In the light of its historic experience the Catholic Church can yield an assurance of truth which Protestant individualism is quite unable to provide.[17] When however he embarks on a discussion of revelation Loisy enters upon more dangerous ground. Here again he places himself in opposition to Sabatier, whom he charges with reducing the whole idea to a level of a 'psychological phenomenon': revelation must rather be seen as both subjective and objective. On the one hand it is the consciousness man has of God – though not 'the consciousness God has of himself in man'; on the other, it is nothing less than the manifestation of God *to* man, a manifestation transcending man alike in origin, content and goal. But what precisely *is* its content? Loisy is convinced that it is not doctrine any more than it is mere sentiment. It is an error, he urges, to regard as 'the essential and indispensable element' in revelation 'a purely intellectual knowledge of theoretical and abstract propositions, such as would be the direct object of divine communications and have to be transmitted from generation to generation like a set lesson in which nothing could for any reason be altered'.[18] A true concept represents it primarily as a work of God in man, or of man with God, the divine being recognizable by man.[19] There is thus a cognitive element in revelation, comprising certain truths (*vérités*) which, though not imparted in the shape of a speculative teaching, can rightly be described as 'divine facts in some manner verified (*éprouvés*) by those who perceive them'.[20] Clearly Loisy is here trying to steer a middle course: religion is much more than mere feeling, but its acknowledged intellectual component is a good deal less than formulated doctrine. The basic religious truths moreover, being pre-theological, are capable of a theological definition which is not necessarily unalterable; in changed circumstances such definition may itself demand alteration: for example, in the light of historical criticism a given dogma may have to be restated. Unfortunately he is less than precise in his indications of what his basic *vérités*, themselves unchanging, really are. Their function, that is, is more specific than their identity; but presumably what Loisy means to imply are the broad affirmations of faith, as distinct from the doctrinal mould into which in the course of history they have solidified.

The article on 'the proofs and the economy of revelation'[21] discusses the evidences of prophecy and miracle. The latter is to be seen not as a violation of natural law – a notion exceedingly difficult, if not impossible, to establish – but as a 'sign' for faith; while the former is less an exact prediction of future occurrences than the proclamation of an 'intimate and consistent harmony of ideas and events within a religious movement progressively accomplished under the guidance of Providence'; for only thus can the Old Testament be judged to prepare, announce and prefigure the New.[22] Hence the truth of religion, Loisy concludes, is demonstrated less by rational argument than by living experience, and maintenance of the integrity of that experience is the *raison d'être* for the Church's authority. 'A religion which ceases to be a church, and a church which foregoes its authority will exist in appearance only.'[23]

Loisy's aim in all these papers, as in certain others published anonymously, as well as in the long preface – in the event unpublished – to the 1903 edition of his *Etudes bibliques*, had already been indicated in the foreword to the *livre inédit*, in which he gave warning that a science of religion was taking shape outside Catholicism and in a spirit contrary to it and that to neutralize this insidious influence, which no external authority could prevent from reaching the more intelligent among Catholic believers, it was necessary to promote just such a science within the Church and in a spirit favourable to Catholicism.[24] But always his personal concern was to claim autonomy for the critical exegete. What he could not allow was that the scope of criticism should be determined by the theologians. History was history, he insisted – *Was ist geschehen*, in Ranke's phrase – and had every right to be pursued independently of a theological *a priori*.[25] Theology must learn to adjust itself to historical fact as scientifically established, the whole point of the new apologetic being to show how this could be done in a way that did not subvert the faith in any essential respect. But the result, in Loisy's own case, was an attempt at theological reconstruction which was soon to force him into open conflict with ecclesiastical authority and to bring the *crise moderniste* to a head.

The occasion for the appearance of the first of the 'petits livres rouges', the famous *L'Evangile et l'Eglise*, is well known. It was a reply to a popular lecture-course of Adolf Harnack's at Berlin which had just been published under the title *Das Wesen des Christenthums*, in which the German liberal theologian had argued that Christianity consists essentially in the gospel as proclaimed by the historic Jesus, which in turn could be summed up in the two-fold doctrine of 'God as Father and the human soul so ennobled that it can and does unite with him'. The text in St Matthew (XI. 27) by which Harnack set so much store, 'No one knows the Son except the Father, and no one knows the Father except the Son, and anyone to whom the Son chooses to reveal him', Loisy considered to belong to a later tradition and not be taken as an original utterance of Jesus. Harnack, that is, was in fact appealing to a witness he had in principle rejected. Loisy judged it opportune therefore to sketch out a history of Christian development, starting with the gospel, in order to show that the 'essence' of the latter – in so far as it has an essence –

had been authentically perpetuated in Catholic Christianity. He was fully aware however that this would necessitate the abandonment of the 'absolutist' theses professed by the scholastic theology on such matters as the formal Dominical institution of the Church and the sacraments, the immutability of dogma and the nature of ecclesiastical authority. But he was not deterred: he had more in mind than the refutation of a Protestant critic. The manuscript of his book he submitted to his friend Archbishop Mignot and received a highly encouraging reply.[26]

The first edition came out in November 1902; a second, which appeared in the following year, carried an additional chapter on the gospel sources, intended to demonstrate that the gospels themselves are expressions of Christian belief as it had shaped itself at the time they were composed. What they indicate is that the general theme of Jesus' preaching was the coming 'Reign of God' or 'Kingdom of Heaven', for which his hearers were urged to prepare themselves in penitence. As against Harnack's view of an 'interior' realm within the individual the gospel conceives the Kingdom as the external goal of history; in no way is it to be confused with the conversion of those who are called into it. Accordingly the gospel did not enter the world as 'an unconditioned absolute doctrine, summed up in a unique and steadfast truth, but as a living faith, concrete and complex', the evolution of which, while stemming from its internal dynamism, is at the same time determined by 'the surroundings wherein faith was born and has since developed'. Any idea of a specific and unalterable 'core' of doctrine is to be dismissed as 'pseudo-theology' based on an insufficiently objective analysis of the sources. Jesus' own outlook, as certainly that of his disciples, was articulated in the eschatological terms familiar in contemporary Judaism. He thought of himself, that is to say, as Messiah, but only by anticipation, as personally *called* to rule over the New Jerusalem; and this is the sole sense in which the expression 'Son of God' could have been applied to him. 'The idea of a divine Sonship was to be linked with that of the Kingdom; it had no definite signification, as far as Jesus was concerned, except in regard to the Kingdom about to be established.'[27]

However, Jesus was mistaken, and in the form in which it was expected the Kingdom did not materialize; on the other hand it did provide the principle or germ of the historic Church. As Loisy pithily phrases it: 'Jesus foretold the Kingdom, but it was the Church that came' – though he added, 'she came, enlarging the form of the gospel'.[28] For the truth is that the Church was as necessary to the gospel as was the gospel to the Church. Hence to reproach the Church for the development of its institutions is to reproach it for having chosen to live. Further, 'there is nowhere in her history any gap in continuity, or the absolute creation of a new system: every step is a deduction from the preceding . . .'[29] The Roman Church itself is historically justifiable as the providential centre of Christian evangelization. What matters is the persistence of a recognizable community. From this need and capacity of vital adaptation have proceeded its dogmatic formularies, as likewise the progressive shaping and centralization of its hierarchy and the development of its sacraments. The entire process has in fact been nothing else than the acquisition by faith of the forms which conditions demanded for its viability. 'Everything by which the gospel sustains its life is Christian.'

Thus if the 'essence' of Christianity is to be found one should seek it in the Church's power of self-perpetuation, as disclosed in the unfolding course – itself unpredictable – of its historic life. Loisy was always at pains to deny that he had any philosophical platform, but on this side of his apologetic there seem to be Hegelian overtones, and it is notable that the British Hegelian, Edward Caird, is cited by him with marked approval.[30] In the section on dogma – which especially aroused the author's critics – it is stated that the development of dogma is not and could not be in the gospel itself, though on the other hand 'it does not follow that the dogma does not proceed from the gospel, and that the gospel has not lived and does not live in the dogma as in the Church'.[31] Again, as the Church's doctrines relate to the general state of human knowledge in the period during which they took shape it must ensue that any large advance in knowledge will render necessary a fresh interpretation of the ancient formularies. But if there is no absolute fixity in dogmatic forms and change is a condition of their survival it is clear that their function is symbolic rather than presentative. 'The efforts of a healthy theology should be directed to the solution of the difficulty, presented by the unquestionable authority faith demands for dogma, and the variability and relativity which the critic cannot fail to perceive in the history of dogmatic formularies.'[32]

Although welcomed by some, *L'Evangile et l'Eglise* was widely denounced for its 'positivism'. The author was accused of having offered a purely naturalistic account of Christianity in both its origins and its development, with the supernatural relegated to the realm of subjective faith. Historic Catholicism was to be seen, that is, as a human phenomenon subject like any other to the principles governing all scientific investigation. Its divine authority, were it deemed to possess any, could not on Loisy's showing be objectively established. Accordingly the archbishop of Paris, Cardinal Richard, personally censured the book on the grounds that it undermined all the basic doctrines of the faith. Unfortunately a sequel to it which appeared a few months later, at the suggestion of friends of Loisy's that he should clarify his position, was even more provocative. *Autour d'un petit livre* (as it was entitled) took the form of a series of open letters to a number of eminent churchmen, clerical (and in one case) lay, dealing with the nature and use of biblical criticism, the study of the gospels, dogma ('What we call revelation can only be man's awareness of his relationship with God'[33]), Christology, the Church and the sacraments. In the event Loisy's explanations only exacerbated controversy and he found himself attacked with increased bitterness. The outcome was that both volumes were condemned by the Holy Office in December, 1903. The author himself made a formal submission and in token of his sincerity offered to resign the lectureship he then held at the Ecole des Hautes Etudes. But as the terms of his submission did not satisfy the pope and a more explicit recantation was demanded, he thereupon took the further step of informing the archbishop of Paris that, in due obedience to the Holy See, he expressly repudiated the errors which the Congregation of the Holy Office had condemned in his writings. *Autour d'un petit livre* was thus in effect his last 'Modernist' utterance, his public comments on the decree *Lamentabili* and the encyclical *Pascendi* being no more than a postscript.

History and dogma

Loisy, as his whole career demonstrates, was primarily a biblical exegete and historian. Between history and theology he drew a firm distinction; biblical exegesis belonged to the former and the theologian entered only upon the heels of the scholar. But the traditional teaching, he contended, reversed this order; the use of history was merely to show how the theological conclusion had been reached, the conclusion itself representing a truth which the historian, if a Catholic, must acknowledge at the outset. Loisy, as we have said, was not indifferent to theology, and his aim as an apologist was to point the implications of modern historical scholarship in regard to it. At the same time one has to recognize that his personal concern was really to secure his own freedom as a scholar, and had he been permitted to pursue his researches unhindered it is likely that he would have been content to remain within the Catholic fold and continue to exercise his priesthood. But the Church refused to accept what appeared to him a simple and unexceptionable division of labour. Biblical history could not be separated from doctrine and authority; on the contrary, it had to be interpreted in accordance with it and indeed under its tutelage. A non-supernaturalistic account of Christian origins which *eo ipso* would eliminate the miraculous was incompatible with a theological doctrine whose content necessarily included events of a supernatural order. A scriptural exegesis which did not anticipate the articulated positions of orthodox dogma was, in consequence, inadmissible. But this Loisy, as a professional historian, could not in his turn allow save at the price of confining himself to points of merely marginal significance. Hence his dilemma, and that also of all Catholic scholars – as Duchesne used candidly to advise his pupils – who wished to prosecute their studies in any but 'safe' areas.

So the whole question was raised of whether religious history can be critically 'pure', or must always bring with it a theological interpretation. Loisy believed the former to be possible and felt that his integrity as a scholar depended on his freedom to distinguish between history and tradition. But between his position and that, say, of a man like Mgr Camus, a member of the Pontifical Biblical Commission and the addressee of one of the letters in *Autour d'un petit livre*, who declared flatly that 'we must take our gospels as they are, as the exact, faithful, unimpeachable expression of that which the apostles saw, heard and related of Jesus',[34] there appeared to be no common ground. However, an attempt at mediation was made by Maurice Blondel in two articles published in *La Quinzaine* early in 1904 under the title *Histoire et dogme: les lacunes philosophiques de l'éxègese*, in which he contrasted what he called respectively 'extrinsicism' and 'historicism' as twin errors. The former, the traditionalist view, he judged to have no real use for historical science and to be interested in history only for apologetic purposes, i.e. to substantiate the testimony of miracles. The Bible is guaranteed *en bloc*, that is, not by its content but by the external seal of the divine. Opposed to such absolutism is the historical relativism with which Loisy, although not named, is plainly identified. Its aim is plausible enough – to investigate the facts for their own sake 'and, instead of seeking dogma and its abstract formula in history, to look for history and history alone even in regard to dogma, which will then come fully alive again'.[35] But the doubt arises whether historical inquiry can ever prove the truth of religious faith. For what, in this context, are the historical facts? 'History' is not only science, it is life; scientific history is represented by the scholar's researches, living history by the continuing tradition of the community. And tradition is neither a fixed deposit nor a progressive surrender to novelty; rather is it, says Blondel, 'the collective experience of Christ verified and realized within us', and as such acts as the effectual mediating principle between dogma and history. But although Blondel and Loisy had corresponded with one another at length on this subject, it is evident that the two men inhabited different intellectual worlds.[36] Loisy did not reply publicly to his critic, but as he commented in his *Mémoires*, he regarded the latter as in no sense an exegete –

had he not frankly admitted his *cécité philologique?* – while his arguments showed that he did not rightly understand the problems involved, especially when he invoked faith to establish fact.

Blondel's views were however taken up by Friedrich von Hügel in an article which also appeared in *La Quinzaine*, with the title 'Du Christ éternel et nos christologies successives',[37] as well as in private correspondence, although it is doubtful whether here again the two disputants ever got to grips with one another, particularly on the specific issue of Christ's human consciousness. But von Hügel certainly had no brief for an outright historical scepticism and summarized his own position by saying that 'although the act of Christian faith necessarily goes beyond the historical facts it nevertheless demands such facts, each of which is open to historical investigation. 'It demands them because that is a condition of all human assent, since our souls are only awakened to the presence of spiritual realities when a contingent and historic stimulus from without excites them. It demands them because all complete and deep religion calls for a factor of this nature. The more complete and profound a religion is, the more it will present this paradox of the permanent seized through the transitory, the eternal manifested in time.'

Von Hügel and Tyrrell

Von Hügel's part in the Modernist movement has been diversely assessed, and that he never incurred ecclesiastical censure has been taken to prove his non-adherence. There was at any rate a marked tendency in some quarters in the years following his death to reduce his role in the movement to a minimum, as is evident, for example, in Bernard Holland's 'Memoir' prefacing his edition of the *Selected Letters 1896–1924* (1927). But the evidence is that most of his contemporaries thought of him as a protagonist, if not, in Miss Petre's expression, its 'arch-leader'.[38] In his general openness of mind to the scientific thought of the day, especially in the historical and biblical fields, he was a decided pace-setter, to a degree which often astonished his closest intimates. On one occasion Tyrrell, after a talk with von Hügel at which Bremond was present, was moved to write to their common Anglican friend A. L. Lilley:

The Baron was just gone. Wonderful man! Nothing is true; but the sum total of nothing is sublime! Christ was not merely ignorant but a tête brulé (*sic*); Mary was not merely not a virgin, but an unbeliever and a rather unnatural mother; the Eucharist was a Pauline invention – yet he makes his daily visit to the Blessed Sacrament and for all I know tells his beads devoutly. Bremond's French logic finds it all very perplexing.[39]

Allowance may perhaps be made for Tyrrell's temperamental exuberance, but the baron's resourcefulness in uniting Catholic piety with radical criticism was something of a marvel to all who knew him. He was well acquainted with the work of contemporary German Protestant scholarship, as in Bernhard Weiss, H. J. Holtzmann and Arnold Meyer – in this respect he was Tyrrell's mentor – endorsing their conclusions on the dating of the New Testament writings, and notably on the authorship and character of the Fourth Gospel; conclusions not admitted by Catholic theologians of his day. Nevertheless he was conscious of the difficulty of determining where exactly to draw the line between the rights of historical criticism and the demands of traditional faith, and it cannot justly be said that he ever succeeded in making himself quite clear on the point. Thus to what extent could religious doctrines be considered true if, under scrutiny, their foundations in history were to vanish? Could they in fact be established independently of their historical grounding? Critical of Blondel's attempt to place tradition alongside if not above science as the warrant of historical authenticity, he at the same time could not dispense with the historical element altogether and posited an historical 'core', by no means exactly definable, which faith must presumably take on trust. So in a paper of 1914 – i.e. after the collapse of Modernism as a movement – he could speak of 'a nucleus of historically assured and historically testable factual happenings' as necessary, though God 'alone knows with entire finality the precise delimitation of this range of happenedness'. For as the body requires the soul, so the soul requires the body. 'There is a real and necessary interdependence between the two, yet they are not simply co-extensive; the soul ranges further than the body.'[40] This position was of course entirely consonant with his realism in philosophy as against all forms of subjectivist idealism or immanentism.

For it was there that von Hügel stood altogether apart from the main current of Modernist opinion. According to *Pascendi* the philosophy of Modernism was essentially immanentist and agnostic. Neither designation however could possibly be applied to von Hügel's philosophical thinking, which even during the Modernist period was resolutely metaphysical and transcendentalist. In later years his dislike of immanentism became almost obsessive, and he tended to discover the offending doctrine everywhere – in Loisy (despite his professed distaste for all philosophizing), in the Italians, in Tyrrell, even in Blondel and Laberthonnière, for all their insistence that their *méthode d'immanence* had no such implications. Between religion conceived on the one hand as a purely intra-human phenomenon, non-evidential save of the aspirations of the human race, and, on the other, as essentially evidential and metaphysical, the effect in man of something vastly more than himself, there was, he held, a complete gulf. And as the years passed the conviction deepened within him, especially under the influence of thinkers like Ernst Troeltsch, Rudolf Eucken and the Edinburgh teacher Norman Kemp Smith, as his posthumous *The Reality of God* (1931) was to make abundantly clear. He still admired, he said, many pages of his 'always well loved' friends, Blondel and Laberthonnière, 'but I have to admit that any fully living interest is now given to thinkers – almost all German, Englishmen and Italians – who are on the way to setting up for us a *critico-realist epistemology*'.[41] Moreover von Hügel's loyalty to the Roman Catholic Church was absolutely unwavering; to him it was the supreme witness to the reality of the transcendent.

But of all the baron's circle no one was more profoundly influenced by him than was the Anglo-Irish Jesuit George Tyrrell. A convert to Roman Catholicism when scarcely out of boyhood, he was still only eighteen when he entered the Society of Jesus. Ordained priest in 1891, he taught philosophy at Stonyhurst before being sent to the Society's London house in Farm Street, Mayfair, where in 1897 he first made von Hügel's acquaintance. The same year saw also the publication of his first book, the devotional addresses entitled *Nova et Vetera*. Other volumes soon followed: *Hard Sayings* (1898), *External Religion* (1899), and the two series of *The Faith of the Millions* (1897–1901), this last consisting mainly of essays contributed by him to the Jesuit periodical *The Month*. A volume called *Oil and Wine* on the other hand did not pass the censorship, while *Lex Orandi* (1903), only scraped by, being in fact the last of his works to appear with the *imprimatur*. Three years later he found himself in the full spate of the Modernist controversy as a result of the publication in the Milan *Corriere della Sera* of extracts, in a garbled translation, of an anonymous 'Letter to a Professor', his own authorship of which he admitted to the General of the Society. To dispel misapprehensions he then published the completed document, with an explanatory introduction, under the title *A Much-Abused Letter* (1906). The upshot of this was his dismissal from the Society and effective suspension *a divinis*. Having now no regularized ecclesiastical status he moved from place to place, usually staying with friends, until he finally settled at Storrington in Sussex, in accommodation made available to him by his loyal supporter Maude Petre. It was there that he wrote the two articles for *The Times* newspaper (30 September and 1 October 1907) attacking *Pascendi*, an act which brought upon him the minor excommunication. Two years later he died of Bright's disease, his burial in the Church of England parish churchyard at Storrington being attended by, among others, his friend Henri Bremond, who was himself disciplined for having conducted the obsequies. The last books to be seen through the press by him were *Through*

Scylla and Charybdis and his abrasive reply, *Mediaevalism*, to a pastoral letter of the archbishop of Malines, Cardinal Mercier. Both came out in 1908. *Christianity at the Cross-Roads* appeared in the following year, posthumously.

Tyrrell's adoption of Modernist opinions was gradual. After an initial period of almost exaggerated orthodoxy, exemplified in some of his early articles in *The Month*, he entered on a phase of what he called mediatorial liberalism, akin to the position maintained by Wilfrid Ward. He had come, that is, to believe in freedom in matters of science and criticism, but not without limitations: ecclesiastical authority commands respect and theology is not to be put at the behest of other disciplines. However, his growing friendship with von Hügel was to have a direct influence upon his intellectual outlook, encouraging him upon more adventurous paths. During his time as a teacher at Stonyhurst he had sought to inculcate what he considered authentic Thomism – the doctrine of St Thomas himself rather than the Suarezian version of it favoured by the Society of Jesus – and had encountered opposition for so doing. In his view Aquinas represented 'a far less developed theology than that of the later scholastics, and by going back to him one escapes from many of the superstructures of his more narrow-minded successors, and thus gets a liberty to unravel and reconstruct on more sympathetic lines'.[42] A deepening distrust of theological rationalism, then already germinating in his mind, was expressed in two articles published, the one in *The Weekly Register*,[43] the other in *The Month*,[44] with the titles respectively of 'A Perverted Devotion' and 'The Relation of Theology to Devotion'. The first of these, which discussed difficulties in the traditional doctrine of hell, was a plea for restraint in regard to the Church's teaching on everlasting damnation and deprecated the sort of theologizing which can draw inferences repugnant alike to faith and ordinary morality. For the doctrine of hell was not unique in this; intellectual problems respecting other doctrines were raised needlessly, 'whereas thousands would willingly submit to these mysteries were they allowed to preserve that agnosticism in their regard which is one of the elements of faith'.

The second of the articles was a clear pointer to the whole subsequent movement of Tyrrell's thinking on the nature of dogma and theology generally. Indeed his apologetic never really changed direction or exceeded the bounds there indicated. His use of terms should be noted. By 'devotion' he means the practical life of religion as commonly experienced; by 'theology', both the dogmatic formulation of religious belief and that broader intellectual understanding of religion in which dogma occupies an authoritative place. Between the substance of religion and its intellectual definition there is thus a distinction similar to that which exists between nature and the science of nature. Theology is abstract and rationalizing in its procedure; it offers no more than the 'bare ribs' of religious truth, to be 'fleshed out' by a liberal recourse to analogy. Analogy, for Tyrrell, is the key-word, and one, he is pleased to recall, with the proper *cachet* of scholastic usage. Man's thought about the supernatural order cannot be other than analogous, and the real fault of anthropomorphism is in not remembering that this is so. The language of practical religion is from this point of view no more defective than that of theology, and has the great counterbalancing advantage of being the utterance of living experience. 'The use of philosophy lies in its insisting on the inadequacy of the vulgar statement; its abuse, in forgetting the inadequacy of its own, and thereby falling into a far more grievous error than that which it would correct.'[45] The *depositum fidei* was not a mere symbol or creed but a concrete religion – that 'left by Christ to His Church'; hence more directly a *lex orandi* than a *lex credendi*. 'The creed is involved in the prayer, and has to be disentangled from it.' Formularies are always to be tested and explained by the concrete religion which they seek to formulate.[46]

With the turn of the century Tyrrell may be said to have entered on his Modernist period, although his personal opinions, as indicated in his private correspondence, were on the whole ahead of the views to which he gave public voice. His interest now was concentrated on the problem of Catholic doctrine as such, its nature and its evolution. *Lex Orandi*, the first of his books to mark the new phase, was in tone devotional rather than theological. Even so his religious pragmatism was already discernible: it is the task of the apologist, he wrote, not only to relate theological statements to other forms of human knowledge but 'to connect the life of religion with the rest of our life and . . . to show that the latter demands the former'. The test of doctrine is in its prayer-value, not in the pseudo-scientific coherence of its systematic expression. The truths of religion, like those of history and science, have life rather than intellectual satisfaction as their end, and their final significance is practical. 'The religiously important criticism to be applied to points of Christian belief, whether historical, philosophic, or scientific, is not that which interests the historian, philosopher or scientist; but that which is supplied by the spirit of Christ.'[47] Little exception could be taken to this statement, and the appeal which Tyrrell made to the theory of analogy was also reassuring. However, the book he next published, *The Church and the Future* (1903), under the pseudonym of 'Hilaire Bourdon' – though he took little precaution to conceal his own identity as its author – was deliberately controversial, not only attacking the official 'Romanist' account of Catholicism, but offering a restatement of it in uncompromisingly 'Modernist' terms. His earlier 'mediatorial liberalism' is now abandoned, since he recognizes that the moderate positions which constituted its platform stood no chance of being accepted under the new pontiff, Pius X, whose rigid conservatism was apparent from the start. Tyrrell denies that the claim of Catholicism to have been divinely instituted can with any certainty be based on the idea that the transformation of Christianity from its 'inspirational' phase into an institution, 'officered and organized after the pattern of a secular monarchy or empire', was foreseen and arranged by Christ in anticipation of the centuries following the decline of the original belief in an imminent *Parousia*, a belief which Jesus himself in all likelihood shared. Catholicism should rather be seen as the embodiment of that Spirit 'which created both Christ and the Church to be different and complementary organs of its own expression, adapted to different phases of the same movement'.[48] Theology, accordingly, is no more than an inadequate analysis or rational presentation of the mysteries underlying the Christian life.

Tyrrell's final views on the problem of the interrelation of revelation, dogma and theology are set out in *Through Scylla and Charybdis*, and principally in the two essays which had not previously been published, namely those on Revelation and on what he calls 'Theologism' – the latter a reply to criticisms made by the French Jesuit J. Lebreton. Revelation is now identified not, as hitherto, with some articulated *depositum fidei*, but with a direct experience, a spiritual vision. This vision is not inexpressible or incommunicable: revelation is actually transmitted in the Church in the form of a record, although as such it is secondary to the experience itself. It is expressed in terms that are spontaneous and imaginative – inspired, as it may truly be claimed, but also, naturally and inevitably, using language and ideas derived from the contemporary cultural environment. The impact of the supernatural order is thus carried *symbolically* into the faith and piety of believers. The symbolism however is not fully commensurate with the original experience, and can neither exhaust it nor even adequately project it. But although subordinate to the primary experience it has authority in so far as it communicates the values disclosed in that experience, and it is the Church's responsibility to maintain it intact. It may be characterized as 'prophetic' truth – truth pragmatically significant for the Christian life. Certainly the particular images and thought-forms adopted – for example, the Messiah-figure, or 'the Second Adam', or the Logos-concept – are not themselves absolutes, since 'prophetic truths' are not statements from which deductive inferences can be made. Indeed the task of theology is to take prophecy not as statement but as experience; it must try, that is, to reach behind the statement to the religious phenomenon itself, using it not simply as verbal but as factual evidence for its own conceptual representations of the supernatural order. When therefore one speaks of the *development* of doctrine – a subject by which Tyrrell's mind was always much exercised – it has to be understood that prophetic truth is not itself capable of development, although as a record of experience it must stand. Where development necessarily does occur is in the interpretation, or re-interpretation, of the revelation-experience itself.

What however is the status and authority of dogma as such? Briefly, Tyrrell answers, as a protective covering for revealed truth – a function which it shares with theology. Theology and dogma nevertheless are not one and the same, the difference being that dogma is authoritatively imposed. 'The Church but declares what the Apostles declared, and that was not theology.' The logical unity of the creed is subsequent to the controversies which rendered dogmatic definitions necessary, and 'heresies do not arise according to any logical plan of succession'. Such definitions – 'dogmas in the secondary sense' (i.e. as distinct from the primary, scriptural image – for example, the Virgin Birth), are clearly at a further remove from the original revelation-experience. Theology, as adopted and imposed by ecumenical decree is, says Tyrrell, 'the Church's *understanding* and translation into common language of the truths which she feels and believes and has revealed to her in prophetic imagery'.[49] Thus to affirm as revealed truth that Christ is consubstantial with the Father is not to claim that the expression itself is inspired or revealed in the way that St Peter's confession, 'Thou art the Son of the living God', constitutes revelation, but merely to signify that it is the rational or philosophical equivalent of a revealed truth. To imply more would be to attribute some sort of divine character to the Aristotelian categories in which the dogma is actually expressed. Hence the meaning of the definitions lies essentially in the truth which they protect and not in the terms of the protective formula itself. As 'divine oracles' their sense is more or less cryptic and enigmatic, and to treat them as miraculous 'theologoumena' is to degrade them to the plane of reason.[50] But Tyrrell maintains that although dogmatic definitions are arrived at by theological debate the infallible authority attaching to them is not so founded. Rather, when a definition is adopted by the Church it is imparted to the faithful not as a theological but as an oracular and prophetic pronouncement. 'Like her Master and His apostles she teaches through the Spirit and not through reasoning, theological or otherwise.' It follows therefore that in Tyrrell's view dogmas as such, like the original 'prophetic truths', cannot develop; where development does occur is in *theology*. But the unifying factor, the power by which revelation, dogma and theology are all essentially one, is the Spirit. It is only by the Spirit's inward guidance that the Church can know, as by instinct, what will or will not nourish her life.

'Former heresies', Tyrrell wrote in his posthumous *Christianity at the Cross Roads* (1910), 'questioned this or that dogma, this or that ecclesiastical institution. Modernism criticizes the very idea of dogma, of . . . revelation.'[51] But he was no less anxious than before to urge the difference between Modernism and Liberal Protestantism, although the symbolo-fideism of A. Sabatier and E. Ménégoz can now be seen to have been a factor in shaping the Modernist outlook. Between Christ and Catholicism the Liberal Protestant, according to the Modernist, sees only a chasm, with no bridge, and Christianity has fallen into the chasm, to remain there, stunned, for nineteen centuries.[52] But the Liberal Protestant position had been shattered at its base by the consistent eschatologism of Johannes Weiss, Loisy and Albert Schweitzer: in other words, the germ of Catholicism was already latent in the apocalyptic 'Kingdom'. Likewise Modernism and Liberal Catholicism, at least as represented by Lamennais, Lacordaire and Montalembert, had really very little in common, although as regards Newman – if the term Liberal Catholic be applicable to him – Tyrrell was apparently less sure. The central issues, he was convinced, related to history and dogma, and the problem had in more recent years so widened as to cover not Catholicism alone but Christianity in general.[53] Yet Tyrrell was still persuaded that Roman Catholicism, for all its accretions and perversions, was the truest form of Christianity and therefore the most authentic expression of the religious impulse itself.

Voluntarism and pragmatism

Loisy and Tyrrell were the outstanding representatives of Modernism, and it is their names above all with which the movement's aims have most readily been associated. The two men however differed markedly in temper as in interests. Except for Lagrange, a life-long opponent, Loisy had no rival among contemporary Catholic scholars as a biblical exegete, and when authority refused him the exercise of his scholar's rights he declared that the attempt to modernize Catholicism – the biblical issue being to him crucial – was but to plough the sands. Tyrrell, on the other hand, was a theologian and apologist for whom the essential question was that of the very nature of religious belief itself. Neither of them was a philosopher, at any rate in the more exact sense. Yet according to *Pascendi* it was philosophy of a distinctive type, viz. immanentism, which lay at the root of Modernism in all its forms. Whether or not the Modernists were right in denying this, immanentist

tendencies were clearly evident in at least some of the thinkers connected
with the movement. At this point therefore one is bound to refer to the part in
it played by Maurice Blondel, who has even been described as its 'spiritual
father'.[54] This assessment is so exaggerated as to be false, but it is the case
that much Modernist writing reveals Blondel's influence. His doctoral thesis
L'Action, published in 1893, had developed a metaphysical system which,
while complying – as its author always insisted – with 'the most minute and
rigorous demands of Catholicism', was intended to respond to those also of
modern thought; and in his subsequent 'Lettre sur les exigences de la pensée
contemporaine en matière d'apologétique' (1896), in which he argued the
need for a new type of apologetic, he characterized his own procedure as a
méthode d'immanence, in opposition to the scholastic procedure which sought
first to establish revelation as an *a priori* possibility and then to demonstrate
its actuality in Christianity – an argument which might appeal well enough to
believers but hardly to the sort of persons to whom apologetic treatises are
usually addressed. A better approach is indicated by the Pascalian motto,
Quelle chimère est-ce donc que l'homme: viz., that for all men revelation poses
an inescapable choice and that moral responsibility is incurred in the
acceptance or rejection of it. Nonetheless the use of the term *immanence*, even
when qualified as a 'method', left Blondel open to misapprehension by
theologians and philosophers trained in scholasticism. Thus his opinions, all
too easily rendered ambiguous by his prolix and elusive way of writing,
quickly became a focus of controversy. Yet it is apparent that he himself was
no Modernist, and with the publication of *Histoire et dogme* in 1904 his
disagreements with Loisy became public. His views could indeed be called
Modernistic in so far as he believed that Christian doctrine and spirituality
were to be understood inwardly and in relation to man's total experience,
without forcing the antithesis between supernatural and natural. But as he
later pointed out, he had no idea 'of belittling the rational intelligence or
undermining fundamental theology', his 'only ambition being to explore
patiently the whole area accessible to reason in questions common to both
philosophy and religion'.[55] In after years, as a devout Catholic deeply
respectful of ecclesiastical authority, Blondel not only mitigated the expression of his views but consistently played down his own earlier connection
with Modernism.

His disciple, the Oratorian Lucien Laberthonnière, editor from 1905 to
1913 of the periodical *Annales de Philosophie chrétienne*, a forum for the
expression of liberal ideas, was more forthright in arguing for an
'immanentist' style of religious philosophy. A volume of essays which
appeared in 1903, offered, he explained, less an exposition of doctrine

than 'a preoccupation and an attitude': the one, to defend Christian belief in the face of modern philosophy; the other, frankly to concede to that same philosophy certain of its essential postulates. The notion of an 'extrinsic' or 'heteronomous' truth, that is, is uncongenial to the modern mind. 'Of whatever order the truth may be by which we have to live . . . it becomes ours, and illuminates us and vivifies us, only to the extent that we ourselves, with all that we are, strive to create it within us.' The authority of religious doctrine depends therefore on the degree to which it is morally appropriated 'as the law of our own being and our own life'.[56] *Moral dogmatism*, founded upon a living experience, must replace that of scholastic rationalism. What Christianity testifies is the active presence of God in humanity itself. If it propounds 'a system of supernatural truths to be believed it is because we have a supernatural life to live'. In a subsequent book, *Le Réalisme et l'idéalisme grec* (1904), an oblique attack on scholasticism, Laberthonnière contrasts the abstract, static character of Hellenic thought with the dynamism and concrete personalism of the biblical outlook. What matters for the biblical writers, he points out, is not the externality of facts – which is secondary – but their inner meaning. This applies to the gospel itself. Christ is there presented, not for the sake of his historic individuality but for 'what he was in himself, for the significance of his acts, the bearing of his words, and for the place which he occupies in humanity and the role he fulfils there'.[57] Thus what the gospel conveys under the form of a history is essentially a *faith*, but a faith which is no more an abstract intellectualism than is the history an empirically verifiable record. Both are the expression of a vital experience. The function of dogma is interpretative, interpretation being 'the essential mode of the Spirit's activity'.[58] History, of itself, cannot yield faith; nor on the other hand is the Church's tradition a dead letter. Christ did infinitely more than cast his truth into the shape of an absolute doctrine. Rather he disseminated it 'as a living thing in hearts that are alive, in order that it might grow there, and bear fruit, and propagate itself'.

Laberthonnière, who stood firmly in the tradition of French voluntarism going back through Gratry and Bautain to Maine de Biran, could be said, as Loisy remarked, to have translated Blondel, whose own literary style was always Germanically opaque, into French. But if he rendered his master's thinking more explicit and intelligible, he suffered consequences which the latter himself was spared. In 1906 both volumes were placed on the Index, and when, later, two other works were refused the *imprimatur* he agreed to make no further attempt to publish. Thus he escaped excommunication at the price of silence.

The pragmatist approach to Catholic doctrine, already implicit in

Laberthonnière's moral dogmatism, became overt in Edouard Le Roy's *Dogme et critique* (1907). A mathematician and, in philosophy, a disciple of Henri Bergson, he argued that the meaning of truth is to be found mainly in the services it offers and the results which its acceptance involves; as too, and more widely, 'by the vivifying influence which it exercises over the whole body of knowledge'. The truth of religious doctrines must be seen in this light, for the problem of religious belief as it presents itself today is created not by this or that doctrine in isolation but by the nature of dogma as such. Credibility cannot be imposed by authority alone, nor, to the modern mind, is it established by appeal to arguments essentially extrinsic to the alleged truth itself. Moreover the very intelligibility of dogmas is rendered the more difficult by knowledge of the circumstances of their historical formation, since this shows them to be an amalgam, on the one hand of scriptural imagery, and on the other of a type of metaphysical thinking long obsolete. In short, Catholic dogma as traditionally expounded rests upon a false intellectualism. It is not, that is, a statement of truth in the speculative or theoretical order, nor does it add anything to the sum of positive knowledge, being in no way comparable to a scientific hypothesis. What, Le Roy contends, religious doctrines properly do is to furnish *rules of practical conduct*, amounting in sum to prescriptive guidance to the religious and moral life as a whole. He gives instances of what he means. The doctrine that God is personal is in effect an injunction: So conduct yourself in your relations with him as you would in your relations with a human person. Again, to affirm Christ's resurrection is to say: Let your relation to the risen Christ be what it would have been before his death, or what it is to your own contemporaries. The dogma in itself is a metaphor incapable of restatement in literal terms, inasmuch as we lack the requisite historical evidence. At the level of speculative interpretation dogmas have only a negative function, in excluding specific errors. Thus to state that God is personal is deliberately to refrain from reducing him to 'a mere law, a formal category, an ideal principle, an abstract entity'.[59] But what in positive terms the divine personality means cannot be said. The doctrine can only indicate a practical attitude, which is all that religion, as distinct from philosophy, in fact demands.

The movement in Italy and Germany

In Italy Modernism adopted political and social as well as scientific aims, as it also acquired a degree of coherence and even of concerted effort which it lacked elsewhere. On questions of history and biblical exegesis, a field in which Salvatore Minocchi (1869–1943) and the Barnabite Giovanni Semeria

(1867–1939) took the lead, the inspiration came directly from France and produced nothing of original merit, although Ernesto Buonaiuti (1881–1946), to whose authorship the anonymous *Programma dei modernisti* (1907) is to be assigned, was among those who insisted that in general the movement's intellectual concern stemmed not from any predominant philosophical interest but from the challenge which critical history inevitably presents to the traditional institutions of Catholicism. Nevertheless Italian Modernism on its intellectual side soon became overtly apologetic and reformist. Minocchi and Semeria, in an interview in the summer of 1903 with Leo Tolstoy, admitted that they attached little importance to Catholicism's 'husk of dogma' and that their personal reason for remaining in the Church was partly to avoid the sort of public scandal commonly associated with 'useless apostasies', but also, and more importantly, to promote their own religious ideals within it.[60] Of the cause of liberal reform, as thus envisaged, the journal *Il Rinnovamento*, which made its début at the beginning of 1907, was the mouthpiece, its principle supporters including a number of young laymen of high social rank such as Alessandro Casati and Tommaso Gallarati-Scotti. How its contributors viewed Catholicism was made apparent at the outset. Christianity, they believed, is primarily a life, the continuance of which depends directly on its freedom of development: to seek to enclose it within the limits of some supposedly definitive system would only be to stifle it. Its forms, necessary in themselves, are bound to change if its vitality is to be transmitted to a new age. A conception of religion which claims in the name of faith permanently to bind the understanding to a particular philosophical or social doctrine is fundamentally wrong. Senator Antonio Fogazzaro (1842–1911), a poet and novelist but likewise a prominent member of the *Rinnovamento* group and a fervent disciple of Rosmini, was a particularly vigorous critic of such *immobilismo*. His novel *Il Santo*, published in 1905, develops the idea that the work of reform really calls for the mission of a great saint, probably a layman of liberal vision and intense spirituality, a St Francis of the twentieth century.

The charge that Modernism was committed to an immanentist theology has usually cited the writings of some of its Italian adherents, especially younger men whose standpoint has been represented as virtually a Christianized humanism. *Il programma*, however, accepted the immanentist label only as meaning that religion is the spontaneous outcome of the irrepressible needs of the human spirit, which finds its satisfaction in 'the inward and emotional experience of the presence of God within us', so that the intellectual case for God's existence – or, more precisely, intellectual justification of faith in the divine – is nowadays to be based less on logical than on moral considerations. 'Immanentism' relates to an apologetic method, not, as *Pascendi* avers, to a metaphysical doctrine: the ontological reality of the supernatural is in no way denied.

Yet the liberal movement in Italian Catholicism was in origin not theological but social and political; theologically it was, as Rivière observes, a *sous-produit* of the latter.[61] On the social side its leader was Don Romolo Murri (1870–1944), a religious conservative, indeed 'un scholastique ferme et inconvertissable', in Loisy's opinion.[62] As founder of the Lega Democratica Nazionale he wished to see Catholics playing a more active role in Italian national politics, thus retrieving the democratic movement from the grip of the anticlericals and nonbelievers. In the first (January 1898) issue of his review *Cultura sociale* he praised 'those who have contributed to the present civil independence and internal political freedom in Italy' and avowed his own determination 'not only to accept but actually to further ends usually held to be beyond the purview of Catholics, and especially of priests: independence from foreign powers, civil liberty, constitutional life, popular franchise and progress in every form of culture and public activity'. Only the Church, the importance of whose existence as a concrete historical institution he consistently stressed, could, he urged, take an effective lead in overcoming social evils. Buonaiuti on the other hand, was entirely opposed to any such enterprise. Not only was he sensitive to the risks which political action by the Church, whose true values, he held, were not of this world, would inevitably run; he was convinced that Catholics should adopt an attitude critical of all temporal causes.[63] For him the 'Modernist' cause turned on intellectual issues only and demanded a radical critique of the kind of orthodoxy which the enthusiasts of the Lega Democratica continued to uphold.

We have already said that the existence in these years of any clearly identifiable Modernist type of thought among German Catholics is questionable. German Catholicism had its own traditions and ethos, less subject than elsewhere to neo-ultramontanist pressures, while the fact that Catholic faculties were to be found alongside Protestant in some German universities resulted in a certain astringency in the cultural air which Catholics who passed through them naturally breathed and which kept them intellectually awake. What is of interest is that, in the circumstances, Catholic intellectuals should have maintained a middle-of-the-road course, avoiding the extremes of either obscurantism or sweeping innovation. But Josef Schnitzer (1858–1939), professor of the history of dogmatics at Munich University, who may fairly be described as a Modernist – he at least had an unconcealed admiration for Loisy – denounced *Pascendi* as a reactionary attack, not on supposed heresy, but on the whole trend of modern philosophy and scholarship,[64] while Thaddäus Engert (1875–1945), of Würzburg, editor of *Das Zwanzigste Jahrhundert*, a 'progressive' periodical, and biblical scholar who, in *Die Urzeit der Bibel* (1907), adopted a critical approach to the history of ancient Hebrew religion, was excommunicated in January 1908. Both now appear as rather isolated figures.

Modernism and Vatican II

The Modernists have been criticized of late for the limitations of their outlook, and except in Italy they were, it has to be admitted, little concerned with the wider issues of the Church and contemporary society, or even with specific matters of ecclesiastical or liturgical reform. Thus by comparison with the range of subjects covered by the Second Vatican Council their interests were predominantly intellectual, though not merely academic. Despite their objections to Protestant liberalism their viewpoint was in large measure determined by the criticism and religious philosophy of the Protestant *avant garde* of their day, especially its unquestioning assumption of secular 'progressivist' values, its positivistic view of history, its restricted conception of the function of biblical criticism and its sympathy with an immanentist metaphysic incompatible, when pressed to a conclusion, with the principles of Christian theism. Yet to be fair we must see the Modernists in relation to what they themselves regarded as the most urgent need of their situation. The outlook of traditional Catholicism, despite certain public pronouncements of Leo XIII, remained mediaeval; of the implications of natural science and historical criticism for the Church's received teaching the *magisterium* seemed to take no account. It is little wonder therefore that not a few Catholics should have looked to contemporary Protestantism for guidance as to how Christian belief and modern knowledge could be reconciled. For Protestant churches, especially in Germany, had been confronted by the problem since the close of the eighteenth century. Indeed it was mainly in Germany and within the ambit of Lutheranism that scientific historical scholarship had arisen and developed. But if behind Catholic Modernism the shadow of Liberal Protestantism was pretty clearly discernible, and if the Modernists were themselves not unaware of this, their anxiety to dissociate themselves from an influence to which they were so far indebted is not difficult to explain since any declared sympathy with neo-Protestantism would have been the gravest of obstacles to the promotion of their opinions among their fellow-Catholics. At the same time there can be no impugning the sincerity of virtually all the Modernists in regarding themselves as loyal Catholics, seeking change only in the higher interest of Catholicism itself. With the religious ethos of Protestantism they had no affinity and the 'liberal' interpretation of Christianity, even in the light of historical scholarship, impressed them as basically false. For they were genuinely convinced that Catholicism alone, once it had freed itself from pre-scientific thought-categories and had accepted the irreversible tendencies of modern philosophy and criticism, could succeed in preserving the values and even the institutions of historic Christianity. The fault of Protestantism, in other words, was its inability to respond to needs of the human spirit, in all their diversity, in the way that Catholicism could do. The humanism of the Catholic tradition, which Protestants were so ready to deplore, was in fact, as Tyrrell always held, its actual strength. Catholicism thus had no reason to fear the appeal to history, since its own roots drew such deep sustenance from the past. But it was necessary to understand history for what it is, and its authentic usage only the most searching and impartial investigation would reveal. It was for this reason that the problem of the relation of historical science to theology was, within the limits of the Modernist debate, the obviously crucial one, and philosophy was an aid only in resolving it.

It is sometimes claimed today that as a consequence of the Second Vatican Council, more than half a century after the suppression of the movement, Modernism has in effect been vindicated and that it is the 'integralists' who in the long term have lost out. There is in this claim a measure of truth. The Modernists raised questions which in their view the Church should answer positively and not merely with warnings that such inquiries reveal a basic lack of faith. But not only was this answer not forthcoming, every effort was made, during the remainder of Pius X's pontificate, to silence the questioners themselves, whoever they might be, with the result that for a generation and more to come serious biblical scholarship in the Roman Catholic Church, though not entirely suppressed as the work of M. J. Lagrange, for example, evidences, was rendered extremely difficult, while theological thinking, dominated as it was by Thomism, moved only, for the most part, on strictly traditional lines. However, although Pius XII's encylical, *Humani generis*, of 1950 was plainly hostile towards certain modern trends in theology, his earlier (1943) letters, *Mystici corporis Christi*, stressing the unity of the Church as the 'Mystical Body of Christ', and *Divino afflante Spiritu*, which, while insisting on the need to follow the literal meaning of Scripture wherever this was possible, nevertheless by recognizing a diversity of forms within the biblical literature went some way towards sanctioning a more critical approach to the exegetical problem. That these latter pronouncements were in fact straws in the wind was made clear when a new ecumenical council summoned in 1962 by Pope John XXIII with the aim of bringing about what he described as an *aggiornamento* within papal Christendom, actually went into session. Issues long considered to have been virtually closed to any radical discussion were reopened. Thus the *Constitution on Divine Revelation*, formulated by Pope Paul VI in November 1965, was indicative of an entirely fresh attempt to deal with the whole problem of revelation – central to the Modernist debate – in a way which the Modernists would undoubtedly have found congenial, even though traditionalist elements remain somewhat awkwardly juxtaposed in it to more progressive tendencies. Again, the Constitution on the Church (*Lumen gentium*, 21 November 1964) seeks to break away from the legalist-institutionalist conceptions hitherto prevailing to one with a more obviously biblical basis – that of (to use its own term) the pilgrim 'People of God'. Once more, this approach was anticipated in Modernist writings, especially Tyrrell's. The Second Vatican Council has been called 'Newman's Council', but perhaps it would be nearer the mark to characterize it as the Council which the Modernists, other than the most extreme, would gladly have welcomed, had they lived to see it. Moreover, after the Council, and quite certainly because of it, access by loyal Catholics today to current scientific, philosophical and critical thought is no longer debarred or discouraged, and indeed a freedom of debate now exists which, in its range and outspokenness on all subjects, moral and social as well as intellectual, is to non-Catholics, in view of the Roman church's record in this respect, still little short of astonishing. Yet although the most fundamental aims of the Modernist movement may have been achieved, it would be a mistake to talk of a revival of Modernism. The ferment of opinion to which that name is historically applied belongs to the past, as likewise does the anti-modernism which in 1907 secured a temporary triumph. Both, that is, need to be seen in historical perspective as phases in a process of continuing change, in which progress and reaction, liberty and restraint, are abiding features.

Notes

1 *Simples réfléxions sur le décret du Saint-Office 'Lamentabili sane exitu' et sur l'encyclique 'Pascendi dominici gregis'* (2nd ed., 1908), pp. 14f.
2 30 September and 1 October 1907.
3 *Simple réfléxions*, pp. 149–52.
4 *Mediaevalism* (1908), p. 106, Cf. *Christianity at the Cross Roads* (1909), p. 3.
5 Lord Acton, *Essays on Freedom and Power*, ed. G. Himmelfarb (1956), p. 244.

6 *Mémoires pour servir à l'histoire religeuse de notre temps*, I (1930), p. 426. Cf. also p. 421. Buonaiuti went so far as to call Newman a 'forerunner, true and characteristic' of Modernism (*Le Modernisme Catholique* [1927], p. 130) – an opinion to be accepted however only with strict qualification.

7 *Mémoires*, II (1931), p. 86.

8 *The Programme of Modernism*, trans. [by G. Tyrrell] with an introduction by A. L. Lilley (London, 1908), p. 16.

9 See *Etudes bibliques* (3rd ed., 1903), pp. 139–69.

10 A full account of it is contained in *Mémoires*, I, pp. 419–77.

11 *Mémoires*, I, p. 421.

12 'Le développement chrétien d'après le Cardinal Newman', in *Revue du Clergé français*, I December 1898, pp. 5–20.

13 As by J. Ratté, *Three Modernists* (1968), p. 131.

14 'La définition de la Religion', *Revue du Clergé français*, I June 1899, pp. 193–209.

15 'La théorie individualiste de la Religion', in *Revue du Clergé français*, I January 1899, pp. 202–15.

16 *Ibid.*, pp. 214f.

17 'L'idée de la Révélation', in *Revue du Clergé français*, I January 1900, pp. 250–71.

18 *Ibid.*, pp. 253f.

19 p. 266.

20 p. 269.

21 'Les preuves et l'economie de la Révélation', in *Revue du Clergé français*, 15 March 1900, pp. 126–53.

22 *Ibid.*, p. 135.

23 *Ibid.*, p. 152.

24 *Mémoires*, I, p. 445.

25 'De même que la critique ne peut ni ne doit définir la portée dogmatique d'un texte, le théologien ne peut ni ne doit en définir la signification historique. Le principe du critique ne lui permet pas de formuler des conclusions de foi. Nul principe du théologien ne l'autorise à formuler des conclusions d'histoire' (*Etudes bibliques*), Préface, p. 36).

26 *Mémoires*, II, p. 133. Cf. p. 156.

27 *L'Evangile et l'Eglise* (5th ed., 1930), p. 89.

28 *Ibid.*, p. 153.

29 *Ibid.*, p. 152.

30 Cf. *Mémoires*, II, p. 179.

31 *L'Evangile et l'Eglise*, pp. 169f.

32 *Ibid.*, p. 205.

33 *Autour d'un petit livre*, p. 195.

34 Poulat, *La Crise moderniste*, p. 172, n. 26.

35 English trans. by A. Dru and I. Trethowan, Maurice Blondel: *The Letter on Apologetics and History and Dogma* (1964), pp. 229 and 232. The original articles are reprinted in *Premiers écrits de Maurice Blondel* (1956).

36 For the whole correspondence see R. Marlé, *Au cœur de la crise moderniste* (1960).

37 1 June 1904, pp. 285–312. The French trans. was made by Henri Bremond.

38 *Hibbert Journal*, October 1925, p. 85. Cf. *Congrès d'histoire du Christianisme*, Jubilé Alfred Loisy (1928), III, p. 227.

39 Tyrrell to Lilley, 14 August 1908. Lilley Papers in the possession of A. R. Vidler. Quoted Vidler, *A Variety of Catholic Modernists* (1970), pp. 117f.

40 *Essays and Addresses in the Philosophy of Religion* (*Second Series*) (1926), p. 109.

41 See the letter (11 July 1921) to Professor R. Guiran of Lausanne (*Selected Letters*, pp. 333f.).

42 Letter to von Hügel, 6 December 1897. See M. D. Petre, *Autobiography and Life of George Tyrrell* (1912), II, p. 45.
43 16 December 1899. Repr. in *Essays on Faith and Immortality*, ed. M. D. Petre (1914), pp. 158–71.
44 November 1899, pp. 461–73. Repr. in *Through Scylla and Charybdis*, pp. 85–105.
45 *Through Scylla and Charybdis*, p. 93.
46 *Ibid.*, p. 104.
47 *Lex Orandi*, p. 55.
48 *The Church and the Future* (ed. 1910), pp. 63f.
49 Letter to von Hügel, 10 February 1907. See *George Tyrrell's Letters*, ed. M. D. Petre (1920), pp. 56ff.
50 *Through Scylla and Charybdis*, pp. 329f.
51 *Ibid.*, p. 10.
52 pp. 40f.
53 p. xxi.
54 G. de Ruggiero, *Modern Philosophy*, trans. A. H. Hannay and R. G. Collingwood (1921), p. 213.
55 *Itinéraire philosophique de Maurice Blondel* (1928), pp. 44f.
56 *Essais de Philosophie religieuse*, pp. xvf.
57 *Le Réalisme chrétien et l'idéalisme grec*, p. 56.
58 *Ibid.*, p. 82.
59 *Dogme et critique*, pp. 25f.
60 Cf. *Civiltà cattolica*, III (1903), pp. 581–3.
61 *Le Modernisme dans l'Eglise* (1929), p. 89.
62 *Mémoires*, II, p. 561.
63 Cf. *Le Modernisme catholique* (French ed., Paris, 1927), p. 98 note.
64 Cf. 'Der Katholische Modernismus', *Zeitschrift für Politik*, V (1913), pp. 1–128. For a bibliography of research bearing on the development of Roman Catholic theology in Germany during the Modernist movement, cf. T. M. Loome, *Liberal Catholicism, Reform Catholicism, Modernism* (1979), pp. 288–90

Bibliographical essay

Of the still unpublished sources for the study of Catholic Modernism the Loisy papers (in 34 volumes) at the Bibliothèque Nationale in Paris (Nouvelles acquisitions françaises, nos. 15634 to 15667) are the most considerable. The main published sources include Loisy's *Choses passées* (Paris, 1913) and his voluminous *Mémoires pour servir à l'histoire religieuse de notre temps* (3 vols., Paris, 1930–1), which are of prime importance, as too are his earlier *Simples réflexions sur le décret du Saint-Office 'Lamentabili sane exitu' et sur l'encyclique 'Pascendi dominici gregis'*, and *Quelques lettres sur les questions actuelles et sur les événements récents* (both dating from 1908); M. D. Petre, *Autobiography and Life of George Tyrrell* (2 vols., London, 1912) and *George Tyrrell's Letters* (London, 1920); B. Holland, *Selected Letters of Baron von Hügel 1896–1924* (with a memoir) (London, 1927): E. Buonaiuti, *Pellegrino di Roma. Le generazione dell'esodo* (1945; new ed. M. Nicoli, Bari, 1964); and of course the various recently published collections of correspondence relating to the movement, notably: R. Marlé, *Au coeur de la crise moderniste. Dossier inédit d'une controverse* (Paris, 1960); *Lettres philosophiques de Maurice Blondel* (Paris, 1961); *Blondel et Laberthonnière, Correspondance philosophique*, ed. C. Tresmontant (1961); *M. Blondel et A. Valensin, Correspondance* (3 vols., Paris, 1957–65); *M. Blondel et J. Wehrlé, Correspondance*, ed. H. de Lubac (2 vols., Paris, 1969); R. Murri, *Carteggio, I, Lettere a Murri, 1889–97* (Rome, 1970); *G. Tyrrell, Lettres à H. Bremond*, ed. A.

Louis-David (1971); *Fonti e documenti, I, dedicato al gruppo radicale romano*, Centro per la storia del modernismo, Istituto di Storia dell Universita di Urbino (1972); *Laberthonnière et ses amis. Dossiers de correspondance, 1905–16*, ed. M. T. Perrin (Paris, 1975).

After years of comparative neglect the Modernist movement has latterly become the subject of a copious literature (although limitations of space prevent allusion here to articles in periodicals – some of them valuable). Among general studies J. Rivière, *Le Modernisme dans l'Eglise. Etude d'histoire contemporaine* (Paris, 1929) remains the most comprehensive. The same author's entry under 'Modernisme' in the *Dictionnaire de théologie catholique*, X (pt. 2, 1935), coll. 2009–47, is also worth consulting. G. Daly, *Transcendence and Immanence: a Study in Catholic Modernism and Integralism* (Oxford, 1980) is one of the best theological discussions of the movement yet to have appeared. Others include E. Poulat, *Histoire, dogme et critique dans la crise moderniste* (Paris, 1962), an indispensable work of reference; A. R. Vidler, *The Modernist Movement in the Roman Church* (Cambridge, 1934) – still a good introductory summary – and *Varieties of Catholic Modernists* (Cambridge, 1970); B. M. G. Reardon, *Roman Catholic Modernism* (London, 1970), which supplies extracts from the principal Modernist writers; M. Ranchetti, *Cultura e riforma religiosa nella storia del modernismo* (Turin, 1963; E. T., London, 1969) – not very satisfactory but of some value for an understanding of the Italian aspect of the movement; and J. Ratté, *Three Modernists: Alfred Loisy, George Tyrrell and William L. Sullivan* (London, 1968). Of the older surveys of the movement – by adherents or detached sympathisers – the following are of permanent interest: A. L. Lilley, *Modernism: a Record and a Review* (London, 1908); P. Sabatier, *Modernism* (Jowett Lectures) (London, 1908); A. Houtin, *Histoire du modernisme catholique* (Paris, 1912) – not 'history' but 'reportage documenté' according to Loisy; J. Kübel, *Geschichte der katholischen Modernismus* (1909); J. Schnitzer, 'Der katholische Modernismus', in *Zeitschrift für Politik*, V (1912), pp. 1–218 (a separate issue, with some modifications, appeared in the same year); M. D. Petre, *Modernism: its Failure and its Fruits* (1918); G. Gentile, *Il Modernismo e i rapporti tra religione e filosofia* (2nd ed., Bari, 1921); and E. Buonaiuti, *Le Modernisme catholique* (French ed., Paris, 1927; Italian ed., *Il Modernismo*, Bari, 1943).

On individual authors the following should be consulted: (Loisy) Sylvain Leblanc [H. Bremond], *Un clerc qui n'a pas trahi* (Paris, 1931); M. J. Lagrange, *M. Loisy et le modernisme* (Paris, 1932); J. Guitton, 'La pensée de M. Loisy', in *Lettres sur la Pensée moderne et le Catholicisme* (Aix, 1936), pp. 63–121; A. Omodeo, *Alfred Loisy: Storico delle religioni* (Bari, 1936); M. D. Petre, *Alfred Loisy: his Religious Significance* (Cambridge, 1944); F. Heiler, *Der Vater der katholischen Modernismus: Alfred Loisy* (1947); A. Houtin and F. Sartiaux (ed. E. Poulat), *Alfred Loisy, sa vie, son oeuvre* (Paris, 1960); R. de Boyer de Sainte Suzanne, *Alfred Loisy entre la foi et l'incroyance* (Paris, 1968); J. Hulshof, *Wahrheit und Geschichte: Alfred Loisy zwischen Tradition und Kritik* (1973); (Tyrrell) J. L. May, *Father Tyrrell and the Modernist Movement* (London, 1932); M. D. Petre, *Von Hügel and Tyrrell: the Story of a Friendship* (London, 1937); A. Loisy, *George Tyrrell et Henri Bremond* (Paris, 1936); J. J. Stam, *George Tyrrell, 1861–1909* (Utrecht, 1938); R. Chapman, 'The Thought of George Tyrrell', in *Essays and Poems presented to Lord David Cecil* (London, 1970), pp. 140–68; E. Leonard, *George Tyrrell and the Catholic Tradition* (London, 1982); G. Schultenover, *George Tyrrell: in Search of Catholicism* (Shepherdstown, 1981); (Von Hügel) M. de la Bedoyere, *The Life of Baron von Hügel* (London, 1951); M. Nédoncelle, *La Pensée religieuse de Friedrich von Hügel* (1935); J. J. Heaney, *The Modernist Crisis: von Hügel* (London, 1969); L. F. Barmann, *Baron von Hügel and the Modernist Crisis in England* (Cambridge, 1972); P. Neuner, *Religiöse Erfahrung und geschichtliche Offenbarung: Friedrich von Hügels Grundlegung der Theologie* (Munich, Paderborn and Vienna, 1977); J. J. Kelly, *Baron Friedrich von Hügel's Philosophy of Religion* (Louvain, 1983); (Blondel) B. Romeyer, *La Philosophie religieuse de Maurice Blondel* (Paris, 1943); H. Dumery, *Blondel et la Religion* (Paris, 1954); H. Bouillard, *Blondel et le Christianisme* (Paris, 1961); A. Dru and I. Trethowan, *Maurice Blondel: 'The Letter on Apologetics' and 'History and Dogma'* (London, 1964) – the best introduction in

English, (Laberthonnière) M. d'Hendecourt, *Essai sur Philosophie du Père Laberthonnière* (Paris, 1947); D. Beillevert, *Laberthonnière l'homme et l'oeuvre* (1972). (The Italians) T. Gallarati-Scotti, *La Vita di Antonio Fogazzaro* (Milan, 1920 [E. T. 1922]; new and corrected ed. 1934); (ed.), *Fogazzaro: Lettere Scelte* (Milan, 1940); V. Vinay, *Ernesto Buonaiuti e l'Italia religiosa del suo tempo* (1956); C. Nelson and N. Pittenger (eds.), *Pilgrim of Rome* (London, 1969), which contains a selection of translated extracts from Buonaiuti's writings; F. Turvasi, *Giovanni Genocchi e la controversia modernista* (Rome, 1974); G. A. Gambaro (ed.), *G. Semeria: saggi clandestini – storico-filosofici* (2 vols., 1967); P. Scoppola, *Crisi modernista e rinnovamento cattolico in Italia* (Bologna, 1961) – which contains a hitherto unpublished article ['Petite consultation sur les difficultés concernant Dieu'] by F. von Hügel.

On the background of Modernism the following will be found useful: R. Aubert, *Le Pontificat de Pie IX 1846–1878 (Histoire de l'Eglise*, ed. Fliche et Martin, vol. 21) (Paris, 1952). E. Lecanuet, *La vie de l'Eglise sous Leon XIII* (Paris, 1930); *Les Signes avant-coureurs de la Séparation: les dernières années de Léon XIII et l'avènement du Pie X, 1894–1910* (Paris, 1930); A. Dansette, *Histoire religieuse de la France contemporaine* (2nd, rev. ed., 2 vols., Paris, 1952; E. T., London, 2 vols., 1961); B. M. G. Reardon, *Liberalism and Tradition: Aspects of Catholic Thought in Nineteenth-Century France* (Cambridge, 1975); G. Fonsegrive, *L'Evolution des idées dans la France contemporaine* (Paris, 1920); J. F. Altholz, *The Liberal Catholic Movement in England: The Rambler and its Contributors* (Cambridge, 1962); M. Ward, *The Wilfrid Wards and the Transition* (2 vols., London, 1934–8); A. Fawkes, *Studies in Modernism* (London, 1913).

Important for the method of Modernist research is: *Liberal Catholicism, Reform Catholicism, Modernism: a Contribution to a New Orientation in Modernist Research*, by T. M. Loome (Mainz, 1979).

6

Russian Religious Thought

GEORGE L. KLINE

1. Introduction

Two of the seven religious thinkers considered in this chapter – Dostoevsky and Tolstoy – are known primarily as novelists. In this they are emblematic of a more general phenomenon of Russian culture over the past two centuries. On the one hand, many of the major Russian literary figures have been preoccupied with religious questions; on the other hand, a number of the major Russian religious thinkers have been gifted, if minor, poets or novelists.

This fusion of the literary and speculative appears to be related to the distinctively non-academic character of Russian religious thought. Most of the thinkers discussed in the other chapters of the present work – from Kant, Schelling, and Hegel, to Royce, James, and Dilthey – were lifelong university professors. There were, to be sure, in nineteenth-century Russian universities and divinity schools professors who taught theology and philosophy of religion. But most of them were compliant followers of one or another West European, Patristic, or Russian master rather than original thinkers. Of the seven religious thinkers here discussed, only Solovyov was a university professor, and that only briefly. In Russia the powerful and original religious thinkers all stood – at least until the end of the nineteenth century – outside the academy.

Compared to their Western European counterparts, Russian thinkers tended to encounter more pervasive resistance and even repression from political and ecclesiastical authorities, based on charges of heterodoxy or the 'subversion of faith and morals'. But such harrassment was not unknown in the West, as we are reminded by the case of Fichte. Despite their difficulties with the authorities, none of the nineteenth-century religious thinkers here discussed went into exile. The contrast with the major Russian religious thinkers of the twentieth century, *all* of whom went into exile after 1917, is striking.

As a group, Russian religious thinkers also tended to take more extreme theoretical positions than most of their Western European counterparts. But there is a conspicuous Western exception – Nietzsche, that 'Russian among the West Europeans'[1] – whose positions, on religion as on other matters, were no less extreme than those of his Russian contemporaries.

Most Russian religious thinkers placed special emphasis upon a cluster of related positive values, values which were broadly cultural as well as more narrowly religious: unity, universality, 'conciliarity' (*sobornost'*),[2] and wholeness (*tsel'nost'*). They harshly criticized the negative counterparts of these values – dividedness, parochialism, self-centredness, and fragmentation. The Slavophiles and neo-Slavophiles saw these disvalues as peculiarly 'Western'. The more generous and judicious Russian thinkers, such as Solovyov, recognized that the positive values too had Western roots: that the religious unity of developing cultures had been stressed by the French Traditionalists, and the unity and wholeness of persons and communities by the German Romanticists. Thus, Russian religious thinkers, here too, mainly developed a series of more or less original variations on Western themes. Both the pronounced religious and ethical impersonalism of Tolstoy, Fyodorov, and (for most of his career) Solovyov and the intense 'personalism' of Dostoevsky and, in his different way, Leontyev, also had Western European roots.

The institutional, dogmatic, and liturgical side of Russian Orthodoxy was sharply criticized by Tolstoy, though defended (with qualifications) by the Slavophiles, Dostoevsky, Leontyev, and – for a period during the 1880s, though not during the 1890s – by Solovyov. The modernizing trends in Western European Christianity were sharply repudiated by Leontyev, who detected a Christian 'humanism' (rightly) in Tolstoy and (wrongly) in Dostoevsky. Like Nietzsche, Leontyev rejected the alliance of Christianity with egalitarianism, democracy, and 'social progress', but, unlike Nietzsche, he was concerned to extricate 'true Christianity' from this corrupting alliance. In the 1890s Solovyov, in contrast, was quite sympathetic to the 'Christian socialism' which he encountered among the French Roman Catholic clergy in Paris.

Most of the Russian thinkers here considered – the only, and partial, exception being Solovyov – exhibit a strong intellectual and emotional resistance to certain aspects of modernity in general and to the modernizing trends of religious thought in particular. But again, this is not an exclusively Russian phenomenon. Some of the seminal thinkers of nineteenth-century

Europe – Kierkegaard, Schopenhauer, Marx, Nietzsche – also display such resistance. And even those twentieth-century thinkers who follow Hegel rather than Nietzsche, Marx, or Heidegger, accepting modernity as 'inevitable', admit that it is a mixed blessing.

2. *The Slavophiles: Alexis Stepanovich Khomyakov (1804–1860); Ivan Vasilyevich Kireyevsky (1806–1856)*

The philosophy of history and 'theology of culture' of the Slavophiles – to use the label first attached to Khomyakov and Kireyevsky (together with Konstantin Aksakov and Yuri Samarin) by their intellectual adversaries, the 'Westernizers', but eventually accepted as their own – was, in one respect, a critical response to a charge which had been levelled by Russia's first philosopher of history, Peter Yakovlevich Chaadayev (1794–1856). At the same time, ironically, the Slavophile position was a further development of a claim made only a few years later by the same thinker.

The charge which the Slavophiles disputed was a blunt one: that the unity, universality, and conciliarity of Christendom had been violated by the *Eastern* Church, beginning with the action of Photius, Patriarch of Constantinople (820–891), in excommunicating Pope Nicholas I. The Eastern Church had broken away from the Western Church and had withdrawn into a growing cultural and religious self-isolation.[3] The Slavophiles flatly denied this, insisting instead that the unity of Christianity was violated by the *Western* Church. As Kireyevsky put it, Rome, 'having the truth and being a living part of the living Church, deliberately broke away from it'.[4] According to Khomyakov, the schism was due not so much to doctrinal differences as to the moral offence of 'fratricide' perpetrated by the Western Church upon its Eastern brother – through the unilateral enunciation of the dogma of the *filioque.*

A quite different claim, one which the Slavophiles hastened to develop and make central to their religious position, was put forward belatedly by Chaadayev in his *Apology of a Madman* (1837)[5] – namely, that Russia might after all have a 'special mission', might indeed be destined to solve a majority of the social problems and to 'perfect the greater part of the ideas' which have had their origin in older societies.[6]

Although he had been forbidden to publish since 1836, Chaadayev was on hand to rebuke his perverse intellectual 'offspring'. In a private letter written in French to Schelling on 20 May 1842, some two decades after their momentous meeting in Karlsbad, he complained that, in contrast to the Christian universalism of Schelling's own Philosophy of Revelation, Hegelianism was being used by Russian nationalists to create 'a retrospective utopia', involving an 'arrogant apotheosis of the Russian people'. This, he felt, threatened to turn Russia away from 'that religious humility, . . . that modesty of spirit which has always been the distinctive trait of our national character'.[7]

Both Kireyevsky and Khomyakov were immersed in German philosophy, the thought of Schlegel as well as that of Schelling. Although their philosophy of history was broadly 'Hegelian', they were critical of Hegel on specific points, e.g. Khomyakov laid at Hegel's philosophical door a portion of the blame for the emergence of a materialist ontology among the Left Hegelians.

Like Chaadayev, they considered themselves 'Christian philosophers'. But they were quite insensitive to the tension in their own thought between Christian universalism, on the one hand, and national-cultural particularism (Russia's 'special path' in world history), on the other. Solovyov, in his anti-Slavophile polemics of the 1880s, emphasized this tension, which he regarded as fatal to the theoretical coherence of the Slavophile position.

As philosophers of Christian history, the Slavophiles were prepared to assert a dialectical relation among the confessions. Roman Catholicism represents unity without freedom; Protestantism – freedom without unity; Russian Orthodoxy – freedom in unity and unity in freedom. This dialectic is explicitly developed by Khomyakov, but its roots are already present in Kireyevsky. And both of the Russian thinkers had Western, particularly German, predecessors, e.g. the Catholic theologian Johann A. Möhler, who, in a work that they both knew, had contrasted *die Vielheit ohne Einheit* ('the plurality without unity') of Protestantism with *die Einheit in der Vielheit* ('the unity in plurality') of Roman Catholicism.[8]

The Slavophiles took over and polemically sharpened Hegel's distinction between understanding (*Verstand = rassudok*) and reason (*Vernunft = razum*): they considered the former to be 'dry, abstract, superficial, analytical, merely logical' and the latter to be 'deep, intuitive, and comprehensive'. The disease of Western 'rationalism' (an aspect of what we might call 'modernity') with its superficiality, fragmentation, and 'formalism', springs from *rassudok* – or, expressed even more abstractly, from *rassudochnost'*.[9] It is this kind of abstract rationality which is isolated from, and opposed to, faith. Kireyevsky even maintained that the principles of Schelling's final system could be grafted onto the 'basic principles of ancient Russian culture' to produce a philosophy which could subject the 'divided culture of the West to the integrated consciousness of believing reason'.[10]

The Slavophiles emphasized that 'faith' or 'believing reason'

(*veruyushchii razum*) is something distinct from assent to dogmas or propositions; it is a kind of integral and integrating knowledge, which is prior to
abstract *rassudok*, and from which the latter is abstracted. What the
Slavophiles, especially Kireyevsky, added to Chaadayev's 'theology of
culture' was a philosophical anthropology, in particular, the linked doctrines
of 'integral knowledge' and the 'wholeness of the spirit'.[11] Kireyevsky
insisted that faith involves the whole person, not just a narrowly 'religious'
aspect of the person.

The Slavophile theory of knowledge has been called an 'ontologism',
namely, the 'assertion that knowledge is a part and function of our "existential" penetration of reality not by thought alone but with our whole being'.[12]
These ideas, which have obvious roots in German Romanticism, were
consolidated by Kireyevsky under the influence of the Greek Fathers of the
Church, especially St Maximus the Confessor. Wholeness of the spirit,
Kireyevsky claimed, had been lost in the Fall, and its recovery was being
impeded by the triumphant *rassudochnost'* of Western Christianity.

Wholeness of the spirit is not something given, but something to be
achieved, an active integration, into a single living whole, of the separate
faculties or powers of the spirit: aesthetic sensitivity, moral intuition,
'enraptured feeling', the 'love of [one's] heart', and also abstract rationality.
In isolation, these elements are partial, incomplete, and mutually
obstructive.[13]

The Slavophile celebration of the power of 'integral knowledge' and the
'wholeness of the spirit' to overcome the superficiality and fragmentedness
of contemporary Western culture, a celebration which is always Romantic,
sometimes, unfortunately, verges on the emptily rhetorical.

It was Khomyakov who provided the fullest elaboration of the related
concept of *sobornost'* ('conciliarity' or 'organic religious togetherness').[14] But
the historical and 'cosmic' dimensions of the concept are nicely set out by
Kireyevsky: 'The sum total of all Christians of all ages, past and present,
comprises one indivisible, eternal living assembly of the faithful, held
together just as much by the unity of consciousness as through the communion of prayer.'[15]

In the specific historical conditions of nineteenth-century Russia,
sobornost' is related to the *obshschinnost'* ('communality') of the peasant
village-commune (*obshchina*). The latter is viewed as the socio-economic,
psychological, and spiritual foundation upon which Russia's 'special path' in
world history will be firmly established. The Slavophiles tended to idealize
the village-commune, but they were openly critical of the Russian Orthodox
Church as an institution which had been 'bureaucratized' and 'Westernized'

by Peter the Great, especially through the St Petersburg institution of the Holy Synod, replacing the Moscow Patriarchate. Such criticisms brought them into occasional sharp conflict with the Tsarist authorities. In fact, although they were able to subscribe to the official slogan '*Pravoslavie, samoderzhavie, narodnost*' ('Orthodoxy, Autocracy, Nationality'), their allegiance was to the purified or idealized essence of each of these elements, not to their current factual existence, as government spokesmen would have it.

A related aspect of Slavophile thought proved, however, quite assimilable to the official xenophobia and chauvinism. According to the Slavophiles, *sobornost'* and 'wholeness of the spirit', once attained, will make it possible for Russian Orthodox believers to understand Roman Catholics and Protestants, but not, of course, *vice versa*. Claims such as this have a ring of condescension, which, when combined with the xenophobia that often tinges Slavophile rhetoric, sometimes produces self-righteous denunciations of the 'distorting influences' of what, in rather sinister terms, Kireyevsky calls an 'alien culture' or 'alien philosophy'.[16] As we shall see, Dostoevsky too sometimes permitted himself such xenophobic Slavophile rhetoric. But the central and lasting Slavophile influence upon Dostoevsky's religious thought is to be found in Khomyakov's doctrine of *sobornost'*.

3. Fyodor Mikhailovich Dostoevsky (1821–1881)

Dostoevsky is unique among the authors discussed in this chapter in that he wrote no books or essays devoted strictly to either philosophical theology or philosophy of religion. Even Tolstoy, whose towering reputation, like Dostoevsky's, rests primarily on his major novels, also published, beginning in 1879, a series of moral-religious tracts as well as his own severely censored version of the New Testament.

While Dostoevsky wrote no treatises, he did compose a number of vivid and impassioned journalistic pieces, which he collected in *The Diary of a Writer* (1873–81). Many of them deal with ecclesiastical, theological, and even philosophical questions. Although Dostoevsky had no formal training in philosophy, he was, during the last decade of his life, in close and continuous contact with two Russian thinkers who did have such training: Nikolai Strakhov (1828–96) and Vladimir Solovyov. He seems to have learned a good deal of philosophy from both of them.[17] And his great novels, in particular *The Brothers Karamazov*, probe deeply into the questions of human freedom, responsibility, guilt, crime, saintliness, community, solitude, immortality, and theodicy.

These novels have been described as 'polyphonic',[18] meaning that they

184

contain a variety of opposed voices, no one of which can be taken as unambiguously representing Dostoevsky's own position at the time of the given work. In Bakhtin's formulation, the 'word' (*slovo*) of a Dostoevskian character lies alongside the 'word' of the author. Ivan Karamazov is often seen – I think rightly – as expressing, with passion, many of the convictions which Dostoevsky had held, with equal passion, thirty years earlier, at a time when, under the powerful influence of the radical critic V. G. Belinsky (1811–48) he had embraced the doctrine and rhetoric of humanitarian socialism. Ivan's doubts are in some sense Dostoevsky's own doubts, present or past. Consider Dostoevsky's own confession, in his notebooks for 'The Legend of the Grand Inquisitor', that his belief in Christ, his 'hosanna [had] passed through a great furnace of doubts'.

To a degree rare among novelists, Dostoevsky gives his characters their heads, permitting them to repudiate or caricature some of his own most cherished convictions. Examples include Myshkin in *The Idiot* (1869) indulging in an intemperate anti-Catholic tirade which contains some of the same polemical points that Dostoevsky was to make later in *The Diary of a Writer*; and Shatov in *The Possessed* (1871) defending a caricature of the Russian religious nationalism which Dostoevsky would embrace toward the end of his life.

In the words of one commentator, Dostoevsky 'created characters, and the characters evolved ideas, often to his own discomfort'; he polyphonically elaborated ideas foreign to him 'as if they were his own, as indeed, artistically speaking, they are'.[19]

Although it is true that Dostoevsky is most – and triumphantly – successful in portraying rebels, seekers, doubters, it would be going too far to conclude (with Shestov) that, in drawing his 'wholly positive' characters, those who have moved beyond doubt and rebellion, are reconciled with the world, and at peace with themselves – Sonya in *Crime and Punishment*, Myshkin, *starets* Zosima in *The Brothers Karamazov* – Dostoevsky lapsed into 'offensive banality'.[20]

Once Dostoevsky had shaken off the spell of Belinsky's secular humanism and utopian socialism, he began to forge a position close to that of the Slavophiles on the linked questions of rationalism and individualism. The 1860s was a period of secularization of both thought and institutions in Russia; the dominant winds of doctrine were anti-clerical, rationalistic, utilitarian, positivistic. Atheism, in Dostoevsky's words, was becoming a kind of religion.

Following his first visit to Western Europe in 1862, Dostoevsky conclud-ed that Protestantism was sliding toward atheism by a process of fragmentation; Roman Catholicism was sliding in the same direction, but by a different route: through socialism. But his more immediate concern was to expose and combat what he saw as the self-enclosed *laissez-faire* individualism which was dominating Western Europe, bringing with it a fateful atomization of spirit, self, and society. To the bourgeois individualist's complacent rhetorical question: 'But am I my brother's keeper?' Dostoevsky answers, out of the fulness of a non-rational, indeed mystical compassion: Every human being is implicated in the sin of existence, which is a mutual aggression: 'All are guilty for all.' To put the point more generally, social ideals are grounded in moral ideals, which in turn gain their vitality from contact with a 'mystical' realm, with 'other worlds'.[21]

The selfish and self-righteous individualism to which Dostoevsky objects is, in his Slavophile view, a product of the dominance of *rassudok* – calculating, analytical rationality. He opposes to such rationalism and individualism the *sobornost'* celebrated by Khomyakov: a merging of individual selves into the 'total charity of the religious collective'; the 'spontaneous togetherness of a congregation at the moment of worship carried over to everyday life'.[22] It was Dostoevsky's conviction, in the words of another commentator, that 'the roots of human interrelationship extend into metaphysical depths; the violation of this organic collectivity of souls is reflected in social upheavals and political catastrophes'.[23]

Dostoevsky's final position was that individual freedom and conciliar community can be harmonized only where each individual self sacrificially transcends its own selfhood and self-interest in the voluntary and loving spiritual togetherness of *sobornost'*. That this might result in a submerging, rather than a harmonizing of selves, was a danger that Dostoevsky sometimes recognized, especially when he was placing chief stress, as in the *Notes from the Underground*, Pt. I (1864) upon the cherished freedom, even arbitrariness, of the existing individual who wants above all things to prove that he is a 'human being and not an organ-stop', not a cog in some deterministic cosmic machine. Of course, the *Notes from the Underground* is a highly polemical work; its extreme, even hysterical defence of free will and arbitrariness is directed against the then dominant, Western-inspired 'rational egoism' determinism, and utilitarianism of N. G. Chernyshevsky (1828–89) and his Russian followers.

The polemic continues in *Crime and Punishment* (1866), where it is directed primarily against utilitarian ethics, striking at two of the most vulnerable aspects of that doctrine: its exclusive stress on consequences as determining the moral quality of an action, and its requirement of 'omniscience', i.e. of impossibly detailed and long-range predictions of the future

consequences of present actions. The whole book is, in a sense, a refutation of
the utilitarian claim that any action – even murder – can be justified so long
as its consequences will bring more pleasure and prevent more pain than the
alternatives. But the murder of the old money-lender which is 'justifiable',
even 'obligatory' in such terms, immediately loses its utilitarian justification
when an unanticipated consequence turns out to be the necessity of murder-
ing the innocent Lizaveta merely because she discovers Raskolnikov *in
flagrante delicto*.

There is, of course, a second motivation, the 'Napoleonic' or 'overman'
motive. Raskolnikov attempts to prove to himself that he is an 'extraordinary man', not bound by the rules which hold for 'ordinary men'. This is
incompatible with the first, 'utilitarian' motive, according to which
Raskolnikov can claim to be moved by love and concern for his suffering
mother and sister. On the first account, as Mochulsky puts it, the murderer is
'a humanist and a Christian who acknowledges his sin and redeems it by
repentance and suffering'; but, on the second account – like Svidrigailov – he
is 'an atheist, a demonic personality, not bound by conscience, who is
incapable of repentance and rebirth'. And the first kind of motivation turns
out in the end to be only a mask, beneath which lies contempt for human life
and a kind of despotism.[24]

Dostoevsky's moral is that extreme individualism, whether of the prudential utilitarian variety or the more frenetic variety assumed by the would-be
Napoleonic overman is, in simple human terms, a social as well as spiritual
disaster.

No less disastrous is the project of the 'man-god', to which those
'possessed' by the spirit of revolutionary destruction are committed. They
are ready to instrumentalize human beings, to march to the 'Crystal Palace'
of the radiant future through a sea of blood. As Gibson remarks: 'Better the
surly rumbling from underground than the flat finality of the Crystal Palace.
Christ might emerge from these blasphemous catacombs [viz. of the
underground man]; there is no place for him among perfected robots.'[25] A
purely secular 'love for man', as Dostoevsky insists, will degenerate into
tyranny; as Kirillov (in *The Possessed*) expresses it: 'Beginning with unlimited freedom, I end up with unlimited despotism.'[26]

Yet two points must be made: first, Dostoevsky could be quite
undiscerning, even obtuse, in matters of politics and the 'middle distance'.
Like the Slavophiles before him, he refused to see any positive value in legal
or constitutional safeguards of individual freedom. The fact that his prejudice against legality and constitutionality was shared by Russian intellectuals of various political persuasions does not, in my judgment, justify

Dostoevsky's position. Second, although, as we shall see (pp. 193, 196 below) Leontyev was sharply critical of Dostoevsky, as well as of Tolstoy, for espousing a 'rose-coloured' humanitarian Christianity, his critique was much more directly applicable to Tolstoy's position than to Dostoevsky's. Nevertheless, the grain of truth in Leontyev's charge is that Dostoevsky *did* place central emphasis on the 'active (sacrificial) love of *man*' rather than – as Leontyev would have preferred – the '*fear* of God', and that, partly as a result of this emphasis, the conception of the 'Kingdom of God on earth' held a lingering fascination for him.

In the major novels, beginning with *The Idiot*, the figure of Christ is at or near the centre; but this is no *pantokrator*, rather a 'human' and suffering Christ, exemplar of sacrificial love. Although, in his later years (and in sharp contrast to Tolstoy) Dostoevsky was 'ardently persuaded of Christ's divinity . . . , that divinity moved his soul and solicited his intelligence most forcefully through its human aspect'. Dostoevsky's conception of Christ 'originates in the Augustinian injunction: "*per hominem Christum tendis ad Deum Christum*"'.[27]

In an often-quoted early letter, written shortly after his release from penal servitude in 1854, Dostoevsky declared 'if the truth really did exclude Christ, I should stay with Christ rather than with the truth' – perhaps a conscious reversal of the Aristotelian dictum that 'truth is dearer even than friends'.[28] But, as Mochulsky makes clear, Dostoevsky's religious convictions at that period were still those of a 'Christian humanist'; his love of Christ was of Christ the man – the 'most beautiful, "sympathetic", and perfect of men'.[29]

But the figure of Christ which stands at the silent centre of the 'Legend of the Grand Inquisitor' is exemplary of the tragic reality of human freedom. Indeed, *The Brothers Karamazov* raises, with unsurpassed dramatic power, the linked questions of tragedy and theodicy. As one commentator puts it: Dostoevsky's novels confront us 'at each moment . . . with tragedy raised . . . to a higher power'.[30] We know that the ghastly stories of the abuse of small children which Ivan recounts to his horrified brother Alyosha were in fact taken from Dostoevsky's scrapbook of newspaper clippings for the year 1876. Ivan draws from this catalogue of horrors the conclusion that no appeal to *future* happiness can possibly justify such overwhelming *present* suffering. Those who offer a 'cheap theodicy' are in fact claiming that the future bliss of all human beings, the future reign of harmony and peace, will retroactively 'justify' or 'redeem' present suffering and violence, including violence directed against innocent children. As Steiner reminds us, it is Dostoevsky's conviction that 'to torture or violate a child is to desecrate in man the image of

God where that image is most luminous'.[31] This is a corollary of his belief that 'love of children, joy in them and close and direct contact with them, is a sign of a special state of Grace. Myshkin and Alyosha have it in common.'[32]

Once the innocent have suffered, it is 'too late in time', 'too late in history' for anything that may occur in the future to justify or redeem that suffering. In that sense, theodicy is impossible, since 'these children *have already been tortured*'.[33] The fact of metaphysical 'demonic' evil – whether perpetrated by political terrorists or by the tormenters of small children – 'wrecks the cheap theodicies (Ivan Karamazov has rendered them unavailable for all time)'.[34]

Dostoevsky's 'natural alignment' is with Kierkegaard, who 'dismissed in the name of Christianity the "world-historical" theodicy which Belinsky had attacked in the name of atheism'.[35] The Belinsky–Kierkegaard–Dostoevsky critique, although doubtfully applicable to Hegel, is clearly and directly applicable to Marx and to all other revolutionary socialists who attempt to justify present evil and suffering, a significant fraction of which they set out deliberately to cause, by an appeal to the remote 'world-historical' future. A similar point had been made as early as 1903 by Shestov, who asked rhetorically how *future* happiness could atone for the unhappiness experienced in the *past* and the *present*. How could the fate of a person who is insulted and humiliated in the *nineteenth* century be 'redeemed' by the fact – if it should turn out to be a fact – that in the *twenty-first* century every last insult and humiliation will have been banished from human life? Shestov adds: 'Dostoevsky does not want universal happiness in the future, he does not want the future to vindicate the present.'[36] Shestov's point is of the first importance; but he might have expressed it more precisely by saying that for Dostoevsky it is *impossible* for any future event or condition to justify present suffering and evil.

Dostoevsky rejected the Augustinian argument that allegedly 'innocent' children are *potential* evil-doers, unable for the moment, though more than willing, to hurt others. This argument will not do, since (in Ivan's example) the eight-year-old peasant boy who is hunted to death by the landowner's dogs as punishment for having thrown a pebble at one of them, slightly injuring its paw, will *never* grow up, will *never* be in a position to actualize his presumed potentiality for evil.

Thus Ivan, who does not deny the Christian morality of active sacrificial love, denies God or, rather, 'turns back his ticket' to God's world, refusing categorically to accept a world in which such horrors and atrocities can take place.

For Dostoevsky the impossibility of a rationalist theodicy means, on the one hand, that reason is not the final court of appeal in human affairs and, on the other, that human existence is marked in its depths by tragedy, an inescapable concomitant of radical freedom. Dostoevsky's censors and critics were quick to point out that his 'official theodicy – the metaphysics of freedom argued by Alyosha Karamazov – failed to give an adequate [theoretical] answer to Ivan Karamazov's fierce recital of the horrors and evils of the world'.[37] But Aloysha's response to the suffering of innocent children is not theoretical; it is intensely practical. He engages himself with a boys' club so that at least *its* members – *these* children – will not be subject to such horrors as Ivan had described.[38]

Dostoevsky's philosophical position does not, like that of his younger friend Solovyov, involve a 'Hegelian' reconcilation with reality. Rather, Dostoevsky teaches us to *endure* a reality which is tragic because irrational, arbitrary, and permeated at its root by freedom. Dostoevsky's final acceptance of suffering, violence, and humiliation is a *tragic* acceptance, neither Stoic nor self-deceiving. In penal servitude, the experience of which helped to bring him back to the 'faith of his fathers', Dostoevsky learned, from the example of his fellow-prisoners, who faced their suffering with quiet courage, that what matters is the ability to 'accept reality with all its horrors' rather than dreaming of a radiant future when 'no one will offend anyone else' – since no conceivable social change can 'banish tragedy from [human] life'.[39]

As for the 'curative' or 'salvific' value of suffering, of which Dostoevsky sometimes spoke, it is important to bear in mind that in *The Brothers Karamazov*, it is *Dimitri* Karamazov, 'behaving strictly in character', who makes this claim. His statement is not intended as a 'metaphysical observation, it is not accepted by Alyosha, nor by the Dostoevsky of 1880'.[40]

The powerful critique of rational theocracy which Dostoevsky puts forward in the 'Legend' raises disturbing questions – quite contrary to his own intentions – about theocracies of every kind, including the Russian Orthodox conciliar community which he championed. Can there be, as Solovyov for a time believed, a 'free' theocracy, combining the moral and spiritual virtues of *sobornost'* with a high spiritual calling? The 'Legend' can be read as casting serious doubt on such a possibility.

Dostoevsky himself, it seems clear, intended the 'Legend' as a direct critique of what he was among the first to recognize as the tyrannical nature of revolutionary socialism, but also as an indirect critique of what he saw as the paternalism inherent in Roman Catholicism. The 'Legend' contains at least two layers of symbolic meaning: 'On the surface lies an exposure of the "Antichrist" principle of the Roman Church and contemporary socialism.' But beneath this 'unjust and unChristian condemnation of Catholicism' there is a 'most profound investigation of the metaphysical meaning of *freedom* and *power*'.[41] Indeed, Mochulsky argues convincingly that there is nothing in world literature to rival the extraordinary and striking force with which Dostoevsky presents Christianity as the 'religion of spiritual freedom'.[42]

One's astonishment at the profundity and universality of Dostoevsky's philosophy of tragic freedom is matched by an equal astonishment at the shallowness and parochialism of the expansionist Pan-Slavism which marks all too many of his journalistic writings of the 1870s. Dostoevsky sought to combine his particularistic nationalism with a kind of universalism through the claim that the uniquely God-bearing Russian people can alone bring together and reconcile the quarrelling nations of Europe. Ivanov puts the point diplomatically when he says that Dostoevsky 'does not draw a sharp enough distinction between the concepts of Nation [or "People" = *narod*] and of the Church . . . despite all his efforts to remain faithful to the "ecumenical" principle, he falls into the error of ecclesiastical nationalism'.[43]

By identifying Russia's special task in world history as the spiritual unification and harmonizing of *all* peoples, Dostoevsky felt that he could avoid the necessity of choosing between the Russian people and mankind as a whole. The Russian people has a special value in the cosmic scheme of things because the path to universally human peace and reconciliation runs through Russian soil.

Shestov – who greatly admired the Dostoevsky of *Notes from the Underground* as a defender of irrational 'existential' freedom and critic of rationalistic system-builders, but deeply distrusted Dostoevsky the Pan-Slavist – remarked drily (in 1903) that, after calling fervently, in his Pushkin Day Address of 1880, for the 'uniting of all parties', Dostoevsky was in fact unable to tolerate 'even the first objection' raised by Russian critics of his project of universal reconcilation and harmony.[44]

Moreover, there was a touch of the xenophobia which we have seen in the Slavophiles (p. 184 above) in Dostoevsky's attitude toward the 'alien' ideologies of Western Europe – secularism, atheism, socialism, utilitarianism, individualism – symptoms, as he would have it, of a one-sided, abstract, and calculating rationality. And there was more than a touch of 'Christian imperialism'[45] in Dostoevsky's aggressive insistence that '*Sooner or later, Constantinople must be ours* . . .'[46] A reconquered Constantinople would resume its medieval name *Tsar'grad* ('King City' – a calque on the Greek *Basilis polis* ['Queen City'] – with the secondary meaning 'City of the Tsar') and would be assimilated into the body of Russian Orthodox culture. This would be a *re*-taking in the sense that nineteenth-century Russia, heir of

Byzantine Christianity, would be restoring this now *Islamic* city to its lost *Christian*–Byzantine glory.

Paradoxically, such warlike words, together with claims that Moscow is the 'third Rome' ('and there shall be no fourth') are to be found in Dostoevsky alongside his praise of the Russian people's mission of humble Christian service to all of mankind.[47] In all of this the influence of Danilevsky's brilliant but xenophobic and chauvinistic tract, *Russia and Europe* (1869) is strong, and not benign.

Dostoevsky has left us an unparalleled example of life lived at 'white heat', a life of frenzied searching, searing doubt, and triumphant affirmation in matters of the spirit, and an unparalleled expression in fiction of those searchings, those doubts, and those affirmations. He is, in a deep sense, a Christian novelist; and it is not going too far to compare him to Dante. Mochulsky, who groups Dostoevsky with the 'great Christian writers of world literature', adds that, 'like Dante, he passed through all the circles of human hell, [a hell] more terrible than the medieval hell of the *Divine Comedy*, guided by the "radiant image of Christ"'.[48]

In Tolstoy we shall encounter a 'pagan' novelist who, nevertheless, both in his fiction and in his tracts, raised religious questions in a comparably compelling, if quite different way. But before turning to Tolstoy we must examine the ideas of the brilliant critic who attacked both Tolstoy and Dostoevsky for their deviations from Russian Orthodoxy as he conceived it. I refer to Konstantin Leontyev.

4. Konstantin Nikolayevich Leontyev (1831–1891)

Leontyev has been called, with considerable justice, the 'Russian Nietzsche' – not in the sense of a Russian thinker influenced by Nietzsche, since he died a year before the appearance of the first Russian commentary on Nietzsche, which initiated an intense preoccupation with Nietzsche's thought in Russia during the 1890s and the early 1900s.[49] Rather, Leontyev was a Russian thinker who, almost two decades before Nietzsche, offered a 'Nietzschean' celebration of 'the aesthetic' and an equally Nietzschean critique of democratic and egalitarian values, 'mass culture', and utilitarian and socialist ideas. Like Nietzsche, he was convinced that all levelling is necessarily a 'levelling down'.

Leontyev's style was often brilliant, although – with the exception of a few late letters on philosophical and religious themes – seldom as aphoristic as Nietzsche's characteristic later style. His polemical writings, like Nietzsche's, were always vigorous and sometimes vehement. Leontyev rejected central aspects of modernity: 'indifferent' secularism, cultural standardization and homogenization, and – more explicitly than Nietzsche – applied science and advanced technology.

From the beginning of his career in the early 1860s until his death in 1891 Leontyev regarded aesthetic values as central. However, he preached an 'aesthetics of [daily] life', which is oriented toward the historical *past* and *present*, in contrast to Nietzsche's 'aesthetics of [high] culture', which is strongly oriented toward the historical *future*. Before his spiritual crisis of 1869–71 Leontyev's 'aesthetic' critique of what he called the 'democratic-utilitarian process' was couched in essentially secular terms. After his crisis a tension began to develop in his thought between the 'aesthetics of life' and his new religious convictions, which were of a 'black' Byzantine severity. In the 1880s, discussing the relation of Christianity to the 'democratic-utilitarian process', he came to distinguish between 'genuine' and 'pseudo' Christianity. The latter, which he characterized as 'rose-coloured', sentimental, humanistic, and even 'anthropolatrous',[50] seemed to him – as to Nietzsche later – a major cause (in Western Europe and, increasingly, in Russia) of the hated drift towards egalitarianism, mediocrity, and cultural homogeneity. Nietzsche, of course, saw *all* Christianity in this light and made no distinction between 'true' and 'false' forms of Christianity.

Leontyev, who charged both Tolstoy (on the whole, justly) and Dostoevsky (quite unfairly) with defending such 'rose-coloured' or 'humanistic' versions of Christianity, even called – in a polemical exchange with Solovyov in 1890 – for a struggle to the death against the 'anti-Christ of democracy'.[51] Nietzsche, in contrast, thought of *himself* as both an 'anti-Christ' or 'anti-Christian thinker' and an anti-democratic thinker, i.e., a cultural and intellectual adversary of both Christianity and democracy. For Leontyev it was only Western pseudo-Christianity that had become allied with democracy and egalitarianism. True Byzantine Christianity, in contrast, was hierarchical, controlled by an anti-democratic 'despotism of form' – where form in turn is the 'despotism of an inner idea'[52] – and remote from humanism and 'anthropolatry'.

In his early writings Leontyev saw 'progress', both socio-economic and moral, as threatening to wash away his prized aesthetic values in a shallow sea of standardized vulgarity and prosiness. His aesthetic rapture over life was explicitly indifferent to moral values. Expressing what Leontyev himself later called an 'aesthetic amoralism', a character in one of his early novels declared bluntly: '*A single century-old magnificent tree is worth more than twenty faceless men*; and I will not cut it down in order to be able to buy medicine [to treat] the peasants' cholera!'[53]

In the historical past of Europe, Greece, and Rome, as well as in the historical present of Greece and the Ottoman Empire (where he served for a decade as a Russian diplomat), Leontyev sees luxuriant diversity and fruitful contrasts – both cultural and socio-political – held within aesthetic limits by the 'despotism of form'. But in the present, and especially in the projected future, of Western Europe he sees only a muting of contrasts and a flattening of diversity into dreary Philistine conformity. He is both horrified and outraged by the thought that

Moses went up to Sinai, that the Greeks built their elegant Acropolises, the Romans waged their Punic Wars, the handsome genius Alexander, in a plumed helmet, crossed the Granicus and fought at Arbela, that the apostles preached, martyrs suffered, poets sang, painters painted, and knights shone in the tourneys, *only in order that the French, German, or Russian bourgeois, in his ugly, shapeless, and comical clothing*, should sit complacently ... upon the ruins of all this past greatness.[54]

Although Leontyev professed a love for the historical ideal of a complex and flourishing 'neo-Byzantine culture', in much the way that Nietzsche professed a love for the high culture of the world-historical future, both thinkers were in fact more clearly characterized by a 'ruling hatred'[55] – of contemporary European civilization, as they would put it, or, as we might say, of essential aspects of modernity.

Leontyev's hostility – he himself referred to it as a 'philosophical hatred' – focused on St Petersburg, the city which Dostoevsky had described as 'most abstract and most intentional', in contrast to the organic historical rootedness of Moscow. Coastal St Petersburg had been built by Peter the Great as a 'window on the West', whereas inward-looking Moscow was the traditional locus of Byzantine–Slavic religion and culture. The 'St Petersburg lawyer' in his black suit and top hat, carrying a briefcase, was Leontyev's key symbol of the hated intrusion of modernity into Russia. Like the Slavophiles and Dostoevsky, he disliked and distrusted judicial systems; indeed, he saw the spreading influence of courts and lawyers as a part of the social and cultural rot which had invaded Russia from the West, and against which he urged a radical remedy: *freeze* Russia to keep it from *rotting*.[56]

The 'freezing', of course, was meant to be socio-political as well as religious and cultural. In Leontyev's view, the creeping 'prosiness' of modernity cannot be resisted, nor the 'poetry of life' maintained, 'without the mysticism and plastic beauty of religion, without the magnificence and threatening power of the state, without a resplendent and firmly established aristocracy'.[57] Furthermore, social injustice, in the form of the 'pressure of classes, despotism, dangers, strong passions, prejudices, superstitions, fanaticism, etc., in a word, everything that the nineteenth century opposes',[58] are essential ingredients in the 'aesthetics' or 'poetry' of life.

Leontyev considers the technology of rapid and efficient transportation and communication – exemplified by what in the 1880s was already familiar:

the railroad and the telegraph, as well as by the still novel telephone – to be destructive of 'all organic life on earth – poetry, religion, the isolation of states and of everyday existence'.[59] He shudders at the thought of a 'grey, impersonal bourgeois or workers' earthly paradise, lighted by electric street-lamps, and talking by telephone from Kamchatka to the Cape of Good Hope'.[60]

Leontyev's philosophical explanation of the decline of nineteenth-century European culture was based on a triadic schema of historical development borrowed from Danilevsky. Historical cultures, like living organisms – he claimed – develop from an infantile stage of 'initial simplicity' to a mature stage of 'flourishing complexity', and then sink through a stage of 'levelling interfusion' to organic death.[61] He maintains that Europe, which had reached the 'flourishing complexity' of its prime during the high Middle Ages, is now far advanced in the terminal process of 'levelling interfusion'. A dreadful 'prosiness' is being introduced by the reigning European *mania democratica progressiva*, with its rage to eliminate monarchy, aristocracy, and inequality generally, along with war and 'the mystical positive religions'.[62]

Leontyev explicitly repudiates the 'feverish preoccupation' with the earthly welfare of the remote future generations of a 'collective and abstract' mankind on the part of both socialists and utilitarians.[63] What Leontyev opposes to such a historical future-orientation is Christian *agapē* – love 'for the nearest, the very nearest, the person encountered, the person at hand – charity toward the living and real human being whose tears we see, whose sighs and groans we hear, whose hand we can actually clasp, like a brother's, in *this present hour*'.[64]

The opposition between 'love of one's neighbour' (*lyubov' k blizhnemu*) and concern for the remote future generations, which Leontyev formulated in 1880, strikingly anticipates the punning distinction which Nietzsche was to make in *Thus Spoke Zarathustra* (1883), when, repudiating *Nächstenliebe* ('love of one's neighbour', literally 'love of the nearest') he advocated *Nächsten-Flucht* ('flight from one's neighbour') and, most passionately, *Fernsten-Liebe* ('love of the farthest off', i.e. 'the most future').[65] Nietzsche might plausibly be charged with being 'feverishly preoccupied' with distant future generations; not, however, with their *welfare*, but with their *cultural creativity* – a quite different matter.

Leontyev insisted that true Christian charity and compassion must not be one-sidedly 'democratic', not directed only toward workers, slaves, and wounded soldiers but also toward the 'high and mighty' – kings, popes, and generals – in all of whom, rather than in the lowly and powerless, Leontyev discerns the 'poetry' of social life.[66]

In his denial that human beings can or should be protected against contingency, risk, or suffering Leontyev also comes close to Nietzsche's position. European 'pseudo-humanism', which attempts to provide such protection, is for Leontyev, naively optimistic, insensitive to the crushing burdens of human existence and its 'unbearable tragic character'.[67] Short-sighted pseudo-humanists wish to eliminate 'those injuries . . . and afflictions which are *useful* to us'[68] – not, of course, socially or economically useful, but useful in a spiritual and ascetic sense, as a discipline and tempering of the spirit.

Genuine Christian humanism, in contrast, is marked by a 'severe and sorrowful pessimism, a courageous submissiveness to the incorrigibility of earthly life'.[69] Leontyev charges both Dostoevsky and Tolstoy with insensitivity to the tragic character of personal and historical existence. In fact, this charge is substantially justified in the case of Tolstoy, but *not* in the case of Dostoevsky, whose Christian vision of human life and history is essentially tragic.[70]

In the works of Dostoevsky, Leontyev distinguishes – though perhaps not sharply enough – between, first, the 'true' Christianity expressed in the major novels, and second, the 'pseudo-Christianity' of Dostoevsky's writings on social, political, and religious themes, especially *The Diary of a Writer* and the Pushkin Day Address of 1880. It was in the latter that Dostoevsky expressed the 'love' of the Russian people for 'the peoples of Europe'. Leontyev responds with a cry of fierce hatred toward contemporary Europe, 'for having ruined everything great, splendid, and sacred in yourself and for destroying with your noxious breath so much that is precious among us unhappy [Russians]!'[71]

Leontyev approves the deep reverence for Russian Orthodox monks which Dostoevsky expresses in *The Brothers Karamazov*, but he disapproves of Dostoevsky's unfriendly depiction of the proud and fanatical ascetic Feraponty. And he is openly critical of *starets* Zosima, self-assured in his 'active love', because that love includes members of secular society. Leontyev prefers the prayers, repentance and 'fear of God' of monks who live in social isolation.[72] (In August of 1891, just three months before his death, Leontyev secretly took monastic vows.)

Tolstoy's reduction of religion to ethics, and of ethics to the 'law of love' and 'nonresistance to evil by force' struck Leontyev as 'saccharine, sentimental, rose-coloured, and utilitarian-moral', alien to the 'mystical-dogmatic' heart of Christianity.[73] Leontyev sees the threat of anthropolatry in a 'Christianity' that is based exclusively, as Tolstoy's is, on '*love* of *man*'. True Christianity is based on *fear* of *God*, which is the beginning and root of wisdom, while love is only its fruit. And 'one must not mistake the fruit for the root, or the root for the fruit'.[74] Put more bluntly: 'One must live to that point, grow to that point, where one genuinely fears God, with a simple, almost animal fear . . . a plain terror of sinning.'[75]

Leontyev candidly confessed to a preoccupation with 'personal salvation'; in this connection he referred to his own 'transcendental egoism' and expressed his 'final wish' – to the ringing of the monastery bells, 'unceasingly reminding us of the eternity which is now so close, to become indifferent to everything in the world except my own soul and the concern for its purification'.[76]

Among the things to which Leontyev found it most difficult to become indifferent was the 'aesthetics of life' – including the aesthetic and sensuous beauty of the Russian Orthodox service of worship. In his last years he came to feel, painfully, that his own severe Byzantine Orthodoxy – 'a religion of disillusionment, a religion without hope for anything earthly'[77] – in fact denied all aesthetic values. In one of his last letters, after commenting bitterly that 'Christian preaching' was joining forces with 'European progress' to 'kill the aesthetics of life on earth, i.e. life itself', Leontyev added, in what appears to have been a tone of quiet desperation, 'We must help Christianity even at the cost of our beloved aesthetics.'[78]

5. (Count) Leo Nikolayevich Tolstoy (1828–1910)

As Merezhkovsky noted in 1901, Tolstoy's genius as a writer of fiction is epic and 'Homeric'[79] in contrast to Dostoevsky's genius, which is dramatic and 'Shakespearian', although the 'Homeric' Tolstoy rejects many central values of the Homeric poems, e.g., military glory and the decisive role of 'leaders' in history.

Tolstoy was a writer of international celebrity when, in the late 1870s, he underwent a profound religious crisis. The fruits of this crisis included the searing manifesto of his Confession (1879) and a series of moral and religious tracts: What I Believe (1884), On Life (1888), Critique of Dogmatic Theology (1891–6), Unification and Translation of the Four Gospels (1892–4), The Kingdom of God is Within You (1893), What is Religion and What is its Essence? (1902), and The Law of Violence and the Law of Love (1908).

Tolstoy's writings before and after 1879 are marked by both continuities and discontinuities. His early fiction raises searching questions about the meaning of individual and social life and the pattern of historical experience, maintaining a steady focus on moral questions. All of this is continued in the didactic works. But there is discontinuity in the extreme political and cultural anarchism of Tolstoy's final period and in the emerging 'tyranny of ethics'[80] which led him to condemn, *inter alia*, most of the world's great literature, including his own novels.

The spiritual crisis of 1879 appears to have been precipitated by desperate reflections upon the related themes of death, violence, and secular culture. As a result of shattering personal experiences, the theme of death came to preoccupy Tolstoy almost to the extent that – as we shall see in Section 6 – it preoccupied Fyodorov. For both thinkers the sheer fact of death drained life of all meaning.

In Paris in 1857, after witnessing a guillotining, Tolstoy wrote in great agitation:

[I]f a man were to be torn to pieces before my eyes, that would not be so repulsive as this efficient and elegant machine by means of which a powerful, fresh, and healthy human being was instantly killed.[81]

In 1860 came the slow and painful death of his beloved older brother Nicholas, followed in the late 1870s by the deaths of two of Tolstoy's small children. Echoes of all of these traumatic events can be found in both the earlier fiction and the later didactic writings.

A subsidiary discontinuity may be seen in the authoritarian tone in which, after 1879, Tolstoy came to reject traditional authorities, both religious and secular. It emerges from the testimony of those who knew him, as well as from the merciless self-dissection of his diaries, that Tolstoy was inclined to intellectual arrogance and coerciveness. He sought to impose the ethics of absolute non-violence through the application of a kind of intellectual violence, brow-beating non-Tolstoyans into an acceptance of his doctrine.

Shestov had noted this trait as early as 1900. Comparing Tolstoy to an Old Testament prophet, Shestov added: 'He does not wish to persuade men but to intimidate them. "Do what I tell you [he says in effect] or you will be [exposed as] immoral, perverse, corrupt creatures".'[82] Gorky, who – unlike Shestov – was personally acquainted with Tolstoy, confirmed this:

He liked to compel [people], to 'compel' them to read, to take walks, to eat only vegetables, to love the peasants, and to believe in the infallibility of Leo Tolstoy's rationalistic conjectures [*domysli*] about religion.[83]

This was what Orwell had in mind when he spoke of Tolstoy's 'tendency toward spiritual bullying'.[84]

Tolstoy's last moral-religious tract, which exhibits its share of 'spiritual bullying', adds a unique element – a kind of emotional blackmail. Tolstoy begins by declaring: 'I . . . , who stand on the brink of the grave, cannot keep silent . . . ,' continues: 'I, with my eighty years, shall never see [the reign of the law of love]', and concludes: 'This is what I wanted to say to my brothers before I die.'[85] The clear implication of such statements is that anyone who refuses to accept Tolstoy's doctrine will be callously rejecting the impassioned plea of an aged and dying man.

As a thinker Tolstoy was self-taught and, perhaps in consequence, eclectic, drawing from varied and even conflicting sources: Rousseau, Kant, Schopenhauer; Buddhism and Taoism. In his approach to religion and morality he is an extreme rationalist, almost a *philosophe*; yet he draws heavily upon such outspoken critics of reason and enlightenment as Rousseau and Schopenhauer.

It was under the powerful influence of both Schopenhauer and Buddhism that Tolstoy, whose earlier life had been marked by 'drunkenness, debauchery, and dueling',[86] came to profess an ascetic contempt for the 'animal self' and its 'material life' – under which labels he included the social and cultural, as well as the physical and biological, aspects of human existence.

Tolstoy claimed to find no more significance in the 'suffering and death in this life' than a peasant would find in the 'calluses on his hands or the exhaustion of his limbs' after a day behind the plough.[87] In 1910, the year of Halley's Comet, he recorded an extreme, though not uncharacteristic position:

The thought that the comet might hook onto the earth and destroy it was very agreeable to me . . . The spiritual life [of human beings] can no more be disturbed by the destruction of the earth than the life of the universe by the death of a fly.[88]

In March 1855, following the death of the despotic Nicholas I, the twenty-seven-year-old Tolstoy, then on duty in the Crimean War, jotted down his excited reflections on the future of Russia and his own role in that future. He spoke of a 'tremendous idea' which he intended to spend his life carrying out – the idea of a 'new religion', the 'religion of Christ, but purged of faith and mystery, a practical religion, not promising future bliss, but providing bliss on earth'.[89] This is a remarkable anticipation of the programme to which, after 1879, Tolstoy returned. The 'purified' or 'true' Christianity which he preached was immanentist and moralistic; Christ was reduced to the role of moral exemplar, but even in that role was inessential (see below, p. 202). Gorky reports that, about 1901, Tolstoy spoke of Christ in a perfunctory way; there was 'no enthusiasm or feeling in his words, no spark of inner fire'.[90]

Even Tolstoy's more formal definitions of religion stress its function as providing a 'rational rule of conduct'. Religion is the 'establishment of a man's relation to that whole [in other formulations: "infinite being" or "infinite existence"] of which he feels himself to be a part, and from which he derives a *guide for his conduct*'.[91] Faith is defined as a 'consciousness of one's relation to the infinite and of the *rule of conduct* which follows from that relation'.[92]

The specific 'guide' or 'rule' which Tolstoy sees at the heart of all true religion is the 'law of love', i.e. the absolute proscription of resistance to evil by force of any kind. The institutionalized religions fail to preach or practice this 'law'; indeed, they actively support the violence of armed conflict, military conscription, capital punishment, etc.

Moreover, Tolstoy charges, the churches are committed to 'religious deception'; their dogmas – specifically including the doctrines of the Trinity, the Resurrection, and the immortality of the soul – are 'irrational' and 'absurd'.[93] In private correspondence he is even blunter, asserting that 'no reasonable man can believe in resurrection'.[94] Echoing Voltaire at his most polemical, Tolstoy rails against the 'dreadful stupidity and cruelty with which the Church's doctrine is filled'.[95] Like the *philosophes*, he considers any faith not founded on reason to be superstitious. The Christian churches, he insists, by stifling the rationality of their members, reduce the latter to a permanently 'stupified condition'.[96]

In contrast, his own 'true Christianity', purged of both dogma and ritual, is fully responsive to the demands of the 'rational consciousness'. Tolstoy sometimes suggests that it is Johannine (cf. Jn. 4.8–16); in any case, it is explicitly and abusively anti-Pauline, chiefly because of Paul's recognition of the legitimacy of state power. Tolstoy was particularly incensed by Rom. 13.1–2; '[T]here is no [political] power but of God; the powers that be, are ordained of God. Whosoever therefore resisteth the power, resisteth the ordinance of God . . .'

Tolstoy the nominalist denies the symbolic meaning of both religious ritual and works of art. The *locus classicus* of his reductive 'making strange' (*ostranenie*) of a work of art is Natasha Rostov's experience of the opera with its *scènes de ballet*. What she perceives is only some 'painted cardboard representing trees' and 'queerly dressed women who moved . . . strangely in [the] brilliant light'. Later there was a 'round hole in the canvas [representing] the moon', and 'one of the women with thick bare legs and thin arms . . . began jumping and striking one foot rapidly against the other'. Finally, a 'man with bare legs jumped very high and waved his feet about very rapidly. (He was Duport, who received 60,000 rubles a year for this art.)'[97]

Tolstoy offers a parallel *ostranenie* of the Russian Orthodox Communion service, couching his description in deliberately non-liturgical terms. The altar is called a 'table' (*stol*), the Communion cloth or corporal is a 'napkin' (*salfetka*), the paten a 'saucer' (*blyudtse*), and the chalice a 'gold cup' (*zolotaya chashka*) or 'gilded cup' (*zolochenaya chashka*). In Tolstoy's account, it is the priest's 'manipulations', along with certain prayers, that are supposed to convert the bread and wine into the body and blood of God. These 'manipulations' consist of the priest's 'raising both arms evenly, despite the resistance offered by the brocaded sack he was wearing, then kneeling and kissing the table'. The name 'Jesus' is repeated over and over, each time with a more audible 'whistling sound', etc.[98] Such reductionist descriptions are clearly intended to destroy the symbolic meaning of the Holy Communion and indeed of any liturgical service whatever.

Tolstoy's project for the 'rational reconstruction' of Christianity was extended to the text of the Gospels themselves. He studied *koinē* Greek and a variety of scriptural commentaries in French and German. His 'edition' of the four Gospels appeared in three bulky volumes in 1892–4.[99] Each page has three parallel columns: the first contains the Greek text, the second the modern Russian translation (authorized by the Holy Synod), and the third Tolstoy's own free interpretation.

Tolstoy drew most heavily from the nineteenth-century commentary of Reuss[100] and the eighteenth-century commentary of Calmet.[101] But his interpretation is tendentious beyond anything in any of his sources. He is at pains to excise from the Gospels whatever is 'extraordinary, enigmatic, and vague'[102] – in the bitter words with which Dostoevsky's Grand Inquisitor had protested against those elements which Christ returned-to-earth had chosen to make central in Christianity. Tolstoy naturalizes and secularizes the Gospel account, removing all traces of transcendence.[103] Although he preferred John to the other Gospels, he reinterpreted even the divine *Logos* as mere human rationality.[104]

In the words of a judicious critic, Tolstoy's Gospel was 'devoid of irrationality, deprived of metaphysical and mystical vision, despoiled of metaphors and symbols, mutilated of its miracles, and sometimes of its parables as well. By killing the letter, he killed also the spirit . . .'[105]

Tolstoy was especially concerned, of course, to eliminate from 'his Gospel' anything that stood in contradiction to Christ's exhortation to 'resist not evil' (Mt.5.39). Examples would include the forceful driving of the money-changers from the temple (Mt.21.12; Jn.2.14–15) and the hard saying 'I came not to send peace but a sword' (Mt.10.34). All such passages Tolstoy either removed or explained away.

That Tolstoy in effect reduced religion to ethics was recognized as early as 1903 by Shestov, who complained that Tolstoy had put 'brotherly love' in place of God.[106] Tolstoy explicitly naturalizes and 'ethicizes' key theological doctrines. Thus he is prepared to accept a doctrine of resurrection only in the metaphorical sense that 'one leaves the tomb of . . . one's individuality' and enters into the 'life of the whole'.[107] And he interprets the 'invisible church' as the aggregate of men of good will, an aggregate apart from which there is no 'salvation'.[108]

Tolstoy deliberately followed Kant's lead in *Religion within the Limits of Reason Alone* in reducing religion to a question of obedience to a rationally grounded moral law.[109] As Kant puts it: 'The uniquely true religion contains nothing but laws, i.e. . . . . practical [viz., moral] principles . . . which we recognize as revealed through pure reason.'[110] In the words of a perceptive commentator, 'For Kant, religion is in principle subservient to morality. The only religious teaching which counts is moral teaching . . .'[111]

This was also Tolstoy's position. But of course Tolstoy went far beyond Kant, reducing the moral law to the 'law of love', i.e. of absolute non-violence, and drawing from this law pacifist and anarchist conclusions which Kant would surely have repudiated.

Tolstoy made significant efforts to acquaint himself with the major world religions: Judaism, Islam, Buddhism, Taoism, and the then new Bahai faith. He claimed to find elements in all of them that could be integrated into his own position; but he felt a special affinity for Buddhism and Taoism. The Taoist doctrine of *wu wei* ('non-acting') was close to his ethics of non-resistance; the *tao* seemed to him much the same thing as *agapē* —[112] an identification which suggests that *agapē* had in fact been drained of its specifically Christian content.

Taoism and Buddhism, like Christianity, were for Tolstoy not sources or sanctions of his ethical doctrine, but *ex post facto* corroborations of the deliverances of his own 'rational consciousness'. He explicitly asserted that 'if there had been neither Christ nor His teaching, I would have discovered this truth [of the "law of love"] myself'.[113] And he welcomed the sceptical conclusions of a German 'higher critic' about the existence of the 'historical Jesus' as showing that the ethics of the Sermon on the Mount come not 'from one temporary and local source, but from the totality of the spiritual life of mankind'.[114]

When Tolstoy the anarchist lists his *bêtes noires*, he lumps cultural, educational, and religious organizations together indiscriminately with military and penal organizations, castigating, 'armies, navies, universities, ballets, synods, conservatories, prisons, gallows, guillotines'.[115] Like Leontyev, as Shestov was one of the first to point out, Tolstoy was ruled more by hatred than by love – in Tolstoy's case by a 'ferocious hatred for the educated classes, for art, for science'.[116]

I suspect that Tolstoy's commitment to cultural anarchism is in fact deeper than his commitment to non-violence, although it is the latter position which he defends in greater detail.[117] To dramatize the absoluteness of his commitment to non-violence, he offers a vivid and extreme example:

The villain raises a knife over his victim; I have a pistol in my hand and can kill him. But I really do not know, and cannot know, whether the upraised knife will effect its evil purpose. It may not, while I most likely *shall* accomplish my evil [sic!] deed.[118]

On a related ethical question, Tolstoy took a position parallel to, although independent of, Leontyev's (see p. 195 above) – one which I find both sound and admirable. Drawing upon the Kantian stress on intentions, and indifference to consequences, as well as the implicit orientation toward the *present* of Kant's deontological ethics, he stoutly resisted the orientation toward the 'world-historical *future*' of the leading socio-political movements of his time. Tolstoy insists that people should 'live not for the future but solely for the present, striving simply to fulfil in the present the will of God revealed to them in love'. He repudiates the 'horrible superstition that it is possible to know the future order of society – a superstition that justifies the use of every sort of violence in support of [the effort to bring about] that [future]order'.[119]

Yet Tolstoy does not share Kant's respect for the human individual as an end in himself and bearer of individual rights. Rather, he equates ethical individualism with egoism, agreeing with Pascal that *le moi est haïssable*, and asserting that 'life as individual existence has been outlived by mankind'.[120] There seems to have been a marked tension between individualism and impersonalism in Tolstoy's own life, one which found expression in his thought. In matters of religion and ethics he appeals to his own highly individual, not to say idiosyncratic, convictions, presenting them as the deliverances of a universal 'rational consciousness'.[121]

In this respect his position, like Kant's, ignores or denies precisely what Hegel had stressed: the presence and efficacy of objective institutions, customs, structures of law and right, culture and symbolism, as the enabling framework within which individual human rights can be guaranteed and individual human potentialities actualized. Tolstoy's conception of the state is almost as nominalistic as Stirner's. 'For anyone who has awakened to the truth [sc., of anarchism]', he writes, 'the entity called a State does not exist . . .'.[122] In sharp contrast not only to Hegel but also to Dostoevsky and the Slavophiles, Tolstoy sees all social groupings, all communities – families, churches, universities, academies, and armies, as well as the state – as fictions or abstractions, deficient in both reality and value. It follows that, for Tolstoy, no institutional change can advance the cause of social harmony. This can be done only by reforming the hearts of individual human beings. And this, in turn, can be done merely by pressing down on the 'Archimedean lever' of absolute non-violence, whereupon 'all the old world will be turned around, all misfortunes will disappear, and men will become happy'.[123]

Tolstoy does in fact often speak as though the reforming of men's hearts were a simple matter. His moral optimism appears to be the obverse of his peculiar blindness to the power of (irrational) evil and to the presence of tragic conflict – both of which Dostoevsky in his major novels had brought vividly to life.[124]

There is much of value in Tolstoy's social and political criticism, in particular his strictures on the future-orientation of radical and revolutionary movements. But most of the social and political alternatives which he proposes strike one as rigid and narrow as well as utopian. With respect to Tolstoy's *cultural* criticism, what Orwell said about his critique of Shakespeare – namely, that although he 'turned all his powers of denunciation against Shakespeare, like all the guns of a battleship roaring simultaneously', Shakespeare emerged unscathed[125] – seems to me to apply quite generally. Tolstoy's striking insensitivity to symbolic meanings, aesthetic values, and cognitive needs renders his critique of traditional religion, 'art for art's sake', and pure science one-sided, superficial, and unconvincing.

We turn now to a no less utopian religious thinker, one who, even more stubbornly than Tolstoy, offered principled opposition to essential aspects of modernity.

6. Nikolai Fyodorovich Fyodorov (1828–1903)

Fyodorov was a solitary and eccentric thinker, but he shared many of the concerns and convictions of other nineteenth-century Russian religious thinkers. He shared Chaadayev's 'theurgical restlessness', and the Slavophiles' concern for 'conciliarity'. He shared Dostoevsky's conviction that *all* men are responsible for evil, and Solovyov's mystical sense of the ideal unity of mankind. He rejected much of what Tolstoy rejected – 'modernity', militarism, high culture, acquisitiveness, sensuality – and preached something parallel to what Tolstoy preached: the reduction of religion to ethics – in Tolstoy's case to the single overriding duty of non-violence, in Fyodorov's case to the single overriding duty of raising the dead. One might say that Fyodorov treated *one* of Tolstoy's obsessions as central. But instead of the obsessive *fear* of death which marked Tolstoy, there was in Fyodorov's religious thought an obsession with the *project* of *vanquishing* death. Tolstoy, who knew Fyodorov well for more than twenty years, is reported to have said, 'I am proud to have lived in the same century with such a man.'[126]

Fyodorov attacked head-on the central and widely shared nineteenth-century assumption that historical progress is valid and valuable, together with the more general assumption that what is new deserves to displace what is old, that the birth and growth of the new requires the decline and death of the old. *Each* human life, Fyodorov insists, is irreplaceable; each person who has died needs and deserves to be restored to life. The living, who have received the gift of life from those now dead, are under an imperative moral obligation to attempt – no matter how staggering the task – to restore life to the no-longer-living. This collective, scientific–technological effort is what Fyodorov calls the 'common cause' or 'common task'.[127] It involves replacing the 'cult of youth' and of women, and the 'lust to procreate', which marks the 'adolescence' of mankind, with a 'cult of the fathers' and the conscious re-creation of the past, which corresponds to mankind's 'maturity'. This in turn means replacing the unconscious process of child-bearing, with its 'false cult of the future' and its 'bad infinity' of reiterated future generations, with a conscious process of resurrecting the dead.[128] Only in this way will it be possible to save the victims of both cosmic and historical 'progress'.

The motivation for the 'common task' is plainly moral. The causes of death, Fyodorov insists, are the same as the causes of non-brotherhood (*nebratstvo*) and of disrelatedness or non-kinship (*nerodstvo*), namely, indifference to the fate of others and insufficient love for them.[129] When a Russian poet died, one of Fyodorov's correspondents wrote to him: 'How can one be reconciled to the death of one so gifted and so young?' Fyodorov's response was characteristic: 'How', he exclaimed, 'can one be reconciled to *any* death?' Fyodorov views death as a 'triumph of blind, non-moral force' and 'universal resurrection', in contrast, as 'a victory of morality'.[130] Since each human being lives at the cost of his ancestors, 'A person who would not return life to those from whom he received it is not worthy of either life or freedom'.[131]

Putting the point in biblical terms, Fyodorov identified Christ's supreme achievement as the raising of Lazarus (Jn.11.43–4), and declared that Bethany, where this miracle occurred, is more precious than Nazareth, or Bethlehem, or Jerusalem.[132] Human beings, in undertaking the project of resurrection, will simply be following Christ's example to the end.

Fyodorov rejects key Western ideas as being either too speculative (non-active) or too individualistic (non-conciliar), or both. Thus, he interprets the Socratic *gnōthi sauton* as meaning 'know *only* thyself' and proposes to replace this egoistic admonition with its conciliar counterpart: 'Know yourselves in the father, and the father in yourselves, and be a brotherhood of sons.'[133] He would replace the contemplative Cartesian *cogito ergo sum* with the activist 'I resurrect, therefore I am.'[134] Nietzsche, for Fyodorov, is the culmination of Western thought, preaching the final destruction of the ancestors in the name of the high culture of the future. In explicit opposition to the Nietzschean *amor fati*, Fyodorov proposes an *odium fati*, an implacable hatred of the 'blind, death-bearing forces of nature'.[135]

According to Fyodorov's own ethical position, which he calls 'supramoralism', one should live *'with all men and for all men'* – in contrast both to egoism – living (only) for oneself – and altruism – living (only) for others.[136]

Philosophy, which has traditionally been either objective or subjective, should now become 'projective', that is to say, it should cease to be a passive account of what *is* and become an active project for bringing about what *ought to be*. Scientists and technicians should stop investigating the causes of phenomena in general and organize themselves into 'task forces' which will investigate the specific causes of non-brotherhood, disrelatedness, and death. Theorists should come to see the world not as a datum (*dannoye*) to be known but rather as a task or assignment (*zadannoye*) to be carried out.

The project is explicitly theurgical. Art and science, in their ultimate union, will constitute a 'real, not a mystical, theurgy [*bogodeistvo*]'.[137] *'In us* [human beings]', Fyodorov declares, 'Gods's word becomes God's deed.' Mankind, he adds, is called to be 'God's instrument' in the 'sacred task' of resurrecting the ancestors.[138]

'*All* matter', Fyodorov declares, 'is the dust of our ancestors'; and 'in the tiniest particles . . . we may find traces of our ancestors.'[139] A perfected science and technology, which will be able to control 'all the molecules and atoms of the external world in such a way as to collect what is dispersed, to unite what is disintegrated',[140] will make possible the literal raising of the dead. This will require a seeking out and recovering of the 'dust of the fathers' from the depths of interstellar space as well as from the bowels of the earth.

Fyodorov himself denies that there is anything mystical in all of this, and explicitly rejects the unduly 'mystical' approach of both Dostoevsky and Solovyov.[141] The raising of the dead will be a redirecting of natural energies, a rational regulation of natural processes. It will not be an act of creation; human beings cannot create, they can only restore or re-create what has already been created (and destroyed). Fyodorov, as Florovsky notes, wanted to replace natural or organic processes such as child-bearing by artificial technological processes such as resurrecting, preferring the conscious and rational character of the latter to the unconscious and irrational character of the former.[142]

When in the early 1880s Solovyov first read an account of Fyodorov's project, he responded with enthusiasm. But on reflection he came to regard Fyodorov's proposal as unduly 'naturalistic', tending toward magic and even necromancy. In Fyodorov's account of the 'divine-human process' (to use Solovyov's own terminology), the 'miracles' of technology replace the miracle of Divine Grace. Zenkovsky, who is generally sympathetic to Fyodorov's ideas, admits that there is in the 'common task' a strain of occultism, stemming from eighteenth-century Freemasonry. But he rejects Florovsky's (and Solovyov's) charge that Fyodorov's project is tinged with necromancy.[143]

Florovsky's reference to Fyodorov's project as a cosmic *mnogoletka* ('many-year plan') on the model of a Soviet *pyatiletka* ('five-year plan'), though witty, is unfair.[144] Florovsky fails to distinguish between the *end* and the *means* which Fyodorov envisages. The scientific–technological *means* are indeed future-oriented, in the way that any technological application of science must be. But Fyodorov's moral and religious *end* is *not* future-oriented, in contrast to the end-in-view of a five-year plan, e.g. attaining a certain level of industrial output by 1989. Fyodorov's end is to be found rather in the *present* and, especially, in the *past*. His project involves the preserving and restoring of achieved human values, in particular the protecting of the lives of those who now live and the recovering of the lives of those who live no longer.

Unfortunately, Fyodorov's concept of life, much invoked, is left undefined. The 'life' which he intends is not, I think, culture-historical; but neither is it purely biological. He has no theory of the human person. Florovsky is right to ask what it is that 'dies and is resurrected': a human being, or only a human body?[145]

Fyodorov failed to raise explicitly the difficult question of what criteria would be invoked to establish the personal identity of the resurrected ancestors. And his answer to a related question, raised by Solovyov, is unsatisfactory. Solovyov protested that Fyodorov wanted to 'resurrect mankind at the [undeveloped] stage of cannibalism'. Fyodorov responded indirectly, in a discussion of Nietzsche's doctrine of eternal recurrence, repudiating the 'precise, blind *repetition* of past life with all of its abominations'.[146] In direct response to Solovyov he said only: 'To resurrect cannibalism, i.e. to resurrect death! What an absurdity!'[147] Perhaps he meant, but he surely did not say, that the process of resurrection will involve a transfiguration, a moral purification, of the resurrected ancestors.

According to Fyodorov, the 'rational regulation' and 'spiritualization' of the cosmos will be carried out in stages, beginning with climate control, proceeding to gravity control, and the construction of orbiting 'space stations', as well as interplanetary and eventually intergalactic exploration and colonization. This will serve both to provide habitats for the resurrected ancestors and to introduce a humanizing control over blind natural forces. Human beings, Fyodorov declared, face the task 'not only of visiting, but also of settling all the worlds of the universe . . . *It was for this that man was created*.'[148]

Once the common task has been carried out, peace will reign in human history, and harmony in the cosmos. The universe as a whole will become a work of art, restored to the 'imperishable splendour' which marked the world before the Fall.

Berdyaev applauds Fyodorov's repudiation of the passivity and resignation traditionally preached by Russian Orthodoxy as well as his religious demand for an active, transforming attitude toward nature.[149] Florovsky, who admits that Fyodorov advanced many vivid ideas and some valid ones, that he made many perceptive conjectures and critical comments, considers him, in the end, a 'stubborn' thinker rather than a 'bold' one.[150]

Fyodorov could be an acute and subtle critic, uncovering genuine, if unsuspected, *aporiai* in the positions which he opposed. His questions were often penetrating, though his answers sometimes tended toward rationalistic simplification and utopianism. In his earnestness and intensity he reminds one of Calvin and Kierkegaard, but he conspicuously lacked Kierkegaardian irony and wit. Like Tolstoy, he is insensitive to the (non-instrumental) value of high culture. He agreed with Tolstoy and Solovyov on many points, but quarrelled violently with the former for defending Buddhism and with the latter for defending Roman Catholicism. His life and work were marked by a fundamental paradox; his was 'a *solitary* dream about the *common* task'.[151]

7. Vladimir Sergeyevich Solovyov (1853–1900)

Vladimir Solovyov, the most important Russian speculative thinker of the nineteenth century, was unusually precocious. He published a substantial essay when he was twenty and a book when he was twenty-one. Over the next seven years he completed three other book-length studies in speculative philosophy, philosophical theology, and philosophy of religion.

He was also remarkably versatile. In addition to major treatises and dialogues on philosophy and theology, he produced sensitive literary criticism and penetrating essays on current social, political, and ecclesiastical questions, as well as highly readable translations of Plato and Kant. He also wrote delightful light verse, humorous verse plays, and verse translations (Virgil, Petrarch, Dante, Schiller, Heine), as well as serious lyric poetry, which, at its best, is subtle and delicately evocative rather than powerful or original. The mystical image of the 'Divine Sophia' (*hē Sophia tou Theou*) which he articulated in theoretical concepts as well as poetic symbols strongly influenced the following generation of Symbolist poets. It was characteristic of Solovyov that on occasion he treated his own mystical encounters with the 'Divine Sophia' ironically or irreverently.[152]

Solovyov was extraordinarily polyglot and erudite. He knew at least three ancient languages and five modern ones in addition to his native Russian. His works of the 1870s exhibit a dazzling mastery of the details of Western philosophical and religious doctrines and his later works an equally dazzling mastery of both Eastern and Western church history, although aspects of his treatment of Byzantium have been criticized as arbitrary and unfair.[153]

Solovyov possessed synthetic powers of a high order and vivid sense of the 'theogonic process'[154] at work in the cosmos and in human history. Sharing Chaadayev's 'theurgical restlessness', he also carried to a new extreme the emphasis on unity, universality, and conciliarity which we have seen in other Russian thinkers. He expressed this both in the concept of 'positive total-unity' (*hen kai pan*) and in the poetic image of the 'Divine Sophia'. Whatever he wrote, his prose style was elegant and lucid.

Solovyov's master's thesis, *Krizis zapadnoi filosofii: Protiv pozitivistov* ('The Crisis of Western Philosophy: Against the Positivists', 1874) draws heavily upon Kireyevsky at several points, among them the conviction that the Byzantine tradition of Russian Orthodoxy had preserved Christian truth and spirituality but had neglected secular culture, whereas Western Europe had neglected Christian truth and spirituality but had developed a flourish-ing secular culture.[155] Slavophile influence is also apparent in Solovyov's treatment of Western philosophy as a hypertrophied form of rationalism; his stress on the 'wholeness' of life and the need for a synthesis of philosophy and religion, which would involve a combining of Western thought with 'Eastern speculation'.[156]

However, Solovyov shows no interest in the *social* theories of the Slavophiles; he has nothing to say about the village-commune (*obshchina*) and little to say about Russia's 'special path' in world history, although he does suggest that Russia will be able to provide the urgently needed synthesis of Eastern and Western values.

The precocious system[157] which Solovyov developed in the 1870s envis-ages a universal synthesis of science, philosophy, and theology, stressing the Platonic tri-unity of goodness, truth, and beauty. 'What the absolute wills as good', Solovyov declared, 'is the same as what it represents as truth and feels as beauty.'[158] Human *making* – whose objective principle is beauty – when purified and unified, assumes the ideal form of 'integral[159] creativity'. Purified and unified *knowing* – whose objective principle is truth – assumes the ideal form of 'integral knowledge'. Purified and unified *doing* – whose objective principle is the good – assumes the form of 'integral society'. Each of these three, in turn, is an integrating synthesis of a triad of subordinate elements: 'integral creativity' of mystical experience (*mistika*), fine art, and technical art; 'integral knowledge' of theology, philosophy, and science; 'integral society' of church, state, and the economy. The inclusive synthesis of integral creativity, knowledge and society constitutes 'integral life'.

In clear contrast to Hegel – and to Plato and Aristotle as well – Solovyov refuses to subordinate doing and making to knowing. He insists that all three human functions are essential components in 'integral life', that all three stand on the same ontological and axiological level.

Solovyov uses a series of Greek terms beginning with 'theo-' to stress the centrality of the religious or 'absolute' element in each of the integrated spheres: 'integral creativity' he calls 'free theurgy'; 'integral knowledge' – 'free theosophy'; and 'integral society' – 'free theocracy'. The last two terms are misleading for different reasons. Following Baader and Schelling, Solovyov uses 'theosophy' to mean a discipline which integrates *theo*logy and philo*sophy*.[160] In his encyclopedia article on *mistika*, he appears to equate 'theosophy' with both mystical theology and mystical philosophy.[161] In any case, it has nothing to do with the forms of 'theosophy' which trace their origins to the 'Theosophical Society' founded by Madame Blavatsky in New York in 1875. The term 'theo*cracy*' misleadingly suggests that Solovyov is concerned with the forms of *political authority*. In fact, in this early period his concern was with *social institutions* generally. Thus a more appropriate term might have been 'theo*praxis*'.

The term 'free' in the quoted expressions seems to mean 'perfected' or 'integrated' – this in contrast to earlier historical forms of theocracy and theosophy in which the 'absolute' order unilaterally controlled the two subordinate spheres: the church dominated both the state and the economy, and theology dominated both philosophy and science. The term 'free' may also be intended to suggest that the integrated elements enjoy a relative autonomy.

Religious elements appear at four key points in Solovyov's early system, in each case representing the highest or 'absolute' component of a given triad: (1) *mistika* is the highest form of human experience, discipline, and 'making'; (2) theology is the highest form of the quest for truth; (3) *mistitsizm* (the philosophy which makes *mistika* – mystical experience – central in the way that empiricism makes *empiriya* – sense-experience – central) is the highest form of philosophy; (4) the church is the highest of social institutions. In placing *mistika* in a triad with fine art and technical art, Solovyov appears to be moving conceptually between skilled shaping (*poiēsis*) and feeling or experience (*aisthēsis*) as components of art. The component of feeling would appear to be minimal in the technical arts, as that of skilled shaping would be minimal in *mistika*, where it would appear primarily as the *askesis* or discipline which is a precondition for, or accompaniment to, mystical experience. One commentator, however, interprets Solovyovian *mistika* as the active art of bringing the divine from Heaven to earth.[162] There is some support for this interpretation in the distinction which Solovyov makes between contemplative and active *mistika* in his encyclopedia article on this subject.[163]

Solovyov left the book 'Philosophical Principles of Integral Knowledge' incomplete and his 'first system' unfinished, perhaps because he came to see that some of his key terms were equivocal and, in consequence, some of his triads artificial. For example, the term 'material' – which marks the lowest stage of each triad, being followed by the higher stages of 'formal' and 'absolute' – is used in at least three senses: (a) 'related to content', (b) 'sensuous' or 'empirical', and (c) 'economic'. The sciences are 'material' only in sense (b), empiricism is 'material' in sense (b) as well as sense (a) – the latter on the Kantian assumption, which Solovyov shares, that our senses provide the 'matter', i.e. *content*, of experience, while the understanding supplies its form, i.e. concepts and categories. But the economy is 'material' only in sense (c), which has only the most tenuous connection with the other two senses.

Solovyov's philosophical theology is elaborate, ingenious, and sometimes fanciful. He takes from Origen the conceit that matter in its present state – a fragmented unity whose parts are external to one another in both space and time – is a product of the Fall. Other key notions, in particular that of the World Soul – the Platonic *psuchē tou kosmou* – in its relation to the Divine Sophia, changed considerably between the earlier and later formulations. Origen had taken the Divine Sophia to be the same as the Logos;[164] Solovyov saw it as the 'produced unity' of the world, parallel to Spinoza's *natura naturata*, while the Logos was the 'producing unity' (*natura naturans*). In his later writings he abandoned his earlier identification of the Divine Sophia with 'ideal mankind'. And he no longer saw the Fall as an act of rebellious freedom on the part of the World Soul, or the temporal world-process as resulting from the World Soul's free supratemporal decision. According to Solovyov, it is because God creates the world not directly but through the mediation of the World Soul that the creation is flawed and the 'theogonic process' marked by 'trial and error'.[165]

The later position has its own *aporiai*: God, in a sense, is said to 'permit' the Fall. 'God loves chaos in its nonbeing [i.e. potentiality], and wants it to exist [in actuality].'[166] More fundamentally, Solovyov envisages not the *redemption* of creatureliness (*tvarnost'*) but its *overcoming*.[167] This is related to his strong sense that the phenomenal world is only *maya*, a veil of illusion (here the influence of Schopenhauer is added to that of Schelling), that only the *trans*-phenomenal is real. 'Not only do I believe in everything supernatural', he once declared, 'but, strictly speaking, I believe in nothing else . . . [T]he [physical] matter which weighs down upon us has always seemed to me to be only some nightmare of dreaming mankind.'[168] What one critic has called Solovyov's 'symbolic illusionism' reduces the symbols and signs of the phenomenal world to shadowy, translucent entities, thus providing – in the tradition of Philo and Origen – a new proof of the 'nullity of all earthly things'.[169]

Solovyov's doctrine of Godmanhood combines the Patristic conception of *Theandria* with the Hegelian–Schellingian conception of historical and cosmic *Werden*. The cosmic process, no less than the historical process, is a series of theophanies. This universal 'divine-human process' has three main aspects: 'the becoming of nature which issues in man, the becoming of history which issues in Christ, and the becoming of the Church which issues in the perfected Kingdom of God'.[170]

The 'rational deduction of the Trinity from the idea of Being',[171] a procedure which Solovyov first sketched in Lecture Six of the *Lectures on Godmanhood*,[172] is a highly technical, and somewhat austere, Hegelian–Schellingian schematization of the three non-temporal positings[173] of Being: from *an-sich* to *für-sich* to *an-und-für-sich* (or *bei sich*). But this 'deduction' fails to establish that the three 'hypostases' of Being are *persons*; at most it establishes that the structure of Being is triadic.

Solovyov claimed to have refuted pantheism, but many commentators have found pantheistic elements in his own position. The early doctrine that 'ideal mankind', or the Divine Sophia, is co-creator of the world, raises serious problems. In addition to the Absolute in being there is an Absolute in process of becoming: a Schellingian 'second Absolute' or *werdendes Absolute*. This temporalized Absolute, which is invoked to account for phenomenal change, is an essential component of the first (non-temporal) Absolute. In Boehmean terms: 'God cannot exist without man.' But this would seem to place an unacceptable limitation upon Divine freedom.[174]

Despite the telling objections which such Russian Orthodox commentators as Trubetskoi and Mochulsky have raised against Solovyov's position, the problems with which Solovyov is struggling are genuine and profound. His position approaches that of contemporary Whiteheadian 'process theologians', who speak of a 'divine relativity' and distinguish between the Primordial and Consequent Natures of God; the latter, like the *werdendes Absolute*, is both in process of becoming and co-created by the temporal world.

By the early 1880s Solovyov had turned to a new project: the reunion of the churches. He was the first major Russian thinker to devote himself to this task and perhaps the most important proponent of ecumenical principles in Europe after Leibniz.[175] Ecclesiastical reunion was the focus of all of his intellectual and spiritual energies for a full decade: 1881–90. As he put it: 'Whatever I write, the end is the same: *caeterum censeo instaurandam esse Ecclesiae unitatem*' ('Moreover, I hold that the unity of the Church must be restored'): adding: '*Primum et ante omnia Ecclesiae unitas instauranda . . .*' ('First and foremost, the unity of the Church must be restored . . .').[176]

All that remained of his earlier (moderate) Slavophile 'messianism' was the claim that Russia's special mission was the reconciling of East and West in general, and the reunion of the Russian Orthodox and Roman Catholic churches in particular. He was now sharply critical of those defenders of Byzantine cultural and spiritual superiority, such as Danilevsky and Leontyev, and by implication Dostoevsky, for whom he had earlier had a certain sympathy. He castigated their 'zoological nationalism' and charged them with turning Russian Orthodoxy into an *attribut de la nationalité*.[177] In response to the urging of Danilevsky and Dostoevsky that Russia 'retake' Constantinople (see Section 3 above), Solovyov exclaimed impatiently: 'What could we bring to it except the pagan idea of an absolute state and the principles of caesaropapism which we have taken over from the [Byzantine] Greeks!'[178] In a poem of 1890, 'Ex oriente Lux', he made the point in vivid terms, addressing 'Holy Russia' with the barbed question:

> *Kakim zhe khochesh' byt' Vostokom:*
> *Vostokom* Kserksa il' Khrista?
>
> (What sort of East would you then be:
> The East of *Xerxes* or of *Christ?*)[179]

One unfortunate aspect of Solovyov's ecumenical efforts, and one which he himself later regretted, was his linking of the reunion of the churches with his utopian project of a 'future theocracy' in which spiritual authority for all of Christendom would fall to the Pope while temporal authority for the united Christian nations would fall to the Tsar. That he was able, even temporarily, to exalt the Tsar to this degree resulted, at least in part, from the fact that he tended to view 'Russian reality' from 'much too high up'.[180]

Solovyov met and corresponded extensively with the Roman Catholic

Bishop of Zagreb, Strossmayer. At the time of those contacts he wrote: 'Primarily I look upon Rome – great, holy, and eternal – as a fundamental and inalienable part of the universal church. I believe in that Rome, I worship it, I love it with all my heart . . .'[181] Because of such sentiments as these, Solovyov acquired the reputation of a 'Papist' and his major works of this period were denied publication in Russia by the 'spiritual censorship'. He published 'The History and Future of Theocracy' in Russian in Croatia, and *La Russie et l'église universelle* in Paris.

Strossmayer forwarded a copy of Solovyov's essay *L'Idée russe* (originally intended as a general introduction to *La Russie et l'église universelle*) to Pope Leo XIII. The Pope responded: 'Bella idea! ma fuor d'un miracolo è cosa impossibile.'[182] Although this reaction was deeply disappointing to Solovyov, he did not abandon his ecumenical project. Nor did he, until the early 1890s, realize that Dostoevsky's penetrating critique of the rule of the Grand Inquisitor, although harsh and unfair as an account of the Roman Catholic church, was nevertheless a just and fair critique of *theocracy* as such. It follows, as Solovyov eventually acknowledged, that 'free theocracy' is a contradiction in terms, and that the words with which Solovyov in 1887 concluded his book on theocracy were emptily utopian: '[T]heocracy's highest good and true end consists in the perfect mutuality of free divine-human union – not in the fulness of *power*, but in the fulness of *love*.'[183]

Solovyov was also one of the first Russian thinkers to extend the ecumenical project to include Protestantism and Judaism. He saw the 'Protestant principle of freedom' as an essential ingredient in the building of the universal church. His final work, 'A Short Story of the Anti-Christ' (1900) contains a moving scene of ultimate reconciliation and union, in Jerusalem in the twenty-first century, among Pope Peter II, the *starets* Ioann, and the Protestant theologian Professor Ernst Pauli. This scene follows the unmasking of the 'Emperor of the World' as the Anti-Christ. And it is Pauli who speaks, as he firmly grasps the hands of Peter II and Ioann: 'So also, Väterchen, nun sind wir ja Eins in Christo.'[184]

Solovyov was the first Russian thinker to see the 'Jewish problem' as primarily a 'Christian problem'. He urged complete equality of civil and religious rights for Russian (and Polish) Jews, protested against the abridgment of such rights, and attacked the general xenophobia and specific anti-Semitism of the later Slavophiles. Moreover, he made a serious and sustained study of Hebrew under the tutelage of Frederick Goetz of Moscow beginning in 1881. After reading all of the Old Testament prophets in the original, he added Hebrew phrases (beginning in 1887) to his own daily prayers. After Solovyov's death Goetz declared that no Christian scholar or writer since Lessing had been so deeply loved and respected by Jews. Solovyov's 'glorious name', he says, will long be remembered 'reverently and with love' by a grateful Jewish people.[185]

The most controversial aspect of Solovyov's relation to Roman Catholicism is his alleged 'conversion' of 18 February 1896. On that day Solovyov did in fact take communion in Moscow from Fr Nikolai Tolstoy (not related to Leo Tolstoy), a Roman Catholic priest of the Eastern rite. However, it is clear from several kinds of evidence that Solovyov was not moving from Russian Orthodoxy to Roman Catholicism[186] or abandoning the 'faith of his fathers'. First, there is his statement of 1892: 'I am as far from Latin narrowness (*ogranichennost*') as I am from Byzantine narrowness or that of Augsburg or Geneva. The religion of the Holy Spirit which I profess is broader and at the same time fuller and richer than all the separate religions.'[187] If it be argued that Solovyov changed his mind between 1892 and 1896, we may cite two statements that date from 1896–7. In a letter to Tsar Nicholas II he calls Russian Orthodoxy 'a most pure and most perfect form of Christianity'.[188] And in a letter to Princess Elizabeth G. Volkonsky, who had indeed 'gone over' to Roman Catholicism (in 1887) Solovyov explains that he has listed his religion on the current census form as 'Russian-Orthodoxly Catholic'.[189]

Two further points are relevant: first, Solovyov never *renounced* Russian Orthodoxy, something which would have been required of a 'convert' to Roman Catholicism; second, he did not receive communion – either from a Roman Catholic or Russian Orthodox priest – at any time after 18 February 1896, until, on his deathbed, he received communion and made his final confession to a *Russian Orthodox* priest.[190] What is more to the theoretical point, Solovyov's act of joining the not-yet-existent *église universelle* is entirely consistent, not only with his ecumenical project, but also with his life-long commitment – philosophical and theological as well as 'mystical' – to 'positive', i.e. 'inclusive', total-unity. Since he did not recognize the division between the Eastern and Western churches, he could hardly 'go over'[191] from one confession to the other. His act of 1896 was 'extra-ecclesiastical and extra-dogmatic', and when he came to realize that one could not in fact 'join' the universal church *before* the union of the Eastern and Western churches, he repented of his own 'non-canonical' act.[192]

Solovyov's last decade was marked by disillusionment with his 'theocratic' project, a withdrawal from ecclesiastical politics, and a return to theoretical philosophy. He wrote a short but powerful book on *The Meaning of Love* (1892–4) and a massive treatise on ethics and social philosophy, *The Justification of the Good* (1897). He accepted the position of editor for philosophy with the Brokgaus (Brockhaus) – Efron Encyclopedia, a standard nineteenth-century Russian reference work, and himself wrote several dozen articles, including those on such Western thinkers as Plato, Plotinus, Duns Scotus, William of Ockham, Nicholas of Cusa, Malebranche, Kant, Hegel, and Comte; on such topics as beauty, evil, knowledge, matter, nature, power, reason, science, time, truth, and Vedanta; and on such Russian thinkers as Danilevsky and Leontyev.[193]

He completed the first three chapters of a work projected in at least three volumes, *Foundations of Theoretical Philosophy* (1897–9).[194] These chapters offer a series of Cartesian meditations, undogmatic in tone, exploratory in method, tentative in conclusions, yet of undiminished wit, perspicacity, and analytical vigour. His boldness of imaginative construction is here tempered by what he called 'the conscientious quest for valid truth, to the finish'. The fragments of his new system do not take him beyond a phenomenalism of both the subject and object of experience, although he clearly intended to move far beyond such a position in the projected but unwritten portions of his work. Here, however, he insists that immediate experience provides no basis for distinguishing between veridical and illusory perceptions or even between dreaming and waking states of consciousness. Solovyov intended to rebuild his speculative system on purged and strengthened theoretical foundations. He did not live to complete the task.

Instead, in the last year of his life, obsessed by a gathering sense of the palpable power of evil in the world, he composed his final work, *Three Conversations: On War, Progress, and the End of History* (1900). This is a skilfully constructed 'Platonic' dialogue, which presents four distinct points of view, of which the two most pronounced and sharply opposed are a Tolstoian ethic of non-resistance to evil ('The Prince') and Solovyov's own Neo-Hegelian critique of this position ('Mr Z.'). There are Fyodorovian motifs in this work, which had been foreshadowed by a number of formulations in the earlier *Meaning of Love* (including the doctrines of the androgyne and the 'syzygy' of mankind with the cosmos). Thus Mr Z. asserts that, if all men must in fact die, 'progress' is an empty concept. He characterizes death as the 'extreme of evil' and even refers, somewhat cryptically, to 'future victories in the collective resurrection[195] of all men'.[196] Equally Fyodorovian is Solovyov's reference to the 'communion of the living with the dead' and the 'living unity of the resurrected past with the realized future in the eternal present of the Kingdom of God'.[197]

But the focus of *Three Conversations* is upon the impending apocalypse and the triumph of cosmic evil symbolized in the figure of the Anti-Christ. Solovyov's apocalypse strikingly combines medieval and modern motifs.

The Anti-Christ appears in the twenty-first century in the aftermath of the great East–West wars of the twentieth century. He is accepted and even revered as the 'humane' and 'liberal' leader of a super welfare-state. He offers 'spiritual authority' to the Roman Catholics, 'sacred tradition' to the Russian Orthodox, and a generously funded 'world institute of free scriptural investigation' to the Protestants in exchange for their 'free' acknowledgement of his absolute authority as Emperor of the World.[198] It is only the tiny remnant of those Christians of the three confessions who dare to *refuse* this offer who are ultimately united, following the downfall of the Anti-Christ.

One learned and acute commentator, who criticizes a number of Solovyov's specific positions, sees courage, nobility, even a kind of 'spiritual heroism' in Solovyov's resolute striving to transform Christian doctrine into Christian practice. He characterizes Solovyov's work as an 'effective and authentic response to the religious yearnings and anxieties of his age', and notes that Solovyov shared with Plato the rare gift of being able to 'touch and move men by thought', to kindle in them the fire of inspiration.[199] An equally learned and acute commentator sees in Solovyov the 'greatest artist of [conceptual] order and organization' – after St Thomas – in the entire history of thought, a thinker who borrows from all systems after purging them of their 'negations'.[200] Thus, in drawing upon the sometimes 'dark and muddy' streams of Western Sophiology, from Boehme to Baader, he purifies them, turning them into 'crystal-clear waters'.

These judgments strike me as sound, as does von Balthasar's further comment that Solovyov thinks in universal terms, at a height not reached by any speculative philosopher since Hegel, and sees all things clearly as 'mutually ordered in graded relationships'. His philosophical and religious thought is a 'work of art' on a large scale – a drama, an epic, and a hymn to the universe.[201]

8. Conclusion

Russian religious thinkers of the nineteenth century display a broad range of ideas and insights, some close to, others remote from Western ideas. Close to certain post-Hegelian trends in Western Europe is the Russians' stress on Christianity as a *historical* force, and their related attempts to elaborate a 'theology of culture'. In the last quarter of the century such Russian thinkers as Fyodorov and Solovyov – anticipating some of the ideas of Teilhard de Chardin – developed a conception of Christianity as a *cosmic* force, capable of transfiguring the natural world. Tolstoy, during the same period, moved in the opposite theoretical direction, attempting to reduce religion to ethics, and ethics in turn to the 'law' of non-violence. In this he was following the lead of Kant, but moving far beyond Kant's own position.

Russian religious thinkers also display a broad range of reactions to modernity and to modernizing trends in religious thought. Among the thinkers who resisted or repudiated major aspects of modernity and of these modernizing trends most actively, ingeniously, and on occasion stubbornly, were the Slavophiles, Dostoevsky, Leontyev and, in their different though related ways, Tolstoy and Fyodorov.

Solovyov stands almost alone as a 'Hegelian' defender of modernity and modernizing trends in religion, one who welcomed the new forms of 'social Christianity' which were emerging in French Catholicism during the 1890s. Yet two factors modify even Solovyov's commitment to modernity: his life-long celebration of both mystical experience and mystical philosophy; and his sudden turn, in the final year of his relatively short life, from a previously serene 'rational' faith in cosmic and historical progress to an anguished sense of impending cosmic and historical doom. Belatedly, he too joined the ranks, at least on this apocalyptic point, of the Russian anti-modernists.

Notes

1 N. F. Fyodorov, *Filosofiya obshchego dela* (Moscow, 1913), vol. II, p. 119. This passage dates from the 1890s.

2 *Sobornost'*, a term made current by Khomyakov, may also be rendered as 'organic religious togetherness'. The root *sobor* means both 'cathedral' and 'council' and, like the Greek *ekklēsia*, is derived from a verb meaning 'to call together' or 'assemble' (*sobirat'*). Cf. the Greek *ekkalein* ('to call out' [citizens to the assembly]).

3 Chaadayev made this and other charges in the first of his *Lettres philosophiques*, composed in 1829, but not published until 1836 (in Russian translation), at which time it brought down the wrath of the educated Russian public as well as the Tsarist authorities upon its author's head.

4 'On the Necessity and Possibility of New Principles in Philosophy', translated by Peter K. Christoff, in James M. Edie, James P. Scanlan, and Mary-Barbara Zeldin (eds.), *Russian Philosophy* (Chicago, 1965, 1969; Knoxville, Tenn., 1976), vol. I, p. 177; cf. also pp. 175, 189ff.

5 The title *Apologie d'un fou* is an ironic reference to Chaadayev's 'instant insanity', which was proclaimed officially in 1836.

6 Peter Yakovlevich Chaadayev, *Philosophical Letters and Apology of a Madman*, translated with an introduction by Mary-Barbara Zeldin (Knoxville, Tenn., 1969), p. 174.

7 P. Ya. Chaadayev, *Sochineniya*, ed. M. O. Gershenzon (Moscow, 1913; reprint Oxford, 1972), vol. I, pp. 245, 246.

8 Cf. Johann A. Möhler, *Die Einheit in der Kirche, oder das Prinzip des Katholizismus* (Tübingen, 1825). The quoted expressions appear in Möhler's table of contents as the headings of chs. 3 and 4, respectively. For a brief but helpful discussion of Möhler's influence on the Slavophiles, and a citation of the relevant literature, see Andrzej Walicki, *The Slavophile Controversy: History of a Conservative Utopia in Nineteenth Century Russian Thought*, translated by Hilda Andrews-Rusiecka (Oxford, 1975), pp.

192–3 and 193n. See also S. Bolshakoff, *The Doctrine of the Unity of the Church in the Works of Khomyakov and Möhler* (London, 1946). Zenkovsky offers a more sceptical view of Möhler's influence on Khomyakov. (Cf. V. V. Zenkovsky, *A History of Russian Philosophy*, trans. by George L. Kline [London and New York, 1953], pp. 184–5.)

9 The adjectival form of *razum* is *razumny* and of *rassudok – rassudochny*, regularly used in such expressions as *rassudochnaya metafizika*, which is roughly equivalent to Hegel's pejorative *Verstandesmetaphysik*.

10 'New Principles in Philosophy', in *Russian Philosophy*, vol. I, p. 213.

11 The Russian expressions are *tsel'noye znanie* and *tsel'nost' dukha*.

12 Zenkovsky, *A History*, p. 219.

13 'New Principles in Philosophy', in *Russian Philosophy*, vol. I, pp. 198, 199.

14 For a thorough discussion of Khomyakov's conception of *sobornost'* see Peter K. Christoff, *An Introduction to Nineteenth-Century Russian Slavophilism*, vol. I: *Xomjakov* (The Hague, 1961), ch. 6. For an interesting parallel between the Slavophiles' concept of *sobornost'* and Tönnies' concept of *Gemeinschaft*, and the contrasting parallel between their concept of 'fragmented Western society' and Tönnies' concept of *Gesellschaft*, see Walicki, *The Slavophile Controversy*, pp. 169–74.

15 'New Principles in Philosophy', in *Russian Philosophy*, vol. I, p. 197.

16 *Ibid.*, pp. 180, 202, 213.

17 Berdyaev had a high opinion of Dostoevsky's powers as a metaphysician, but not as high as the English translation of his book on Dostoevsky makes it appear. He did not call Dostoevsky 'Russia's greatest metaphysician' (Nicholas Berdyaev, *Dostoevsky*, translated by Donald Attwater [New York, 1934, 1957], p. 11), but rather *velichaishii russkii metafizik* (N. Berdyaev, *Mirosozertsanie Dostoyevskogo* [Prague, 1923], p. 7), i.e. 'a major [or 'very great'] Russian metaphysician'. The misleading translation is widely quoted, e.g. by George Steiner, *Tolstoy or Dostoevsky* (New York, 1959), pp. 287, 294.

18 See Mikhail Bakhtin, *The Poetics of Dostoevsky*, translated by R. W. Rotsel (Ann Arbor, Mich., 1973).

19 A. Boyce Gibson, *The Religion of Dostoevsky* (Philadelphia, 1973), pp. 63, 65.

20 Lev Shestov, *Dostoevsky and Nietzsche: The Philosophy of Tragedy* (1903), translated by Spencer Roberts, in *Dostoevsky, Tolstoy and Nietzsche* (Athens, Ohio, 1969), pp. 216, 217. Shestov's judgment of Myshkin is particularly harsh: Myshkin is a 'pitiful shadow', a 'cold, anemic specter', who is 'nothing but idea, i.e., a void' (*ibid.*, p. 216). Vyacheslav Ivanov is both more charitable and more judicious, seeing in Myshkin a 'spirit that assumes flesh' rather than a 'man who rises to the spiritual' (*Freedom and the Tragic Life: A Study in Dostoevsky* [New York, 1952, 1957], p. 90.) – A note on terminology: although the Russian word *starets* is derived from the same root as *stary* ('old') and *starik* ('old man'), it connotes not age but spiritual authority. For this reason I have avoided the commonly used translation 'elder', preferring to keep the Russian term.

21 See Reinhard Lauth, *Die Philosophie Dostojewskis in systematischer Darstellung* (Munich, 1950), p. 218. – 'Other worlds' in Dostoevsky's Russian is *miry inye*, an inversion typical of the Russian Bible. The expression thus carries an aura of the sacred not conveyed by its English counterpart.

22 Gibson, *The Religion of Dostoevsky*, pp. 123, 131, 210.

23 Konstantin Mochulsky, *Dostoevsky: His Life and Work* translated by Michael A. Minihan (Princeton, 1967), p. 511.

24 *Ibid.*, pp. 282–3, 285.

25 *The Religion of Dostoevsky*, p. 29.

26 Cf. Mochulsky, *Dostoevsky*, p. 563.

27 Steiner, *Tolstoy or Dostoevsky*, p. 291.

28 *Pis'ma*, ed. Dolinin, vol. I, p. 142.

29 *Dostoevsky*, p. 153.

30 Ivanov, *Freedom and the Tragic Life*, p. 11.
31 *Tolstoy or Dostoevsky*, p. 203.
32 Ivanov, *Freedom and the Tragic Life*, p. 95.
33 Steiner, *Tolstoy or Dostoevsky*, p. 204; italics added.
34 Gibson, *The Religion of Dostoevsky*, pp. 212–13; cf. also pp. 176, 180.
35 *Ibid.*, p. 206.
36 *Dostoevsky and Nietzsche*, p. 207; cf. also p. 238, and Gibson, *The Religion of Dostoevsky*, pp. 5, 176.
37 Steiner, *Tolstoy or Dostoevsky*, p. 316.
38 Gibson, *The Religion of Dostoevsky*, p. 193, n. 37.
39 Shestov, *Dostoevsky and Nietzsche*, pp. 316, 318.
40 Gibson, *The Religion of Dostoevsky*, p. 176, n. 14.
41 Mochulsky, *Dostoevsky*, pp. 619, 620.
42 *Ibid.*, p. 622.
43 *Freedom and the Tragic Life*, p. 57n.
44 *Dostoevsky and Nietzsche*, p. 165.
45 Mochulsky, *Dostoevsky*, pp. 331, 562.
46 Dostoevsky, *Diary of a Writer*, June 1876.
47 *Ibid.*
48 *Dostoevsky*, p. 652.
49 For a sketch of the early reception of Nietzschean ideas in Russia, see my '"Nietzschean Marxism" in Russia' in *Demythologizing Marxism* (Boston College Studies in Philosophy, II), ed. F. J. Adelmann, S. J. (The Hague, 1969), especially sec. 2 (pp. 168–9).
50 Leontyev characterized 'anthropolatry' in his 1882 critique of Tolstoy's 'What Men Live By' as 'a new faith in *earthly man* and in earthly mankind – in the ideal, *self-sufficient, autonomous* worth and dignity of the individual' (*Sobranie sochinenii*, [Moscow, 1912], vol. 8, p. 160).
51 *Soch.*, vol. 6, p. 274.
52 *Soch.*, vol. 5, p. 197.
53 *Soch.*, vol. 1, p. 306; italics added.
54 *Soch.*, vol. 5, p. 426.
55 Solovyov used the expression 'ruling hatred' in his obituary notice on Leontyev (1892). Cf. V. S. Solovyov, *Sobranie sochinenii*, 2nd ed. (Moscow, 1911–14; reprinted Brussels, 1966), vol. 9, p. 402. Another commentator spoke in similar vein of Leontyev's 'miso-Europeanism'. Cf. S. N. Bulgakov, 'Pobeditel'-pobezhdyonny: Sud'ba K. N. Leontyeva' (1916), in *Tikhiye dumy* (Moscow, 1918), p. 120.
56 Leontyev, *Soch.*, vol. 7, p. 124.
57 *Soch.*, vol. 6, p. 213.
58 *Soch.*, vol. 8, p. 93.
59 Letter to Rozanov, 30 July, 1891, in *Russkii vestnik*, No. 285 (June 1903), p. 414.
60 Quoted in K. R. Medvedsky, 'Filosof-Khristianin: Osnovy mirosozertsaniya K. N. Leontyeva', *Russkii vestnik*, No. 242 (Jan. 1896), p. 241.
61 *Soch.*, vol. 5, p. 197.
62 *Soch.*, vol. 7, p. 267; vol. 8, p. 203.
63 *Soch.*, vol. 8, pp. 189, 207, 210–11.
64 *Ibid.*, p. 207.
65 Friedrich Nietzsche, 'Also Sprach Zarathustra' in *Werke*, ed. K. Schlechta (Munich, 1956), vol. II, p. 324. The section in question bears the title 'Von der Nächstenliebe'.
66 Leontyev, *Soch.*, vol. 8, pp. 171, 211.
67 *Ibid.*, pp. 163, 193.
68 *Ibid.*, p. 203.

69 *Ibid.*, p. 189.
70 Cf. N. A. Berdyaev, *Konstantin Leont'ev: Ocherk iz istorii russkoi religioznoi mysli* (Paris, 1926), p. 232.
71 Leontyev, *Soch.*, vol. 8, p. 212.
72 *Ibid.*, pp. 195–8, 204.
73 Letter to Rozanov, 13 Aug., 1891, in *Russkii vestnik*, no. 285 (June 1903), p. 416.
74 *Soch.*, vol. 8, pp. 159, 183.
75 Letter to A. A. Aleksandrov, 24 July, 1887, in *Bogoslovskii vestnik*, vol. 23, no. 3 (1914), pp. 458–9.
76 *Ibid.*, p. 456.
77 Leontyev, 'Chetyre pis'ma s Afona', *Bogoslovskii vestnik*, No. 12 (1912), p. 707. 'Four Letters from Mt Athos' is a partly fictional, partly autobiographical work in epistolary form, written in 1884. The 'letter' here quoted is dated 23 July, 1872.
78 Letter to Rozanov, 27 May 1891, in *Russkii vestnik*, no. 285 (June 1903), pp. 418–19. English translation in George Ivask (ed.), *Against the Current*, pp. 228, 229.
79 Steiner lists a number of persuasive parallels between Tolstoy and Homer, including 'the pastoral setting; the poetry of war and agriculture' and 'the luminous, all-reconciling background of the cycle of the year' (*Tolstoy or Dostoevsky*, p. 74).
80 Zenkovsky, *A History*, p. 392,
81 Letter to V. P. Botkin, Paris, 5 April, 1857: in Tolstoy, *Polnoe sobranie sochinenii* (Moscow, 1949), vol. 60, p. 167.
82 Lev Shestov, *The Good in the Teaching of Tolstoy and Nietzsche* [1900] (trans. by Bernard Martin) in *Dostoevsky, Tolstoy and Nietzsche* (Athens, Ohio, 1969), p. 69.
83 Maxim Gorky, 'Lev Tolstoi. Pis'mo' ('Leo Tolstoy. A Letter') [1910] in *Polnoe sobranie sochinenii* (Moscow, 1973), vol. 16, p. 295.
84 George Orwell, 'Lear, Tolstoy and the Fool' [1946] in *The Orwell Reader* (intro. by Richard H. Rovere) (New York, 1956), p. 308.
85 'The Law of Violence and the Law of Love' (trans. by James P. Scanlan), pref., secs. 13, 19: in *Russian Philosophy*, vol. II, pp. 213, 224, 234. Orwell had detected such 'emotional blackmail' in Tolstoy and had called it 'tyrannous'. (Cf. 'Lear, Tolstoy and the Fool', p. 314.)
86 Shestov, *Tolstoy and Nietzsche*, p. 80.
87 'Chto takoye religiya, i v chem sushchnost' yeyo?' ('What is Religion and What is its Essence?'), sec. 17: in S. L. Frank (ed.), *Antologiya russkoi filosofskoi mysli* (New York, 1965), p. 45. A complete English translation is included in *Lift Up Your Eyes: The Religious Writings of Leo Tolstoy* (intro. by Stanley R. Hopper) (New York, 1960), pp. 267–314. This passage is on p. 314.
88 Letter to N. N. Gusev, 14 January, 1910: *Soch.*, vol. 81, p. 44.
89 *Dnevnik* (Diary), 4 March, 1855; *Soch.*, vol. 47, p. 37.
90 Gorky, 'Lev Tolstoi. Zametki' ('Leo Tolstoy. Notes'), sec. 7: *Soch.*, vol. 16, p. 264.
91 'Chto takoye religiya?' secs. 2, 3: *Antologiya*, pp. 25, 26; and *Lift Up Your Eyes*, pp. 272, 273; italics added.
92 'The Law of Violence', sec. 14: *Russian Philosophy*, vol. II, p. 225; italics added.
93 It was Tolstoy's rejection of the doctrine of the Resurrection, in particular, which caused Solovyov to charge him with being a Buddhist and not a Christian. See Konstantin Mochulsky, *Vladimir Solov'ev: Zhizn' i uchenie* (Vladimir Solovyov: Life and Doctrine) (Paris, 2nd ed., 1951), pp. 249, 253, 254.
94 Letter to Muhammed Sadig, 22 May, 1903. *Soch.*, vol. 74, p. 132 (original in English).
95 Letter to A. I. Dvoryansky, 13 December, 1899: *Soch.*, vol. 72, p. 264.
96 'Chto takoye religiya?' sec. 16: *Antologiya*, pp. 43–4; and *Lift Up Your Eyes*, p. 312.
97 *War and Peace*, pt. 8, chs. 9–10.

98 *Resurrection*, pt. 1, ch. 29.

99 The first edition was published (in Russian) in Geneva in order to avoid the Imperial censorship. With the relaxation of the censorship laws after 1905 the work became publishable in Russia, where the second edition appeared in 1907–8.

100 Cf. Eduard Wilhelm Eugen Reuss, *Geschichte der Heiligen Schriften des Neuen Testaments* (Halle, 1842).

101 Dom August Calmet, *Commentaire sur l'Ancien et le Nouveau Testament* (22 vols., Paris, 1715–16). Tolstoy also consulted several other – mainly Protestant – German commentaries. For details, see Nicolas Weisbein, *L'Évolution religieuse de Tolstoi* (Paris, 1960), ch. 6, pp. 182–219. Weisbein provides helpful summaries of Tolstoy's 'free interpretations' of the Gospels, offering several columns of biblical text in parallel with Tolstoy's versions. There is a complete English translation by Leo Wiener in *The Complete Works of Tolstoy*, vols. 14 and 15 (London, 1904; rpt. New York, 1968).

102 *The Brothers Karamazov*, pt. 5, ch. 5.

103 When, in conversation with Leontyev at the Optyna Pustyn monastery in 1890, Tolstoy referred to 'my Gospel' (*moyo Yevangeliye*), Leontyev reacted with outrage. (Reported by V. V. Rozanov in *Okolo tserkovnykh tsen* [St Petersburg, 1906], vol. II, p. 116.) Although 'Tolstoy's Gospel' was not published in full until 1892–4, an abridged version had appeared as a single slim volume in Geneva in 1890.

104 Cf. Weisbein, *L'Évolution religieuse*, p. 447.

105 Renato Poggioli, 'A Portrait of Tolstoy as Alceste', in *The Phoenix and the Spider* (Cambridge, Mass., 1957), p. 100.

106 *Dostoevsky and Nietzsche*, p. 226.

107 Weisbein, *L'Évolution religieuse*, p. 435.

108 *Ibid.*, p. 451.

109 See Gary R. Jahn, 'Tolstoy and Kant', in George J. Gutshe and Lauren G. Leighton (eds.), *New Perspectives on Nineteenth-Century Russian Prose* (Columbus, Ohio, 1982), pp. 60–70.

110 Kant, *Die Religion innerhalb der Grenzen der blossen Vernunft* [1793] in *Gesammelte Werke* (Berlin, 1907), vol. 6, pp. 167–8.

111 Quentin Lauer, S. J., *Hegel's Concept of God* (Albany, N.Y., 1982), p. 25.

112 See A. I. Shifman, *Lev Tolstoi i vostok* (Leo Tolstoy and the Orient), 2nd ed. (Moscow, 1971), p. 45. Cf. Tolstoy, *Soch.*, vol. 40, p. 351.

113 Letter to M. A. Engelhardt, between 20 Dec., 1882, and 20 Jan., 1883; *Soch.*, vol. 63, p. 116. English version in *Tolstoy Centenary Edition* (trans. by Aylmer Maude) (London, 1934), vol. 14, p. 379.

114 Letter to P. I. Biryukov, 1 August, 1899: *Soch.*, vol. 72, p. 164. The book in question is S. E. Verus [Titus Voelkel], ed., *Vergleichende Übersicht . . . der vier Evangelien* (Leipzig, 1897).

115 'The Law of Violence', sec. 8: *Russian Philosophy*, vol. II, p. 221.

116 Shestov, *Tolstoy and Nietzsche*, p. 71.

117 For a critical account of Tolstoy's ethics of non-violence (or 'non-resistance to evil by force') see my *Religious and Anti-Religious Thought in Russia*, esp. pp. 25–9.

118 'The Law of Violence', sec. 17: *Russian Philosophy*, vol. II, p. 231.

119 *Ibid.*, secs. 14, 17: pp. 224–5, 232.

120 *Soch.*, vol. 26, p. 380.

121 Since Russian (like Latin) lacks both definite and indefinite articles, Tolstoy's expression *razumnoe soznanie* can mean 'rational consciousness', '*a* rational consciousness', or '*the* rational consciousness'.

122 This is the epigraph, written by Tolstoy, which precedes sec. 15 of 'The Law of Violence'. (This epigraph, like the numerous other epigraphs used by Tolstoy, is omitted in the Scanlan translation.)

123 Shestov, *Tolstoy and Nietzsche*, p. 36.
124 Cf. Nicholas Berdyaev, 'The Worth of Christianity and the Unworthiness of Christians' (trans. by Donald Attwater), in *The Bourgeois Mind and Other Essays* (London and New York, 1934), p. 122.
125 'Lear, Tolstoy and the Fool', p. 315.
126 The source of this tribute is a letter to Fyodorov, ca. 1890, from Tolstoy's friend the poet Afanasy Fet (1820–92). The letter was first published by V. A. Kozhevnikov in an appendix to his monograph, *Nikolai Fydorovich Fyodorov: Opyt izlozheniya ego ucheniya* . . . (Moscow, 1908). For bibliographical details see George M. Young, Jr., *Nikolai Fedorov: An Introduction* (Belmont, Mass., 1979), pp. 201–2, n. 2, 203–4, n. 5.
127 In Russian *obschcheye delo*; *obshcheye* means both 'common' and 'universal', *delo* means both 'cause' and 'task'. Fyodorov clearly intends to exploit the dual meanings of both terms.
128 Fyodorov uses the term *voskreshenie* for his own theurgical–Promethean project of immanent resurrect*ing*; he reserves the traditional term *voskresenie* for the transcendent resurrection of which God is the agent.
129 *Filosofiya obshchego dela* (The Philosophy of the Common Task) (Verny [Alma Ata], 1906), vol. I, pp. 136–7.
130 *Ibid.*, p. 339.
131 *Ibid.*, p. 338.
132 *Filosofiya obshchego dela* (Moscow, 1913), vol. II, pp. 23–7.
133 *Ibid.*, vol. I, p. 407.
134 *Ibid.*, p. 137.
135 *Ibid.*, vol. II, p. 162.
136 *Ibid.*, vol. I, p. 96.
137 *Ibid.*, p. 416.
138 *Ibid.*, p. 67; italics added; *ibid.*, vol. II, p. 387. Cf. also vol. I, p. 213.
139 *Ibid.*, vol. I, p. 329; italics added.
140 *Ibid.*, p. 442.
141 *Ibid.*, p. 439.
142 Florovsky, *Puti russkogo bogosloviya* (Paris, 1937), pp. 325, 326.
143 Zenkovsky, *A History*, p. 601; cf. Florovsky, *Puti*, p. 326.
144 *Puti*, p. 325.
145 *Ibid.*, p. 324.
146 *Filosofiya obshchego dela*, vol. II, p. 103, n. 2; italics added.
147 Cf. Kozhevnikov, *Nikolai Fyodorovich Fyodorov*; quoted in Sergei Bulgakov, *Dva grada* (Moscow, 1911), vol. II, p. 271.
148 *Filosofiya obshchego dela*, vol. I, p. 416.
149 'Religiya voskresheniya', *Russkaya mysl*, no. 36 (July, 1915), pp. 99–100.
150 *Puti*, p. 330.
151 *Ibid.*, p. 322; italics added.
152 See especially the long poem *Tri svidaniya* ('Three Encounters', 1898); Russian text in *Sochineniya* (Brussels, 1970), vol. 12, pp. 80–6. Solovyov's three 'encounters' with, or mystical visions of, the 'Divine Sophia' occurred in Moscow (1862), London (1875), and the Egyptian desert (1876).
153 Cf. Mochulsky, *Vladimir Solov'ev*, pp. 139, 141.
154 The expression *teogonicheskii protsess* is one of many which Solovyov borrowed from Schelling (*theogonischer Prozess*). Others include *mifologicheskii protsess* (*mythologischer Prozess*), *umstvennoe sozertsanie* (*intellektuelle Anschauung*), and the key term *vseyedinstvo* ('total-unity' or 'all-unity') modelled on Schelling's *All-Einheit* and *All-Einigkeit*. Schelling's *mystischer Empirismus* is the model for Solovyov's *mistitsizm* (see below, p. 210).

155 Cf. Alexander Koschewnikoff [Alexandre Kojève], 'Die Geschichtsphilosophie Wladimir Solowjews', *Der russische Gedanke*, vol. 1 (1929–30), p. 320.
156 Cf. Mochulsky, *Vladimir Solov'ev*, p. 54.
157 For a detailed exposition and critique of Solovyov's 'first system', see my article 'Hegel and Solovyov', in *Hegel and the History of Philosophy*, ed. J. J. O'Malley, K. W. Algozin, and F. G. Weiss (The Hague, 1974), pp. 159–70. This system is set forth primarily in three works: (1) the unfinished but architectonically complex and detailed *Filosofskie nachala tsel'nogo znaniya* ('Philosophic Principles of Integral Knowledge', 1877), (2) the doctoral dissertation, *Kritika otvlechennykh nachal* ('A Critique of Abstract Principles', 1877–80), (3) *Chteniya o Bogochelovechestve* ('Lectures on Godmanhood', 1877–81).
158 *Lectures on Godmanhood* (abridged trans. by George L. Kline), *Russian Philosophy*, vol. III, p. 69.
159 Solovyov's terms *tsel'ny* ('integral') and *tsel'nost'* ('wholeness') are stronger synonyms for Hegel's *konkret* and *Konkretheit*. In Hegel's speculative usage 'concrete' means 'many-sided, adequately related, complexly mediated'. Solovyov's *tsel'ny* also means 'harmoniously unified or integrated'.
160 Cf. Hans Urs von Balthasar, *Herrlichkeit: Eine theologische Aesthetik* (Einsiedeln [Switz.], 1962), vol. II, pt. 2, p. 659.
161 *Sobranie sochinenii*, 2nd ed. (St Petersburg, 1911–14), vol. 10, p. 244.
162 von Balthasar, *Herrlichkeit*, p. 707.
163 *Soch.*, vol. 10, pp. 243–6.
164 E. N. Trubetskoi, *Mirosozertsanie Vl. S. Solov'eva* (Moscow, 1913), vol. I, p. 362.
165 von Balthasar, *Herrlichkeit*, pp. 680, 686.
166 The original is in French: '. . . Dieu aime le chaos dans son néant et Il veut qu'il [sc. 'chaos'] existe' (*La Russie et l'église universelle* [1889] in *Vladimir Soloviev: La Sophia et les autres écrits français*, ed. Fr François Rouleau (Lausanne, 1978), p. 252.
167 Mochulsky, *Vladimir Solov'ev*, p. 100.
168 Letter to N. N. Strakhov, 12 April, 1887: *Pis'ma*, ed. E. L. Radlov (St Petersburg, 1908), vol. I, pp. 33–4.
169 Florovsky, *Puti*, p. 318.
170 von Balthasar, *Herrlichkeit*, pp. 654ff.
171 *La Russie*, Bk. III, ch. 1: in *La Sophia*, pp. 240–4.
172 *Soch.*, vol. 3, pp. 83–96; trans. in *Russian Philosophy*, vol. III, pp. 62–6.
173 The term here translated 'positing' is *polozhenie* in Russian, *position* in French. Both appear to be modelled on the German *Setzung*.
174 Trubetskoi, *Mirosozertsanie Solov'eva*, vol. I, pp. 307f, 362f.
175 See [Mgr.] Jean Rupp, *Message ecclésial de Soloview: Présage et illustration de Vatican II* (Paris–Brussels, [1975]) esp. pt. 5: 'Un Levier pour l'oecuménisme'.
176 Letters to A. A. Kireyev, 1883 and 1884: *Pis'ma*, vol. 2, pp. 107, 118.
177 *L'Idée russe*, in *La Sophia*, p. 101.
178 *Ibid.*, p. 88.
179 *Soch.*, vol. 12, p. 28; emphasis added.
180 Cf. Fedor Stepun, *Mystische Weltschau: Fünf Gestalten des russischen Symbolismus* (Munich, 1964), p. 17.
181 Letter to Ivan Aksakov, March 1883: *Pis'ma*, vol. 4, p. 21.
182 Letter to his brother Michael, 1888: *Pis'ma*, vol. 4, pp. 118–19. (In translation: 'A fine idea! But apart from a miracle it is something impossible.') There are unconfirmed reports that Solovyov had a secret audience with Leo XIII at the Vatican in May 1888. (Cf. Mochulsky, *Vladimir Solov'ev*, p. 171 and n. 1.)
183 *Soch.*, vol. 4, p. 633; italics added.
184 *Soch.*, vol. 10, p. 218. ('And thus, Holy Fathers, we are now one in Christ.')
185 F. Gets (Goetz), 'Ob otnoshenii Vl. S. Solov'eva k evreiskomu voprosy' ('On V. S.

Solovyov's Attitude toward the Jewish Question'), *Voprosy filosofii i psikhologii*, Bk. 56 (1901), p. 198.
186 As is claimed by such otherwise perceptive and judicious Roman Catholic commentators as von Balthasar and Falk. Cf. von Balthasar, *Herrlichkeit*, p. 649n., and Heinrich Falk, S. J., 'Wladimir Solowjows Stellung zur katholischen Kirche', *Stimmen der Zeit*, vol. 144 (1948–9), esp. pp. 428–35.
187 Letter to V. V. Rozanov, 28 Nov., 1892: *Soch.* (Brussels, 1969), vol. 11, p. 416.
188 *Soch.*, vol. 11, p. 453. This letter is undated, but internal evidence – including a reference to incidents leading up to the Spanish–American War of 1898 – places it in 1896–7. (Cf. *ibid.*, p. 454.)
189 In Russian: *pravoslavno-kafolicheskii*. The letter was written in December 1896 or January 1897. (*Soch.*, vol. 11, p. 448.)
190 Cf. S. M. Solovyov, *Zhizn' i tvorcheskaya evolyutsiya Vladimira Solovyova* (Brussels, 1977), pp. 346–7. This informative book, by Solovyov's nephew, Fr Sergei M. Solovyov (1885–1946), a Roman Catholic priest of the Eastern Rite, was completed in the Soviet Union in 1923 but not published until 1977.
191 Stepun aptly remarks that Solovyov's move with respect to Roman Catholicism was not an *Übertritt* but a *Hinzutritt*, a move beyond the space separating the historical confessions into the space of a 'mystical universalism' (*Mystische Weltschau*, p. 28).
192 Mochulsky, *Vladimir Solov'ev*, pp. 218, 220.
193 These articles are reprinted in *Soch.*, vol. 10, pp. 227–523 and vol. 12, pp. 547–620.
194 There is an abridged translation by Vlada Tolley and James P. Scanlan in *Russian Philosophy*, vol. III, pp. 99–134.
195 Solovyov uses the term *voskresenie* rather than Fyodorov's *voskreshenie* (see n. 128).
196 *Tri razgovora*, *Soch.*, vol. 10, pp. 173, 183, 184.
197 *Ibid.*, pp. 219, 187.
198 *Ibid.*, pp. 210–12.
199 Florovsky, *Puti*, pp. 319, 318.
200 von Balthasar, *Herrlichkeit*, p. 651.
201 *Ibid.*, pp. 647f, 649, 658.

Bibliographical Essay

The major historical survey of Russian religious thought is Fr Georges Florovsky, *Puti russkogo bogosloviya* ('Ways of Russian Theology') (Paris, 1937, xerographic reproduction, Ann Arbor, Mich., 1975). Only the first half of this book, dealing with pre-nineteenth-century developments, has as yet appeared in English (1979). Florovsky's erudite and brilliantly written study offers penetrating criticisms of individual thinkers, some of which are unduly severe. A broader survey, which places religious thought in the context of speculative philosophy, is Fr Vasily V. Zenkovsky, *A History of Russian Philosophy*, 2 vols. (London and New York, 1953), translated by George L. Kline from *Istoriya russkoi filosofii*, 2 vols. (Paris, 1948, 1950). Zenkovsky is more sympathetic than Florovsky to most of the thinkers discussed in the present chapter, although his treatment is by no means uncritical. A more personal and speculative approach is to be found in Nicolas Berdyaev, *The Russian Idea* (London, 1947; New York, 1948; Ann Arbor, Mich., 1962), translated by R. M. French from *Russkaya ideya: osnovnye problemy russkoi mysli XIX veka i nachala XX veka* (Paris, 1946). Berdyaev treats nineteenth-century religious thought in the context of ethics, social philosophy, and the philosophy of history. Like Florovsky, he tends to assume in his readers the kind of detailed knowledge of Russian history and culture which Zenkovsky, for the most part, is at pains to provide.

Original editions of the works of the seven individual thinkers discussed in this chapter will be listed first, followed by selected translations and monographic studies. The passages in Florovsky and Zenkovsky devoted to each of the thinkers will also be indicated.

The Slavophiles (Khomyakov and Kireyevsky)

A. S. Khomyakov, *Polnoe sobranie sochinenii*, 4th ed., ed. Yu. F. Samarin, 8 vols. (Moscow, 1911–14); I. V. Kireyevsky, *Polnoe sobranie sochinenii*, ed. M. O. Gershenzon, 2 vols. (Moscow, 1911). Both are complete works, including correspondence, and, in Khomyakov's case, poetry.

Translations include: A. S. Khomyakov, *The Church is One*, translated by W. J. Birkbeck, first published in *Russia and the English Church during the last Fifty Years: Correspondence between William Palmer and M. Khomiakoff, 1844–1854*, ed. Birkbeck (London, 1895), vol. I, pp. 193–222; reprinted as a separate volume, London, 1948, New York, 1953. Khomyakov, 'On Recent Developments in Philosophy: Letters to Yu. F. Samarin', translated by Vladimir D. Pastuhov and Mary-Barbara Zeldin, is in James M. Edie *et al.* (eds.), *Russian Philosophy* (Chicago, 1965, 1969; Knoxville, Tenn., 1976), vol. I, pp. 221–69. His 'To the Serbians: A Message from Moscow', translated by Peter K. Christoff, is in the latter's book, *An Introduction to Nineteenth-Century Russian Slavophilism: A Study in Ideas*, vol. I: *A. S. Xomjakov* (The Hague, 1961), Appendix (pp. 247–68). Khomyakov's 'On the Western Confessions of Faith' (original in French) translated by Ashleigh E. Moorhouse, is in Fr Alexander Schemann (ed.), *Ultimate Questions: An Anthology of Modern Russian Religious Thought* (New York, 1965), pp. 31–69.

Kireyevsky's 'On the Necessity and Possibility of New Principles in Philosophy', translated by Peter K. Christoff, is included in *Russian Philosophy*, vol. I, pp. 171–213 and is reprinted in Christoff, *An Introduction . . .*, vol. II: *I. V. Kireevskij* (The Hague, 1972), Appendix pp. 346–75).

The earliest monograph on Khomyakov, and still one of the liveliest, is N. A. Berdyaev, *Aleksei Stepanovich Khomyakov* (Moscow, 1912; reprinted Westmead, Eng., 1971). Unfortunately, it has not been translated into English. Albert Gratieux, *A. S. Khomiakov and the Slavophile Movement*, 2 vols. (Belmont, Mass., 1982), translated by Elizabeth Meyendorff from *A. S. Khomiakov et le mouvement slavophile*, 2 vols. (Paris, 1939), is a scholarly and judicious study. Andrzej Walicki, *The Slavophile Controversy: History of a Conservative Utopia in Nineteenth Century Russian Thought* (Oxford, 1975), translated by Hilda Andrews-Rusiecka from *W kręgu konserwatywnej utopii: Struktura i przemiany rosyjskiego słowianofilstwa* (Warsaw, 1964), despite having originally been published in Communist Poland, and containing scattered laudatory references to Marx and Lenin, is a solid, erudite, and philosophically sophisticated study. The two volumes of Christoff's projected four-volume study of Slavophilism mentioned above (a third volume, on Konstantin Aksakov, has recently appeared [Princeton, 1982]) offer a careful and detailed exposition and assessment of Slavophile religious thought, in the context of Slavophile ethics, social philosophy, philosophical anthropology, and philosophy of history. See also Florovsky, *Puti*, pp. 249–60, 270–81; Zenkovsky, *A History*, pp. 180–227.

Dostoevsky

Polnoe sobranie khudozhestvennykh proizvedenii, 13 vols. (Moscow–Leningrad, 1926–30), includes the major fiction as well as *The Diary of a Writer* and critical articles. The 10-volume *Sobranie sochinenii* (Moscow, 1956–8) contains the complete fiction, but does not include *The Diary of a Writer* or Dostoevsky's critical articles. *Pis'ma*, ed. A. S. Dolinin, 4 vols. (Moscow, 1928–59), is a complete annotated edition of Dostoevsky's letters.

All of Dostoevsky's novels have been translated into English (first by Constance Garnett, then by David Magarshack, Sidney Monas, *et al.*). *The Diary of a Writer* was translated by Boris Brasol, 2 vols. (New York, 1954). 'Winter Notes on Summer Impressions' was translated by Kyril Fitzlyon as *Summer Impressions* (London, 1955).

Russian Religious Thought

Among the huge number of monographs of Dostoevsky those of special importance for the understanding of his religious thought include: Vyacheslav Ivanov, *Freedom and the Tragic Life: A Study in Dostoevsky* (New York, 1952; reprint, 1957), translated by Norman Cameron, apparently from a German version, *Dostojewski: Tragödie, Mythos, Mystik* (Tübingen, 1932), which in turn was translated by Alexander Kresling from Ivanov's manuscript. Portions of this work had appeared in Russian journals beginning in 1911. This perceptive, if sometimes involuted, account by a noted Russian classical scholar and Symbolist poet stresses the role of Dostoevsky's poetic 'myths' and introduces the category of 'tragic novel' or 'novel as tragedy'. Nicholas Berdyaev, *Dostoevsky* (New York, 1934; reprint, 1957), translated by Donald Attwater from *Mirosozertsanie Dostoyevskogo* (Prague, 1923), is a uniformly stimulating, if occasionally idiosyncratic study, organized around such themes as: man, freedom, evil, love, revolution, socialism, and Russia. Konstantin Mochulsky, *Dostoevsky: His Life and Work* (Princeton, 1967), translated by Michael A. Minihan from *Dostoyevskii: Zhizn' i tvorchestvo* (Paris, 1947), is a magisterial work, which offers an illuminating and balanced account of Dostoevsky's life, art, and ideas (including religious views) in their complex interrelationships. George Steiner, *Tolstoy or Dostoevsky: An Essay in the Old Criticism* (New York, 1959), is a lively account, which develops the distinction first drawn by Dmitri Merezhkovsky in 1901 between Dostoevsky as Christian dramatic poet and Tolstoy as pagan epic poet, stressing the unity of poetry and metaphysics in both authors. Steiner reads the major European languages but not Russian. A. Boyce Gibson, *The Religion of Dostoevsky* (Philadelphia, 1973), is a sympathetic, subtle, and judicious treatment of Dostoevsky's religious and theological views by a philosopher who learned Russian in order to read Dostoevsky. See also Stewart Sutherland, *Atheism and the Rejection of God: Contemporary Philosophy and 'The Brothers Karamazov'* (Oxford, 1977); Florovsky, *Puti*, pp. 295–300; Zenovsky, *A History*, pp. 410–32.

Leontyev

Sobranie sochinenii, 9 vols. (Moscow, 1912–14; xerographic reproduction, Ann Arbor, Mich., 1967) includes Leontyev's philosophical and religious essays, but does not include his important correspondence, which was published fragmentarily in various Russian journals before 1917. Translations of brief excerpts from several works, arranged topically, may be found in *Konstantin Leontiev: Against the Current (Selected Writings)*, ed. George Ivask, translated by George Reavey (New York, 1969), especially the section entitled 'Philosophy', pp. 133–229. An abridged translation of 'The Average European as an Ideal and Instrument of Universal Destruction' by William Shafer and George L. Kline is in *Russian Philosophy*, vol. II, pp. 267–80.

Nicholas Berdyaev, *Leontiev* (London, 1940, reprint 1968), translated by George Reavey from *Konstantin Leont'ev: Ocherk iz istorii russkoi religioznoi mysli* (Paris, 1926) is a sympathetic study, which emphasizes Leontyev's critique of religion and culture, as well as his 'aestheticism'. See also George L. Kline, *Religious and Anti-Religious Thought in Russia* (Chicago, 1968), pp. 35–54; Florovsky, *Puti*, pp. 300–5; Zenkovsky, *A History*, pp. 434–52.

Tolstoy

Polnoe sobranie sochinenii, ed. V. G. Chertkov *et al.*, 90 vols. (Moscow, 1929–1958; xerographic reproduction, Ann Arbor, Mich., 1967), is a complete annotated edition of all of Tolstoy's works, including his fiction, moral–religious treatises, diaries, and letters. *Sobranie sochinenii*, 12 vols. (Moscow, 1958–9) contains only the fiction.

227

GEORGE L. KLINE

All of Tolstoy's fiction and most of his moral–religious writings have been translated into English (a few volumes by Constance Garnett, twenty-one volumes by Louise and Aylmer Maude). A convenient anthology is *Lift Up Your Eyes: The Religious Writings of Leo Tolstoy*, ed. with an introduction by Stanley R. Hooper (New York, 1960). An abridged translation of 'The Law of Violence and the Law of Love' by James P. Scanlan is in *Russian Philosophy*, vol. II, pp. 213–34.

Of the many monographs on Tolstoy the most important for our purposes are Nicolas Weisbein, *L'Évolution religieuse de Tolstoï* (Paris, 1960), a meticulous study, which makes copious use of Tolstoy's diaries and correspondence; and George Steiner, *Tolstoy or Dostoevsky*, listed under Dostoevsky above. See also Kline, *Religious Thought*, pp. 11–12, 21–34; Florovsky, *Puti*, pp. 423–4; Zenkovsky, *A History*, pp. 386–99.

Fyodorov

Filosofiya obshchego dela (The Philosophy of the Common Task) ed. V. A. Kozhevnikov and N. P. Peterson, vol. I (Verny [now Alma Ata], 1906), vol. II (Moscow, 1913) (both volumes reprinted Westmead, England, 1970), consists mostly of writings not published during Fyodorov's lifetime. Thus, the editorial responsibilities of Kozhevnikov and Peterson were heavier and more sensitive than those of the editors of the other editions of collected works listed here. Each section is identified by the initials of the editor who prepared it for the press. A third volume was planned, but only fragments of the material which it was to have contained have been published.

A translation of 'The Question of Brotherhood . . .' (from *Filosofiya* . . ., vol. I, pp. 2–32), by Ashleigh E. Moorhouse and George L. Kline is in *Russian Philosophy*, vol. III, pp. 16–54. Excerpts drawn from *Filosofiya* . . ., vol. I, pp. 45–149, under the title 'The Restoration of Kinship Among Mankind', translated by Ashleigh E. Moorhouse, are in *Ultimate Questions*, pp. 175–223.

George M. Young, Jr., *Nikolai Fedorov: An Introduction*, (Belmont, Mass., 1979) is a vivid and sympathetic account, which places Fyodorov helpfully in his time and place, and judiciously assesses his sometimes complex relationships with Dostoevsky, Tolstoy, and Solovyov. Taras D. Zakydalsky, *N. F. Fyodorov's Philosophy of Physical Resurrection* (doctoral dissertation, Bryn Mawr College; University Microfilms, Ann Arbor, Mich., 1976), is a philosophically acute examination of certain theoretical problems which are raised by Fyodorov's project of physical resurrection, including the establishing of criteria of personal identity, and the relation of 'isomorphic' to 'isohylic' resurrection. See also Florovsky, *Puti*, pp. 322–30; Zenkovsky, *A History*, pp. 588–604.

Solovyov

Sobranie sochinenii, ed. S. M. Solovyov and E. L. Radlov, 2nd. ed., 10 vols. (St Petersburg, 1911–13); reprinted, Brussels, 1966, with two additional volumes (Brussels, 1969, 1970) containing unpublished and uncollected articles, selected correspondence, and the complete poetry. *Pis'ma*, ed. E. L. Radlov, 4 vols. (St Petersburg, 1908–11, 1923) is the complete correspondence. *Vladimir Soloviev: La Sophia et les autres écrits français*, ed. with introduction by Fr François Rouleau (Lausanne, 1978), contains the previously unpublished early dialogue on the Divine Sophia (written in Cairo and Sorrento, February–March, 1876), as well as previously published articles and letters written in French, and the text of *La Russie et l'église universelle* (Paris, 1889).

Seven of Solovyov's books have been translated into English, and there is a nearly complete edition of his works in German. Of special importance for present purposes are the following:

228

Peter P. Zouboff, *Godmanhood as the Main Idea of the Philosophy of Vladimir Solovyev* (New York, 1944), which contains a complete, but philosophically unsatisfactory, translation of the *Lectures on Godmanhood*. A new translation of portions of the *Lectures*, by George L. Kline, is included in *Russian Philosophy*, vol. III, pp. 62–84. Selections from *Foundations of Theoretical Philosophy*, translated by Vlada Tolley and James P. Scanlan, appear in *ibid.*, pp. 99–134. See also *Three Conversations concerning War, Progress, and the End of History, Including a Short Story of the Antichrist* (London, 1915), translated by A. Bakshy from *Tri razgovora: O voine, progresse, i kontse vsemirnoi istorii*; and *Russia and the Universal Church*, translated from the French by H. Rees (London, 1948). A useful collection is *A Solovyov Anthology*, arranged by S. L. Frank, translated by Natalie Duddington (London and New York, 1950; xerographic reproduction, Ann Arbor, Mich., 1973).

The most illuminating, comprehensive, and judicious of the many commentaries on Solovyov's thought is Konstantin Mochulsky, *Vl. Solovyov: Zhizn' i uchenie*, 2nd ed. (Paris, 1955); unfortunately, it has not yet been translated into English (or French or German). Ludolf Müller, *Das religionsphilosophische System Vl. Solovjevs* (Berlin, 1956) is a careful systematic account by a leading Protestant commentator of Solovyov's philosophy of religion and philosophical theology, in their relation to his philosophy of history. The long chapter on Solovyov in Hans Urs von Balthasar, *Herrlichkeit: Eine theologische Aesthetik* (Einsiedeln [Switzerland], 1962), vol. II, pt. 2, pp. 645–716, is an appreciative and philosophically penetrating discussion by an eminent Roman Catholic theologian and philosopher. Although von Balthasar does not know Russian, he has made full and fruitful use of the existing French and German translations of Solovyov's writings. See also Florovsky, *Puti*, pp. 308–21, 462–70; Zenkovsky, *A History*, pp. 469–531.

7

British Agnosticism

JAMES C. LIVINGSTON

A God understood would be no God at all.

Sir William Hamilton

Who art Thou Lord? We know Thee not; We only know Thy work is vast, And that amid Thy worlds our lot, Unknown to us, by Thee is cast.

'Charles Darwin: A Memorial Poem'
George John Romanes

the Unknowable seems a proposal to take something for God simply because we do not know what the devil it is.

F. H. Bradley

I

At the close of the last century the philosopher James Seth remarked that 'if one were asked to name the two most characteristic attitudes of the latter half of the nineteenth century, one would be safe in answering – Evolutionism and Agnosticism'. Seth went on to observe how noteworthy and surprising it was that an age which saw such remarkable achievements in science 'should be also the Age of Agnosticism, the epoch of the creed *Ignoramus et ignorabimus*'.[1] The late Victorians, too, were struck by this fact, and it constituted a major point of debate between Anglicans and other theists, positivists, and the agnostics themselves concerning the very possibility, the limits, and the effects of this rapidly advancing temper of mind.

We only recently have come to recognize that major shifts in what people believe and in the way they live their lives are traceable not only or even primarily to intellectual causes. This is apparent to us now in assessing the spread of secularization in England in the latter half of the nineteenth century. The forces of industrialization and urbanization, as well as the impact of scientific discovery and technology were decisive in changing patterns of behaviour and ways of perceiving and thinking. Nevertheless, whether as cause or effect, ideas play their role in advancing cultural change and this is evident in the shifting religious climate in Britain in the last decades of the nineteenth century. What is of interest, however, is that the dominant figures in this chapter of religious history were not the professional theologians or clerics; they were, rather, the lay prose writers – Mill, Arnold, Huxley, and Spencer – the Victorian sages, major and minor, who were absorbed with the cultural significance of an emerging scientific and secular society. Beatrice Webb recalled that in those decades it was the men of science who were the leading British intellectuals and that it was they who stood out as men of genius with international reputations; also that it was they who were routing the theologians.

Until recently the religious histories of the period have been largely the work of Anglican churchmen, concentrating their attention on the ecclesiastical changes and theological developments within the Church of England. The standard narratives focus on the Anglican classics from Thomas Arnold to Charles Gore and on the disputes from *Essays and Reviews* (1860) to *Essays Catholic and Critical* (1926). One need not deprecate this Anglican historical tradition – the Church did in fact reveal a commendable resiliency in its encounters with science and modern social and philosophical currents – in making the judgment that this was but a chapter in a larger religious drama of the struggle in Victorian Britain between scientific naturalism and the quest for a spiritual interpretation of life. The reconceiving and modernizing of Anglican thought must, then, be understood as a significant event, but only that, in a broader historical development: the emergence and the challenge of a secular, agnostic frame of mind.

This new empirical and secular temper was articulated by a group of thinkers in Britain who came to find the received religious tradition intellectually suspect and socially irrelevant. These men included not only the scientific empiricists who looked to Mill's *System of Logic* as 'a sacred scripture', but also those critics of scientific empiricism – Carlyle, Arnold, T. H. Green – who felt that modern men could neither do without religion nor do with it as it was. Nevertheless, the noteworthy and culturally significant fact is the crucial role and historical persistence in British religious thought of the empiricist tradition, or what has been called 'the agnostic principle'. It dominates the discussion of religion in Britain from Mill to Antony Flew. It is Britain's most important contribution to the *philosophical* discussion of religion in the last two centuries.

Like so many movements of thought in the nineteenth century – one thinks for example of Hegelianism – Agnosticism is commonly thought to be long dead. This is due, in large part, to the fact that the works of the great agnostics – Hamilton, Mansel, Spencer, even Leslie Stephen and Huxley – are no longer read. However, this essay will suggest that the agnostic controversy not only marked an especially important chapter in modern intellectual and religious history, in that the agnostic debates succeeded in posing serious problems for religious belief but also, and more importantly, helped to create a temper of mind antipathetic to *traditional* religious belief – one which has continued to be widely held to this day. This cast of mind was a significantly new social phenomenon. It is further suggested that contemporary philosophical debate concerning religious belief reveals a marked similarity to the agnostic disputations of a century ago in that the issues under discussion today are often but an echo of what was argued and concluded then. That is to say, the agnostic controversy was instrumental in establishing a temper of mind and certain philosophical positions and claims against which and beyond which theology, in some very important ways, has progressed little.

Before examining Agnosticism in the context of nineteenth-century British religious thought it will be helpful to define our terms, i.e., to say something about the difficulties associated with the meaning and use of the word 'agnostic', and to say something of the causes and beginnings of the movement. An issue on which the participants in the numerous debates were in substantial dispute – from the 1850s onward – was the exact meaning of the terms 'nescience' and 'agnostic'. Whether, for example, there could be an absolute or complete nescience or Agnosticism and, if not, what a mitigated Agnosticism implied in the regions of theology, metaphysics, or science.

In the course of the controversy the word Agnosticism came to be used as a synonym for atheism, infidelism, scepticism, positivism, materialism, pantheism, and know-nothingism. While some agnostics shared some doctrines in common with thinkers claiming one or another of these labels, Agnosticism cannot be identified with any one of them, nor did the chief agnostics (Spencer, Huxley, Stephen, Tyndall) accept any of these designations as defining their own position. It was, in fact, Huxley's irritation at being labelled as 'infidel' by the Rev. Henry Wace, Principal of King's College, London, and his being embraced as a 'Positivist' by Frederic Harrison that prompted him to write his famous article, 'Agnosticism', in 1889. There he explains how he came to invent the word and what he meant by it. While the question of the beginnings of nineteenth-century British Agnosticism is disputed,[2] it is clear that Huxley not only coined the term but gave it its wide currency and stamped it with his own particular meaning. Since Huxley recorded his recollection of the matter, it is worth citing his description in full:

When I reached intellectual maturity and began to ask myself whether I was an atheist, a theist, or a pantheist, a materialist or an idealist, a Christian or a freethinker, I found that the more I learned and reflected the less ready was the answer, until at last I came to the conclusion that I had neither art nor part with any of these denominations except the last. The one thing in which most of these good people were agreed was the one thing in which I differed from them. They were quite sure that they had attained a certain 'gnosis' – had, more or less successfully, solved the problem of existence; while I was quite sure that I had not, and had a pretty strong conviction that the problem was insolvable. And with Hume and Kant on my side, I could not think myself presumptuous in holding fast by that opinion.[3]

Hume was the dominant influence on Huxley's Agnosticism, but Hamilton's essay on 'The Philosophy of the Unconditioned', which he read about 1840, left an indelible impression upon him as a young boy. He later spoke of Hamilton's essay as 'the original spring of Agnosticism'.[4]

Huxley also explains the circumstances of his invention of the term 'agnostic', which occurred at a meeting of the Metaphysical Society one evening in 1869:

Every variety of philosophical and theological opinion was represented there, and expressed itself with entire openness; most of my colleagues were –ists of one sort or another and however kind and friendly they might be, I, the man without a rag of label to cover himself with . . . So I took thought, and invented what I conceived to be the appropriate title of 'agnostic'. It came into my head as suggestively antithetic to the 'gnostic' of Church history, who professed to know so much about the very things of which I was ignorant; and I took the earliest opportunity of parading it at our Society . . . To my great satisfaction, the term took.[5]

The term agnostic did indeed 'take'. The periodicals and newspapers in the 1880s were absorbed with the debate. At the universities it became the predominant creed among the undergraduates and the younger dons. On the whole, Agnosticism appealed to the educated classes, whereas militant atheism and secularism had a greater attraction among some segments of the working class. Nevertheless, the word became a byword of persons of all stations. The fact was humorously conveyed by a cartoon in *Punch* depicting a young cook undergoing an interrogation by her future mistress. On being asked to what religious denomination she belonged, the girl confidently replied: 'Please ma'am, I'm an agnostic.'

The term Agnosticism came to take on a variety of meanings which led to innumerable squabbles. Nevertheless, it is clear that it originated in the doctrine that metaphysical, hence theological, knowledge is impossible in view of the inherent limitations of the human mind – a doctrine derived from Hume and Kant by way of Hamilton, Mansel, and Spencer. Huxley was to give to the term a wider, less philosophically precise, application which, for all its difficulties (pounced on by his antagonists), more truly represents the spirit and aims of the leading agnostics in the last three decades of the century, as well as today. The belief which he held and preached with such zeal and success – and which he shared with Spencer, Leslie Stephen, Tyndall, among the most illustrious agnostics – included three very basic principles. These he summarized in a little-known article published in 1884. Since he invented the word, he wrote that he had a certain 'patent right' on it and, in any case, was entitled to say what it originally meant. The word, for him, involved (1) metaphysical nescience, (2) the application of scientific method to the study of all matters of experience and (3) the rejection of much of Christian doctrine as unproven or unprovable.[6] These constitute the first principles and the faith of Agnosticism to the present day. They also give a clue to its origins and the success of the movement.

Agnosticism, far more so than the British Secularist movement, was dominated by the rising intellectual aristocracy, by men who came from the educated middle class and disliked the polemics of working-class atheism.[7] Its philosophical descent cannot be traced out in detail, but two sources predominated and, in each case, produced a distinctive form of Agnosticism in the period after 1850. On the one hand, there was the empiricist tradition from Locke through Hume. It was this philosophic tradition that informed the critique – particularly the epistemological principles – of what can be called 'Left-wing' Agnosticism, i.e., the writings and influence of Huxley, the Stephens, and Tyndall. Here Hume's influence is paramount. Passages in Huxley and Leslie Stephen often appear to be but paraphrases of the notorious criticism of metaphysics found in Hume. This form of Agnosticism was closely associated with Victorian scientific naturalism. The other source of Victorian Agnosticism was Kant, as interpreted by Hamilton and applied in the work of Mansel and Spencer. It is this line of descent that can properly be called 'Right-wing' Agnosticism. It was an Agnosticism that, as Kant had put it, 'found it necessary to deny knowledge in order to make room for faith'.

The sources or causes of modern British Agnosticism, especially those represented in the writings of Huxley and the 'Left-wing', cannot, however, be understood fully in terms of philosophical influences alone. There were also, from the 1830s on, a series of damaging attacks, either direct or indirect, on orthodox Christian belief – particularly on the Bible — from the physical and historical sciences: Charles Lyell's *Principles of Geology* (1830–3); Robert Chambers' *Vestiges of Creation* (1844); Darwin's *Origin of Species* (1859); *Essays and Reviews* (1860); Bishop Colenso's *The Pentateuch Examined* (1862–3); Huxley's *Lay Sermons* (1870); Edward Tylor's *Primitive*

JAMES C. LIVINGSTON

Culture (1871); Tyndall's *Belfast Address* (1874) and *Fragments of Science* (1879); Stephens' *Essays on Freethinking and Plainspeaking* (1873); W. K. Clifford's *Lectures and Essays* (1879); and the multiple volumes of Spencer's *Synthetic Philosophy* (1862–96). The response to many of these assaults was to say in effect: 'If these men of learning find such superstitions and falsehoods in and contradictions with the records of our religion and in our received theology, who am I to challenge their undoubted knowledge?' The seeds of doubt were sown concerning the veracity of the biblical texts and, *eo ipso*, of the central doctrines of Christian belief.

The scientific and historical studies contributed to what was, perhaps, the most potent dissolvent of orthodox belief, viz., relativism. Darwin's *Origin* and Tylor's *Primitive Culture*, while sidestepping Christianity, undermined, by their theories of development, its explanatory and authoritative grounds. It was not difficult to infer from these works their agnostic conclusions concerning any claim to absoluteness or uniqueness. Walter Pater read Darwin and in 1866 reflected:

Modern thought is distinguished from ancient by its cultivation of the 'relative' spirit in place of the 'absolute' . . . To the modern spirit nothing is, or can be rightly known, except relatively and under conditions. The philosophical conception of the relative has been developed in modern times through the influence of the sciences of observation. Those sciences reveal types of life evanescing into each other by inexpressible refinements of change.[8]

A third, and fundamentally important, source of the attraction of Agnosticism was ethical. If the Bible and the Creeds were shown to be false or doubtful, how morally reprehensible to continue to recite the Creeds and propagate the biblical doctrine! There was hardly a moment during the mid and late Victorian decades when the ethical issue of belief, and particularly of subscription to the Creeds and Articles of the Church of England, was not controverted in the periodicals and the press. The unremitting presence of this issue took its toll on the morale of the laity as well as the clergy. In the 1870s churchmen were called upon to answer a relentless series of attacks on the moral justification for holding their religious beliefs. Perhaps the sharpest and most uncompromising rebuke and challenge came from W. K. Clifford, in his essay 'The Ethics of Belief'. According to Clifford, one has a moral duty to inquire into the evidence – for example, the biblical sources – of one's belief, for assent to false or untested beliefs, no matter how seemingly trivial, prepares one to accept more of the same and weakens others:

If I let myself believe anything on insufficient evidence, there may be no great harm done by the mere belief; it may be true after all, or I may never have occasion to exhibit it in outward acts. But I cannot help doing this great harm towards Man, that I make myself credulous, and lose the habit of testing things, and inquiring into them . . . The credulous man is father to the liar and the cheat.[9]

It was not, however, only a question of the morality of believing on false or insufficient evidence. The doctrines themselves – original sin, sacrificial atonement, and especially the biblical theodicy and eternal damnation – were judged morally offensive. Charles Darwin's highly personal objection to eternal punishment was typical:

I can hardly see how anyone ought to wish Christianity to be true; for, if so, the plain language of the text seems to show that the men who do not believe – and this would include my father, brother, and almost all my best friends – will be everlastingly punished. And this is a damnable doctrine.[10]

A London writer rightly judged that 'there is no one thing which oppresses the mind of thoughtful men at the present day more than the popular idea that Christianity is committed to the affirmation of the everlasting damnation of the overwhelming majority of mankind . . . It is one of the most fruitful sources of unbelief.'[11]

At a time when science was revealing how very much we actually do not know, and calling for a learned modesty, even ignorance, how pretentious appeared the dogmatic pronouncements of ecclesiastics and theologians on the profound questions of the origin and moral governance of the world! 'It is enough', wrote Leslie Stephen, 'that [the theologians] defend the nature of God Almighty with an accuracy from which modest naturalists would shrink in describing the genesis of a black-beetle.'[12]

There was, finally, a factor which contributed to the attraction of Agnosticism among the spokesmen for the new class of scientific professionals: a social and political consideration which had to do with what groups or institutions in Britain would, through their leadership and power, determine matters of public policy, e.g., public health and education. This was a potent, if less obvious, motive in the Victorian conflict between science and religion and explains the attraction of Agnosticism for those opposed to the hold which 'Ecclesiasticism' had over matters affecting the social and political life of the British people. Men like Spencer, Tyndall, Galton, and Huxley were especially alert to the adverse effect which the ecclesiastical establishment was having on the application of science to social problems. The 'Prayer controversy', which kept rekindling through the 1860s and 70s, is illustrative. During the wet summer of 1860 when the harvests were threatened, Bishop Wilberforce instructed his clergy to offer an appointed prayer for good weather for the preservation of crops. Several bishops followed his example. Huxley saw Wilberforce and the successive representatives of dogmatic Ecclesiastical Christianity as standing in the way of the scientific spirit and its application. 'The future of our civilization . . . depends', he wrote, 'on the result of the contest between Science and Ecclesiasticism which is now afoot . . .'[13] Some clerics, such as Charles Kingsley, opposed Wilberforce's use of prayer and were commended by John Tyndall, who wrote that Kingsley was doing 'service to public character, by encouraging a manly and intelligent conflict with the real causes of disease and scarcity, instead of a delusive reliance on supernatural aid'.[14]

The debates over the efficacy of prayer, over natural selection, or the narrative of the Gaderene swine were, then, more than disputes over ideas. Rather, they 'manifested the tensions arising as the intellectual nation became more highly differentiated in functions, professions, and institutions. It was a clash between established and emerging intellectual and social elites for popular cultural preeminence in a modern industrial state.'[15]

II

While the philosophical origins of modern Agnosticism are traceable to the British empiricists from Locke to Hume and to the philosophy of Kant, the immediate sources of nineteenth-century British Agnosticism are found in the writings of Hamilton, Mansel, and Spencer. Sir William Hamilton (1788–1856) was a follower of the Scottish realism of Thomas Reid. He was, however, profoundly influenced by his reading of Kant whom he did not, it is now generally conceded, fully understand. According to Hamilton, 'the mind can conceive and consequently can know, only the *limited*, and *the conditionally limited*'; that is, the mind cannot know the Infinite or Absolute which 'can be conceived only by a thinking away from, or abstraction of, those very conditions under which thought itself is realized'. 'Consequently', he insists, 'the notion of the Unconditioned is only negative.'[16]

For Hamilton, thought necessarily supposes conditions and relations, e.g., mind and matter; and the knowledge of certain facts is always conditioned by our knowledge of other facts. 'To think', writes Hamilton, '*is to condition*; and conditional limitation is the fundamental law of the possibility of thought.' Just as 'the eagle [cannot] outsoar the atmosphere in which he floats; so the mind cannot transcend that sphere of limitation, within and through which exclusively the possibility of thought is realized'.[17]

As the mind cannot transcend its conditionedness, so God as the Absolute or Unconditioned is not constituted by necessary relations, and thus, as Unconditioned, cannot be known. To think of God, as have philosophers such as M. Cousin, as Absolute *cause* is to conceive of Deity in terms of some necessary relation to the world. Assuming such a hypothesis, one of two alternatives must be admitted: 'God, as necessarily determined to pass from absolute essence to relative manifestation, is determined to pass either *from the better to the worse, or from the worse to the better.*'[18] According to Hamilton, the dilemma of philosophical theology is unavoidable. Either God is independent of the world for His being and perfection, on which theory philosophical knowledge of God founders; or God is dependent on the world for His manifestation or perfection and the above difficulties concerning the Divine possibility must be faced. Mill and the British Hegelians were soon, of course, to grasp that nettle and to usher in the modern debate over panentheism.

Hamilton's conclusion is that philosophy thus teaches us

the salutary lesson, that the capacity of thought is not to be constituted into the measure of existence; and we are warned from recognizing the domain of our knowledge as necessarily coextensive with the horizon of our faith. And by a wonderful revelation we are thus, in our very consciousness of our inability to conceive aught above the relative and finite, inspired with a belief in the existence of something unconditioned beyond the sphere of all comprehensible reality . . . True, therefore, are the declarations of a pious philosophy: – 'A God understood would be no God at all;' – 'To think that God is, as we can think him to be, is blasphemy.'[19]

Hamilton's logical speculations were put to the test by Mill and others and *logically* found wanting. Nevertheless, his plea for a 'learned ignorance' had a profound impact on men like Huxley. Hamilton's appeal was not to be found in his speculations but in such compelling passages as the following:

The recognition of human ignorance is not only the one highest, but the one true, knowledge; and its first-fruit . . . is humility. Simple nescience is not proud; consummated science is positively humble . . . The grand result of human wisdom is . . . an articulate confession, by our natural reason, of the truth declared in relevation, – that *now* we see through a glass darkly.[20]

It was H. L. Mansel (1820–71), Waynflete professor of moral and metaphysical philosophy at Oxford, afterwards Dean of St Paul's, who applied Hamilton's epistemological doctrines more directly to the problems of a Christian theology of revelation in his Bampton Lectures of 1858 on *The Limits of Religious Thought*. Mansel boldly staked his case for Christian revelation on metaphysical agnosticism. The motto of the book is taken from Hamilton: 'No difficulty emerges in theology, which had not previously emerged in philosophy.' Thus for Mansel the crux of the matter is that 'the primary and proper object of criticism is not Religion, natural or revealed, but the human mind in relation to Religion'; and the ground of the mind's impotence in relation to religion is Hamilton's 'great principle', viz., that the Ultimate, being unconditioned, is incognizable and inconceivable.

Earlier Mansel had made use of Hamilton's doctrine in controverting F. D. Maurice's neological use of the word 'Eternal' in the latter's effort to temper the severity of the orthodox teaching on eternal damnation. Maurice interpreted 'Eternal' as devoid of all temporal associations. Mansel responded that a consciousness which does not embrace a succession of states

represents no human conception at all . . . We can conceive representatively in thought only what we have experienced presentatively in intuition . . . The term Eternity, in this sense, expresses not a conception, but the negation of a conception, the acknowledgment of the possible existence of a Being concerning whose consciousness we can only make the negative assertion that it is not like our consciousness.[21]

Mansel argues that all human knowledge implies consciousness of relation, i.e., of some thing, hence conditionedness. What a being or condition may be like *out* of human consciousness, our consciousness cannot tell us. The principle applies as well to the Divine personality as to the future life. To speak of an Absolute or Infinite Person is inconceivable. Yet our fundamental religious experience points to an infinite Personal Being, who as a free agent can, for example, hear and answer prayer. The dilemma only forces Mansel to conclude that 'the limits of positive thought cannot be the limits of belief':

If, then, it can be shown that our religious instincts and feelings necessarily require us to believe in a Personal God, we are not justified in rejecting that belief on account of any apparent difficulties raised by the Philosophy of the Unconditioned. We may believe that a Personal God exists: we may believe that He is also absolute and infinite as well as personal; though we are unable, under our present conditions of thought, to conceive the manner in which the attributes of absoluteness and infinity coexist with those which constitute personality.[22]

Our positive conceptions of God's attributes, derived as they are from the imperfect representation of them in the analogous attributes of human nature, is what Mansel meant in calling such concepts *regulative*, not *speculative*, truths. In theology the limits of speculation do not issue in a necessary suspension of belief in regulative truths.

We are required to believe and to act upon much that we cannot comprehend; and our belief and practice must take such a form as is adapted to the constitution of our own minds, even though it may also be related to a possible ultimate truth which our present faculties are unable to seize. Hence it is that ideas and images which do not represent God as He is may nevertheless represent Him as it is our duty to regard Him. They are not in themselves true; but we must, nevertheless, believe and act as if they were true . . . a conception which is speculatively untrue may be regulatively true.[23]

It is important to stress that Mansel's position is not to be confused with pragmatism or the 'as if' philosophy of Hans Vaihinger. He clearly indicates that a regulative conception, while not derived from the immediate perception of the object itself, is *'from that of something else, supposed more or less nearly to resemble it'* (italics added).[24]

If man aspires to understand God he is drawn inevitably to the phenomena of human consciousness and, hence, to 'a more or less refined Anthropomorphism', which, far from unsound, 'is one that meets us in almost every page of Holy Scripture'. According to Mansel, it is in Revelation that God has given men those symbols by which He wills us to think of Him and by which He guides our conduct. In Revelation God graciously condescends to meet our limits and the spiritual needs of our nature. To talk, then, of the conflict between the object of reason and revelation is unmeaning: religion is, after all, the relation between God and man. But to compare, and thus discern conflict between two ideas, it is necessary to have a positive and distinct idea of both – a condition which Mansel has shown us our minds lack: 'The Coexistence of the Infinite and the Finite, in any manner whatever, is inconceivable *by reason*; and the only ground that can be taken for accepting one representation of it, rather than another, is that one is revealed, and the other is not revealed.'[25] However, does not our sense of absolute dependence (Schleiermacher) or our moral obligation (Kant) serve as direct intuitions of God? Mansel insists that these two sentiments are fundamental to all religion and that they give rise to the two sublime acts of personal religious life: prayer and the sense of sin which seeks release in expiation. They do not, however, yield a direct intuition of God as absolute and infinite.

Mansel's rejection of natural theology, his refusal to allow reason the right to determine what Revelation is or must be, and his denial that man has any moral or mystical 'point of contact' with God have their historical affinities in his contemporary, Kierkegaard, and his doctrine of the 'infinite qualitative distinction' between time and Eternity and later in Karl Barth's 'positivism of Revelation'. Mansel's anti-rationalism also has a certain likeness to Rudolf Otto's stress on the radical otherness of God and that awe and wonder experienced in the presence of the numinous or holy – a position not uncongenial to some contemporary philosophers who, following A. J. Ayer, accept a non-cognitive view of religious belief.

Like Butler before him and Barth after him, Mansel failed, as James Martineau and Leslie Stephen pointed out, to appreciate that his *tour de force* was a two-edged sword; that there were those who, convinced of the impotence of reason in matters theological, would remain agnostic concerning the claims of Revelation as well. Mansel thus reminded Huxley of 'the drunken fellow in Hogarth's contested election, who is sawing through the signpost at the other party's public house, forgetting he is sitting on the other end of it'.[26]

For all its limitations, Mansel's Bampton lectures focused attention on *the* fundamental modern question of religious knowledge *vis-à-vis* the logical status of the theistic, revelatory claims of the Bible. What is the nature and status of biblical revelation? Mansel's answer was anathema to both the Coleridgeans and Broad Church theologians (Maurice, Stanley, Hort) and to the empiricist disciples of Mill. Maurice was provoked by Mansel's seeming defence of biblical revelation as a communication of regulative doctrines rather than as the revelation of the living God. He responded in an emotionally charged and confused book entitled *What is Revelation* (1859). For Maurice, the biblical drama chronicles the existential encounter with the living God in His dealings with men and nations. God is not Spencer's Unknowable nor is He known only regulatively, symbolically, analogically; He is encountered existentially, 'personally'.

Maurice regarded Mansel's dogmatic presentation of the revelation of the Incarnation – something like Kierkegaard's portrayal of the Absolute Paradox in the *Philosophical Fragments* – as lacking the vital reality of an encounter with an historical person. Maurice objected that Mansel's treatment of Christ was but 'an additional, hard and insoluble difficulty, which we must receive in addition to all the other difficulties, because God commands us in His book to receive it'.[27] On the contrary, what is disclosed in the revelation in Christ is the very living, suffering, reality of God – 'He that hath seen me hath seen the Father.' To Maurice's thinking, Mansel was a modern day Arian – and equally as great a threat to the faith.

Maurice, of course, for all his rhetorical probity and profundity, failed to understand the problem with which Mansel was wrestling, viz., the epistemological question of the status of putative statements of fact claiming metaphysical truth. Mansel's problem was the one initiated by Hume and pursued by Mill and the agnostic empiricists from Huxley to Ronald Hepburn in our own day.[28] Mansel wrote that the Incarnation is 'the manifestation of God *in the flesh*', the 'assumption of a nature in which the manifestation is adapted to human faculties and limited to a mode in which man is capable of receiving it'.[29] Mansel's position, contrary to some critics, does not preclude his use of a form of analogy in his regulative use of revelatory language, as will be noted in his dispute with Mill.

Mansel's *philosophical* contemporaries were as outraged by his book as were Maurice and the Broad Churchmen. Mill is, perhaps, the paradigm case. He could not abide Mansel's 'morally pernicious' claim that it is not necessary to suppose that the infinite goodness of God 'is not the same goodness which we know and love in our fellow-creatures, distinguished only as infinite in degree'.[30] Mill takes his stand 'on the acknowledged principle of logic and of morality, that when we mean different things we have no right to call them by the same name . . . Language has no meaning for the words Just, Merciful, Benevolent, save that in which we predicate them of our fellow creatures.'[31] 'What belongs to it as Infinite I do not pretend to know', Mill concedes, 'But I know that infinite goodness must be goodness and that what is not consistent with goodness is not consistent with infinite goodness.'[32]

Mill's logical empiricist conclusion is the direct precursor of that represented more recently by Antony Flew in the significant 'Theology and Falsification' debate (1955). Mill writes:

If what I am told respecting [God] is of a kind which no facts that can be supposed added to my knowledge could make me perceive to be right; if his alleged ways of dealing with the world are such as no imaginable hypothesis respecting things known to him and unknown to me, could make consistent with the goodness and wisdom which I mean,[33] then one is speaking vacuously or insincerely.

'I will call no being good', Mill concludes, 'who is not what I mean when I apply that epithet to my fellow creatures; and if such a being can sentence me to hell for not so calling him, to hell I will go.'[34]

There is some doubt whether Mill thoroughly grasped Mansel's understanding of analogy. It has been argued that Mansel's doctrine does steer between the pitfalls of anthropomorphism and a pure Agnosticism; that he did not deny a resemblance between God and man, or hold that such a resemblance is limited to St Thomas' analogy of proportionality. Rather, that Mansel holds that many things which, for example, are to God just might *appear* unjust to men. 'It was not the connotation of the term "justice" which differed in the case of God and in the case of man, but the *denotation*; the *particular things* which God saw to be just did not coincide with the particular things which men supposed to be just.'[35] According to Mansel, in one sense a phrase such as 'the love of God' is utterly unimaginable; yet the believer does trust that there is something in the ineffable mystery of God's providence that is the prototype of what men experience as love in their encounters with their fellows.

Mansel's position has striking affinities to one proposed more recently by I. M. Crombie.[36] Like Mansel, Crombie recognizes the logical oddness of theological speech, since we are not talking about an object that falls within our normal experience. Nevertheless, there are human experiences of limitation which we all genuinely feel and, while we are not able to conceive positively the kind of being that would be free from such limits, they properly represent the 'reference range' by means of which a concept of God can be specified. For Mansel such experiences as contingency, dependence, and moral obligation represent such a 'reference range'. Crombie similarly writes that our concept of an Infinite Spirit stands for 'the abstract conception of the possibility of the removal of certain intellectual dissatisfactions which we may feel about the universe of common experience'.[37] For both thinkers such an 'undifferentiated theism' provides a sufficient referent for the term God. Yet Mansel and Crombie would agree that such an 'undifferentiated theism' does not give us any *knowledge* of the positive attributes of God. For such knowledge, both agree, one must resort to the language of symbol and parable, i.e., the language of concrete and authoritative revelation, in which certain objects and events are viewed as manifestations of the Divine. Crombie's conclusion might easily be read out of Mansel:

The things we say about God are said on the authority of the words and acts of Christ, who spoke in human language, using parable; and so we too speak of God in parable – authoritative parable, authorized parable; knowing that the truth is not literally that which our parables represent, knowing therefore that now we see in a glass darkly, but trusting, because we trust the source of the parables, that in believing them and interpreting them in the light of each other, we shall not be misled, that we shall have such knowledge as we need to possess for the foundation of the religious life.[38]

The problem here, of course, is that outside the circle of faith the attribution of positive Divine qualities has no meaning, since they do not have that independent experiential grounding demanded by the 'agnostic principle' set forth by Mill and carried forward since by his disciples.

The controversy between Mansel, Maurice, and Mill unquestionably exposes one of the central issues of modern theological debate. In their very different ways Mansel and Maurice perceived the challenge that philosophical empiricism posed for the Christian doctrine of Revelation. Their creative responses have begotten their counterparts in the twentieth century in, e.g., Karl Barth and the theologies of 'Encounter' (Brunner, Buber). The fundamental limitation of both Mansel and Maurice was their failure, unlike their Broad Church colleagues, to take seriously the historical–critical questions concerning Scripture. Mansel, like Barth a century later, encouraged the conservative clergy of his day to remain satisfied that the whole tradition of orthodox doctrine was immune from criticism. While Maurice refused to join the conservatives in attacking the then radical historical–critical conclusions proffered by the writers of *Essays and Reviews*, neither did he take seriously the implications of their work. He could continue, for example, to accept uncritically the Johannine reports of the words of Christ. It is correct, then, to conclude that while 'Maurice attained genuine freedom from biblical literalism . . . he never squared this with his quite uncritical realism about "biblical facts". He left thus as many problems as he resolved.'[39]

In the Prospectus of *A System of Philosophy*, published in 1860, Herbert Spencer (1820–1903) outlined the intellectual programme which was soon to attract large numbers of the late Victorian educated class. In the precis of the *First Principles*, which was to serve as the initial volume in the series and was to become the 'Bible of Agnosticism', Spencer wrote that he was 'carrying a step further the doctrine put into shape by Hamilton and Mansel'.[40] It was aptly remarked that Mansel was the Charagus, the teacher, of the agnostic chorus, Spencer was its Coryphaeus, its leader. Spencer moved from Theism to Agnosticism by means of Hamilton and Mansel long before he was introduced to evolutionary theory; the latter had nothing to do with his becoming an agnostic.[41]

Spencer's philosophy of the Unknowable, derivative as it is from Mansel's Bampton Lectures, requires little elaboration. Where he notably differed from Mansel was in his insistence that the Unknowable must be conceived not only as a negation of the knowable but as something positive. This got him into some metaphysical confusions that prompted thinkers like Bradley, Sidgwick, and James Ward to ridicule the grotesqueness of his agnostic doctrine. While asserting the Unknowable *not* to be known, Spencer elsewhere confidently declared, e.g., that it was 'the fundamental reality which underlies all that appears', and was 'the omnipresent Causal Energy or Power of which all phenomena are the manifestations'. How he warranted his knowledge of the existence and the particular attributes of the Unknowable is left unclear and this muddle led him into controversies both with those who thought his agnostic metaphysics incoherent and those who felt that he simply had not carried his speculations concerning 'the Infinite and Eternal Energy' far enough, i.e., to their logical conclusion in a 'Christian Agnosticism'.[42]

Spencer's speculations on the Unknowable resulted in one of the most celebrated of the late-Victorian religious controversies, the so-called 'Quadrangular Duel' of 1884. Spencer initiated the debate in an article entitled 'Religion: A Retrospect and Prospect'. Science was forcing theology to abandon its anthropomorphic notions and, Spencer prophesied, the theistic conception of the future would be one 'which has been enlarging from the beginning [and] must go on enlarging, until by disappearance of its limits, it becomes a consciousness which transcends the forms of distinct thought, though it forever remains a consciousness'.[43] Passages such as this were pounced on by the positivist Frederic Harrison, by the sceptic James Fitzjames Stephen, and the Catholic apologist Wilfrid Ward. A lengthy argument ensued. Harrison and Ward agreed that Spencer was simply putting a bit of spiritual unction into Ignorance; that all his religion came to was a negation – that 'there is a sort of something, about which we can know nothing'.[44] Harrison would have liked to have seen the new *Imitatio Ignati*: 'Your men of science have routed our priests, and have silenced our old teachers. What religious faith do you give in its place? And [Spencer] replies, his full heart bleeding for them, and he says, "Think of the Unknowable".'[45]

It was Stephen, however, who attacked Spencer with merciless logic as well as withering invective. 'I do not clearly understand', he wrote,

what is meant by 'a consciousness' or how a conception 'by disappearance of its limits' can become a consciousness; or how if this takes place, it can be known that the state of things so created will 'remain forever'. I should have thought that if the conception of God were proved to be an incoherent absurdity, the word 'God' would fall into disuse.[46]

He likened Spencer's Infinite and Eternal to a gigantic soap bubble which, blown thinner and thinner, had become a pure transparency. For Stephen it seemed *religiously* a matter of perfect indifference whether a man asserted, 'Of this at least I am sure: I am in "the presence of an Infinite Eternal Energy from which all things proceed", or "I am *not* in the presence of an Infinite Eternal Energy from which all things proceed."'[47]

The physicists also had great fun with Spencer's Absolute Force. Since it was a Force which was unknowable, i.e., not likened to any known forces or energies, P. G. Tait said that the only recorded instance of its action was the famous Baron Munchausen's journey to the moon by pulling himself up by his boots!

Spencer's metaphysics deserved the derision it received. Yet to acknowledge that his work was repudiated in his lifetime and that his massive and tedious books are no longer read is not to gainsay either his success or his importance. Spencer's talent for joining an apparent scientific method with a deep, natural piety in an effort to discover a reconciliation of science and religion within an evolutionary world-view was enormously appealing to his age. His reverent humility before the mystery of existence largely explains the attraction of his Agnosticism, not only to his contemporaries but to those sharing the modern temper as well.

Spencer's importance in modern religion lies, then, in the crucial role which he played, primarily with Huxley, in the transformation of Agnosticism as a distinct but philosophically limited metaphysical creed into a more inchoate but prevalent byword of everyday thought, a kind of axiom among people imbued with a secularist outlook. Frederic Harrison forecast this future of a secular Agnosticism in our time: 'When the agnostic logic is simply one of the canons of thought, agnosticism as a distinctive faith will have spontaneously disappeared.'[48]

III

While 'Right-wing' Agnosticism did include non-theists, it also numbered many theists like Samuel Laing[49] as well as those espousing a 'Christian Agnosticism' – men such as the apologist H. G. Curteis.[50] The latter group included numerous parish clergy. The Rev. W. J. Dawson's words are typical of a widely expressed sentiment of the time: 'We are all Agnostics. The term really expresses humility of mind . . . And so it is in religion. We may be bad theologians and yet good Christians; Agnostics, yet believers . . . The true attitude toward these [Christian] mysteries is a reverent Agnosticism.'[51]

The 'Left-Wing' agnostics shared the metaphysical nescience of Mansel and Spencer but they did not embrace the positive religious doctrines or feelings of either. They were, rather, the heirs of Hume and the leaders and propagandists of Victorian scientific naturalism. Darwin, Huxley, Morley, Leslie and Fitzjames Stephen, and Tyndall all explicitly denied the charge of atheism. Yet all rejected Christianity and only the latter appears to have accepted Spencer's doctrine of the Unknowable and to have infused the concept with some of the same mystical piety.[52]

What distinguishes the Agnosticism of the 'Left-Wing' is its *historical* and, more especially, its *sociological* and *ethical* critique of Christian belief. The style and tone of the religious prose writings of these men also are strikingly distinct from that of Mansel, Spencer, and their followers. The rhetoric of Huxley and the Stephens is more personal and passionate; it is punctuated with bursts of bitterness and scorn. The aspiring rationalism also reveals an undercurrent of pessimism and sadness, not unlike that found in some of the writings of Russell and Camus.

Darwin's espousal of Agnosticism was not unrelated to his ethical objections to certain Christian teachings, but it appears to be more closely associated with his loss of belief in design. In a letter to J. D. Hooker he confessed that his theology was a muddle and that, while he could not view the world as the result of blind chance, he could 'see no evidence of beneficent design or indeed of design of any kind in the details'.[53] A few years later he wrote to a student acknowledging what 'a poor argument' design was and recommending that 'the safest conclusion seems to me that the whole subject is beyond the scope of man's intellect'.[54] In 1876 he was to confess: 'I for one must be content to remain an Agnostic.'[55]

Darwin's metaphysical agnosticism concerning the origin and moral governance of the world was shared by Huxley and Stephen. Statements which reflect the legacy of Hume, Kant, and Mansel abound in their essays. However, Darwin's metaphysical puzzlement is not what is most characteristic of the Agnosticism of the Stephens and Huxley. They are more troubled by questions of evidence, with the moral warrant of Christian belief, and with its declining social relevance. They saw themselves as propagandists for Agnosticism and confessed to enjoying the role of *provocateur*. It was the passionate personal note in their writings that, in part, explains their success and the widening acceptance of the agnostic profession.

Leslie Stephen (1832–1904) was convinced that if men were guided by reason and experience they simply ought to be agnostic. This is what disturbed and disillusioned him about his clerical friends, whom he saw as having the greatest opportunity for influencing the minds of the younger generation. Instead, Broad Churchmen were, in his view, taking refuge in a most immoral form of scepticism, viz., that 'which assumes that as truth is unattainable it can do no harm to tell lies',[56] or that if there is no 'conclusive' evidence for a certain belief a man has a right to hold either the negative or positive creed. Against both the liberal clergy and the pragmatist William James, Stephen argued that such a man 'has a right to hold *neither*. By Agnostic I do not mean a negative creed, but an absence of all opinion; and that I take to be the only rational frame of mind.'[57]

Stephen was critical of the matter as well as the manner of Christian belief. Doctrines such as the resurrection, the atonement, and eternal damnation he found both illusory and immoral. With Huxley he was moved by the Psalmists' words read in the funeral service and felt they were grand and real, but he was outraged by the words of St Paul which he could view only as 'desperately trying to shirk the inevitable . . . to cover up the terrible reality under a veil of well-meant fiction'.[58]

Stephen recognized in religious beliefs the original impress of man's moral instincts. They were the means by which those instincts found expression. But the danger was in prolonging the association when the belief had become a mere shadow. Belief in hell was an example. Stephen explains the modern psychological process as he sees it:

To make your threats effective at all, you must exaggerate the dream indefinitely to compensate for its unreality. Then it shocks and revolts instead of governing the conscience, and you imagine expedients for softening the shock which you have produced . . . You will find that a mere rose-coloured dream fails to satisfy the deepest instincts which lie at the root of your religion. And meanwhile the whole vision has become so shadowy and uncertain that its hopes and its terrors cease alike to have any tangible influence.[59]

Stephen believed, as did Marx and the social Darwinists, that the course of history – and not particular philosophical arguments – was proving Christianity incompatible with intellectual and social progress. It was, he observed, withering away, having lost its power of assimilation and growth. The long philosophic warfare over the ancient creed was, moreover, 'but the superficial symptom of a deeper social struggle, and the fate of the creed is bound up with the fate of the organization by which it is defended'. Stephen was convinced, certainly erroneously, that Christianity was thoroughly allied with the conservative forces of society. 'Its influence', he wrote, 'is rigorously dependent upon the strong conviction of the governing classes that the old creed is bound up with the old order.'[60]

Newman's criteria of warranted belief, *securus judicat orbis terrarum*, was also Stephen's. Except that the *orbis terrarum* 'must not mean that part of the earth's surface which is overlooked by the spire of St Mary's or the dome of St Peter's'. The true deposit of faith was, for Stephen, 'that body of scientific truth which is the slow growth of human experience through countless ages, and which develops by the labour of truth-loving men, and under the remorseless pressure of hard facts'.[61]

This was, of course, Huxley's creed as well. He, too, foresaw a growing secularity in which supernatural explanations would fade away: 'The Phraseology of Supernaturalism may remain on men's lips, but in practice they are Naturalists . . . Parish clerks doubt the utility of prayers for rain, so long as the wind is in the east; and an outbreak of pestilence sends men not to the churches, but to the drains.'[62]

Huxley (1825–95) frequently asserted that he had no *a priori* objections to the existence of the supernatural; his denials were simply directed against 'the evidence adduced in favour of this, or of that, extant form of Supernaturalism'.[63] There is reason to doubt that this was in fact the case, and his critics cited passages that contradicted his disclaimers.[64] Nevertheless, his case against Christianity was largely built up from an examination of the evidence for particular historical claims. His most famous text case was the narrative of the Gadarene swine. It became for him the touchstone not only of belief in miracle, but in the veracity of the Synoptic Gospels, and in Christ's authority. Huxley simply argued, like Hume in the *Inquiry*, on the grounds that experience teaches us that natural explanations of phenomena are more probable and hence more reasonable than are supernatural or miraculous explanations. Thus he did not think it unreasonably sceptical to say that 'the existence of demons who can be transferred from a man to a pig does thus contravene probability'[65] when put to the test of the Humean canons of credible testimony. Much more, however, is to be inferred from disbelief in the Gadarene story. If the story is discredited, all the other stories of demonic possession fall under suspicion. Furthermore, since Jesus taught demonical possession, Huxley concluded that 'exactly in so far, for me will his authority, in any matters touching the spiritual world be weakened'.[66] To Huxley 'the Gadarene miracle either happened, or it did not'. Whether it had a moral or religious significance, as Principal Wace argued, 'has nothing to do with the fact that it is a purely historical question whether the devil-possessed pigs did, or did not, rush over the cliffs'.[67]

Today Huxley's historical positivism appears myopic and crude. He was blind to the possible meanings or spiritual truths in the metaphorical and mythological interpretations of the biblical narratives. Huxley thought, for example, that he had devastated Wace when he raised doubts whether Jesus had preached the Sermon on the Mount as we know it, when all Wace was concerned to maintain was that the Sermon afforded a true depiction of Jesus' essential teaching. William Irvine correctly remarks that Huxley's method of historical criticism was 'an elaborate and mistaken attempt to make Christianity a needle in a haystack of conflicting evidence'.[68] This aspect of his work reveals a lack of what Matthew Arnold called 'critical tact'. Huxley furthermore espoused the radical critical positions earlier held by Strauss, Baur, and Volkmar as 'the main results of Biblical criticism' at a time when they long had been abandoned by the new generation of Continental and British scholars of the highest repute.

The real force of Huxley's criticism is not to be found in his metaphysical and historical criticism of miracles or the narratives of the New Testament. It is to be found, rather, in his analysis of the theological arguments and particularly the language of his theological antagonists. In this aspect of his critical writings on religion he stands as an important precursor of the twentieth-century analytical critics of religion. Examples can be found throughout his work, but perhaps most tellingly in the essay he wrote in the last days of his life – his critique of A. J. Balfour's *The Foundations of Belief* (1894). In his rebuttal of Agnosticism, Balfour had sought to discredit the philosophy of Huxley, Spencer, and Tyndall by comparing what he judged to be their metaphysical beliefs with those of Theism. Huxley successfully demonstrated that the doctrines Balfour attributed to Agnosticism did not, in most instances, correspond with the doctrines of the leading agnostics. More significantly, he showed that Balfour was using confused and illogical language. Balfour, for example, asserted that for theists 'Creative reason is interfused with infinite love.'[69] Huxley subjects his vast metaphysical claim to logical analysis: '"Reason" and "love" are names for mental phenomena of totally distinct kinds. It seems to me that if I were to say that algebra is interfused with infinite odours, I should make quite as comprehensible a statement.'[70] Furthermore, 'if the qualification "infinite" destroys all analogy with the finite, then the use of the word becomes delusive'.[71]

Huxley's principal legacy to contemporary religious criticism rests on his successful championing, with W. K. Clifford, L. Stephen, and John Morley, of a powerful morality of knowledge. It had been enunciated earlier by Locke who wrote that

there is this one unerring mark of [the lover of truth], viz., the not entertaining any proposition with greater assurance than the proofs of it is built upon will warrant. Whoever goes beyond this measure of assent, it is plain, receives not truth in the love of it; loves not truth for truth's sake, but for some other by-end.[72]

Huxley called the new ethic of belief 'the Agnostic principle'. It simply affirmed

that it is wrong for a man to say that he is certain of the objective truth of any proposition unless he can produce evidence which logically justifies that certainty . . . That which Agnostics deny and repudiate, as immoral, is the contrary doctrine, that there are propositions which men ought to believe without logically satisfactory evidence; and that reprobation ought to attach to the profession of disbelief in such inadequately supported propositions.[73]

The Victorian agnostics sometimes (in a few cases entirely) failed to recognize that not all questions ultimately were scientific questions and that it was not possible to answer all inquiries by a single all-embracing method; that different questions implied different types of evidence and diverse warrants. Nevertheless, what they meant by scientific method or 'the agnostic principle' was simply that there be commonly accepted standards of assessment of any putative factual claims. Huxley and his friends insisted that the religious apologists not simply fall back on intuitive claims or what Fitzjames Stephen called 'increasing the bulk and weight of evidence by heating it with love'; or claim that ordinary warrants do not apply in similar cases. What they repudiated was a double standard in which commonly accepted warrants were followed, only to be rejected in cases of cherished traditional beliefs.

What also disturbed Huxley and his colleagues was the argument, widespread in their day, that unfounded beliefs should be propagated and doubts suppressed if such actions served moral ends. 'It is utterly beside the mark', Huxley asserted,

to declaim against these conclusions on the ground of their asserted tendency to deprive mankind of the consolations of the Christian faith and to destroy the foundations of morality

. . . The point is not whether they are wicked; but, whether from the point of view of scientific method, they are irrefragably true. If they are, they will be accepted in time whether they are wicked, or not wicked.[74]

The 'dreadful consequences' arguer was asking the agnostics, in effect, to abstain from telling the truth or to confess to a belief lacking the evidence to justify it. This the agnostics, rightly, refused to do.

The 1880s were the high point of agnostic disputation. In the years following the agnostic creed came under increasingly sustained criticism; however, the agnostic temper of mind had by then deeply affected British thought. The changing philosophic climate was captured by F. W. H. Myers. In 1886 he wrote that

just as the old orthodoxy of religion was too narrow to contain men's knowledge, so now the new orthodoxy of materialistic science is too narrow to contain their feelings and aspirations; and consequently . . . just as the fabric of religious orthodoxy used to be strained in order to admit the discoveries of geology or astronomy, so now also the obvious deductions of materialistic science are strained or overpassed in order to give sanction to feelings and aspirations which it is found impossible to ignore.[75]

First of all, it became abundantly clear that the agnostics – Huxley, Stephen, Tyndall – carried with them a bag full of *a priori* assumptions, especially concerning religious belief. W. E. Hodgson's complaint was widely voiced: 'The attitude of Mr Huxley to orthodox religion long ago ceased to be that of a man who does not know whether it is truth or untruth that orthodoxy proclaims . . . *Controverted Questions* shows him to be sure that orthodoxy is the embodiment of almost unmitigated error . . .'[76]

The critics R. H. Hutton and W. H. Mallock likewise saw the fatal weakness in the agnostic's failure to carry out logically their agnostic method, particularly in the field of ethics. Mallock, in one of the most trenchant critiques of the entire agnostic position, reverts at length to Huxley's powerful indictment of man's brutish nature, his 'blind prey to impulses', and then concludes that Huxley's Agnosticism is really cowardly, not because it refuses to believe enough, but because it refuses to deny enough since it does not deny the meaning and reality of moral duty. Mallock chides Agnosticism for professing that it gives up 'all that it cannot demonstrate', while 'it is keeping back part, and the larger part of the price – not however from dishonesty, but from a dogged and obstinate cowardice, from a terror of facing the ruin which its own principles have made'.[77]

A century later it is evident that the Victorian churchmen were wrong in believing that morality could not possibly survive the removal of its theological underpinnings. But Mallock and Hutton and others were correct in exposing the often unexamined or pseudo-scientific grounding of the agnostics' own moral beliefs and assumptions. The new philosophical climate was reflected in the transformation of George Romanes in the 1880s from dogmatic scientific naturalist. The Left-wing agnostics, he came to believe, were not radical enough. In his Rede Lecture at Cambridge in 1885, Romanes called for a 'pure agnosticism', one which would be applied equally by both the harbingers of the new science and the new theology. He was especially critical of the dogmatic negations of men like W. K. Clifford.

The Victorian belief in the unity of truth and of intellectual method and inquiry was now and henceforth to be challenged. 'My whole contention', writes Romanes,

has been the men of science, as such, have no business either 'to run with the hare of religion', or 'to hunt with the hounds of antitheistic negation' . . . If a man of science is profoundly interested in the great questions of religion, he should recognize that they have no more bearing upon his professional occupation than have the questions of politics, literature, art, or any other department of rational thinking.[78]

The metaphysical and epistemological assumptions underlying the scientific empiricism of the agnostics were critically examined by the now-dominant school of British Idealists (see Ch. 8, 'The British Idealists') and by figures such as W. G. Ward,[79] St George Mivart,[80] Henry Sidgwick,[81] A. J. Balfour,[82] and, most thoroughly, by James Ward.[83] W. G. Ward, Mivart, and Sidgwick all focused their criticism on the suppositions of the empiricists' psychology – on their 'intuitions' with regard to 'states of consciousness' and memory. Huxley had asserted that one can trust one's present act of memory because in innumerable past cases the avouchments of memory have proven true. 'You find fault', Ward chides Huxley, 'with objectivists for gratuitously and arbitrarily assuming first principles: was there ever a more gratuitously and arbitrarily assumed first principle than your own? . . . Professor Huxley cannot legitimately even guess that *anything whatever* has been "verified by experience" unless he first knows that certain acts of memory testify truly.'[84] Mivart argued similarly with regard to the agnostics' belief in an enduring self.[85]

Sidgwick summed up the matter when he observed how much 'one is amazed at the audacity of claiming a special trustworthiness for the intuitions of empirical psychology'.[86] The agnostics' bag full of intuitive universal facts, including the uniformity of natural laws and causes, provoked Sidgwick to ask: on what grounds do the agnostics disallow claims to similar intuitive faculties in other departments of logic?

One of the most sustained criticisms – despite Huxley's analytical dismantling of the positive, theological side of the argument – of Agnosticism's failure to examine the premises of its scientific foundations was carried out by A. J. Balfour. Balfour (1848–1930) considered it unjustified that new developments in science were being used to bolster the *philosophical* systems of naturalism and materialism. The ordinary view of scientific philosophy was that science makes statements about the general laws of phenomena based entirely on observation, which is also the evidence of scientific truth. This was the essence of Mill's thesis in the *System of Logic*. For Mill and the agnostics the problem of knowledge did not emerge until one crossed the boundary into metaphysics. In his *Defence of Philosophic Doubt*, Balfour argues to the contrary, that when the systematizing of our modes of experimental inference is accomplished, the problem of knowledge actually remains unsolved. For example, take the law of universal causation. Balfour denies the empiricists the right to say that this law 'is the uncontradicted result of observations extending through centuries':

For the fact that mankind has been observing . . . for centuries cannot be to any of us a matter of direct observation or intuition. It therefore must be an inference from experience; the only experience it can be inferred from is the immediate and limited experience of each individual; this, therefore, either at one remove or two, is the only possible empirical foundation for the law of causation, or any other general principal.[87]

Balfour was quick to observe the fundamental incoherences in scientific empiricism. Yet he acknowledged that, despite the limitations of science in its premises and inferences, everyone has 'an implicit and indestructible confidence' in its truth. And so it is, and should be, he argues, in the case of religion. 'If Religion is thought to stand in this respect on a level with Science . . . the same remarks, *mutatis mutandis*, may properly be applied to it . . . Religion is, at any rate, no worse off than Science in the matter of proof.'[88]

Like Newman and William James, Balfour saw the importance of certain non-rational psychological and cultural predispositions which served as causes and grounds of belief. But, unlike Newman, he refused to accord these causes the rank of rational proof or certitude. His Humean conclusion was that 'I and an indefinite number of other persons, if we contemplate religion and science as unproved systems of belief standing side by side, feel a practical need for both . . . We are in this matter, unfortunately, altogether outside the sphere of Reason.'[89]

James Ward (1843–1925) agreed with Balfour's faith in science *and* religion, but he did not share his scepticism. Ward's *Naturalism and Agnosticism* proved to be the decisive *dénouement* of nineteenth-century British scientific Agnosticism. Ward showed that Naturalism and Agnosticism go hand in hand, being the complementary sides of the dominant philosophy of many scientists. 'Agnosticism . . . has reacted upon naturalism, inducing in it a more uncompromising application of scientific method to all the phenomena of experience . . . Naturalism in its turn has reacted upon agnosticism inducing in that a more pronounced scepticism, or even the renunciation of higher knowledge as a duty.'[90] Ward goes on to demonstrate that this agnostic monism tends to degenerate into a materialism, which even Huxley was wise enough to renounce. Ward remarks that the 'champion of Agnosticism, runs his ship high and dry on the idealistic side and there capitulates: "Our one certainty", [Huxley] acknowledges, "is the existence of the mental world."'[91] In brief, Ward concludes that

taking agnostic naturalism just as it presents itself, we have found it to be really inside out. Instead of the physical world being primary and fundamental . . . the precise opposite is implicit in its own structure. The things known, material permanence, mechanical necessity, natural law, will not account for the knower; can we find anything in the knower that will account for them is now the question. If we do, it must be something teleological.[92]

Ward believed that human experience required a philosophy that encompassed richer dimensions of existence than science allowed. For Ward the psychologist, feeling and action were intrinsic to cognition. What experience discloses is not a dead mechanical world but a world of action, freedom, and faith – a spiritual world of conative subjects striving for ends and realizing values. In short, a nature teleological throughout. With Ward we are at the threshold of the new philosophical world of vitalism, pragmatism, and existentialism – the world of Bergson, William James, and Kierkegaard. Ward considered man's primordial faith and striving to be the very source of his scientific knowledge and the ground of his enduring trust in science. He asserted that 'almost every forward step in the progress of life could be formulated as an act of faith – an act not warranted by knowledge – on the part of the pioneer who first made it'.[93] In existentialist fashion he concluded that 'we trust and try first, not understanding until afterwards: our attitude in short is not unlike that of Anselm's famous *Credo ut intelligam*'.[94]

Two events now can be seen as harbingers of the demise of dogmatic scientific Agnosticism and the emergence of a richer, more radical empiricism in late nineteenth-century Britain. Both events were associated with saints of agnostic orthodoxy. One was the publication of Huxley's *Evolution and Ethics* in 1893. Up to this time the agnostics all had agreed that human morality could be explained in terms of the scientific laws governing the course of evolution. Huxley now broke decisively with this view and argued that the direction of the evolutionary process often is contrary to what we regard as morally right. Furthermore, our moral responsibilities cannot be fully explained in scientific terms. On this point Huxley wrote: 'Cosmic evolution may teach us how the good and evil tendencies of man may have come about; but, in itself, it is incompetent to furnish any better reason why what we call good is preferable to what we call evil than we had before.'[95]

Leslie Stephen and Spencer considered Huxley's book a desertion of the agnostic coalition. Spencer complained that Huxley's position now 'involves the assumption that there exists something in us which is not a product of the cosmic process, and is practically going back to the old theological notions which put man and nature in antithesis'.[96] This was not true, but Huxley's views on the human mind and on ethics did leave him vulnerable to the devastating attacks of James Ward, the Idealists, and the radical empiricists.

The second event came earlier and was associated with J. S. Mill (1806–73). In 1874 Mill's *Three Essays on Religion* were published. They shocked and angered Morley and Stephen, since Mill clearly was abandoning some of the most sacred agnostic convictions. In 'The Utility of Religion' Mill wrote that, in the case of Agnosticism,

it is not enough to aver . . . that there can never be any conflict between truth and utility; that if religion be false, nothing but good can be the consequence of rejecting it . . . [For] when the only truth ascertainable is that nothing can be known, we do not, by this knowledge, gain any new fact by which to guide ourselves; we are at best, only disabused of our trust in some former guide-mark which, though itself fallacious, may have pointed in the same direction with the best indications we have. . . . It is, in short, perfectly conceivable that religion may be morally useful without being intellectually sustainable.[97]

Mill's essay is surprisingly compatible with what John Henry Newman (See Ch. 3, 'Newman and the Tractarian Movement') was arguing with great subtlety in his book, the *Essay in Aid of a Grammar of Assent* (1870). Newman, too, was concerned with the role of the imagination, the will, and of probabilities in the act of reasoning and assenting.[98] For Newman, assent must be contrasted with scientific inference, for the concrete reasoning of the individual in matters of a moral or ultimate nature is not reducible to the formal demonstrations of science. According to Newman, conditional inferences can move to unconditional assent through the cumulation and convergence of probabilities, 'probabilities too fine to avail separately, too subtle and circuitous to be converted into syllogisms, too numerous and various for such conversion.'[99] He called this act of reasoned judgment the illative sense, the power of inferring truth from converging lines of evidence, none of which separately would justify certitude.

In the new philosophical climate of the 1880s and 90s, the scientific agnostics' criteria of evidence and truth seemed more and more restrictive and unreal. The importance of the role of intention and action in the life of belief were once again recognized. R. H. Hutton criticized W. K. Clifford for failing to take account of this in his overly scrupulous ethic of belief. Hutton insisted that differences of temperament affect judgments of evidence. Not, he claimed, that personal differences affect 'the estimates formed of *particular evidence*; but that what it does affect is *the choice of the evidence* which is allowed to fall in the shade'.[100]

This line of argument was soon to be most forcefully and felicitously presented by William James (see Ch. 9, 'James and Royce') in 'The Will to Believe', the classic critique of the agnostic dogma that 'it is wrong always, everywhere and for everyone to believe anything upon insufficient evidence'. James denied Clifford's charge that Christians were holding their beliefs on insufficient evidence and thus were guilty of dishonesty and hypocrisy. The evidence, for James, was on the whole sufficient. The point, he claimed, was that Clifford and the agnostics 'believe so completely in an anti-Christian order of the universe that there is no living option: Christianity is a dead hypothesis from the start'.[101]

The problem lay in the agnostics' deficient and restrictive account of experience. As William Irvine observed: 'While the older empiricists were using the test of experience to refine truth into a rather dry and austere question mark, newer empiricists were using the same test to make it a tropical forest of abundance, variety, and vividness.'[102] The agnostics had long been insisting that experience alone can give data from which to draw reasonable conclusions. James, Bergson, and Ward took them at their word and showed them what a fertile reality experience, in fact, is.

The old theology and its methods of verification were now dead. Yet neither could man's search for and experience of spiritual reality and truth be realized when restricted to the rules of verification and the assured results of natural science. Pragmatists and Personal Idealists alike agreed with T. H. Green that 'No deliverance indeed is to be looked for from without.'[103] Persons cannot disinterestedly seek external verification for their religious beliefs. We can, Green insisted, only *make* our certitudes in and through experience. 'Though the failing heart cries out for evidence', he advised that one should 'live on as if there were God and duty, and they will prove themselves to you in your life. The witness which God has given of Himself in the spiritual history of mankind you will in this way make your own.'[104] There is a close resemblance between Green's lecture on 'Faith' and the position advocated a century later by the empiricist H. H. Price in his Gifford Lectures on *Belief*.

The Victorian thinker who perhaps best understood the hopeless alternatives of his age between a dying religious orthodoxy and a spiritually barren scientific naturalism and Agnosticism was Matthew Arnold. He is a writer who still is able to instruct us in the uses of language and experience in the religious life.[105]

Arnold (1822–88) attempted to do for his age what Coleridge (see Ch. 1, 'Coleridge') had done for his and what Rudolf Bultmann has sought to do for our own, viz., to ground Christian belief in radically empirical or existential bases which would withstand the onslaughts of modern scientific reductionism. Arnold was committed to an effort of mediation between Christianity and the modern empirical and secular temper. He was not eminently successful in his own time – although *Literature and Dogma* sold well and had a greater influence among the lay public than did the writings of the professional theologians of the time. His religious writings were forgotten in the middle decades of the twentieth century – during the hegemony of Logical Positivism and Neo-Orthodoxy. Now we are in a position to see that the lack of interest in Arnold's form of mediation was due in large measure to what Noel Annan has called the curious strength and hold which the old-fashioned positivism had, and continues to have, in Britain – the result being that other modes of experience continue to be called upon to produce grounds conforming to the canons of scientific empiricism, or be demoted to the status of emotion or subjective taste.

In his prose writings of the 1870s Arnold turned to religious criticism 'precisely in order to combat the fragmentation of consciousness which he saw recorded in his own poetry and which was later to be widely accepted . . . by (I. A.) Richard's distinction between the scientific and emotive use of language'.[106] Arnold was aware that the question of truth was critical to the modern problem of language but that the truth of religion was doomed if it made claims for its language that were of the same logical type as that appropriate to the natural sciences. Therefore he sought to establish Christianity's truth on a more variegated sense of language and on a wider, more radical empiricism – on the unassailable ground of human experience.

Modern critics from T. S. Eliot to Lionel Trilling have failed to do justice to Arnold's religious reconstruction, and this is largely due to their acceptance of the disjunction between scientific and poetic language made commonplace in Richard's first edition of *Science and Poetry*, and to the conferring on scientific discourse the pride of place. For example, Trilling asserts that Arnold reduces Christian language to poetry, i.e., to pseudo-statement, and pseudo-statement is, for Trilling, confined within the bounds of feeling, it does not speak of facts, cannot be verified, hence cannot be true.

When one turns to *Literature and Dogma* and the other prose writings on religion, one is immediately struck by the importance Arnold places upon setting forth the truth of Christianity – against both the uncritical supernaturalists and the positivists and agnostics. In the Preface to the popular edition of *Literature and Dogma*, Arnold affirms that the object of the book 'is to reassure those who feel attachment to Christianity . . . but recognize the growing discredit befalling miracles and the supernatural'. Such persons are to be reassured not by hiding the discredited grounds of belief 'but by insisting on the natural truth of Christianity'.[107] Arnold believed that religious apologetics based on the traditional historical and metaphysical proofs were doomed and that on this point the agnostic critics were right. However, for Arnold Christianity derived its power from the characters of certainty and grandeur which belong to Christianity in its natural truth.

Arnold explains what he means by the 'natural truth' of Christianity:

By this truth things must stand, not by people's wishes and asseverations about them. 'The God of all of us is the God that we all belong to whether we will or no.' The Eternal that makes for righteousness is such a God; and he is the God of Christianity. Jesus explains what this God would have of us; and the strength of Jesus is that he explains it right. The natural experimental truth of his explanation is their one claim upon us; but this is claim enough. Does the thing, being admittedly most important, turn out to be as he says? If it does, then we 'belong to him whether we will or no'.[108]

Arnold's stress on the experiential truth of Christianity had, of course, its precursors in British theology – from the Cambridge Platonists, through Butler and Coleridge. This tradition required a quite different understanding of experience and language than that held by the scientific naturalists. Arnold understood not only the uniquely evocative power but also the truth inherent in the symbolic and metaphorical use of language. The educated religious man can accept much of what his religion teaches as literal statement. But the rest he cannot so accept. Of the latter, Arnold insists,

he may rehearse as an approximate rendering of it; – as language *thrown out* by other men, in other times, at immense objects which engaged their affection and awe and which deeply engage his also; objects concerning which, moreover, *adequate statement is impossible* . . . It is a great error to think that whatever is thus perceived to be poetry ceases to be available to religion. The noblest races are those which know how to make the most serious use of poetry.[109]

The reason is that the language of myth and metaphor often can 'cover more of what we seek to express than the language of literal fact and science. The language of science about it will be *below* what we feel to be the truth.'[110]

For Arnold myth and metaphor are the means by which people represent imaginatively their understanding of human existence, means which reveal genuine and indispensable dimensions of experience and reality with their own modes of verification. The literal, 'materialized myths' of Christianity are not the logical grounds of Christian belief. For Arnold the symbol, the idea is the fact, for though couched in poetic, figurative, mythical language, it is grounded in authentic religious experience. William Robbins points out that

what the imagination seizes on as poetically true, what conduct accepts as morally true, has for [Arnold] a practical and experimental truth superior to that of a logically verifiable proposition, which is to be contrasted to an emotionally verifiable experience. Nor is this experiential verification merely an emotional response akin to wishful thinking. Arnold believes Christianity has, in Spinozist idiom, 'all the grandeur of a natural law'.[111]

The 'linguistic turn' of philosophy in the period since World War II has freed our notions of experience from the tyrannical hold of scientific positivism. This is reflected in the revised edition of Richard's *Science and Poetry*. There he acknowledges that science cannot answer certain religious questions, not because they are meaningless, but because 'they do not belong to its province'. He then adds: 'Nor can philosophy or religion answer them in the sense in which science has taught us to expect answers to its questions. As the senses of "question" shift, so do those of "answer" and those of "fact", "truth", "belief", and "knowledge" with them.'[112]

Richards concludes by acknowledging the truth of Arnold's position:

There are many feelings and attitudes which, though in the past supported by beliefs now untenable, can survive their removal because they have other moral, natural supports and spring directly from the necessities of existence . . . Our protection, as Matthew Arnold insisted, is in poetry . . . The poetic function is the source and the tradition of poetry is the guardian of the supra-scientific myths.[113]

Here the older Victorian belief in the unity of truth and of method is rejected. Here Romanes' 'pure agnosticism' which decried the dogmatic presumptions of both science and theology finds a new voice, one which was to gain wider recognition through those philosophical analysts influenced by the later work of Wittgenstein. But while there are affinities between Arnold's variegated understanding of the uses of language and truth and some contemporary Wittgensteinian analysts, Arnold's position must be seen, rather, as a precursor of another type of empiricism, one quite distinct from the classical British empiricism of the Victorian agnostics. Arnold's religious writings are in the tradition of the radical empiricism which we now associate with James, Dewey, Whitehead, and Henry Nelson Wieman. It is an empiricism not limited to the traditional domain of sensory data, but one in which concrete human experience in its broadest dimensions, including moral, aesthetic, and religious experience, is a valid medium of disclosure of the world of reality.

V

While the epistemological and metaphysical assumptions of the Victorian agnostics and the more recent logical empiricism of, for example, an A. J. Ayer, have undergone trenchant criticism from James Ward at the turn of the century to Quine, Wittgenstein, and Wisdom in the mid-twentieth century, the challenge of the 'agnostic principle' to religion persists and gives evidence of continued vigour and influence. The heritage of Mill, Huxley, Clifford, and Stephen is carried forward today in the critiques of theology in the philosophical work of such writers as Antony Flew, Alasdair MacIntyre, Ronald Hepburn, and Kai Nielsen. The lines of continuity are undisguised and often avowed.

The 'agnostic principle', as Antony Flew calls it[114] is, perhaps, most succinctly stated in its current form by Kai Nielsen:

Whatever it is that we are allegedly asserting if we are making a genuine factual assertion, it must be possible to show what it would be like for the assertion to be true or probably true and what it would be like for the assertion to be false or probably false. If that condition did not obtain, if God-talk does not lay itself open to experiential confirmation or disconfirmation in this way . . . it, no matter how emotively meaningful, is without factual significance and makes no genuine truth-claim.[115]

Since, it is maintained, religious assertions or factual claims, e.g. 'God loves us as a father loves his children', are not open to the usual empirical tests or verification, nor appear to be falsifiable, they remain uninformative and therefore one's attitude toward such beliefs should remain, at the least, agnostic.

The legacy of nineteenth-century Agnosticism is apparent in a variety of current theological positions and religious attitudes that can properly be called 'theological agnosticism'. The most evident and popular form is reflected in those numerous individuals who have no religious affiliation, or are ecclesiastically inactive, but who, nevertheless, are not disposed to reject belief in God. They believe in God but vaguely express their belief in terms such as 'Infinite Spirit' or 'the Transcendent' – terms which imply ignorance, and perhaps indifference, concerning the real nature or attributes of God.

There are growing numbers of people, many of them committed Christians, who have adopted a 'worldly', 'religionless' or 'secular' interpretation of faith and of Christianity and are explicitly agnostic about God. Their beliefs centre on the stories about Jesus or some other paradigm events and the moral intention to carry out a certain way of life based on what Ronald Hepburn calls a 'tightly cohering extended parable or myth that vividly expressed the way of life chosen, and inspires the believer to implement it in practice'.[116] Such forms of 'theological agnosticism' have been proposed not only by Hepburn, but in a Christian context by R. B. Braithwaite in *An Empiricist's View of the Nature of Religious Belief* (1956), and by Paul Van Buren in *The Secular Meaning of the Gospel* (1963), among others.

One of the surprising legacies of the Victorian age was, as James Seth observed, a profound sense of pious ignorance about God, a feeling of His radical otherness, unfathomableness, or even absence. This sentiment was expressed not only by Mansel and Spencer but by poets such as Tennyson and Arnold, as well as by the Left-wing agnostics. There was a sense abroad that to attempt to fully explain or understand God was to be guilty of a crude anthropomorphism, was to engage in idolatry. As both Mansel and Karl Barth have insisted, to claim *knowledge* of God is not, in fact, to know God – for God and man are, after all, incommensurable.

We see two lines of continuity with this Right-wing form of Victorian Agnosticism in more recent theological reflection. Thomas McPherson has suggested one. He maintains that the Right-wing Victorian agnostics and the contemporary logical empiricists are correct: theology is not a cognitive enterprise and theological beliefs cannot be tested like ordinary phenomena. Theologians are wrong in attempting to engage in metaphysics and natural theology. 'The things that theologians try to say belong to the class of things that just cannot be said. The way out of the worry is retreat into silence.'[117] The agnostics and positivists may be the enemies of theology but they are the friends of religion. For religion is in essence, as Rudolph Otto has argued, a deep feeling of awe and reverence before the numinous, mysterious experiences which derive from our sense of creatureliness. Huxley gained such a sense of religion from Carlyle's *Sartor Resartus*, which had led him 'to know that a deep sense of religion was compatible with the entire absence of theology'.[118] Thus Huxley would have agreed with McPherson that the positivist branding of *theological* assertions as 'nonsense' need not be anti-religious. 'It can be interpreted as an attack on those who in the name of religion are perverting religion. It can be interpreted as a return to the truth about religion.'[119]

Finally, there is today the Barthian form of Agnosticism concerning any knowledge of God derived from natural theology, the rejection of reason's right to determine what God's revelation is or must be – which, as we have indicated, has its precursor in Mansel. These contemporary forms of 'theological agnosticism' all remain highly problematical. If the simple believer wishes to speak of an 'Infinite Spirit', he is using a name which calls, certainly, for some intelligible meaning. The 'theological agnosticism' of a Van Buren or Braithwaite raises the question of why one myth or set of stories is chosen over another – why, for example, Jesus? Is psychological adequacy sufficient? Does not the religious person want his beliefs to be cognitively meaningful, e.g. to make claims about what in fact is the case in a world of competing claims?

The Right-wing 'theological agnosticism' of either a McPherson or a Barth faces equally grave problems. To reduce religion to ineffable, numinous experience precludes the possibility of any defence of one religious view over any others. All religions appear to be on a par. The notion of judging one experience against another as a *true* experience would be illicit. The Barthian doctrine of revelation must, surely, ask the question: If a revelation is some form of knowing, does this not imply that one must make discriminating judgments between competing revelations, all of which are mediated through some phenomenal means, be it a person, a book, or an institution? And does not such a judgment require reason, that is, some general philosophical suppositions above evidence and the assessment of assertions and claims?

The agnostic controversy which has continued in Britain since the middle of the last century has, in the judgment of this writer, demonstrated that the Right-wing forms of 'theological agnosticism' have not proven adequate because they have failed to give convincing accounts of how their beliefs and assertions have the right to be taken as informative or true. The important legacy of the Left-wing agnostics, of the 'agnostic principle', as formulated by Huxley and Stephen, is that they have, in their twentieth-century counterparts – e.g., Flew – kept this criticism of the theological tradition alive. This is no small contribution to religious thought and life. Yet this tradition of Agnosticism is, finally, inadequate. Its commitment to a positivistic empiricism rightly opens it to Romanes' charge against Clifford: Left-wing Agnosticism fails as a 'pure' Agnosticism. It fails to adequately appreciate the rich and various uses of language and modes of human experience as well as the ways in which theistic language is actually used by believers. 'God' is not a word which falls within the believer's normal discourse concerning phenomena, despite the recalcitrant anthropomorphism. Theistic language is language stretched beyond its normal logical coherences – but this is true as well of the language of the poets, artists, and metaphysicians. It is to the credit of the Right-wing agnostics that they recognized this. A genuine theism both 'religiously available' yet finally repelled by talk of God as 'a magnified non-natural man', such a theism must live with this tension without any simple resolution.

Persons both responsive to religious experience and scrupulous about the difficulties involved in the language and truth-claims of theology find that neither a restricted, scientific Agnosticism nor a 'positivism of Revelation' will suffice. A theology acceptable to such persons requires both a more radical empiricism *and* a radically agnostic frame of mind. These persons are the enemies of positivism, whether it be religious or scientific – and they find warrant in a long tradition of biblical monotheism. A man sensitive to this complex temper has written:

JAMES C. LIVINGSTON

A genuine agnosticism, which is neither indolent indifference nor that of despair . . . means the repression not of another man's self-confidence, but of my own. Nor does repression of my own self-confidence mean treating my most assured convictions as quite probably mere illusions. It means taking care to avoid the assumption that what I don't know isn't knowledge.[120]

If the agnostic controversy has taught us to be more agnostic about claims both outside and within our own circle of faith, it has served us well.

Notes

1 J. Seth, 'The Roots of Agnosticism', *The New World*, 3 (1894), 458.
2 Nineteenth-century writers and contemporary students of Agnosticism both rightly point to its philosophical roots in Locke, Hume, and Kant. However, the immediate origin is variously assigned to 1829, the year Sir William Hamilton published his essay 'Philosophy of the Unconditioned' in *The Edinburgh Review*; to 1858, the year Henry Mansel's Bampton Lectures on *The Limits of Religious Thought* appeared; and, more frequently, to 1862, the year Herbert Spencer published his *First Principles*.
3 T. H. Huxley, *Essays Upon Some Controverted Questions* (London, 1892), pp. 354–5. In all citations that follow, the place of publication is London unless otherwise indicated.
4 T. H. Huxley, 'Mr Balfour's Attack on Agnosticism', *The Nineteenth Century*, 37 (1895), 534.
5 Huxley, *Controverted Questions*, p. 356.
6 T. H. Huxley, 'Agnosticism: A Symposium', *The Agnostic Annual*, ed. Charles Watts (1884), pp. 5–6.
7 See Susan Budd, *Varieties of Unbelief* (1977).
8 W. Pater, *Appreciations* (1910), p. 66.
9 W. K. Clifford, 'The Ethics of Belief', *The Contemporary Review* 29 (1877), 294. For an account of this aspect of Victorian religious controversy, see James C. Livingston, *The Ethics of Belief: An Essay on the Victorian Religious Conscience* (Scholars Press, 1974).
10 *The Autobiography of Charles Darwin*, ed. Nora Barlow (1958), pp. 86–7.
11 D. G. Rowell, *Hell and the Victorians* (Oxford, 1974), p. 354.
12 L. Stephen, 'An Agnostic's Apology', *An Agnostic's Apology* (1892).
13 T. H. Huxley, 'Mr. Balfour's Attack on Agnosticism', *The Nineteenth Century* (1895), 530.
14 J. Tyndall, 'Reflections on Prayer and Natural Law – 1861', *Fragments of Science*, vol. II (1879), p. 6.
15 F. Turner, 'Rainfall, Plagues, and the Prince of Wales: A Chapter in the Conflict of Religion and Science', *The Journal of British Studies*, 13 (1974), 65. This essay is an excellent exploration of this theme.
16 W. Hamilton, 'On the Philosophy of the Unconditioned', *Discussions on Philosophy and Literature, Education and University Reform* (1852), p. 12.
17 *Ibid.*, p. 14.
18 *Ibid.*, p. 35.
19 *Ibid.*, p. 15.
20 Hamilton, *Philosophy of the Unconditioned*, pp. 36–37, 601–2.
21 H. L. Mansel, *The Limits of Religious Thought* (1858), p. 16.
22 Mansel, 'Man's Conception of Eternity' [1854], *Letters, Lectures and Reviews* (1873), p. 111.
23 Mansel, *Limits of Religious Thought*, 5th ed. (1867), pp. xi–xii.

24 *Limits of Religious Thought*, pp. xivf.
25 Mansel, 'Man's Conception of Eternity', p. 113.
26 L. Huxley, *Life and Letters*, vol. I, p. 202.
27 F. D. Maurice, *What is Revelation?* (Cambridge, 1859), p. 220.
28 For an excellent example of a recent critique of the kind of theology of revelation espoused by Maurice, see Ronald Hepburn, *Christianity and Paradox*, Chs. 3–4, 'Encounters' (1958).
29 Mansel, *An Examination of the Rev. F. D. Maurice's Strictures on the Bampton Lectures of 1858* (1859), p. 106.
30 J. S. Mill, *An Examination of Sir William Hamilton's Philosophy* (1865), p. 100. For a similar criticism of Mansel, see Goldwin Smith, *Rational Religion* (Oxford, 1861).
31 Mill, *Examination*, p. 101.
32 *Ibid.*, p. 102.
33 *Ibid.*, p. 103.
34 *Ibid.*, p. 103.
35 Edwin Bevan, *Symbolism and Belief* (1938), p. 334.
36 In A. Flew and A. MacIntyre (eds.), *New Essays in Philosophical Theology* (1955), pp. 109ff.
37 Crombie, 'The Possibility of Theological Statements', *Faith and Logic*, ed. Basil Mitchell (1957), p. 66.
38 Crombie, *New Essays*, p. 122–3.
39 Claude Welch, *Protestant Thought in the Nineteenth Century*, vol. I (New Haven, 1972), p. 257.
40 Spencer, *First Principles* (1862), p. v.
41 David Duncan, *The Life and Letters of Herbert Spencer* (1908), p. 398.
42 See, e.g., H. G. Curteis, 'Christian Agnosticism', *The Nineteenth Century*, 15 (1884).
43 H. Spencer, 'Religion: A Retrospect and Prospect', *The Nineteenth Century*, 15 (1884), 8.
44 F. Harrison, 'The Ghost of Religion', *The Nineteenth Century*, 15 (1884), 502–3. See also Wilfrid Ward, 'The Clothes of Religion', *The National Review*, 3 (1884).
45 Harrison, 'The Ghost of Religion', p. 503.
46 J. F. Stephen, 'The Unknowable and the Unknown', *The Nineteenth Century*, 15 (1884), 905.
47 Stephen, 'The Unknowable', p. 908.
48 F. Harrison, 'The Future of Agnosticism', *The Fortnightly Review*, 45 N.S. (1889), 155.
49 Samuel Laing, *Modern Science and Modern Thought* (1885), *Problems of the Future* (1889), and other works.
50 See Curteis' *Scientific Obstacles to Christian Belief* (1885).
51 As reported in the *Christian World*, 31 March, 1892. The sentiment, however, did not only become familiar among ordinary parish members. Words, such as those expressed by Baron von Hügel, were commonplace in the contemporary works of philosophical theology: 'indeed, we are all Agnostics in our better moments . . . Such an Agnosticism is but the sense of mystery – the consciousness of how much greater is the world of reality . . . than is or can be, our clear definable, transferable analysis and theory of it.' *The Reality of God and Religion and Agnosticism*, ed. E. G. Gardner (1931), p. 108.
52 J. Tyndall, *Address Delivered Before the British Association at Belfast* (1874), pp. 64–5. W. H. Mallock satirizes this aspect of Tyndall in the person of Mr Stockton in *The New Republic* (1877).
53 F. Darwin and A. C. Seward (eds.), *More Letters* (1903), vol. I, p. 321.
54 F. Darwin (ed.), *The Life and Letters of Charles Darwin*, vol. I (1887), p. 307.
55 Barlow (ed.), *The Autobiography*, p. 94. Cf. F. Darwin, *Life and Letters*, vol. I, p. 304.
56 L. Stephen, 'The Broad Church', *Essays on Freethinking and Plainspeaking* (1873), p. 40.
57 N. Annan, *Leslie Stephen* (1951), p. 317.

58 L. Stephen, 'Dreams and Realities', *An Agnostics Apology* (1893), pp. 91–2.
59 Stephen, *Agnostics Apology*, p. 119.
60 L. Stephen, 'The Religion of all Sensible Men', *Agnostics Apology*, pp. 65–6, 364.
61 L. Stephen, 'Newman's Theory of Belief', *Agnostics Apology*, p. 239.
62 T. H. Huxley, 'Prologue', *Controverted Questions* (1892), pp. 34–5.
63 Huxley, 'Prologue', p. 35.
64 See, e.g., T. Vincent Tymms' 'Agnostic Expositions', *The Contemporary Review* (May 1889).
65 T. H. Huxley, 'Agnosticism', *Controverted Questions*, pp. 344–5.
66 T. H. Huxley, 'Agnosticism and Christianity', *Controverted Questions*, p. 485.
67 *Ibid.*, p. 473.
68 W. Irvine, *Apes, Angels, and Victorians* (1955), p. 324.
69 T. H. Huxley, 'Mr. Balfour's Attack on Agnosticism II', in Houston Peterson, *Huxley: Prophet of Science* (1932), p. 318. This essay was not published by Huxley because he was unable, due to his fatal attack of influenza, to correct the proofs. It was first published in Peterson's study.
70 T. H. Huxley, 'Mr Balfour's Attack', p. 318.
71 *Ibid.*, pp. 318–19.
72 J. Locke, *An Essay Concerning Human Understanding*, ed. A. S. Pringle-Pattison (Oxford, 1934), Book IV, ch. XIX.
73 T. H. Huxley, 'Agnosticism and Christianity', p. 450.
74 T. H. Huxley, 'Prologue', *Controverted Questions*, p. 34.
75 Introduction to *Phantasms of the Living*, by E. Gurney, F. W. H. Myers, and F. Podmore (1886), vol. I, pp. liv–v.
76 W. E. Hodgson, 'The Controverted Question', *The National Review*, 20 (1892), 329, 331.
77 W. H. Mallock, 'Cowardly Agnosticism', *The Fortnightly Review*, 45 N. S. (1889), 540.
78 G. Romanes, 'Mr Mivart on the Rights of Reason', *The Fortnightly Review*, 45 (1886), 333.
79 *Essays in the Philosophy of Theism* (1884).
80 *Lessons from Nature* (1876).
81 See, e.g., 'The Verification of Beliefs', *The Contemporary Review*, 17 (1871) and the paper read before the Metaphysical Society, 'The Incoherence of Empirical Philosophy', 14 January, 1879. This paper was later published in *Mind* in 1882.
82 *Defense of Philosophic Doubt* (1879) and the more popular *Foundations of Belief* (1894).
83 *Naturalism and Agnosticism*, 2 vols. (1899).
84 W. G. Ward, 'The Rule and Motive of Certitude', *Essays on the Philosophy of Theism*, vol. I (1884), p. 4.
85 St G. Mivart, 'On One Point in Controversy with the Agnostics', in H. E. Manning (ed.), *Essays on Religion and Literature*, Third Series (1874), pp. 218–19.
86 H. Sidgwick, 'The Verification of Beliefs', p. 589.
87 A. Balfour, *Defense*, p. 71.
88 *Ibid.*, pp. 315, 319.
89 *Ibid.*, pp. 319–20.
90 J. Ward, *Naturalism and Agnosticism*, vol. I (1906), pp. 20–1.
91 *Ibid.*, vol. II, p. 229.
92 *Ibid.*, p. 229.
93 J. Ward, *The Realm of Ends*, 2nd ed. (Cambridge, 1912), p. 415.
94 *Ibid.*, p. 416.
95 T. H. Huxley, 'Ethics and Evolution', *Collected Essays*, vol. 9, p. 80.
96 D. Duncan, *The Life and Letters of Herbert Spencer* (1908), p. 336.
97 J. S. Mill, *Collected Works*, vol. 10 (1969), p. 405.
98 J. S. Mill, 'Theism', *Collected Works*, vol. 10, p. 483.

99 J. H. Newman, *Grammar of Assent* (1947), p. 219. For an analysis of the controversy between Newman's position in the *Grammar of Assent* and the agnostics such as Leslie, Fitzjames Stephen, and W. K. Clifford, see the author's *The Ethics of Belief: An Essay on the Victorian Religious Conscience* (1974).

100 R. H. Hutton, 'Wilfrid Ward's "Wish to Believe"', *Contemporary Thought and Thinkers*, vol. 1 (1894), p. 367.

101 W. James, *The Will to Believe and Other Essays* (1897), p. 14.

102 W. Irvine, *Apes, Angels, and Victorians* (1955), pp. 257–8.

103 T. H. Green, *Faith and the Witness of God* (1883), p. 88.

104 *Ibid.*, p. 98.

105 For the treatment of Arnold the author has drawn, in part, on his analysis in 'Matthew Arnold and His Critics on the Truth of Christianity', *Journal of the American Academy of Religion*, 41 (1973).

106 W. Madden, *Matthew Arnold: A Study of the Aesthetic Temperament in Victorian England* (Bloomington, 1967), p. 195.

107 M. Arnold, *The Complete Prose Works of Matthew Arnold*, vol. VI, pp. 142–3.

108 *Ibid.*, vol. VIII, p. 159.

109 *Ibid.*, p. 132.

110 *Ibid.*, vol. VI, p. 189.

111 W. Robbins, *The Ethical Idealism of Matthew Arnold* (1959), p. 80.

112 I. A. Richards, *Science and Poetry* (1970), p. 60.

113 *Ibid.*, p. 78.

114 A. Flew, *The Presumption of Atheism* (1976), ch. 2.

115 K. Nielsen, *Contemporary Critiques of Religion* (1971), p. 40.

116 R. Hepburn, 'Scepticism and the Naturally Religious Mind', *Christianity and Paradox* (1958), p. 195.

117 T. McPherson, 'Religion as the Inexpressible', *New Essays in Philosophical Theology*, ed. A. Flew and A. MacIntyre (1955), p. 133.

118 L. Huxley, *Life and Letters of T. H. Huxley*, vol. I, p. 220.

119 McPherson, 'Religion', p. 139.

120 A. E. Taylor, *The Faith of a Moralist*, vol. II (1930), p. 405.

Bibliographical Essay

Unless otherwise indicated, works cited in the bibliography were published in London.

1. Primary sources

The following works of Hume and Kant are crucial for an understanding of the late nineteenth-century agnostic controversy and the continuing philosophical debate over religious belief:

David Hume, *Enquiry Concerning Human Understanding* (1748). See especially sections X and XI. *Dialogues Concerning Natural Religion* (1779). Immanuel Kant, *Critique of Pure Reason* (Berlin, 1781; Smith ed., 1929).

A. The Right-wing agnostics and their critics

Sir William Hamilton, *Discussions on Philosophy and Literature, Education and University Reform* (1852). This work contains the essay 'On the Philosophy of the Unconditioned' which originally appeared in the *Edinburgh Review*, 1 (1829).

Henry Mansel, *The Limits of Religious Thought* (1858). The important 5th edition was published in 1867; rpt. 1973.
Letters, Lectures and Reviews ed. by H. W. Chandler (1873). Contains Mansel's first critique of F. D. Maurice in 'Man's Conception of Eternity' (1854), and his defence of *Limits* against Henry Calderwood and others.
An Examination of the Rev. F. D. Maurice's Strictures on the Bampton Lectures of 1858 (1859).
Herbert Spencer, *First Principles* (1862).
J. S. Mill, *An Examination of Sir William Hamilton's Philosophy* (1865). The classic empiricist critique of the Hamilton–Mansel agnostic doctrine.
Goldwin Smith, *Rational Religion* (1861). Important contemporary critique of Mansel.
F. D. Maurice, *What Is Revelation?* (Cambridge, 1859; rpt. 1975) Maurice's unfortunate effort at rebutting Mansel.

B. The Left-wing agnostics and their critics

Richard Bithall, *The Creed of A Modern Agnostic* (1883) and *A Handbook of Scientific Agnosticism* (1892) are derivative works of secondary importance but reflect a popular form of agnostic writing, as do the articles by Charles Watts, E. Lynn Linton, S. Laing, G. J. Holyoake and F. J. Gould in the *Agnostics Annual* (1884–1900).
W. H. Clifford, *Lectures and Essays*, ed. by Leslie Stephen and Sir Frederick Pollock (1879) contains such important essays as 'The Ethics of Belief' and 'The Unseen Universe'.
Charles Darwin, *The Autobiography*, ed. by Nora Barlow (1958). Darwin's autobiography includes an important section on his religious belief and espousal of Agnosticism.
T. H. Huxley, *Essays Upon Some Controverted Questions* (1892).
This volume contains most of Huxley's important writings on religion and Agnosticism published during the 1880s. These essays also appear in Huxley's *Collected Essays*, vols. IV and V (1893–4) which were reprinted in 1968 (New York). See also *Collected Essays*, vol. VI, *Hume* (New York, 1968). *Christianity and Agnosticism: A Controversy* (n. d.) includes several of Huxley's essays on Agnosticism, also published in the above volumes, but contains as well essays by Henry Wace, W. C. Magee, W. H. Mallock, and Mrs Humphrey Ward.
John Morley, *On Compromise* (1874) is a powerful statement of the new agnostic ethic of belief. See especially the chapters on 'The Possible Utility of Error' and 'Religious Conformity'. Morley's studies of *Diderot, Rousseau*, and *Voltaire* also reflect his criticism of religious thought.
Leslie Stephen, *Essays on Freethinking and Plainspeaking* (1873; rpt. 1969) and the essays collected in *An Agnostic's Apology* (1893; rpt. 1969) include Stephen's most important critical writing on religion and Agnosticism during the 1870s and 1880s.
John Tyndall, *Fragments of Science* (1879; rpt. 1970). Volume two includes such important essays as 'The Belfast Address' and 'Reflections on Prayer and Natural Law'.
For examples of positive responses to Agnosticism by theistic writers see H. G. Curteis, *Scientific Obstacles to Christian Belief* (1885) and Samuel Laing, *Modern Science and Modern Thought* (1885) and *Problems of the Future* (1889).
The best sources for a study of the debates between the agnostics and the leading theistic writers during the last third of the nineteenth century are the pages of the *Fortnightly Review*, *The Contemporary Review*, and *The Nineteenth Century*. See especially *The Nineteenth Century* for 1884 and 1889.
Among the most important nineteenth-century critiques of Agnosticism and its philosophical and historical presuppositions are the following:
R. H. Armstrong, *Agnosticism and Theism in the Nineteenth Century* (1905).

British Agnosticism

Arthur Balfour, *Defense of Philosophic Doubt* (1879) and *Foundations of Belief* (1894).
Robert Flint, *Agnosticism* (1903).
R. H. Hutton, *Criticisms of Contemporary Thought and Thinkers* (1894) and *Aspects of Religious and Scientific Thought* (1899).
William James, *The Will to Believe and Other Essays* (1897).
James Martineau, *A Study of Religion* (Oxford, 1888).
St George Mivart, *Lessons from Nature* (1876).
George Romanes, *Mind and Motion and Monism* (1895).
Henry Wace, *Christianity and Agnosticism* (1895).
James Ward, *Naturalism and Agnosticism* (1899).

II. Secondary Sources

On the development of mid- and late nineteenth-century British religious thought, including Agnosticism and the challenge of unbelief:

Earlier studies, rationalist in outlook, are A. W. Benn, *The History of Rationalism in the Nineteenth Century* 2 vols. (1906; rpt. 1966) and J. M. Robertson, *A History of Free Thought in the Nineteenth Century* 2 vols. (1929). Despite their limitations, these works remain valuable for their compendious references to sources.

Leonard E. Elliott-Binns, *English Thought: The Theological Aspect* (1956) and the shorter work from which it evolved, *The Development of English Theology in the Later Nineteenth Century* (1952). Both are interpretations of the advance of liberal theology. Clement C. J. Webb's *A Study of Religious Thought in England from 1850* (1933) focuses on the role of theological idealism in meeting scientific and historical–critical developments. The best recent introduction to the main currents of British religious thought of the period is B. M. G. Reardon's *From Coleridge to Gore: A Century of Religious Thought in Britain* (1971). The early chapters of Owen Chadwick's *The Victorian Church*, Part II (1970) also deal with the multifarious challenges to traditional belief. O. A. J. Cockshut's *The Unbelievers: English Agnostic Thought 1840–1890* (1964) and Basil Willey's *Nineteenth Century Studies* (1949; rpt. 1966) and *More Nineteenth Century Studies* (1956; rpt. 1966) contain urbane, lucid, and often insightful chapters on several of the Victorian agnostics and 'honest doubters'. For a brief study of the moral crises occasioned by the challenge to belief, see James C. Livingston, *The Ethics of Belief: An Essay on the Victorian Religious Conscience* (Tallahassee, 1974). Noel Annan's intellectual biography of *Leslie Stephen* (1951; rpt. 1984) is a penetrating study of the intellectual and moral background and crosscurrents that produced not only Stephen but others who shared his rationalism and Agnosticism. Frank M. Turner's *Between Science and Religion: The Reaction to Scientific Naturalism in Late Victorian England* (New Haven, 1974) is a discerning exploration of the thought of several men who sought a way between Christianity and scientific naturalism, including Sidgwick, Romanes, and James Ward.

D. W. Dockrill has written two valuable articles on the beginnings of English Agnosticism: 'The Origin and Development of Nineteenth Century English Agnosticism', *Historical Journal* (University of Newcastle, New South Wales, 1971), and 'T. H. Huxley and the Meaning of "Agnosticism"', *Theology* (1971).

On the more radical British secularist and atheist movements, the reader should consult, Susan Budd, *The Varieties of Unbelief* (1977) and Edward Royle, *Victorian Infidels: The Origins of the British Secularist Movement, 1791–1866* (Manchester, 1974), and the primary works and studies cited by these scholars.

The following works survey the important period of transition in British religious thought from 1889 to 1920: J. K. Mozley, *Some Tendencies in British Theology: From the Publication of Lux Mundi to the Present Day* (1951); A. M. Ramsey, *From Gore to Temple* (1960); and Thomas A. Langford, *In Search of Foundations: English Theology 1900–1920* (Nashville, 1969).

III. The contemporary debate

For the twentieth-century discussion of Agnosticism, in the light of more recent developments in logical empiricism and linguistic analysis, the following works are important. A. J. Ayer, in *Language, Truth, and Logic* (1935), argued that since all religious discourse is literally nonsensical, theism, agnosticism, and atheism are all false, for they assume the question of God is a genuine question. Since they are not intelligible, any form of religious utterance can be neither true nor false. Ayer's position would call for a suspension of judgment. For a very different kind of defence of 'theological agnosticism', in the tradition of British empiricism, see Ronald Hepburn, *Christianity and Paradox* (1966), and R. B. Braithwaite, *An Empiricist's View of the Nature of Religious Belief* (1956). Kai Nielsen, in *Contemporary Critiques of Religion* (1971) and numerous other works, argues that belief in God is not reasonable or justified but he does not champion atheism. For a defence of the plausibility of atheism see, Antony Flew, *The Presumption of Atheism* (1976). In *Faith and Reason* (1983) Anthony Kenny objects to Flew's atheistic presumption and defends an agnostic suspension of judgment. For a variety of positions on the question, consult the essays in A. Flew and A. MacIntyre, *New Essays in Philosophical Theology* (1955) which includes T. McPherson's 'Religion as the Inexpressible', a contemporary expression of British Right-wing Agnosticism. The contemporary Left-wing agnostics can be faulted for the fact that their agnosticism often is not radical enough, as evidenced by a covert, if not overt, commitment to a scientific positivism. The weakness of contemporary Right-wing Agnosticism is its implicit consent to a conceptual and religious relativism or a fideism. This is evident, for example, in the writings of some followers of the late Wittgenstein: D. Z. Phillips, *The Concept of Prayer* (1965), *Faith and Philosophical Enquiry* (1970), and the essays by Phillips, Norman Malcolm, and Peter Winch in *Religion and Understanding* (1967), ed. by D. Z. Phillips. For a critique of this so-called 'Wittgensteinian Fideism', see K. Nielsen above.

IV. Bibliographical guides

No single, comprehensive bibliographical guide for research in British religious thought in the late nineteenth and early twentieth centuries exists. The most adequate recent guide is *Victorian Prose: A Guide to Research*, ed. by David DeLaura (New York, 1973). This *Guide* contains extensive bibliographical essays on Carlyle, Newman, Mill, and Arnold, as well as excellent surveys of studies on 'The Victorian Churches', including religious thought, and an essay, 'The Unbelievers', by John Bicknell, which includes superb annotated bibliographies on the general literature of unbelief, as well as on the leading agnostics, Huxley and Stephen.

8

The British Idealists

H. D. LEWIS

I

Idealism was the type of philosophical thought which dominated British philosophy, and thereby a great deal of philosophy in other parts of the world, in the second half of the nineteenth century and especially towards the close of the century; indeed, so extensive and powerful was the influence of this movement that many of its practitioners came to believe that it was finally established as the philosophy of the future, allowing of refinements and new applications but no question of its fundamental principles. It had come to stay. Rarely has confidence been so ill justified. Until very recently little attention has been paid in our time to idealistic thinkers in this country or indeed in other parts of the world. Even when they are mentioned with respect they are rarely examined or read or given a place in the curricula of universities in the main part of the present century. One figure alone, namely F. H. Bradley, kept his place in the interests of philosophers, and that for the most part was confined to a few devoted admirers. He was paid a grudging respect but largely disregarded. Other notable figures passed almost entirely out of the interest of contemporary philosophers, and they were treated with outright contempt.

There have persisted throughout this period some very gifted idealistic thinkers, such as, in our time, Brand Blanshard, R. G. Mure, T. M. Knox, H. J. Paton, and Errol Harris. Others, without subscribing wholly to idealist principles have accepted them in certain regards and drawn much from them for the inspiration of their own work, for example A. C. Ewing and C. A. Campbell. All these have done notable work, but it has been left to drift along at the edges of the main current of philosophical thought without making any impact upon it, and often subjected to undeserved disrespect, even in cases like those of Campbell and Ewing where the writers engaged themselves very positively with the prevailing trends in philosophical thinking.

This neglect, the habit of simply disregarding traditional idealism, in the form it took in the nineteenth century without seeking even to refute it, or consider carefully what merits and faults it had, has been, in my opinion, a source of great impoverishment of philosophical thinking, for although idealist thought is open to serious objections, as I hope to show, it has also a great deal to teach us which is exceptionally relevant to some of our most basic and urgent problems.

The sad situation to which I have referred has been not a little corrected in quite recent years by a renewed interest in the philosophy of Hegel from which much of nineteenth century thought took its start. Professor J. N. Findlay's *Hegel – A Re-examination* was a landmark in this reversal of attitudes, and he may well be regarded, both by his written work and by his participation in philosophical discussions in other ways, as the prime rehabilitator of Hegel, but he has been very ably supported by a number of other scholars and translators, such as T. M. Knox and H. B. Acton, with such effect that the study of Hegel has again won a central place in philosophical thinking, although much of it continues to be almost wholly disregarded in some very influential philosophical quarters of our time. With the renewal of interest in Hegel has come a better regard for other post-Kantian philosophers, but the tide is still rather slow in coming up to the work of thinkers such as Bosanquet or Pringle-Pattison or G. F. Stout who were regarded as very considerable figures in the philosophical world of the turn of the century.

The reasons for the distaste for idealist philosophy in our time are many. In some measure the idealist writers were themselves to blame, for on occasion they lapsed into obscure jargon or the exploitation of verbal ambiguities, and they were prone to make, with great confidence, high flights of speculation for which it was by no means clear what the method of assessment was to be. They sometimes also represented a form of seriousness, which became very alien to the prevailing philosophical temper, and a somewhat inflated style of writing.

But perhaps the most important factor in the discrediting of idealist philosophy, or the widespread disregard of it, was the changed temper of mind which was brought about by the First World War. H. J. Paton has pointed out[1] how much intellectual leadership was lost, and what a sharp break with the past was involved, in the death of so many of the brightest of the young people of the period in the war that began in 1914. But the terrible ravages of war, the abandonment of many cherished traditions and restraints, and above all a deep sense of disillusionment with the bright, and often superficial, optimism of the late nineteenth century, summarized in a typically sententious way by a leading idealist teacher of the time in the words 'The universe is homeward bound' – all this brought into existence a much tougher temper and an extensive impatience with speculative thinking which could not, like science, be brought to the test of hard fact here and now. Philosophers, like other writers, felt it was time they came back to earth, the poetry of Wilfred Owen, Siegfried Sassoon and Herbert Read replaced that of Rupert Brooke as fitting the mood of the time, the cynicism of Lytton Strachey found a ready response; and a realist movement in philosophy, already under way as a strictly philosophical reaction in the work of a very influential Oxford philosopher and teacher, Cook Wilson,[2] found a more explicit and more boldly acceptable expression in the work of Bertrand Russell and G. E. Moore and in due course of Wittgenstein than whom, whatever view we take of the merit of his work, no one has had more influence on philosophical thinking in our time. With the popularizing of this new mood in the positivist work of the Vienna Circle and its exposition in A. J. Ayer's early masterpiece of exposition, his now celebrated *Language, Truth and Logic*, all metaphysical thinking fell under the general ban as literal nonsense in which no one could indulge and retain the respect of his philosophical colleagues generally. The story of this alleged 'Revolution in Philosophy', the abandonment of any kind of speculative thinking, the emergence of very cautious analytical philosophy, the preoccupation with language as the major clue to the treatment of philosophical questions, has often been told, both by those who welcomed the change and by their critics. There is little need to repeat it here, but it will explain how it came about that philosophical works which were very celebrated in their day, from T. H. Green's *Prolegomena to Ethics* to F. H. Bradley's *Appearance and Reality* and Samuel Alexander's *Space, Time and Deity*, came to be thrust aside as of no account, indeed appallingly misleading, by the more influential philosophical thinkers and writers of our time and even more completely by the younger men who took their cue so completely from their tough-minded but narrowly dogmatic mentors that they never even bothered to look at the works which had been so admired a few generations earlier or even commend them to their pupils.

The result has been that, although there have been, mainly in the early part of this century, a few celebrated 'refutations' of idealism, of which the famous essay[3] of that name by G. E. Moore is the most celebrated, this great movement of thought and determinant of attitudes, has not been so much refuted or critically examined as thrust aside as of no account and left almost wholly to the small, isolated band who continued to find it stimulating and helpful. The time for a careful reassessment is certainly due.

This is all the more necessary because a great deal that is being maintained and practised today, under the name of analytical or linguistic philosophy, has much in common with the actual teaching of some leading idealists, notably perhaps in the areas of logic and the study of perception. But there has also been a widespread renewal of interest in metaphysical philosophy, variously understood, and the abandonment of a severely reductionist empiricist approach to philosophy. Few adhere strictly now to the sort of rigid empiricism which had its classical expression in the works of David Hume. The ranks of philosophy are thought to be much wider than providing a linguistic underpinning of the philosophy of Hume; and with this return to a broadening of scope and interest, one hopes that the disciplines to which we have been subjected, and the insistence on clarity of thought and expression, will help in the examination now due of what is of real merit and what is the result of incautious enthusiasm in the works of the late nineteenth-century idealists.

A further reason for undertaking such an examination, in an exhaustive way which a paper of this length cannot attempt, is the extension of informed study about other cultures than our own, and especially in this case of Indian philosophy and religion. Hinduism in particular has a great deal in common with idealist philosophy and the few practitioners of idealism have found, and continue to find, a warmer response in Eastern countries, and especially India, than in other parts of the world. A study of idealism in the nineteenth century will provide very valuable clues to the understanding of Hindu practice and speculation, and it is from Indian philosophers that we often find the best guides both to what notable idealists taught (see the fine book on Bradley by S. K. Saxena[4] of Delhi University) and to the way idealist logic has suggestive points of affinity with logic and epistemology as studied today – and as anticipated in remarkable ways in the long tradition of Hindu philosophy itself.

Some intimations of the movement of thought which was to develop into British idealism in the strict sense may be found as early as the work of Coleridge who acquired a considerable interest in German, and especially Kantian, philosophy, getting lost, as Hazlitt (a little bemused by his friend even in his most appreciative moments) was inclined to think 'in the labyrinthe of the Hartz forest and in Kantean philosophy'.

But the effect of this was very restricted and did not extend much beyond literary persons like Coleridge's own associates. The really important beginning of the new movement came with the work of Professor James Frederick Ferrier of St Andrews. His major work was *The Institutes of*

Metaphysic (1854). This had been preceded by a number of articles on the philosophy of consciousness which were collected and published, along with other papers, in his *Lectures on Greek Philosophy and Other Philosophical Remains* in 1866. He did not draw much directly upon Hegel and does not seem to have been much attracted to him, and his method of presentation, in his main book, *The Institutes of Metaphysic*, is made a little tedious, notwithstanding the attractiveness of his style, by persistent contrasts with psychological doctrines which he was concerned to rebut. His main themes are derived, in an almost *a priori* way, from his initial doctrine that any intelligence must have some cognisance of itself. By a series of deductions he arrives at the conclusion that there must be 'a supreme and infinite and everlasting mind in synthesis with all things'. This is very close to what the major idealists were to hold later in the century.

The influence of Hegel began to make itself firmly felt in British thought with the publication (in 1865) of James Hutchinson Stirling's *The Secret of Hegel*. The main theme of this book was the relation of Hegel to Kant. It is a difficult book but it helped to make Hegel's work better known and throws light upon it. The aim of reconciling religion and philosophy was also brought into prominence.

It was, however, in the work of T. H. Green, sometimes described as 'the father of British idealism', that the movement got seriously under way and began to be the dominant influence which it had established for itself so completely in the closing stages of the nineteenth century. Green (1836–82) taught at Oxford, first as a Fellow of Balliol College and in due course as the White's Professor of Moral Philosophy. He was firmly supported by the Master of Balliol at that time, Edward Caird and his brother John Caird, Principal of the University of Glasgow. Edward Caird presented his ideas mainly in the form of a critical exposition of Kantian philosophy as leading to the position in due course taken up by British idealists. This means that, although Caird produced very readable and illuminating expositions of Kant which should not be neglected by students of Kantian philosophy, he is not an altogether reliable guide, as he tended to see and to present Kant through the eyes of the speculative idealist which he himself had become. His influence on thought, and attitudes, in his day, was considerable, and his reputation stood very high. But he did not set the course for idealist philosophy in general in quite the same way as T. H. Green. In spite of a style which sometimes became cumbersome and very involved, Green wrestled more, on his own account, with the difficulties which his central themes presented, in the moral and political field as much as in general metaphysics, and set the pattern for later writers who shared his outlook and concerns.

Much has been written, sometimes very sharply, about the cumbersomeness of Green's philosophical style, and this is no doubt one factor in the lack of interest taken in his book, at one time very celebrated, *Prolegomena to Ethics*, by teachers of philosophy today. It is not a style to emulate, but it has to be remembered that this book was not finally prepared for publication by Green himself, but by A. C. Bradley who prepared the text of the book out of notes of Green's lectures. In addition, Green was a most painstakingly honest thinker; he did not, like some later idealists, take refuge in obscure metaphors or the ambiguities of certain terms. He writes in plain English, but so concerned was he to come to terms with the philosophers he criticized, especially Hume and Mill, and to make all concessions to opposing views with some of which he retained a great deal of sympathy, that he is found qualifying his own affirmations, in relative clauses and sometimes long parentheses, and it is difficult to keep firm hold of the thread of his main contentions. In some ways, however, and to those who cultivate the necessary patience, the sometimes tortuous thinking of T. H. Green is very instructive, not least when it is most at fault; and it was for this reason, I believe, that Professor H. A. Prichard, approaching problems in moral philosophy in a very different way, found Green's works irresistibly fascinating and, as I heard him say, read them countless times over.

The philosophy of T. H. Green, and thereby the whole subsequent idealist movement, owed much directly to Kant as well as to Hegel. But what gives it its distinctive themes and character, especially in the form of speculative idealism, was the concern which Hegel had to correct what he took to be one fundamental inadequacy at the centre of Kantian philosophy. This concerns the bifurcation to which Kant was led in due course between the world as it appears to us, not just individually but as creatures only capable of viewing the world in a certain way, and the world of reality as it truly is, phenomenal reality on the one hand and noumenal reality on the other.

The way Kant himself came to make this distinction is as follows. He was much impressed with the difficulties Hume had raised for any *a priori* thinking and for our awareness of the world as more than the flow of our own fleeting or transitory impressions. It was Hume who, in the famous words, awakened him from his dogmatic slumber. We cannot construct the world, as some of the pre-Kantian rationalists had tried, by the exercise of reason alone proceeding from some elementary first principles of reason itself. In some way the world is over against us, it has some kind of solidarity, events take place in a predictable way which gives us an ordered environment in which we can function and which we may manipulate. If there were merely passing sensations we could find no objectivity or meaningful world, and we could not effectively distinguish ourselves from the passing scene to which our experience in its totality had been reduced.

To cope with this Kant insisted that the world which can become an object of knowledge must have system and order and that whatever we apprehend at a particular moment must be given its place in a system of things which make it intelligible. Kant also believed that he could deduce from the nature of the sort of experience of the world which we have what must be the main principles or modes of its unification. This is the famous transcendental deduction of the categories, but one has not to follow Kant in all the aspects of this deduction to appreciate the importance that must be attached to the organizing of ingredients of our experience which will make it the apprehension of some objective reality, and not a dream, and enable us to survive and communicate with one another on the basis of our manipulation or intervention in the way things happen in the world around us.

But this had, for Kant, correctly it seems to me, the further presupposition that, along with the unity or system which the world of our experience must have, there has to be unity also on the subjective side. If our experiences were just a matter of sliding along the course of our passing presentations, whatever their ultimate nature or source, we could be aware of nothing but the passing scene; and so we arrive at the notion that the kind of experiences we do in fact have presupposes a subject which remains constant throughout the flow of experience and is then distinct from any of its passing ingredients. There must be an abiding self or subject.

But the subject, by the very nature of the reasoning which establishes it, as a necessary condition of experience, cannot itself be an item in the world whose apprehension it makes possible, or one further object among the many things which in due course we come to apprehend. It just cannot be an object in this sense at all or be subject to the modes of unification by which we find that awareness of an intelligible world is made possible. It seems thus to be just subject and nothing more, and in some of the ways in which Kant presented this, the subject, the 'pure ego', tends to become merely an abstract condition of our having our sort of experience, a 'necessary focus' as it is put in one place, and thus to forfeit any genuine concrete reality of its own. The world around us is ordered, for example, in space and time as some sort of initial 'given magnitudes', in Kant's terms, without which nothing could come about as we apprehend it. But the self or subject is not itself subject to these conditions. Not only is it not spatially extended, an object for which a firm location can be found and which can be identified, among other characteristics by its location, but it does not seem to have duration either. At the same time it is said to be abiding and permanent. It must be capable of apprehending its experiences as a whole and place the various items of experience in their place and identify them by holding them together in their inter-relations in one comprehensive apprehension. The difficulty of this position led to the somewhat extravagant notion of a self or subject which is not itself in time but which also is, in some way, abiding and constant enough to be the focus or centre of all that we do apprehend in the events of the world around us. The culmination of this is the notion of a timeless self, although it is by no means clear that Kant would always want to conceive of it in that way.

These problems are bound up with another feature of Kant's epistemology and metaphysics, namely the view that the principles on which our world is organized and becomes intelligible are relative to the special way in which our own minds are conditioned to apprehend them. We may thus, on the one hand speak properly of subjects of experience and not just subjective states or apprehension – 'a world of objects' as it is sometimes put – but we are also forced to recognize some subjective aspect of all this processing and system. The world I apprehend is not relative to me as an individual, but it is relative to our 'faculty of cognition', to the way *we* order things or to our minds as the creatures that we are and there is moreover something essentially incomplete or inadequate about the way the world is shaped for things to be ingredients in a world of our objective experience. There are questions, for example, about beginning and end in space or time; and there always lurks in the background the ghost of the problem which led Berkeley to his more openly subjective idealism, namely that however coherent and ordered and predictable events may be in our own kind of experience, they are also in some way fleeting and variable according to very subjective factors. There are perspectival distortions which vary from moment to moment and which lead to the idea that the world of our immediate experience, however coherent, has no permanent or solid reality other than the necessary ways in which we in fact do experience them, and even when we speak of 'necessary' ways, there also seems to be something arbitrary about this also, since, in the last analysis, we *find* that experience is the sort of ordered presentation which we can understand and manipulate, but find it hard to say why it has to be so beyond noting how unintelligible and chaotic it would be otherwise. This led Berkeley to the supposition that we could rely on God, as the author and sustainer of all, to guarantee the consistency of all that happens in the world around us, but others have hankered for the postulation of some reality of things other than the way they present themselves to us and which in some fashion directly warrants their appearing as they do. Beyond the table, as it presents itself as an item in the kind of experience *we* have, is the table as it really is as an item in an independent reality not relative to the way we apprehend things at all, and Kant, concerned about this problem, was led to the view that, along with the reality as we experience it, there must also be the reality of 'things in themselves' distinct from objects as apprehended by us. This alleged 'thing in itself' tended to be a distinct reality or world, and this is what is meant by the bifurcation of reality in Kant's system to the phenomenal world, as relative to our 'faculty of cognition' and its modes, and the noumenal world of objects existing in their own right and in a more final way.

As we are limited to apprehension of objects in the kind of world we are predisposed to apprehend or experience, we can have no knowledge, in the proper sense of what 'things in themselves' are like, we can never push beyond the boundaries of the world as we experience it, however much we must also postulate the other reality of the world of things in themselves. The latter can never be proper objects of knowledge for us although Kant tried also to maintain, by the postulates of Practical Reason, or what he sometimes called 'Faith', that we could have some kind of assurance, not knowledge proper, of the world beyond in the form at least of finding God a requirement of certain features of *moral* experience and along with this a postulate of immortality. The arguments Kant uses here, as is generally acknowledged, are somewhat strained and artificial and hardly adequate to the weight they have to bear. But there is also the problem, if we think of physical things as being in some way also 'things in themselves', of establishing some relation between the 'real' external world and the world as we apprehend it, a causal one perhaps.

These are features of Kant's philosophy which seemed to be left in a somewhat unsatisfactory state. He himself appears to have been very uncertain just where to place the subject or 'pure self' presupposed in all the kinds of experience we have. There are reasons for doubting whether he would place it outright in the world of things in themselves. But if we are not to do that, we are left with either 'an imaginary focus' or an unspecified subjective condition of unified experience of which nothing whatsoever can be known and which seems to have no actual or concrete reality; and, as it seems firmly not to be in time, which is a mode or condition of the phenomenal world *we* apprehend, there appears to be no alternative to regarding it at least as 'a timeless self'.

It is, nonetheless, the existence or postulation of this 'timeless self' that makes morality possible and sets us up as free moral agents, for everything in the phenomenal world, including our own passing desires, is subject to invariable laws. Freedom is not found in the phenomenal world, but only in the timeless noumenal world. Kant was very concerned about postulating freedom as a condition of moral obligation; if I have a duty then this must be something I am capable of fulfilling, the 'ought' implies 'I can', and this becomes a pivotal key notion in Kantian ethics. But how is the 'timeless self', not properly in the world at all, to be an agent accountable for what we do in the course of our lives? At times there is a suggestion of some once and for all choice of our way of life, but in the main it must be said that Kant left the position as a whole here in a very unsatisfactory state, since he did not seem able to give the self – or at least 'the pure self' which is free – sufficient body to be an agent properly effective in the world around us.

Kant does indeed speak of 'a phenomenal' as well as a noumenal self, and this former is where our desires are placed and our dispositional nature. But as an element in the world of phenomena the self is not free and a moral agent. Kant tended to concede to the hedonist the last word where our desires are concerned. They are determined by what we find pleasurable and come about by this necessity. It is not for these that we are accountable, and this in turn leads to further complications in ethical thinking, especially when we have to consider the content of our particular obligations, the precise things it is our duty to do from moment to moment. For Kant finds it impossible to ascribe proper and inherent worth to natural aspirations and their fulfilment as part of the hedonistic phenomenal world, and he thus concludes that nothing has worth in itself besides the good will as exercised by the free noumenal self. But if nothing has worth in itself besides the good will, 'shining like a jewel by its own light', it would seem that we have no obligation other than that to maintain the moral goodness of the good will itself, and thus the content of all that we can be required to do must be educed somehow out of the goodness of the will itself.

There are various ways in which Kant seeks to do this, above all variations on the theme of the principle of universalization, so to will that my maxim should also become universal law. But while this gives some guidance, it becomes in practice very difficult to apply without some standard or criterion or judgment which goes beyond the intrinsic goodness of the good will itself; and the renewal of this principle in much idealist thought, and especially in the moral and political thought of T. H. Green, was a source of particular difficulty in late nineteenth-century thought and practices. But with the Kantian bifurcation, however he may have understood the status of the 'pure self', the difficulties multiply, and not least when the principles involved are brought to bear upon the tasks of finding out a proper way to live in the actual world around us – and of properly understanding our practical and political commitments.

It is to these difficulties that Hegel addressed himself, and the main move that he made, at least for our understanding of his influence on later idealism, was to reject the finality of the distinction we draw, in Kantian philosophy, between the world of phenomena and the world of noumena, of things as they appear in our experience and things as they really are. There is only one world, the entire universe, and just as it was in virtue of being rational creatures, the self co-ordinating the world of its own experience, that we have a unified objective world to apprehend, so also it is by virtue of the same rational necessity that the seeming contradictions in the world as we apprehend it are to be resolved and superseded in the notion of one universe which we, with our limited intellects, cannot properly encompass and which must therefore leave us with partial and incomplete, and thus essentially inadequate, understanding, but which is nonetheless in principle capable of exhaustive rational explanation. 'The real is the rational and the rational is the real', as the famous text has it. There will still remain a division between the incomplete world of things as they seem to us and the full and true reality of things as they are in their proper place in the one unified system of things to which we cannot fully attain. But it is now a partial distinction, however much we must remain subject to it, not an ultimate distinction of principle; and so, for the sharp distinction of things as they seem and things in themselves, we have degrees of apprehension of ingredients in the one reality, distorted unavoidably for us by their incompleteness but still having a measure of truth and reality made more adequate as they point to the principle of the one reality of which they are an inadequately apprehended part. There is nothing in our experience which is wholly unreal, but nothing, as we apprehend it, is fully real except in its place in the one system which is the whole universe and which is rational throughout in the sense that, could we but trace it, the necessity of everything being what it is is prescribed by the nature of the exhaustive rational system of which it is a part – or, as it came to be put more boldly later, 'an appearance'.

It was this rational monism that Hegel contributed especially to nine-teenth-century idealism, but in the work of the main originator and mentor of British idealism, namely T. H. Green, the independent influence of Kant remained a very formative influence. Green retained, as inherited from Hegel, the notion of one monistic system in which the whole universe consists, but in presenting this in more specific detail and argument he took over many notions more expressly from Kant than from Hegel. How did he go to work?

Green begins the positive presentation of his major themes from exactly the same position as Kant, namely that we are aware of an ordered world and that this requires the postulation of an abiding – and, as Green very explicitly says, timeless – subject which makes it possible for us to relate our presentations to one another and not be confined to the transitory impression. The world for us is made possible or sustained by the self or subject.

But, it is argued, in addition to the world as each individual subject apprehends and unifies it, there is the world of nature at large which has also to be regarded as a unified world. What can sustain this? The same principle must be invoked again, and so, in addition to each individual subject of experience, we have what Green calls a Spiritual Principle in Nature making possible the organization of our individual worlds.

This is a curious argument, in some respects reminiscent of Berkeley when he ascribed the coherence of our experience to the way the world, dependent in perception on being perceived, was also sustained by an infinite mind. But there are differences, mainly due to the different way in which Green supposes that the world is maintained for each one initially by an abiding subject. He does not appeal to considerations which are thought to lead directly to the view that colours and sounds etc. cannot be conceived to exist except as seen and heard. His concern is expressly with the unity of our experience, and while Berkeley had at least a legitimate problem in asking what could cause or account in some way for the reliable coherent way in which things happened in our experience, Green seems to think that the unifying activity of the subject is all we need, and for this reason, since experience is already sustained by the activity of each subject in his own case, it is not clear what remains to call for the sustaining activity of the Eternal Spiritual Principle in Nature. It looks as if the world were being accounted for twice over.

One has also to ask what is the relation of the Eternal Spiritual Principle to the individual subjects of experience and the cosmos as each one finds it. The answer draws a great deal upon the way Hegel had come to conceive of the world and its shaping as some process whereby thesis and antithesis have been resolved in some more complete synthesis. But Green does not give prominence to this particular notion of thesis and antithesis. What he does is to give special place to the ideas of history and progress, ideas which had also been brought to the centre of the speculative stage by the spread of Darwinian ideas and the importance ascribed to evolution. He thus comes to the conclusion that the truth about the relation of the Eternal Spiritual Principle to the world at large is that the former 'reproduces' itself in the world and in nature. It is not very clear what we are to understand by reproduction here, nor what sort of independence it allows to otherwise finite reality. Green does not provide much in the way of a clue himself. But the upshot is clear.

This is that we have to view the course of history as throughout a spiritually or divinely ordered process leading to greater fulfilment of the Spiritual Principle and thus guaranteed to proceed to ever greater perfection. This was well attuned to accord with the prevailing optimism of the Victorian era and helped to extend and strengthen it. The belief was widespread that progress was inevitable, that the course of history clearly reflected this and that we were ourselves at that time on the verge of substantial advances in the elimination of major ills like slavery, poverty and related deprivations, major conflicts and so forth. Green himself took a prominent part in major reforms and was eager to support changes in education and slum clearance, although, for a reason to be specified, he found this difficult to reconcile with aspects of his teaching. It was perhaps understandable that great confidence should persist during a period of relative calm and much prosperity for at least sections of the community. It was an expectation to be rudely shattered with the outbreak of the First World War, and not much recovered since that time.

There is perhaps a good case to be made for the view that our control of our natural environment and resources today, the radical changes in means of transport and communication, make possible for us the elimination of major ills, like war and poverty, and set us on a path of unprecedented prosperity for most people. But the same advances which give us this agreeable prospect have also brought new complications and the very real danger that, instead of helping us to a period of much greater general prosperity, they have made possible misery, fear, and the likelihood of almost total mutual destruction. Until certain obstacles are overcome and new arrangements made in the relations of peoples and governments, it seems that despair and fear are more appropriate than happy optimism. Indeed so sharp is the change that highly influential thinkers in the early part of the present century, notably religious and theological writers, passed to the other extreme, often with the same assurance and lack of analysis, of assuming that human beings were inevitably depraved and that, whatever they may seem to achieve provisionally and outwardly, mankind is doomed to barbarous and destructive self-seeking, we are incurably and totally corrupt.

All this raises issues which cannot be properly investigated here. But just as the gloomy prophets of doom in the twentieth century tended to rest their case on partial and rash generalizations, so it was that the comfortable optimism of the late nineteenth century was based mainly on *a priori* considerations and a mood of cheerfulness induced by a partial survey of appropriate evidence and considerations. Green himself provides very little evidence from the course of history itself, the rise and fall of its many civilizations, the long periods of confusion and reversal of fortunes; and he offers very little in the way of a close analysis of what we should understand by progress and the ways in which it is to be measured.

The most that he offers are a few illustrations, as in the comparison between Greek and Christian ideals and views of motivation.[5] The Greeks, so he affirms, had the notion of promoting what is inherently good and beautiful in the community, but only on a limited scale for their own community only, or indeed for an elite or privileged section of it. But with the coming of Christianity we have the extension of such expectations, not for the gifted or privileged few but for all – 'weak things and things that are despised hath God called'. How far this can be sustained in practice or taken to be generally true of the spread of Christianity, is a moot point. But we are in any case moving at the level of great generality far removed from clear and comprehensive historical evidence. Green seems to have taken it as firmly established, on the basis of his general metaphysical reasons for regarding our lives as the scene of the reproduction of itself by an Eternal Spiritual Principle, that the course of history would involve unmistakable stages of rising on stepping stones of our dead selves to higher things.

A further peculiar feature of Green's metaphysics is closely bound up with his epistemology. He stresses, as we have seen, the unity and essential inter-relatedness of experience as we have it in our apprehension of the world. But we have also to take account of some 'given' element in experience also. This presents considerable difficulty, for we find it exceptionally difficult to think of any ingredient of experience that is not already accorded some place in the system by which we apprehend and make sense of our environment – we see everything in perspective, for example, and find it hard indeed to think this away altogether. This is why the notion of sense-data has been so much frowned upon in recent years. Not even an artist, trained to see things in a more realistic way than others, can eliminate altogether the way we accord some placing, and thereby some character, to what we apprehend in perception. All the same, however disposed we may be for reasons of this sort to be suspicious of the sense-datum theory, and however difficult it may be to specify, notwithstanding the magnificent work of Professor H. H. Price, just what we would regard as a bare sense-datum or in the curious terminology of some contemporary writers, 'raw feels', something along the lines of what is meant by 'the given' element in experience seems unavoidable. Why, in the absence of this, should we see the world or particular things in it, in one way rather than another, green and not red, round, over there and not here, and so forth. We do not choose to see things as they are, not even in dreams, we see them as they seem to us to be, 'over and against us' or presented in one way and not another.

It may seem odd, as common sense and ordinary language philosophers have stressed in our time, to say that we see patches of colour flying by or that we sit on a sense-datum – we see horses at the race and sit on a chair. But whatever may be said for this approach to the subject and the extraordinary difficulty of framing a sense-datum theory in a satisfactory way, it seems unavoidable in any plausible account of perception to take account of ingredients, perhaps an entire visual field, which are presented as the distinctive and definitive characteristics of objects in our environment. If we leave this out, what do we have? Nothing, it would seem, but the inter-relatedness of things, and this is indeed the position in which Green himself in due course came to rest. Reality is in fact 'one all-inclusive system of unalterable relations'.

This hardly does justice to the quality of being over-against us which in some way must be accorded to the external world and the rich and colourful variety, the changes and particularity, which is an obvious feature of the world in which we actually find ourselves. Whatever account be finally offered of the 'given' element in experience, whether it be in terms of sense-data or some of the theories which seem to have ousted this notion at the moment, we just have to reckon with some aspect of the world around us which is not as bloodless and abstract as things dissolved eventually into their relations to one another.

The same must be said, even more forcibly in my view of the matter, of the distinctness of persons. For Green, the subject in experience seems to be reduced to some formal principle of unification – and timeless at that – by which presentations are held together, virtually 'the imaginary focus' of Kant; and in this way the finality of the individual person is eroded in favour of the view that we are at best 'centres of unification', as a fairly moderate later idealist was to say.[6] It is only in our place in the unifying function of the whole that we exist and function; and the more we expand our experience and identify with our true nature in the unifying function of the whole, the more we become identical with one another and with the one whole of reality in which we exist. The more perfectly the Eternal Spiritual Principle 'reproduces' itself in us the less significant are we in any distinctness that may be accorded to us. In a metaphor which became popular later, the more we all enlarge our peepholes upon the world, the more is our experience strictly the same and we ourselves merge in one another in the unity of the whole.

A later, but very different, idealist was to insist that the subject in experience must be 'a something'[7] and not a mere abstract principle of unification. This sets us on a very different course, but it was not the one followed in the main stream of idealist thinking after Green. It was Green who set the main pattern for others and determined thereby the ways in which most thinkers in Britain – and many other parts of the world – viewed their problems and exercised considerable influence on the attitudes of people in general in the closing stages of the nineteenth century – and the beginning of this one.

The metaphysical side of Green's thought, to which I have been alluding, was matched by and extensively influenced by what he maintained on moral and political questions. Here there were two main themes. In the first Green sets himself in sharp opposition to the prevailing hedonism of philosophical thought just before his day, but at the same time proceeding on the initially subjectivist factor of satisfaction of desire as the ultimate determinant of all valuation. But, whereas Kant had thought of the desiring side of our nature as subject to a mechanical determination on the basis of what we had empirically found to be pleasurable, Green brought the Kantian view of the self as a centre of unification to bear more closely, not only on the theory of knowledge and perception, but on our understanding of our desiring nature. The process of unification permeates the latter as well, and so we have to view ourselves, not as the scene of isolated warring forces or unrelated desires, but as a system or 'universe',[8] in a later term, of desires where the strength of our desires at any particular time was determined by their place in our general anticipations and what would satisfy, not this or that desire as an atomic passing ingredient in our natures, but our desiring nature as a whole. There was an 'end of the self as a whole' or what would meet our desiring nature as a whole, the satisfaction of the whole person and not of warring impulses in isolation.

This is how it comes about, Green and his followers would argue, that desires which might be very strong in themselves have not much place in our characters or influence on our conduct, because they are isolated or belong to a weak 'universe' of desire. I may have a strong desire for some food or drink which I also know will not agree with me, or, in extreme cases as when I come upon a poisoned well in the desert, will be certain to do me great harm, but I do not satisfy it or think seriously of doing so. I think ahead, I look beyond the passing scene and immediate satisfaction, to what will satisfy me as a rational being or as a whole, and in this way there becomes possible for us also the emergence of desires, in art or literature for example, which never present themselves for brutes incapable of the rationality which characterizes us as human beings. The more coherent our natures become in this way, the more we aim at fulfilment of ourselves as a whole, the better our moral evaluations will be and the more estimable our conduct. Judgments of value must be made on the basis of the satisfaction of our desiring nature as a whole, but the same impulse takes us further than the satisfaction of this or that individual to what will satisfy our general natures as human beings and thus provides for us the notion of an end to be attained which is shared by and includes the satisfaction in similar terms of other members of society. So that what is eventually good is what will satisfy me as a member of society where the ruling principle is what will satisfy 'human nature as a whole'.

A problem which this presents is why, if the initial criterion is satisfaction of desire, I should give pride of place, not to what will best satisfy me as an individual but to what will satisfy society as a whole or the general desiring nature of man. Green in fact thought that the conflict would never in fact become an urgent one, since the same rationality which induces me to give prominence to my own satisfaction as a whole operates also to induce me to include the satisfaction of others on the basis of the satisfaction of human nature as a whole; but in finding this somewhat easy transition from my own satisfaction as an individual to an 'end of man' or the fulfilment of my desiring nature in which I share the aspirations of other members of society, and thus overcoming one major difficulty in his position, Green is much influenced by a further feature of his theory which he derived more directly from Kant and Rousseau than from Hegel and the 'one all-inclusive system of relations'.

This is the conviction that there is no genuine goodness other than the good will. If this were the case how could we ever come to discover any content for moral action and our obligations. This difficulty is peculiarly sharp when we stand upon the principle that the goodness of the will, or moral worth in the strict sense, depends upon our devotion to duty or 'conscientious action', as it is sometimes put. The most we can aspire to, in these terms, is the cultivation, in ourselves and in others of the goodness of the will itself, its purity or integrity in being especially concerned with the fulfilment of obligation, and, as this presupposes freely willed action, there does not seem to be much we can do about it in the case of the goodness of other persons. The most we can do is to ensure the purity of our own motivation.

Green is not unaware of this difficulty, and he returns again and again to the question 'But what in particular ought I to do?' setting out on the same quest in various directions, in one futile attempt after another, but always returning to the point where he started. The *reductio ad absurdum* of this particular circling around the one notion of the good will comes in one place where Green, discussing the situation of Jeanie Dean in Scott's *The Heart of Midlothian* seems forced to admit that Jeanie has no real problem about the morality of telling a lie to save Effie's life, convinced as she is of the innocence of her sister, since nothing in the moral quality of Effie's life will be affected if she is unjustly put to death. Indeed, if the goodness of the will is all, or if, as Green seems to think at times, the good will unfolds itself directly in specific requirements or defines its own content, there can never be any problem of moral perplexity or of being genuinely mistaken about what we should do, a view which Green himself forcibly puts in the insistence that if we are wrong in the course we pursue as our duty it must be because our motives are 'not pure enough' – the yellow streak will show.

This is an extraordinary line to be taken at any time. Conscientious persons have done in the past many things, in the course of what seemed to them their duty, which we would consider appalling today; and in the complexities of our age we have notorious difficulties in deciding where the course of our duty lies, in matters of war and peace, for example, or in personal problems or family ethics, or in legal and medical matters, and in economic matters affecting the just distribution of material goods. Many of these problems were sharpening themselves in Green's day, in the aftermath of the industrial revolution and the existence, as he himself put it, of 'a dispossessed proletariat'. It is astonishing that he never admitted this, notwithstanding that it forced itself so much upon his attention in the very reforms, slum clearance, fuller educational opportunity and the freedom of slaves, which he himself set out to further. He never achieved a satisfactory answer to this problem or found himself able to think in terms of any notion of duty, along the lines later stressed in this century by G. E. Moore, H. A. Prichard or W. D. Ross, other than the devotion to duty itself, and this leaves us with very little which we can suppose ourselves called upon to do in this or that particular respect.

This in turn is closely bound up with the notion that genuine goodness must be 'non-competitive', a 'common good', as it was also put, in which the heightening of my share in no way diminishes that of others. That there are attainments which can be singled out as of special worth in this way, besides the goodness of conscientious action itself, may be admitted. In the attainment of knowledge I do not diminish the common stock of others, but rather am most likely to extend it. But all this also depends on material conditions and opportunities which bring us at once to the sphere where the good of one person has to be weighed against the good of others. The alleged 'non-competitive' character of inherent moral worth affords no way of evading the problem which is sometimes very acute – just what in particular ought I to do? It is not enough to give the answer 'Just do your duty', for our inquisitor, and we all fill that role at times, is already resolved to do his duty, to join the resistance movement in an oppressed or invaded country or to try to placate the enemy by collaboration, but he remains troubled as to which of various seemingly appropriate courses of action is the one he *really* ought to take.

A position like that of Green thus leaves us with little incentive or direction where some positive action or reform is concerned, and it is this reluctance to interfere in any way with the freedom of the individual to pursue whatever course seemed appropriate to him, and meddle as little as possible in the lives of one another, that affords us one of our major clues to the line taken by Green, and by most idealists after him, in social and political theory. This in turn is bound up with the persistence of the individualism of an earlier age in a great deal of the political thinking of the nineteenth century. This is the individualism which, in the case of Locke, ascribed to persons an imprescriptible and inalienable right to 'life, liberty, and property'. In defence of Locke some have tried to ascribe more importance than used to be the case to his qualification 'provided there is as good left over for others'. But it was in the spirit of the right of the individual not to be subject to influence or restraints to which he did not himself consent that Locke's teaching exercised such widespread influence in America as in Europe in his day and for a long time after. In essentials, notwithstanding his plea for a strong undivided government, Thomas Hobbes, in an earlier time had insisted that a wise government will interfere as little as possible in the concerns of the citizens beyond keeping the peace and making life secure – the 'like debt', as Hobbes put it, we all owe to the State.

It was these notions that Rousseau in due course inherited and which he accepted in very thorough fashion in his early work. He became later acutely conscious of our indebtedness to a community, without which we would remain, in his own words, 'stupid and limited animals', and thereby of the need for much positive State enactment. But how justify this without a firm abandonment of the initial individualism? That was a price which Rousseau was never fully prepared to pay, and so we find him involved in the toils and ambiguities of the famous notion of the General Will by which men were to be forced to be free, in the strict sense that, in being required and compelled to comply with laws to further the positive good of the community, they remained 'as free as before' and 'obeyed themselves alone'. The upshot of this, as I have attempted to show elsewhere,[9] is to prepare the way for that sort of social despotism where public enactment takes no account of peculiar and varying needs but imposes upon all the uniformity of a way of life in which there is little scope for individual initiative or varieties of needs and attainment. We are to be shut in in the world of our own thoughts without the stimulus to independent thinking which effective social existence makes possible. The great prophet of freedom and of the rights of the individual, thus unwittingly attacked freedom at its tenderest spot and prepared the way for the sort of regimentation and collectivism, in its most extreme form in Hitlerism but often matched in the rigours and ruthlessness of Communist regimes, of which the free world today stands in such fear.

Unhappily T. H. Green and his disciples fell into exactly the same confusion. The only true good is a 'common good' and that, translated into political principles, meant a non-competitive good in the form of action or policies on which we were all agreed. The purity of the General Will required of us to restrict political action to matters on which we could agree because they affected all of us in the same way. But this in effect requires the surrender of major issues and colourful variety to an alleged collective will against which there was no justifiable appeal. Green himself found it very difficult to justify resistance to the State in any conditions or the right to help the run-away slave. His heart was in the right place but he was prevented from paying much attention to it by the tight hold on his attitudes of a theory of the basis of government which easily culminates in the unrestrained despotisms of authoritarian regimes in our day.

This peculiar swing from what is initially a special concern with freedom to the opposite extreme of a repressive uniformity has been described in greater detail in some of my other publications, and I have tried to indicate closely how this came about in Green's attitude to some of the major practical and political issues of his day.[10] Here it must suffice to point out in addition how easily this accords with the general dissolution of the distinctness of persons into their function within the unifying activity of a more comprehensive unit, the State or society. In some instances the State came to be regarded as some super-structure altogether beyond or above the life and rights of individual members. There is no appeal beyond the will of the community, and while there is more than one way of reaching this conclusion, the general course of post-Hegelian idealism, and of the work of notable British idealists, tended to favour this ascendency of the State and society at the expense of individual rights and variety. In combination with other factors, this led in Germany and European communities associated with it to a peculiarly tyrannous and ruthless despotism. The effect of this feature of idealism on British thought was counteracted by many other factors, but the strength of the tendency towards the suppression of individual freedom, and the tension it created in the mind of a lover of freedom, is very sharply defined in the case of T. H. Green. It is more subtle, and to that extent more dangerous, in the work of later writers where the drift towards some kind of collectivism is obscured by less explicit and more ambiguous metaphorical language which became a more distinctive feature of subsequent idealism than the tortured convolutions of Green's attempt to arrest the drift of his thought into a social philosophy where the freedom he valued was put in the gravest peril. This is what lent so much importance at a later date to the powerful blast against the collectivist trend in idealist thinking by L. T. Hobhouse who, at the height of the First World War, published his excellent *The Metaphysical Theory of the State* in 1916 as his own contribution to the struggle for freedom and democracy which was then being waged, as it has since, in an appallingly bloody way.

For the present we must leave this aspect of the implications of the monistic view of the universe and our place in it and turn to some of the more notable extensions and modifications of British idealism in the work of later writers than Green. In essentials, the germ of almost everything of importance in strictly idealist teaching may be found in the work of T. H. Green, the initiator and also the mirror of almost all that was to follow. It is in the work of Bradley (1846–1924), a more outstanding and powerful creative thinker, that the more significant modifications may be found, but his work also contains much that comes directly from the more naive and simplistic arguments of Green.

The key to Bradley's most distinctive contribution to idealism is found in his much discussed theory of relations. Green, as we have seen, was content to think of the universe as a system of 'unalterable relations'. But Bradley was fully aware of the inadequacy of thinking in terms of mere relations. The world has some qualitative character as well, a reality at least more solid than mere relations. 'I still insist', he declares, 'that for thought what is not relative is nothing. But I urge, on the other hand, that nothings cannot be related, and that to turn qualities in relation into mere relations is impossible . . . If you mean that . . . relations can somehow make the terms upon which they seem to stand, then, for my mind, your meaning is quite unintelligible . . . relations must depend upon terms, just as much as terms upon relations.'

The 'terms', although essential, are nothing in themselves, subsisting as it were in their own right and also happening to be related to one another. We cannot think away the relations from what constitutes the term, there are no isolable entities. Not only do we not discover such entities, they are logically impossible. The relation is constitutive of the entity, and we cannot therefore have a strictly pluralistic universe. But neither can we have a wholly abstract one. As Bradley also puts it:

We may briefly reach the same dilemma from the side of relations. They are nothing intelligible, either with or without their qualities. In the first place, a relation without terms seems mere verbiage; and terms appear, therefore, to be something beyond their relation. At

least, for myself, a relation which somehow precipitates terms which were not there before, or
a relation which can somehow get on without terms, and with no differences beyond the mere
ends of a line of connection, is really a phrase without meaning. It is, to my mind, a false
abstraction, and a thing which loudly contradicts itself.

But how the relation can stand to the qualities is, on the other side, unintelligible. If it is
nothing to the qualities, then they are not related at all . . . The problem is to find how the
relation can stand to its qualities; and this problem is insoluble.

That is where Bradley really takes his stand. There is something essentially
unsatisfactory about the way we have to think about the world around us. We
must have relations, there can be nothing which is not essentially related to
other things, but there must be some quality of things which is not reducible
to their relations.

The same sort of insistence, and the dilemma to which it leads, runs
through the whole of Bradley's work on Logic and the logical writings of
Bradley's closest and most famous disciple, Bernard Bosanquet. In his
account of perception and judgment, and in the famous chapter I of his *Logic*,
Book II, Part II, Bradley insists on some 'thisness' or something which is
immediately 'felt' as reality impinging upon us, but we cannot isolate this or,
as Bosanquet put it, get at a datum unrelated or uninterpreted. However
much we may try to think away the interpretation of what is presented, or the
'raw feels' in the somewhat inelegant term of today, we find that we are
bound to place it in some way, even if very minimal, in a system of things.
Even an artist trained to see things more as they are than in our normal
perspective, cannot dispense with some kind of viewpoint or framework.
The 'given' and the relation thus seem essentially bound up with one
another, and this alleged internality of relations, much disputed by later
critics of idealism like G. E. Moore and Bertrand Russell, leaves us in an
insoluble dilemma. Every quality in relation has, in consequence, a diversity
within its own nature, and this diversity cannot immediately be asserted of
the quality. Hence the quality must exchange its unity for an internal
relation. But, thus set free, the diverse aspects, because each is something in
relation, must each be something also beyond. This diversity is fatal to the
internal unity of each, and it demands a new relation, and so on without limit.
In short, qualities in relation have turned out to be as unintelligible as were
qualities without one. The problem from both sides has baffled us.

Whether the problem is as insoluble as Bradley thought is debatable. But
for him it led to the further conclusion that 'the relational way of thought',
and that is unavoidable for us, 'must give us appearance, not truth'. It is a
makeshift, a device, a mere practical compromise, most necessary but in the
end most indefensible. We have to take reality as many, and to take it as one,
and to avoid contradiction. There are various consequences of this. One of

them is that there cannot be 'a plurality of independent reals'. On the other hand we cannot think away the world of our experience. 'Everything which appears must be real. Appearance must belong to reality . . . the real is individual. It is one in the sense that its positive character embraces all differences in an inclusive harmony.' The world as we have to think of it is a phenomenal world of appearance, our intellect cannot rest content with it in the last analysis. But it is not 'mere appearance', or a complete delusion. We find some clue in the insistence, which Bradley comes to very firmly that there is no reality other than experience, neither in some independent physical world nor in a subject 'standing separate' from experience. But the unity in diversity which we find in experience as we have it is also essentially unacceptable to our thinking, and, while not to be dismissed as nothing or wholly unreal, it must be thought to have its proper reality in some more ultimate unity which eludes our grasp altogether. We can have 'an idea of its main features', but 'fully to realize the existence of the Absolute is for finite beings impossible'. In the terms made familiar by the most distinguished follower of Bradley in our own century,[11] the phenomenal and contradictory character of reality, though final for us, leads to the notion of a 'supra-rational' character of ultimate reality in which the imperfections of the world as we must think of it are taken up and resolved in some way which is altogether beyond our comprehension.

This, presented very boldly here, requires us to take present reality with all seriousness as genuine reality, and not a world of dreams, but also brings us to the recognition of a mysterious ultimate nature of reality in its fulness, a transcendent to which everything points.

The hard problem, if we think in these terms, is to think out a satisfactory way of relating the world of appearance, as it must be for us, and the ultimate from which it derives its genuine reality; and, however much Bradley may have thought that sentience provides the model for the transcendent and perfect unity in difference from which the world of appearance is torn and has 'ragged edges', we cannot avoid the conclusion that everything there is, or everything that happens, is only ultimately or fully real in its place in a transcendent harmonious whole in which contradictions and imperfections, unavoidable in our limited experience and conspectus, are resolved and disappear. Nothing is ever just what it seems to be for us, and when we realize this we rest content in the knowledge that what is bewildering and unsatisfactory for our understanding, and can weigh us down if viewed exclusively as finite and 'final phenomenal truth', is ultimately resolved in the perfection and complete harmony of the Absolute from which it is 'torn' or of which it is a genuine, and to that extent, real appearance.

We thus avoid the absurdity of thinking of the world as mere appearance, but serious problems remain and they persisted as a source of serious perplexity for all adherents to the doctrine of Absolute Idealism. For while the alleged suprarational character of ultimate reality relieves us of the strain of giving an exhaustive rational account of all there is, including evil, we are not able to escape the implications of ascribing to everything its place in one absolute and perfect whole of being.

There are many forms which this difficulty takes. One, connected with the theory of 'internal relations', is to come to terms with the brute fact of the world, as we encounter it, being what it is. There is some aspect of the 'givenness' of things, whether or not it leads to a distinct plurality, which remains a feature of our experience which will not go away in the insistence on some transcendent unity of all things. Then there is error and evil; there cannot be either in the absolute, and yet they appear to be very positive characteristics of much that we encounter in our finite existence. Several idealist writers struggled hard to reconcile themselves to the conviction that all evil would eventually be found to be an element in a whole which, could we but penetrate its secret, was perfect through and through. All evil tends to be in this way a form of good, and this is peculiarly hard to sustain when we recognize the positive character of evil. Heroic efforts to overcome these difficulties were made by some thinkers closer to our time, A. S. Pringle-Pattison,[12] A. E. Taylor,[13] Henry Jones[14] and others. But they leave us, all the same, with the impression that they are desperately trying to force the reality of evil into a mould into which it will not go.

We come close to finding what is of lasting worth in these doctrines of absolute idealism when we consider the modification of the doctrine in the work of thinkers of a later time than that of the heyday of Absolute Idealism, such as A. C. Ewing and C. A. Campbell. For, in the latter's insistence on the 'finality' of phenomenal truth for us, we come closer to the understanding of the transcendent, as it had taken shape in earlier religious and metaphysical thinking, namely, not as a completion or continuation of finite existence, but as an essentially mysterious, but distinct, reality, distinct from the contingent finite world which depended upon it, or the created world. Idealist thinking at its best, as in the penetrating analyses of Bradley, notwithstanding the difficulties of the doctrine of internal relations, helps to highlight the need to recognize, in the ultimate antinomies of finite experience, some more ultimate reality which is complete and perfect in itself, as finite being cannot be, but which is the final source or sustainer of all there is. In this way, as was well brought out by C. A. Campbell, the note of the numinous character of transcendent reality, the *mysterium tremendum* which is pervasive in all else there is, the account of the idea of the Holy in Rudolf Otto's work, has its very effective complement in the work of Bradley and those who adhered most closely to his account of the Absolute; and to this extent, read in conjunction with one another they are illuminating and much advance the subject, yet their proper import has to be taken in the context of a more radical distinction between finite and infinite being than Bradley was able to recognize.

This comes sharply to a head when we consider the distinctness of sentient beings and especially of persons. On any form of idealist doctrine, finite persons, and the whole course of their lives, must be thought of finally in their place in the one whole of being in which all reality consists. This is very hard to accept, especially for those, like myself and many other recent writers, who consider the subject of experience, however much involved in having its particular experiences, to have a quite distinct and irreducible identity incapable of being reduced to any pattern or connectedness of experience, or of being merged in the being of others.

This issue is too vast to be examined on its own account here,[15] but it must be pointed out how very closely all this bears on the question of freedom and accountability. The traditional line in mid-stream British idealism was the presentation of freedom as self-determination. This is contrasted with mechanical determination, or what often passed in these writings as determinism, whereby the self was simply the scene of warring impulses, each with its independent force. As we have seen earlier, however, in the case of T. H. Green, the rational self permeates our desiring nature and enables us to have aims that will satisfy us as a whole, including more elevated desires. The contrast between this and warring impulses is clear, but the fact remains that the measure of such self-determination as we achieve is, in the last analysis, predetermined by just how rational we are by nature. The self-determination will be more complete in some cases than in others, and moreover, in terms of the ideal being itself constituted by what will satisfy our desiring nature as a whole, the more we are free the more our conduct is estimable. When, however, we think of properly *moral* freedom, we consider the wicked and dissolute to be as free as the saintly. The sinner is as responsible for his sins as the saint for his virtues.

In addition, on idealist principles, and the main stream from Green to Bradley and his disciples, the self-determination of each agent is prescribed, in the last analysis by his place in the whole scheme of things, the Absolute of which they are appearances. None of this seems adequate to a view of freedom as a condition of responsibility in which the agent himself is to be properly praised or blamed, and where he may rebelliously take his own line and deliberately choose to do good *or* bad. It is very hard, on a typical idealist view, to find a proper place for genuine moral evil and guilt. Bradley did his best in the impressive first chapter of his *Ethical Studies*. But it is hard to reconcile his main theme with his own insistence in that chapter that a person is to be praised or blamed for something which is properly *his own*.

It is in this context that it is very significant that the thinker of our own time who has done most to present afresh the transcendent or supra-rational character of Bradley's metaphysics, namely C. A. Campbell, is also the thinker who has presented what is far and away the best case we have in our time, perhaps at any time, for a genuinely open freedom of choice, combined with penetrating criticism of freedom as self-determination. But, if Campbell is to stand by this defence of free will, the corrective to a Bradleyan supra-rational is bound to make the distinction between limited finite existence and the supreme transcendent reality on which it depends a more complete one. The break with the monism of absolute idealism is bound to be more complete.

This goes also for the work of another writer who owes a great deal to idealist thought, and who has written some of the best books about idealism,[16] namely A. C. Ewing. For most of his professional life he uneasily accepted the idea of moral freedom as self-determination, but in his closing years, as reflected in his posthumously published work,[17] he came down firmly on the side of the libertarian view.

The idea of the moral end itself as the fulfilment of our nature as a whole found a more ready response in Campbell's work,[18] and he has presented one of the most plausible cases for it, but on the basis of a sharp distinction between moral and non-moral good which is not effectively heeded in idealist ethical thinking as a whole. The failure to provide some more ultimate and genuinely objective standard than our own desiring nature culminated, in the work of Bradley and others, in the tendency to make society the final arbiter and present all moral obligation, in the well-known terms of a famous chapter of Bradley's *Ethical Studies*, as only the duties of my station. Bosanquet was to carry this strain from Green's original thinking further in his collectivism and a typical version of the doctrine of the 'general will' derived, via Green, from Rousseau.

To place the achievements of Bradley in their proper perspective, we have therefore to take our cue from those features of the work of writers most indebted to him who broke away most completely from the dominant monistic strain in his thought. When this is done the supra-rational comes effectively to its own, but this will also mean a sharper break, in moral and religious thinking, with those features of main-stream idealism which accorded most closely with oriental thought, especially Hinduism. The real divide comes with the status accorded to the finite individual and the seeming distinctness of persons.

Other major religious issues, such as the problem of pain and suffering, as it presents itself for a religious attitude, appear also in a much better light[19] when the transcendent numinous reality is regarded as distinct and ultimate in itself, and not the all-inclusive transformation of finite existence in a monistic system. It is for this reason that particular interest attaches to the work of a number of thinkers who are firmly in the idealist tradition but who also presented, in the late nineteenth century, a pluralistic view in which the finality of the distinctness of persons is vigorously affirmed. I close this section with brief indications of this in the work of three very outstanding thinkers of this period.

James Ward (1848–1925) stands firmly in the idealist tradition, but in a form that has much closer affinity with Leibniz than with Hegel. He favours a distinctly theistic idealism, in which there was a strong panpsychic element but where the point of most significance was the distinct existence of particular beings, or monads, as Leibniz would have them, and also, in sharp contradiction to Leibniz, interaction between them. This is a very substantial and important departure from traditional idealism where everything is ultimately an appearance or element of the one being of God or the Absolute. It very much simplifies the insistence on the freedom and responsibility of the individual person, and it accorded well with the work of a notable colleague of James Ward at Cambridge, F. R. Tennant who, in his general and excellent work in his two volumes of *Philosophical Theology* and still more explicitly in his *The Concept of Sin*, shifted the emphasis, in theology and philosophy of religion, from the notion of some inevitability of sin to man's freedom and accountability. Few studies of this subject have come to terms more effectively, both in respect to the teachings of the Bible and to the philosophical analysis of ethical notions, than Tennant's short and readable *The Concept of Sin*. In these respects both Ward and Tennant prepared the way for the very outstanding contribution to this issue in the work of a thinker already mentioned who falls strictly outside our period, namely C. A. Campbell. He took his start from Bradley and presents most effectively the way our thought is driven to the recognition of a supra-rational character of ultimate reality in a way which also admits of the recognition of our distinct identity as ethical and responsible creatures. The analysis of what it is to be a responsible subject, involved in all the experience we have but exhibited pre-eminently as agent in responsible choices between genuinely open alternatives, has rarely been surpassed, perhaps never. No student of British idealism can afford to overlook the substantial contribution to this way of thinking in philosophy, as well as the limitations of it which call for modification in our thought about the distinctness of persons and their freedom made by the most outstanding disciple of Bradley in our own time who provided also the most important modification of the whole tenor and central theme of the idealism to which he himself subscribed so extensively, namely C. A. Campbell. To see the idealist movement in correct perspective, and to appreciate the strains to which it never ceased to be subject, even in the work of its most committed adherents, very close attention should be paid to the variation in idealist approaches and emphases in the line that takes us from James Ward through F. R. Tennant to C. A. Campbell and A. C. Ewing.

There is one further point to be stressed, in what must be a very brief reference to James Ward, namely that his account of the subject of experience is severely Kantian in one respect, namely in finding the subject not to be immediately apprehended in some form of self-awareness or self-ascription, but rather inferred as the thinker which all thinking and all experience involves. But Ward was also most insistent that the subject could not be merely a condition of experience or imaginary focus; the self, he maintained must be 'a something'. It is a further step from this, but in my view a natural, if not inevitable one, to recognizing the way the self is aware of itself in the very fact of having any kind of experience. But if we take this step, unavoidable it seems to me if we are to do justice to the ethical and religious implications of the distinctness of persons, we are departing in one very radical way from the main course of British, and indeed most other, forms of idealism in the nineteenth century.

Some account should also be taken, in this context, of the notable contribution of James Ward to psychology and especially the countering of the associationist psychology of Alexander Bain subjected in different terms to severe criticism also by F. H. Bradley. The most important feature of Ward's contribution to this subject is his notion of a presentational continuum of which particular presentations are partial modifications and not discreet objects. The significance of this radical corrective to associationist psychology for the philosophy of mind in general, including the importance of attention in connative activity, as well as in direct studies of perception, is very extensive.

Mention must be made, finally, of the work of J. E. McTaggart (1866–1925). He does not fall easily into any classification. Owing a great deal to Hegel, but reacting strongly against some fundamental notions and procedures of Hegel, he seems to belong more to the tradition of Ward and

Campbell; he lays stress on the reality and finality of individual minds, although he does not, like Campbell, understand this to mean the possibility of genuinely open choice. McTaggart remained a determinist, although he held that this was compatible with moral judgment and obligation. But where McTaggart departed most sharply from other idealists, both those of the camp of monistic absolute idealism and those who stood by the thesis of a pluralistic universe of discreet individual minds, is in his rejection of any notion of an ultimate, supreme or transcendent mind, or any other overarching reality besides the finite individual minds such as we know ourselves to be. His system has no room for God and all that this entails for religion. In *Some Dogmas of Religion* McTaggart attacked the belief in a personal and omnipotent God. He did maintain however that, independently of the will of an ultimate sustainer of the universe, finite minds were essentially immortal or indestructible. They are also bound to one another in love. Apart from this community of individuals, for whom love is the basic emotion, there is no reality. What appears to us as extended material objects is really minds or part of the content of minds. There is good and evil in this pluralistic spiritual universe, but the good is steadily gaining the day and we shall exist eventually in a 'timeless and endless state of love', 'knowing nothing but our beloved, because they love, and ourselves as loving them'. In the two volumes of *The Nature of Existence* McTaggart presents these themes in terms of exceptionally subtle and splendidly marshalled arguments, mainly of an *a priori* nature but very impressive as a remarkable indication of what may be accomplished in this way by a metaphysical thinker of the highest order. But whether we can ultimately arrive at the soundest views of ourselves and our place in the universe by these exquisite variations on themes of severely abstract analyses and requirements of thought, whether so much can be spun out from rationality itself, remains the major question mark we must place against these pluralistic forms of post-Hegelian idealism as much as against the more typical monistic form, and indeed against Hegelian philosophy also and the precursors of it in modern, and yet earlier, forms of severe rationalism. Perhaps, what we have to learn most of all from the brilliant ingenuity of idealist philosophy, and its truly determined and often most illuminating effort to relate itself to the reality that we actually know, is that, without being narrowly empiricist or formally hide-bound in any other way, in the fashionable analytic and linguistic philosophy or any other, we must resist the lure of the one sure method and cultivate the art of looking more effectively, in the first place, at what we find ourselves and the world around us to be like, and then proceed cautiously to consider how this points to and shapes itself into some bolder and more inclusive view of the universe. This is perhaps the true lesson of the vigorous positivism to which we have been subjected in our time and the aversion, in the earlier part of this century, to all metaphysical and speculative philosophy. That was an understandable but misguided reaction, but we forget at our peril the salutary warning against the distortion of what we find in fact to be the case that comes about from hastily completing our systems by preconceived notions and forcing whatever else we encounter into the structures we have already set up independently of them. By all means let us try to see ourselves and the world in their wholeness, and discern as far as we can the structures that extend beyond this and such visions as we have of that ultimate form of reality that eludes our present proper comprehension; but let us also do this on the basis of what we find, not in reason alone but in actuality also, to be the inescapable reality of what is most immediately present in our experience of ourselves and the world around us. The 'first look' of common sense philosophy may not be enough, we need to see things in the proper perspective and with due and modest sense of their limited placing, we must be bold to look beyond the immediate scene, but not in disregard of what, with our best understanding and reflection, we find it to be. Metaphysics, and the 'spiritual discernment' of religion which can have so vital a part in it, like charity, begins at home.

II

The main views of leading idealist philosophers on specific religious issues were very largely determined by their philosophical systems; indeed they were little more than translations of their basic philosophical ideas into new formulations and further modes of expression. Even the corrective which Bradley supplied to the very attenuated religion of T. H. Green was largely a philosophical correction of those aspects of Green's teaching which gave it its most distinctively religious feature. Of religion as a mode of being and experience with an initial, self-sustaining character of its own, of which metaphysics had to take account as an ingredient to be reckoned with in the proper formulation of a metaphysical system, they had little notion.

This can be seen particularly clearly in the case of T. H. Green who leaves us with little doubt that, granted the soundness of his philosophical claims, little else mattered in religion beyond the reformation of major philosophical notions in the terminology of more familiar religious language.

Green himself came from a traditional Christian background, his father was an Anglican rector and he himself at one stage thought seriously of seeking ordination. He signed the thirty-nine articles as required to take the degree of M.A., but he sat very lightly to creeds and institutions. 'Saving of souls is one thing', he wrote,[20] 'making a fuss about an institution and a creed quite another.' He once declared that 'a modified unitarianism suits me very well'.[21] But he never thought of leaving the Church of England. He did not think of himself as in any way outrageously unorthodox, and, while anxious that justice should be done to dissenters, in education and similar matters, he was by temperament and habit disinclined to challenge the establishment. None of this, however, imposed a particular strain upon him. For he understood the substance of traditional affirmations and the point of his religious observances in a very open way in terms of the major philosophical views in which his own serious thoughts were crystallized; and, without any insincerity or the lack of the courage of his opinions, he found it easy to move, as he thought the tide of enlightened opinion was moving, towards the acceptance of 'the essence of Christianity', in the term that gained much currency at the time, in the form of very general notions about the essentially spiritual nature of all existence and our mission to be the instruments of some divine process, conceived in that way. Subject to that understanding, there was no serious objection to the discriminating use of traditional language and observance and the retention of their power.

This becomes clear at almost every point where Green makes explicit reference to religious matters or pleads the cause of religion as a matter of prime importance for all. Though he might not, being restrained and modest in his ways, put it so himself, he would regard himself as a deeply religious and devout person, and was generally so regarded by those around him.

The combination of piety, on the one hand, and very great openness, on the other, may be seen well in the few papers in which he dealt expressly with religious matters and, especially, in his essays on 'Christian Dogma'[22] and his address, 'The Witness of God'.[23] The first of these opens with the insistence that 'the vital essence of things necessary for salvation'[24] was fully available to St Paul, not only independently of the Gospels as actually written, 'but in spite of ignorance (this is the necessary inference from his own language) of the facts of our Lord's life prior to his death'. Green deplores especially the practice of appealing to specific scriptural 'propositions', taken to contain in themselves 'some absolute truth', as the foundation of dogma. This is for him 'enfeebled Christianity' and a very false notion of 'inspiration'. In this we may readily concur. There has been from time to time a habit of appealing to proof-texts, and, more extensively, a proneness to derive credal affirmations from isolated complete passages. This seems quite unwarranted. But it does not follow that an explicit body of belief may not be derived from sensitive and judicious apprehension of the message of the Scriptures as a whole and of the specific presentation of Jesus, as a historical figure, and of his role in Christian experience. This is not the place to develop this theme. The point for the moment is that Green does not entertain any serious alternative to the purported scriptural basis of dogma other than the ascription of absolute truth to every scriptural proposition. Indeed it is very uncertain whether the Synoptic Gospels mattered at all for him.

How then did dogma come about? It began, according to Green, in 'authoritative tradition', linked closely to the oral communications of Christ and crystallized in 'the consent of the apostolic churches, conveyed through their bishops'.[25] It would be idle 'to deprecate the value' of these creeds, for they gathered up 'the various elements of the Christian consciousness, as represented by various churches . . . in a quite different phase from that presented to us in the writings of the New Testament. It is not that the creeds assert anything that may not be deduced with tolerable fairness from those writings, but they convey it in a different form, and the difference, primarily one of form becomes a difference of substance.'[26] It was, as Tertullian had taught, 'independent of the written scripture' and 'a necessary complement', but it 'soon came, by an insensible instinct of self-preservation, to affiliate itself to them, and to refashion the parent after the superstitious child's likeness'.[27]

In pursuance of this theme, and with much uncertainty as to where the ultimate basis of Christian belief may be found, Green embarks on a somewhat sweeping survey of the course of Christian doctrine culminating in the view that, with 'the Nicene Council', 'the manhood [of Christ] had been taken into God',[28] a process made complete in the dogma of Chalcedon. These aberrations were corrected by Luther who restored 'the primary fulness of the intuition, which had become abstract and empty in its dogmatic evolution'.[29] This came about especially, notwithstanding his continuing to be haunted by 'the ghost of scholasticism' because 'according to his proper idea', faith 'was the absorption of all merely finite and relative virtues', as such, in the 'consciousness of union with the infinite God'.[30] But this was in turn corrupted by the 'obtrusion of mysteries', and the 'dogmatic expression in those "mysteries" of original sin and incarnation, which again involve the paradox of guilt without free agency and the presence of a double consciousness of Christ'.[31] The theory which best retains 'the fulness of the christian reference is that of the "inward light"',[32] and the proper implication of this is that 'Christian dogma must be retained in its completeness, but it must be transformed into a philosophy'.[33]

We are therefore told that

Christ, as an object of intuition, must undergo a similar process. To the twelve apostles he was a visible person, and, as such, a saviour of the Jews only. By St Paul he was known under those attributes which gentile (at least Alexandrian) philosophy had learnt to ascribe to the spirit or wisdom of the world, and as such he became the Christ of the gentiles. These attributes, however, were still referred to the historical Jesus. He was the reality of which the idea involving the attributes was the objective reflex. To the modern philosopher the idea itself is the reality – the idea is at once the complement of the intuition and its justification.[34]

These are also the central themes of 'the Witness of God'. 'As the primary Christian idea is that of a moral death into life, as wrought for us and in us by God, so its realization, which is the evidence of its truth, lies in christian love, a realization never complete, because for ever embracing new matter, yet constantly gaining in fullness'.[35]

'The church has been the witness of Christ . . . not as the depository of a dogma . . . but as the slowly articulated expression of the crucified and risen life.'[36] Again we are told:

The glory of christianity is not that it excludes, but that it comprehends, not that it came of a sudden into the world, or that it is given complete in a particular intuition, or can be stated complete in a particular form of words, but that it is the expression of a common spirit, which is gathering all things in one. We cannot say of it, lo, here it is, or lo, there; it is now but was not then. We go backward, but we cannot reach its source; we look forward, but we cannot see its final power. We do it wrong in making it depend on a past event, and in identifying it with the creed of a certain age, or with a visible society established at a certain time.[37]

In the gospel of St John we have 'that final spiritual interpretation to the person of Christ, which has for ever taken it out of the region of history and of the doubts that surround all past events, to fix it in the purified conscience as the immanent God'.[38]

We can sympathize with the sort of things which Green was anxious to avoid, the confounding of 'the formula with the reality', or the making of Christian witness into the mere 'depository of a dogma', or reducing the true life of religion to 'artificial schemes of salvation, or the forensic substitution without us of Christ's merits for our sins'. On the other hand it is by no means clear that anything of substance is retained, either in the way of distinctive historical fact or a unique disclosure, that could not be taken care of just as well in the over-all philosophical notion of an eternal spiritual principle renewing or 'reproducing' itself in our lives and in history, 'vouchsafed as a sign' in the life and death of Christ but with such generality as to take out of the sign all genuine distinctiveness. Philosophical understanding is paramount at least in matters of belief, a 'past event' of little importance in itself, even if we had more reliable knowledge of it than the allegedly total ignorance of St Paul.

When we turn to Bradley it is by no means easy to determine where exactly he stood in relation to normal religious observances and commitment. I think he would regard himself, and be regarded by others, as a profoundly religious person. There are religious overtones to almost everything he says, and his background was a distinctly Christian one, his father being a preacher much in demand and admired for his literary style. But this does not make it easy to place Bradley himself in relation to ordinary Christian commitment. He mentions God freely in some contexts. But he also makes a sharp distinction between God and the Absolute. It is the Absolute alone that is ultimate and complete in itself, it carries the sort of finality and eternal self-sustaining character we normally ascribe to God, and it is in that context, as indicated already, that we find the main significance of Bradley's work for religious understanding. He certainly does not ascribe to God the full reality of the Absolute. But, then, none of us are real for him in that sense. Is it the case that God does have, in a far greater degree than we have, the limited, appearance-type of reality that we have? Are we to think of him as a being in the sense in which each of us is a particular being, notwithstanding that our being owes itself entirely to its place in the Absolute? Is there, if we may put it very starkly, a supreme though finite existent to whom we stand in a special relation, a being we should adore and in some way worship, but who exists or functions alongside the Absolute, in the sense in which we do, though like ourselves finally merging its reality in the Absolute itself?

These are very difficult questions to answer. The main problem for Bradley was that we normally think of God in theistic terms and approach him as a person. But this has limitations similar to those which Bradley finds in morality. The latter come about in part because of conflicting claims upon us, calling upon us, Bradley seems to think, to find some place for evil in our general conspectus of goodness itself. 'The opposition [of Good and Evil] in the end is unreal, but it is, for all that, emphatically actual and valid.'[39] 'Evil and Good, in short, are not ultimate, they are relative factors which cannot retain their special characters in the whole.' But the main contradiction, and that from which the initial one stems, seems to be that the moral will must, it is alleged in the first place, have its worth expressly in the inner commitment to the good, in essentials a morality of duty for duty's sake which was also found wanting in Bradley's *Ethical Studies*. This, in turn, comes about from supposing that a morality which makes moral worth centre in this way on conscientiousness itself must be an empty one. On the one hand, 'the intensity of a volitional identification with whatever seems best appears to contain and to exhaust the strict essence of goodness'.[40] 'That a man is to be judged solely by his inner will seems in the end undeniable.'[41] But this seems also to contradict 'the very notion of goodness'. 'For a will must after all do something and must be characterized by what it does.'[42] It must have some material and not just a formal reality. 'A formal act which is not determined by its matter, is nonsense.'[43] 'If the act is not morally characterized and judged by its matter, will there in the end be a difference between the good and the bad.'[44] 'The excellence which is barely inner is nothing at all.'[45] But the excellences at which we must aim in practice depend on our dispositions and upbringing; these are 'the common virtues' of life by which individuals are estimated. Our conceptions of what is worth aiming at, as well as our capacity to make the effort 'depends on the strength of some "natural gift"'.[46] This, however, contradicts what appears to be the very essence of morality. 'Morality has proved unreal unless it stands on, and vitally consists in, gifts naturally good', 'morality, in short, finds it essential that every excellence should be good, and it is destroyed by a division between its own world and that of goodness'.[47] Some discord is then 'essential to morality'.[48]

For these problems there is, as gifted writers early in the present century made very plain, a relatively simple solution in the radical distinction we draw between strictly moral good and non-moral good, the latter including virtues in the form of dispositions or qualities of character. But, in the absence of this very vital distinction in moral philosophy, we are led, according to Bradley, to look for some 'unattainable unity' in a higher form of goodness which 'ends in what we may call religion'.[49]

This, in turn, comes about because 'for religion all is the perfect expression of a supreme will, and all things therefore are good'.[50] 'That which is evil is transmuted and, as such, is destroyed, while the good in various degrees can still preserve its own character.'[51] The finite self does in this way attain its perfection. 'The finite self is perfect, not merely when it is viewed as an essential organ of the perfect whole, but it also realizes for itself and is aware of perfection.'[52] For 'where a whole is complete in finite beings, which know themselves to be elements and members of its system, this is the consciousness in such individuals of their own completeness'.[53]

On the other hand, it is not possible for religion in this way 'to pass wholly beyond goodness'. It must contain goodness and with it 'the opposition required for practice'. In a difficult pronouncement, Bradley declares that 'the moral duty not to be moral is, in short, the duty to be religious'.[54] In the end we are forced to admit that the contradiction remains. For if the whole is still good, it is not harmonious, and if it has gone beyond goodness, it has carried us also beyond religion. The whole is at once actually to be good, and, at the same time, is actually to make itself good. Neither its perfect goodness, nor yet its struggle, may be degraded to an appearance. But, on the other hand, 'to unite these two aspects consistently is impossible'.[55]

305

This is the core of the contradiction which pervades religion itself. The centre of religion, we are assured, is faith. The whole and the individual are good for faith, but faith is also essentially practical, and must recognize an opposition to the good to be overcome. 'This inner discrepancy, however, pervades the whole field of religion.'[56] Accordingly, 'the religious consciousness rests on the felt unity of unreduced opposites', and for this reason 'its dogmas must end in onesided error, or else in senseless compromise'.[57] 'Like morality, religion is not ultimate.'[58]

This leads to the further view that, while 'man is on the one hand a finite subject, who is over against God, and merely "standing in relation"', 'on the other hand, apart from man God is merely an abstraction', or, as we are also told, 'God is again a finite object.'[59] 'Hence, God, if taken as a thinking and feeling being, has a private personality. But, sundered from those relations which qualify him, God is inconsistent emptiness; and, qualified by his relation to an Other, he is distracted finitude.'[60]

In religion there is thus 'a practical oscillation'. 'We may say that in religion God tends always to pass beyond himself. He is necessarily led to end in the Absolute which for religion is not God. God, whether "a person" or not, is, on the one hand, a finite being and an object to man. On the other hand, the consummation sought by the religious consciousness, is the perfect unity of these terms.'[61] 'The unity implies a complete suppression of the relation, as such; but with that suppression, religion and the good have altogether, as such, disappeared. If you identify the Absolute with God, that is not the God of religion. If again you separate them, God becomes a finite factor in the Whole.'[62] 'We may say that God is not God, till he has become all in all, and that a God which is all in all is not the God of religion.'[63]

We can follow the course of these arguments, and we can recognize much of their power once we grant certain assumptions, including what seems to me some radical misunderstandings about our ethical situation. But the question remains – just how is the talk about God and religion to be taken? Is it seriously intended, when, for example, Bradley deplores the failure of the churches in his day to stress enough the wrath of God, that there is a being, as actual at least as ourselves, whose anger is provoked by our wickedness? Or is this only the best way in which we can represent to ourselves the way in which we can most adequately think of ourselves and our place in relation to the Absolute?

I much suspect that the latter is the case, not in the familiar sense that there is some symbolic or analogical character to all we say about God, but in the sense that in the last analysis the meaning evaporates altogether out of our inescapable but quite inadequate religious affirmations. We have, I suspect, to take quite seriously, the intentions of Bradley when he declares bluntly: 'God is but an aspect, and that must mean but an appearance, of the Absolute.'[64]

There is thus a sense in which A. E. Taylor, in a fine appreciation of Bradley the man as well as the philosopher,[65] could plausibly maintain that Bradley 'could reasonably speak of himself, when all deductions have been made, as a Christian', but Taylor tells us also that

while the conception of the meeting of the divine and the human in one 'by unity of person' lay at the very heart of his philosophy, he was wholly indifferent to the question whether the ideal of the God-Man has or has not been actually realized in flesh and blood in a definite historical person. Like Hegel, he thought it the significant thing about Christianity that it had believed in the incarnation of God in a definite person, but also, like Hegel, he seemed to think it a matter of small importance that the person in whom the 'hypostatic union' was believed to have been accomplished should be Jesus the Nazarene rather than any other, and again whether or not the belief was strictly true to fact. The important thing, to his mind, was that the belief stimulates to the attempt to the achievement of 'deiformity' in our own personality.[66]

Bradley would, in conversation, Taylor assures us, describe himself as a Christian and indeed as an Anglican, though not a practising one. But his final position seems as far removed from central Christian themes as that of Green when he confessed that a 'modified unitarianism suits me very well'. On another central theme, namely immortality, Bradley's view is at least more explicit though a little wavering. He assures us that 'there is no way of proving, first, that a body is required for a soul',[67] and that thus 'a future life is possible';[68] but for various reasons[69] 'a future life must be taken as decidedly improbable'.[70]

There are theologians of our own time, still considered not to be unorthodox, who would not be troubled by the last admission. It seems to me, however, that little is salvaged out of the Christianity we derive out of the New Testament when neither life after death nor the historicity of Jesus, as the author and perfecter of our faith, are taken to be of much importance. The distinctness of a specifically Christian commitment seems to be absorbed in both cases into a philosophical spiritual view of the universe which, nonetheless, has, in the case of Bradley especially, very considerable importance for a proper understanding of the Christian faith.

The difficulties which were encountered by the more monistic type of idealist philosopher, in seeking to accommodate his views to our normal familiar assumptions and to traditional Christian thinking, were not so acute for the idealists who favoured a more pluralistic view of the universe. James Ward's position is here much closer to what we normally assume, namely that we are distinct existences, however dependent on some one ultimate supreme reality. God and the world are distinct, and our faith, a philosophical faith for Ward, in an ultimate unity of things, reflected in science and in the reference which goes beyond the reach of science, is in no way incompatible with what we normally assume about personal existence and responsible agency. In a very crucial statement, in his essay on 'Faith and Eternal Life',[71] Ward makes this very explicit. He writes: 'Volumes have been written in our times on the psychology of religious experience, but few, if any of them, have held fast to what, as I think, is fundamental to any experience at all – the duality of subject and object.'

This, as I have said earlier, eases very much the problem of the proper regard we have for one another, as distinct existences and our accountability for moral action. In other respects it seems to intensify the problem of the central incarnational factor in Christian belief. The monistic idealist coped with this on the basis of the special instantiation of the presence of God in all things. There is little temptation for the pluralist to go that way, and to that extent he is in closer accord with the traditional Christian view of a once-for-all incarnation in a particular individual. But the traditionalist view is fraught with very difficult problems of its own reflected in the long and familiar controversies of Christian theology. We do not find very much to help us at this stage in the writing of non-monistic idealists, least of all in James Ward.

This is mainly because Ward had early found himself much repelled by dogmatic doctrinal controversies and especially the seeming debasement of the moral quality of life in much of traditional Christian dogma. It was this aversion to traditional dogma that brought about the major turning point in his career. He was brought up in a conventional evangelical faith and set himself to prepare for the congregational ministry by sustained and very committed study at Spring Hill College, near Birmingham – later to be incorporated in Mansfield College, Oxford. From very early years he had taken a keen interest in science and in careful observations of the world of nature around him. This, as happened to others at that time, brought him into some conflict with a view of the world allegedly derived from the Bible. But this was not a major issue for Ward. He made the obvious adjustment very easily and stressed how much the essential claims of religion passed beyond science as such without being overtly in conflict with it. But the inherent difficulties of traditional dogma troubled him more, and at one critical stage he wrote: 'The doubting phase is pretty well passed from me now. I reject the whole system of Christian dogma from beginning to end and rationalize its history.' He was concerned about 'the ethical worth of Christianity' but 'was uncertain as to anything else in it'. This crisis led to his retirement, after one year, from his charge of a Congregational Church at Cambridge and his commitment to an academic career of great distinction at Cambridge. His ideas did however develop and mellow, but still with little regard for traditional dogma.

This was crystallized in an impressive, though still somewhat elusive, statement of his views in a paper read to the Cambridge Theological Society as late as 1924, one year before his death. It is entitled 'The Christian Doctrine of Faith and Eternal Life'. His main theme here is that eternal life must be thought of primarily as something we enjoy or attain here and now. That, as he understands it, is the emphasis we find in the New Testament, the contrast in St Paul between the old life and the new being much stressed. 'In short', Ward writes, 'we miss the meaning of "eternal" in the New Testament, if we associate it with time at all, and especially if we interpret it as referring simply to a future life everlasting.'[72] The difficulty here is to gauge the import of the word 'simply' in the last phrase. It seems to imply that, while we must avoid the notion of a future existence as simply a reward for good works in this one (a matter which Ward stressed in many places), our continued existence in some form is assured, subservient though that is to the deeper meaning of 'eternal life'.

We have an even firmer note in a significant statement about the object of faith and 'divine Personality' in the same context. Ward writes:

At first, merely a vague sense of a 'something beyond' and a feeling of helpless dependence – and this much is found among men everywhere – at length religion culminates in the Christian's faith in an indwelling presence as the source of a new life of peace and power – an experience without any sense of vagueness or isolation. The 'something beyond', the 'not-ourselves' has become for him a divine Personality, anthropomorphically so regarded indeed; for we can none of us understand what a person neither finite nor changeable can be. But a personality appreciative of the eternal values is the highest that we know; and we can hardly suppose that the divine Personality of whose presence the genuine Christian is assured – if it is anything at all – is not something higher (not something lower) than this. But it must be something and a something beyond himself is evidenced already by the childish anthropomorphisms of the savage which the Christian has outgrown. It is the *object* of his faith, and of its supreme reality he is convinced by the love which it awakens and the new life which it imparts.[73]

This passage sums up well both the caution and the confidence which characterized Ward's Christian commitment. In the letters reproduced in the fine memoir by his youngest daughter with which the posthumous volume of essays opens, we read much of Ward's awareness of the perils of misunderstood ritual and dogmatic formulations divorced from sensitive insight and living experience. This concern was very marked during the tempestuous period of his coming to give up the ministry. He did not abandon it and continued to speak with some acerbity of the famous councils of the Church, including Nicaea. But, with all the insistence on the practice of the faith, he did not reduce the substance of Christian commitment entirely to ethics. His God was a genuine personal presence. 'The profession of a creed', he declared, 'is a poor substitute for the living faith of the New Testament.' But of the full cognitive force of this faith we are left in some doubt. Nor does he help us to determine whether, behind the travesties and crudities he forcefully rejected in traditional dogma there may be still some truths to be better apprehended.

Although Ward does not take us very far on the latter course, his teaching did prepare the way for others, owing much to his pluralism and his account of the subject of experience, to advance further in the reassessment of what had seemed vital in traditional Christian experience.

It is not easy to estimate the bearing of McTaggart's views on what seem the most basic religious issues. He was an atheist and with this rejection of the idea of God go all the usual problems about the relation of God to the world, including traditional Christian controversies about the sense in which God may be said to be incarnate in Christ. If there is no God, there can be no incarnation. It would be wrong however to conclude that McTaggart had nothing to say that was relevant to Christian and other religious dogmas. He maintained that dogma was important, though not perhaps in the way dogma would normally be understood. His view of dogma is difficult to assess but it has significance in the context of recent philosophical controversy. At the same time he found serious flaws in traditional dogma, and he had pertinent things to say about some familiar solutions to the problem of evil. He himself came to rest in the view that we need have no regret about the abandonment of the belief in God. As Professor Peter Geach puts it, in an acute but sometimes perplexing study of McTaggart,[74] we can get by in religion (according to McTaggart) with 'the system of persons perceiving one another . . . [in] a timeless and endless state of love'.[75] 'Love will not cease, and love is enough.'[76]

This raises many problems which can not be fairly discussed without close reference to elaborate and difficult metaphysical arguments and intricacies of a system and mode of philosophizing peculiar to McTaggart. Professor Geach makes a good case for the claim that study of this can be helpful for the understanding of other more traditional religious views. But it seems also plain that the sort of religion which would be consistent with McTaggart's metaphysics is very far removed, not only from the more overtly theistic religions, but from many others, not excluding Buddhism, which have some kind of reference beyond limited finite existence at the core of them.

The British Idealists

Notes

1 'Fifty Years of Philosophy', in H. D. Lewis (ed.), *Contemporary British Philosophy* (London, 1956), vol. III, p. 337.
2 His main writings were published posthumously under the title, *Statement and Inference* (2 vols., Oxford, 1926).
3 'The Refutation of Idealism', *Mind*, XII (1903).
4 *Studies in the Metaphysics of Bradley* (London, 1967).
5 *Prolegomena to Ethics*, Chapter V.
6 For example, A. S. Pringle-Pattison in his contribution to the symposium on Finite Individuality in the *Proceedings of the Aristotelian Society*, vol. XVII (1917–18).
7 James Ward. See below, p. 298.
8 See J. S. Mackenzie, *Manual of Ethics* (London, 1929), pp. 43–7.
9 *Freedom and History* (London, 1962), Chapters III, IV and V. Cf. also my 'Freedom and Authority in Rousseau', *Philosophy*, LIII (1978), 353–62.
10 See *Freedom and History*, pp. 92–104. Cf. also *Thomas Hill Green and the Development of Liberal–Democratic Thought* by I. M. Greengarten (Toronto, 1981), Chapter V.
11 C. A. Campbell. See especially his *Scepticism and Construction* (London, 1931).
12 *The Idea of God* (Oxford, 1917).
13 *The Faith of a Moralist* (London, 1932).
14 *A Faith that Enquires* (London, 1922).
15 I have referred at more length, in Chapter XIV of my *The Elusive Mind* (London, 1969), to the symposium to which three very notable idealists contributed in 1918, Bosanquet adhering more strictly to the traditional line in idealist thought, the others (G. F. Stout and A. S. Pringle-Pattison) struggling to ascribe to individuals the independence which they seem to require to be distinct persons and exercise moral responsibility. On this topic I can do no better here than refer to what I have already written about the way this crucial issue in idealist thought came very sharply to a head in this famous symposium ('Do Finite Individuals possess a Substantive or an Objective Mode of Being?', *Proceedings of the Aristotelian Society*, vol. XVII (1917–18), pp. 479–581).
16 *Idealism* (London, 1934). It remains the best all-round critical survey of Idealism.
17 *Value and Reality* (London, 1973).
18 See his 'Moral and Non-Moral Values', first published in *Mind* (1935), and reproduced as Chapter IV of his *In Defence of Free Will* (London, 1967), and 'Moral Intuition and the Principle of Self-Realization', *The Hertz Annual Philosophical Lecture* delivered before the British Academy in 1948 and also reproduced in *In Defence of Free Will*, Chapter V.
19 The treatment of suffering in Chapters XIII and XIV of C. A. Campbell's *Selfhood and Godhood* (London, 1957) has rarely been surpassed.
20 *Works* (London, 1886), vol. III, p. xxxvi.
21 *Ibid.*, p. xxxv.
22 *Ibid.*, pp. 161–85.
23 *Ibid.*, pp. 230–52.
24 *Ibid.*, p. 161.
25 *Ibid.*, p. 163.
26 *Ibid.*
27 *Ibid.*
28 *Ibid.*, p. 173.
29 *Ibid.*, p. 179.
30 *Ibid.*
31 *Ibid.*, p. 181.
32 *Ibid.*, p. 182.
33 *Ibid.*

34 *Ibid.*, p. 183.
35 *Ibid.*, p. 236.
36 *Ibid.*, p. 239.
37 *Ibid.*, p. 241.
38 *Ibid.*, p. 242.
39 *Appearance and Reality* (Oxford, 1897), p. 381.
40 *Ibid.*, p. 382.
41 *Ibid.*
42 *Ibid.*, p. 383.
43 *Ibid.*, p. 385.
44 *Ibid.*
45 *Ibid.*, p. 387.
46 *Ibid.*, p. 384.
47 *Ibid.*, p. 387.
48 *Ibid.*, p. 388.
49 *Ibid.*, p. 385.
50 *Ibid.*, p. 390.
51 *Ibid.*
52 *Ibid.*
53 *Ibid.*
54 *Ibid.*
55 *Ibid.*, p. 391.
56 *Ibid.*, p. 392.
57 *Ibid.*
58 *Ibid.*, p. 393.
59 *Ibid.*, p. 394.
60 *Ibid.*
61 *Ibid.*, p. 395.
62 *Ibid.*, p. 295.
63 *Ibid.*, p. 397.
64 *Ibid.*
65 *Mind*, XXXIV (1925), 1–12. The whole of this number of *Mind* is devoted to Bradley. *Ibid.*, p. 12.
66 *Ibid.*, p. 10. See also Gordon Kendal, 'F. H. Bradley: an Unpublished Note on Christian Morality', *Religious Studies*, XIX (1983), 175–83.
67 *Appearance and Reality*, p. 455.
68 *Ibid.*, p. 446.
69 *Ibid.*, pp. 447–8.
70 *Ibid.*, p. 448.
71 *Essays in Philosophy* (Cambridge, 1927), Chapter XII.
72 *Ibid.*, p. 352.
73 *Ibid.*, p. 355.
74 *Truth, Love and Immortality: An Introduction to McTaggart's Philosophy* (London, 1979).
75 *Ibid.*, p. 165.
76 *Ibid.*

The British Idealists

Bibliographical essay

A very clear and concise account of the course of idealist philosophy in general is to be found in the article by H. B. Acton, under the subject of idealism, in Paul Edwards' *The Encyclopedia of Philosophy* (New York, 1967), vol. IV. The best comprehensive survey of idealist thought is still *Idealism: A Critical Survey* by A. C. Ewing (London, 1934). The same author has also provided excellent examples of idealist texts in his book, *The Idealist Tradition from Berkeley to Blanshard* (Glencoe, Ill., 1957). A very short but clear account of various forms of idealism is provided by R. F. Hoernlé in his *Idealism* (London, 1924). *Prolegomena to an Idealist Theory of Knowledge* by Norman Kemp Smith (London, 1924) also provides an excellent introduction to the subject. Looking outside the British tradition the student should consider especially Josiah Royce's *The World and the Individual* (London and New York, 1899, 1901) and his *Lectures on Modern Idealism* (New Haven, Conn., 1919). Brand Blanshard is probably the most distinguished recent advocate of idealist views. The two volumes of his *The Nature of Thought* (London, 1939) are very comprehensive and splendidly written. Much further light is thrown on idealist notions, their merits and their difficulties, in the volume about Blanshard in the famous Schilpp series, The Library of Living Philosophers, *The Philosophy of Brand Blanshard* (Open Court, 1980). A good account of German idealism is found in Nicolai Hartmann's *Die Philosophie des Deutschen Idealismus* (English text, *Ethics*, trans. Stanton Coit, 3 vols., London, 1932). *The Works of Thomas Hill Green* (3 vols., London, 1888) contains all the known writings of T. H. Green except the introduction to Hume in *Hume's Works* edited by T. H. Green and T. H. Grose (London, 1886) and *The Prolegomena to Ethics* (Oxford, 1883) based on Green's notes for his lectures and published posthumously under the editorship of A. C. Bradley by the Oxford University Press. The first volume of the *Works* contains a very full introduction to Hume's *Treatise of Human Nature*, which includes a general survey of empiricism in Locke and Berkeley and a detailed investigation of Hume's ethical theories. There is also an extensive discussion of Herbert Spencer and G. H. Lewis on the 'Doctrine of Evolution'. The second volume contains Green's lectures on Kant and Logic, the latter mainly a critical discussion of Mill. A lecture on moral freedom paves the way for the *Lectures on the Principles of Political Obligation* which have also been published as a separate book (London, 1911). In the third volume we have a very full memoir devoted mainly to Green's intellectual development and based extensively on his own correspondence. Other 'Miscellanies' include the discussions of religious topics noted above and several others in like vein, and also many papers on education and an unusual essay on the value and influence of works of fiction in modern times.

There have not been many first-rate studies of T. H. Green. Among the best are W. D. Lamont's *Introduction to Green's Moral Philosophy* (London, 1934) and J. Pucelle's *La Nature et l'Esprit dans la Philosophie de T. H. Green* (2 vols., Louvain, 1961).

On the philosophies of Kant and Hegel there is a massive literature of which there is a good account in the *Encylopedia of Philosophy*, edited by Paul Edwards, in the articles on Kant by W. H. Walsh, on Hegel by H. B. Acton, and on Hegelianism by S. T. Crites, the latter making special reference to the influence of Hegel on T. H. Green. A similar account of the writings of Bradley and of works about him may be found in the informative article by H. B. Acton in the same work. A book not mentioned by Acton but which seems to me very illuminating is S. K. Saxena's *Studies in the Metaphysics of Bradley* (London, 1967). The number of *Mind*, xxxiv (Jan. 1925) devoted to Bradley shortly after his death will be found very helpful and suggestive.

The main philosophical works of James Ward are *Naturalism and Agnosticism* (2 vols., London, 1899) and *The Realm of Ends* (Cambridge, 1911). His *Psychological Principles* (Cambridge, 1918) is equally notable. There is a fine biography of Ward by his daughter in *Essays in Philosophy*, edited by W. R. Sorley and G. F. Stout (Cambridge, 1927). This exhibits well the progress of Ward's religious ideas. The *Monist*, XXXVI (1926) has a complete list of Ward's writings.

The most important of J. E. McTaggart's works, for our purposes, are *Some Dogmas of Religion* (London, 1906), *Human Immortality and Pre-Existence* (London, 1916) and *The Nature of Existence* (2 vols., Cambridge, 1921, 1927). A very elaborate and exhaustive study of McTaggart is found in C. D. Broad's *Examination of McTaggart's Philosophy* (2 vols., London, 1933, 1938). Professor Peter Geach in a short recent study, *Truth, Love and Immortality: An Introduction to McTaggart's Philosophy* (London, 1979), challenges many of Broad's interpretations and is himself engaged on a full study of McTaggart.

9

William James and Josiah Royce

JOHN E. SMITH

William James and Josiah Royce were colleagues and friendly critics of each other's thought for some twenty-five years in the Department of Philosophy at Harvard during a time which has been called the 'Golden Period' of American philosophy. James, the elder of the two, was responsible for bringing Royce to Harvard from the University of California in 1882. Thus began a philosophical exchange – 'the battle of the Absolute' – which revolved about Royce's defence of Absolute Idealism and James' claim that such a 'block universe' is unable to do justice to the pluralistic, contingent and unfinished character of the cosmos and human life. Both men were deeply interested in religion as a dimension which belongs to the nature of life itself. Royce's approach took him in the direction of metaphysics and concern for the relation between certain basic religious ideas and a comprehensive theory of reality. James, by contrast, regarded metaphysical and theological articulation as secondary, because both are dependent on the elemental experiences of individual persons participating in the religious life. Royce's conception of religion was social through and through as is evidenced by his central conception of the Beloved Community. James, on the other hand, saw the locus of religion in the individual soul and always harboured the suspicion that 'organized religion' means religion at 'second-hand'. The sequel will first treat each thinker separately and then pass on to the consideration of these points at issue between them.

William James' intellectual career is itself a fine exemplification of the humanistic and religiously oriented philosophy in which he deeply believed. True to his conviction that philosophical beliefs are unavoidable – everyone carries some view of the general shape of things, no matter how chaotic, 'under his hat' – he passed through an intellectual development which began with the study of physiology and medicine, moved on to the field of psychology to which he contributed a classic work, *The Principles of*

Psychology,[1] and issued in the development of his pragmatic philosophy and what he called 'radical empiricism'. As he pointed out, the move to philosophy was inevitable because, as he believed, the persistent questions of freedom, of God, of the nature and destiny of the human self, of faith and salvation cannot be settled on the basis of physiology or psychology, even if these studies are not without their contribution to the answering of such questions.

The key to understanding James' thought is found in his insistence that all thinking takes place in and through the life of the individual person who is interested in the world and responds to it as an integral self possessed of will and what he liked to call a 'passional nature'. Although he did not deny, as has often been mistakenly assumed, the existence and importance of the theoretical stance, he insisted that it be seen as *one* interest among others encompassed by the many other concerns of the concrete individual seeking to live a worthwhile life. He was fond of contrasting views of the universe which purport to tell a scientific truth while disregarding man's personal interest in the outcome, with his vision of things which takes into account the human desires, concerns and needs that come into play when a person is grappling with the problems of finding and realizing himself in an unfinished world filled with risks and surprises.

James' commanding ideas, his conception of God and 'piece-meal supernaturalism', the working of the unseen world through the subconscious, his idea of freedom in a pluralistic universe, his belief in the force of belief itself, must be understood against the background of his ideas about what constitutes rationality. The extent of his break with the modern rationalist tradition is epitomized in the title of an important essay, 'The Sentiment of Rationality'.[2] In seeking to define the philosopher's aim of arriving at a 'rational' view of things, James asked, by what marks can the *rationality* of any philosophical theory be recognized? His answer is that a rational conception is one that fills us with a strong feeling of ease, peace, rest and the sense of being able to think fluently. The transition, he said, from a state of perplexity to one of comprehension affects us in a way which is at once a relief and a pleasure. The 'sentiment' of rationality is called forth by conceptions of the cosmos which provide us with a sense of understanding, of no longer being in the dark, of being delivered from confusion and disorientation. James, in short, was defining rationality through the way in which we are *affected* by different *conceptions* of things, and, in the end, he was saying that no theory or belief will succeed in getting itself believed or accepted as a 'rational' belief unless it affects us in the way just described. One sees here clearly the influence of the psychologist concerned for the psychology of belief and not only its logic.

In order to avoid the confusion that may arise from the fact that James saw the sentiment of rationality as arising in both a *theoretical* and a *practical* way, it is essential to understand that in both cases we are dealing with *conceptions* of the universe; the former way has to do with the way of conceiving things which satisfies the intellect and the latter with the conception which satisfies the will and our active nature. On the theoretical side the sentiment is evoked by our ability to apprehend the unity of things through categories and laws of nature, and also to understand these same things in their plurality and concrete individuality. The most 'rational' view is the one which does equal justice to both features of reality: no view will be accepted as satisfactory which attempts to ground itself in one aspect to the exclusion of the other. Hence, we shall not find rationality in a barren monism that omits or submerges the qualitative individuality of things, nor in a merely empirical 'sand-heap world' hardly superior to the chaos with which we began.

Now, said James, suppose we regard the theoretical goal attained so that 'our world can now be conceived simply, and our mind enjoys the relief',[3] would that settle the matter? James' answer is, no, because of the ineluctable human tendency to seek an 'other' for every datum, including the demand for a completed system of reality. This tendency leads to the question why there was anything at all and to the consideration advanced by Schopenhauer that the non-existence of this world is just as possible as its existence.[4] James, in short, not unlike the response of Kierkegaard to Hegel, is maintaining that the 'brute fact' of existence will always present an ultimate barrier, a final opacity, which thought cannot fathom. If the theoretical approach remains incomplete, perhaps the practical can provide a better vantage point. What conception of the universe, James asked, will awaken our 'active interests' or 'esthetic demands' in such wise as to call forth the sentiment of rationality on these grounds? Here the pragmatic turn is clearly in evidence. There is, says James, one relation of greater practical importance than any other and that is the relation of a thing to its future consequences. Expectation requires familiarity; we are baffled by the unusual and disoriented by having but few clues as to what is likely to come next. A philosophical conception, therefore, must, *'in a general way at least banish uncertainty from the future'*.[5] James regarded this condition as an absolute prerequisite based upon the human need to have 'expectancy defined'; man cannot exist and find his way in a world where anything you please may happen.

Seeing the future as staying within reasonable bounds, however, is not enough; what is needed, in addition, is a conception of the future which is congruous *'with our spontaneous powers'*.[6] No philosophy which extinguishes our active powers either in an 'Unconscious' or in a self-defeating Will can evoke the sentiment of rationality. What is needed is the conception of a world which gives us something to press against, tasks to be done which allow for the relevancy of human effort in the course of events. The watchword is 'What is to be done?' and this word expresses James' firm commitment to purpose, effort and activity, what Santayana called 'the strenuous life'. James was, however, pointing to something more subtle than an appeal to action; his deeper claim is that all great periods in the renewal, reformation and development of the human mind have been based on the belief that 'the inmost nature of reality' is congenial to and harmonizes with *powers* which every man possesses. Thus Christianity took seriously the weak and tender in human life and overcame a paganism that scorned these virtues. Luther and Wesley likewise triumphed in their missions because of their appeal to what is in the power of every man – to repent and to have faith. The element of faith is of the first importance throughout James' thought. Faith is, for the man of courage, the pathway to the future. Where doubt is theoretically possible, faith is called for and the mark of its presence is a willingness to act on behalf of a cause without an advance guarantee of its success. Faith appears in both the secular and the religious contexts; in the former, faith is the willingness to believe in the *possibility* that a given belief can be justified or that a certain goal can be attained, and, in the latter, it is the acceptance of and trust in the transforming powers of the 'unseen order' which James took to be the hallmark of all religion.

Numerous critics attacked James on the ground that it is intellectually and morally wrong to believe anything on 'insufficient evidence'. James insisted to the contrary that our normal state of affairs is one in which we are constantly required to believe in some possibility in advance of compelling evidence and that in many cases it is the acting on this belief which alone can place us in a position to obtain the evidence if it is forthcoming. Let us consider two cases: both have relevance for James' philosophy of religion, although the second is of a far more intimate kind. If it is a question whether there exists a vein of silver in a certain mountain, no answer can be given unless there is an antecedent belief in the possibility that such a vein exists which is sufficiently powerful to prompt an investigation. James' point is that only if we act in accordance with this belief by, for example, starting mining operations, can we put ourselves in a position to see the evidence one way or the other. In this case, of course, the belief has nothing to do with the existence of the evidence itself but only with our coming into its presence. There is, nevertheless, the need for the antecedent faith in the possibility as the motive for investigation. Faith in the religious situation is similar in that, as James frequently pointed out, there is no way of testing the belief that 'love never faileth' at arm's length; one must become engaged in a loving response and it was his contention that responding in this way itself contributes something to the verification of the belief.

We come now to a second sort of situation where, as James says, we are faced with 'a certain class of truths in whose reality belief is a factor as well as a confessor'.[7] Although James' illustration concerns an Alpine climber who can save himself from death only by succeeding in leaping across a wide chasm, the point in question he regarded as applicable to moral and religious beliefs as well. Faith in one's ability to perform is a crucial factor in bringing about success, and, in his own formula, *'faith creates its own verification'*.[8] The latter situation clearly differs from the former in that, at the outset, the silver is either in the mountains or it is not, faith notwithstanding. Whereas in James' unfinished universe, the leap is not already 'there' but is yet to come and without some faith it will not come at all. The question then is, how does his thesis work in the specifically religious situation where the leap in question is the 'leap of faith'. Fortunately, James tried to explain and defend his thesis in two essays, 'Reflex Action and Theism' (1881)[9] and 'Philosophical Conceptions and Practical Results' (1898);[10] in both papers the problem concerns the superiority of Theism as opposed to Materialism whether in scientific or in philosophical dress.

'Reflex Action and Theism' presupposes the conception of rationality previously set forth and presents the novel thesis that the reflex action theory of the self developed by the physiology and psychology of the time does *not* in fact issue in the exposure of belief in God as mere superstition. On the contrary, James argued, that theory leads to the conclusion that the God of Theism forms the most adequate possible object for minds like our own to envision as the basis of the universe. On the reflex theory, trains of thought (Department Two) are middle terms standing between an incoming sensation (Department One) and an outgoing nervous discharge which is the response or act itself (Department Three). For James, such a triadic structure must be seen as *teleological* because our theoretical faculty functions exclusively for the sake of ends which do *not* exist in the world of impressions received by the senses, but depend instead entirely on our emotional and practical subjectivity. It is important to notice the singular character of James' argument; the reflex theory can be seen as pointing to a harmony between the human mind and the structure of reality, so that a God, 'whether existent or not' must be understood as 'the only ultimate object that is at the same time rational and possible for the human mind's contemplation'.[11] Hence, quite apart from what James called an 'objective warrant', Theism has a subjective anchorage in its congruity with our nature as thinkers in this universe. What might appear to be a simple retreat to subjectivity must be seen instead in the light of James' contention – a coping-stone for his entire outlook – that a 'remodelling' of the world is inescapable because we have no organ to record or appreciate an order of things simply given or a world which just contains everything. All intellectual endeavour, physics no less than metaphysics and theology, involves such remodelling of the world in accordance with human interests and purposes. The mind, he said, is not a 'reactionless sheet' which is there merely for the purpose of recording what the world writes upon it. The sciences satisfy our theoretical impulse for rationality; religious and philosophical beliefs, including belief in God as the 'deepest power in the universe' and a 'mental personality' not ourselves, satisfy our will and passional nature. To be regarded by us as 'rational', a conception of the real world must satisfy Department One by not omitting any facts; Department Two by overcoming inconsistencies and establishing rational transitions; and Department Three by providing for our emotional powers an object to react to and to live for. Failure on any one of these heads, means 'irrationality'. James' contention is that materialism and agnosticism can never satisfy Department Three and, therefore, both are 'irrational', whereas Theism alone satisfies all three Departments. We must not suppose that, on James' view, Theism alone represents the 'choice' of a point of view, while the other alternatives are forced upon us through the channels of sense experience and rational thought. All cosmic formulas represent an interest and the expression of purposes; materialism, as James saw it, is the *choice* of the barest and most abstract world as *the* reality and thus excludes from the facts it acknowledges all that is most characteristic of man and his concerns.

The particular conception of God associated by James with the Theism he was defending remained fairly constant throughout the two decades that separate 'Reflex Action and Theism' from *The Varieties of Religious Experience*. If there is any significant shift, it is more one of emphasis than of substance. In the *Varieties* where James had to do justice to a multiplicity of facts about a plurality of religions, East as well as West, he was inclined to speak of an 'unseen order' as the fundamental conception of the divine rather than the 'mental personality' which he associated with the western Theism discussed in his papers of the 1880s and 1890s. On the other hand, as will become clear, in referring to the 'More' in reality which is continuous with the subliminal self described in the *Varieties*, James was not thinking of a purely impersonal order but rather of a purposeful power akin to personality. In any case, there are two points on which James never wavered in his conception of God; first, the divine reality is the deepest power in the universe and it is *not ourselves*, but a real and distinct source of transforming power, and, second, that power 'makes a difference' in affecting the lives of individuals in specific instances. Ever critical of the classical theological attributes of God which seemed to him no more than 'dictionary-adjectives', James sought for the 'originals of the God-idea', the God of the 'particular experiences' described in the *Varieties* in the form of conversations with the unseen, responses to prayer, changes of heart, deliverances from fear and assurances of support. On the basis of these 'originals' James sought to identify those features of the idea of God which are 'practical' in the sense of 'making a difference' in some person's life somewhere and somewhen. On this account, such attributes as the 'simplicity' or the 'aseity' of God call forth no sense of reality and awaken no response. By contrast, the 'omniscience' of God and the divine justice have experiential connections to which we can point; as omniscient God 'sees us in the dark' and through his justice he 'rewards and punishes what he sees'. The same holds true for the concepts of ubiquity and eternity; they spawn confidence and help to banish fear. James' rejection of classical metaphysical theology thus has two sides; on the one hand, he was opposed to the 'intellectualist' approach by which he meant defining God's attributes *a priori* from a theoretical or neutral standpoint, and, on the other, he insisted on the need for a divine attribute to have a 'practical' significance in the form of sustaining some connection with man's hopes, fears, desires and concerns.

The full force of James' insistence on the primacy of the practical and the experiential in religion and metaphysics can be seen in his determination of the 'real meaning' of materialism or Theism. The former, he claimed, is not essentially a doctrine concerning the essence of matter, but rather the assertion that there is no moral order and no ultimate hope. Nor is Theism essentially an affair of the 'inner essence' of God, but rather the affirmation of an external moral order and a foundation for hope. One can readily see in these interpretations what James called the 'principle of practicalism' at work. The meaning of a world view is found not in what it asserts about the nature of a world in the past, but in the *consequences* for human life which follow from the kind of world which that view declares to be real. The emphasis is all prospective, a lure for the future.

Although it may well be doubted whether the best-known of James' ideas, 'the will to believe',[12] was actually as important for his thought about religion as many have supposed, the basic idea he had in mind cannot be passed over. James' main thesis is that we have a *right* to adopt a believing attitude in religious matters, despite the fact that 'our merely logical intellect' may remain uncoerced. As James pointed out later in reflecting on this essay, it might more properly have been entitled, 'The Right to Believe' because he was attempting to offer a justification *of* faith. Since not all hypotheses proposed for belief are dependent upon our 'passional and volitional nature' – for example, if we are in bed with a roaring fever, we can *say* that we are well, but, says James, we are *powerless to believe* what we say – it is necessary to indicate what sort of beliefs bring the will to believe into play. Hypotheses are either 'alive' or 'dead' depending on the extent to which they appear as real possibilities to those to whom they are proposed; belief in the Book of Mormon, for example, is a dead hypothesis when proposed to a Roman Catholic believer or an orthodox Calvinist, whereas it may be very much alive for a person having no religious affiliation and seeking for some form of faith. A decision between two hypotheses James called an 'option'. Options are further determined according to whether they are living or dead, forced or avoidable, momentous or trivial. A live option embraces two live hypotheses; a forced option is one that cannot be avoided because it presents a dilemma based on a disjunction that excludes the possibility of not choosing, and a momentous decision is one usually involving a unique opportunity or a decision which cannot be reversed. James called an option 'genuine' when it is live, forced and momentous.

On the assumption that our aim in life is to follow truth and not simply to avoid error (the latter was, for James, *not* the same as the former), James argued that our passional nature may legitimately, and, indeed, must decide in the case of genuine options which cannot be settled on intellectual grounds and where leaving the question open – itself a passional decision – means running the risk of losing the truth. It is clear that James had chiefly in mind questions of speculative philosophy, moral issues, personal relations and matters of religious belief. In all these cases, James contended, some initial faith or willingness to believe in the *possibility* of a fact coming to be or of a belief receiving experiential support is essential as a contributing factor to the outcome. For every individual, the transforming power of love or forgiveness can be experienced – verified – only *subsequent* to actually loving and forgiving which in turn, require an antecedent faith in the possibility of success. Most important for James was the religious hypothesis which says that the best things are the more eternal and that we are now better off for believing this affirmation. On James' view, the man who remains sceptical in the face of the religious hypothesis until there is 'sufficient evidence' is simply yielding to his fear of being duped rather than trusting in the hope that the hypothesis may be true. Underneath this line of reasoning was James' belief that with regard to the things that matter most, we are always and everywhere faced with 'insufficient evidence' as long as we approach them from a theoretical standpoint. This standpoint, however, is inadequate to meet genuine options where the kind of evidence needed can only be obtained *after* one has been willing to believe in its possibility and has placed oneself through action in a position to experience the outcome.

The major source for James' interpretation of religion is, of course, the *Varieties of Religious Experience*,[13] a book whose full impact has sometimes been lost because of an overemphasis on its illustrations and autobiographical accounts coupled with a failure to see these in the light of the philosophical interpretation offered in the closing chapters. James himself was not unaware of his own contribution to this result. In presenting his 'Conclusions' in the final lecture, James not only referred to these reflections as a 'dry analysis' and an 'anti-climax'[14] in comparison with the 'palpitating documents' of first-person experience that make up the main body of the work, but he found himself, upon re-reading the manuscript, 'almost appalled at the amount of emotionality'[15] expressed in the illustrations. On the other hand, it needs to be remembered that James repeatedly explained that he purposely chose the more extravagant examples as providing more profound information than could be gained from soberer illustrations. In this he was correct, but the disparity between the dramatic evidences of religious experience and their theoretical or conceptual analysis must not lead us to lose sight of the connection between the two. The 'Conclusions' represent no mere appendix but were intended to interpret the massive detail preceding them.

These conclusions embrace both the circumscription of the religious life theoretically and practically on the basis of the evidence presented, and James' own hypothesis concerning the reality on the 'farther side' of experience, or a venture into what he called 'over-belief'. James found essential to all religion the belief that the visible world is part of a more spiritual universe on which it depends for its significance, and that a harmonious relation, including perhaps some form of union, with the unseen world is our true destiny. Prayer and one's communion with the spiritual universe – 'God', the 'Law' – is a process wherein there is a passage of spiritual energy which shows itself in the world of ordinary events. Religion, on the side of its effects means a new zest in life which appears as a gift and may manifest itself either in 'lyrical enchantment' or in an active earnestness and even heroism. There is in addition a deep sense of peace and of having been delivered from peril which expresses itself in love to other people.

The nature of the divine or spiritual reality cannot be expressed in terms of a single quality, but must be understood as a group of qualities. In making this point, it might appear that James was mainly concerned to reflect the diversity manifest in the plurality of different religions, and it is likely that this fact was important in determining his view. It is curious, however, that instead of focusing on differences between historic religions, he attributed the complexity of the divine to the fact of diversity in human personality. Not everyone has the same problems and, consequently, he maintained a 'god of battles' is appropriate for one kind of person and a 'god of peace and heaven' for another. We have here another outcropping of James' concern to take differences of 'temperament' seriously, in religion no less than in philosophy, and indeed we should not be surprised at this concern if we take note (as is not often done) of the subtitle of the *Varieties* – 'A Study in Human Nature'.

A most basic feature of James' interpretation of religion would be lacking if we failed to take note of his individualistic emphasis and its implications. A principal reason, we are told,[16] why he was bent on exalting feeling while subordinating the intellect, was his concern for individuality which, for him is founded in feeling. First-person participation in, and living through, experience are fundamental and can never be replaced by theory or knowledge about. For James, theory was always secondary; 'if you wish to grasp [religion's] essence', he wrote, 'you must look to the feelings and the conduct as being the more constant elements.'[17] An important consequence of linking individuality with feeling and of finding in feeling the root of religion, was that James, in the end, had to see the social dimension of religion, the religious community, as secondary and derivative. As we shall see, this consequence marks one of the sharpest points of contrast between him and Royce.

In answering his own question, Is there 'a common nucleus' to which all religions bear testimony above and beyond conflicts of creed or doctrine?, James pointed to two structural features manifest in all religious traditions. One he called an 'uneasiness' or sense that there is 'something wrong about us' in our natural situation, and the other a 'solution' or the sense that we are 'saved from the wrongness' by becoming related in a certain way to the unseen world. That such a schema is indeed relevant for understanding the historical religions becomes evident when one considers that every one of them contains some vision of an ideal fulfilment for man which, when taken as a norm for appraising actual human existence, results in a diagnosis of man's predicament and the disclosure of some flaw which stands in the way of that fulfilment. Thus the Buddha cites the misdirected infinitude of desire as the cause of suffering, and the Hindu sages emphasize the ignorance concerning the true nature of things which prevents man from realizing himself. In both cases and despite the significant differences between these traditions, there is the diagnosis of a 'wrongness' and the quest for some form of deliverance, a way of overcoming the flaw. For James, the individual who acknowledges and criticizes the wrongness from which he suffers becomes aware of 'a better part' of himself, a germ which may signal the basis of a new life if indeed there is a higher power to develop it. When, as James says, the stage of solution or Salvation arrives, the individual identifies himself with the germinal higher part – something he could not do at the outset – and becomes conscious of its continuity with a 'MORE' of the same quality which is operative beyond him in the universe. It was James' contention that the phenomena described in the many examples he cited – the divided self and its struggles, the change of personal centre stemming from the surrender of the lower self, and the appearance of an exterior helping power with which we are in unity – can all be understood in terms of the uneasiness-solution model. From the standpoint of the individual, the practical problems involved take the form of what Kierkegaard would have called 'existential movements' – the realization of the reality of the higher part of the self, the determination to identify oneself with it, and to see it as continuous with the 'rest of ideal being'. James frankly acknowledged that the preceding analysis leaves us with essentially 'psychological phenomena'; the remaining task is to ask about the 'truth'[18] of their content. And it is not without significance that he added in a note, 'the word "truth" is here taken to mean something additional to bare value for life . . .'.[19] This addition may come as a surprise to those accustomed to thinking of James' 'pragmatism' as asserting the identity of 'truth' and 'value for life'. The fact is that he was concerned to offer an hypothesis concerning the 'More' or the unseen power which would be in accord with both a common body of doctrine derivative from a science of religions and the demands of a psychology with scientific stature.

Setting aside claims to offer a 'coercive argument', James proposed instead an hypothesis which in his view, is consonant with the facts of religious experience, is general enough to be applicable to many different religious traditions, and is continuous with what would be regarded as a scientific account of the matter. James was fond of insisting that theologians had, on the whole, lost their scientific contact and thus furthered the struggle between science and religion. The concept essential for describing the 'More' with which the hypothesis is concerned is that of the *subconscious self*, an entity which James regarded as 'well-accredited' from a psychological standpoint. Not unlike his idea of the 'fringes' of experience, or background which is essential for a full understanding of what is focal and explicit, the idea of the subconscious self points to an unmanifested self against which the conscious self stands out in relief. He saw the subconscious self as having in many instances a decisive influence on the concrete life and destiny of the individual, and, in interpreting mysticism especially, he spoke of it as a region which 'invades' conscious life and transforms it. The hypothesis is that the 'More' – the unseen world, the sacred order, etc. – with which the religious person feels connected is, on its 'hither' side, 'the subconscious continuation of our conscious life'.[20] James saw in this notion of a *continuation* a way of doing justice to the scientific requirement that recognized psychological facts be cited and also to the theological claim that a reality or exterior power is involved. What comes from the subconscious has all the marks of external control and yet, since the control is 'the higher faculties of our hidden mind',[21] the sense of union is at the same time a veridical sense of being united with a power beyond. This sense is, in James' language, the 'cash value' of his piecemeal supernaturalism, something literally true and a fact which makes a difference in human life. In short, it is the divine at work.

James made no attempt to deal with the special details of belief characteristic of particular religious traditions. These 'over-beliefs', as he called them, are of great importance, but a 'science' of religions requires that we confine ourselves to what is common and generic. Within these limits, James declared that there is a positive content to religious experience which is literally and objectively true and this content is identical with the fact that the conscious person is *'continuous with a wider self through which saving experiences come'.*[22] Having stated his hypothesis with respect to the 'hither' side of the relation, James concluded with a statement of his own over-belief concerning the nature of the 'far' side of the religious reality.

The wider self involves us in a dimension other than that of the sensible world; James called it the mystical or supernatural region, the birthplace of ideal impulses. That region itself, however, he did not regard as ideal; on the contrary, insofar as the unseen world affects individuals and transforms their lives it must be regarded as a present reality. For the Christian, this reality is God, understood not only in the sense of the reality encountered in experience but in the wider sense of a 'World-ruler' or ground and sustainer of a moral order transcending a cosmos which may some day freeze or burn up. Although James' account is quite short and even abrupt at this point, he seems to have thought that until we come to have faith in the God of the 'far side', the cosmic power, we have not as yet brought a *'real hypothesis'* into play. Such an hypothesis would have to involve new facts and this consequence brings us face to face with James' fundamental over-belief: the world from the truly religious standpoint is *not* the materialistic world taken over again but now seen in a rosier light; it is a world with a different natural constitution in which novel events take place requiring conduct of a sort different from that appropriate in the 'scientific' world. Here we see James' pragmatism at work and the reason for this objection to a certain form of idealism. He rejected, usually with Royce's view in mind, the conception of God as an all-covering blanket thrown over the world, but leaving it essentially as it was before. Instead, James' 'piecemeal supernaturalism' demands particular differences at particular points in the lives of individuals; the ubiquity of God is either too much or not enough. James wanted to see God at work as it were, *hic et nunc*. It was this insistence which led James' contemporaries to say that his God is probably an American!

In passing on at this point to Royce's philosophy of religion, one must resist the temptation to proceed by contrast with the view of James. Royce's position should first be seen in itself and that understanding will provide a basis for further comparisons. In approaching Royce's massive writings on religion and its relation to philosophy, it is helpful to keep two fundamental ideas in the foreground. One is his belief that religion serves as a goad to philosophy in the sense of presenting ideas and insights which stand in need of clarification and require articulation against the background of a general theory of Being. The other is the idealist principle basic to Royce's thought from beginning to end, namely, the appeal to a whole of experience which in the nature of the case is not presented as such but which must be invoked in order to render intelligible some fragment or part which is before us. This principle figures in every one of his arguments from the early proof of the Absolute (1885) to the doctrine of the Beloved Community in his last major work *The Problem of Christianity* (1913).

In *The Religious Aspect of Philosophy*,[23] Royce set forth what is essential to religion in a three-fold pattern; religion must contain a moral code but, since that by itself does not take us beyond command and law, it must add a second element, one of devotion, of reverence and of love by holding up something for the individual to live and die for; the third and most important factor, from the vantage point of the philosopher at any rate, is the presence of belief or religious doctrine. 'A religion', said Royce, 'tells us about the things that it declares to exist'[24] and, consequently, there cannot be a religion without theoretical elements in it. This emphasis is both valid and important especially in view of the many attempts on the American scene to reduce religion to morality, or to minimize the importance of religious ideas by maximizing religion's 'practical' function. Royce maintained this emphasis throughout his thought and ultimately defined the 'problem' of Christianity as that of providing for the mind of his time an intelligible account of three basic ideas – sin, atonement and the Kingdom of God as developed into a doctrine of the Church. If, as some have maintained, he put too much stress on this intellectual content, it cannot be said that he ever sought to avoid the philosophical problems it presents. Religion and philosophy find themselves mutually involved because, as Royce put it, 'Religion invites the scrutiny of philosophy and philosophy may not neglect the problems of religion.'[25] This mutual relationship was later elaborated by Royce in his Gifford Lectures, *The World and the Individual*.[26] There he distinguished three approaches to the study of religion: first, the assessment of the argument for God from design in the light of modern science, second, a description of the religious consciousness as something valid in its own right because man is essentially a religious animal, and third, what Royce called 'the fundamental Philosophy of Religion', or the interpretation of religion in the light of a theory of Being or the nature of things. He adopted as his own the third approach and sought to understand Nature, Man and God in the light of an original voluntaristic idealism in the tradition of Schopenhauer and Fichte. In accord with this tradition, Royce began with human knowledge and the identification of Being with Being *known*, which is to say that reality is defined in terms of what would make it possible for us to have a complete knowledge of it. Into this tradition, however, Royce introduced a novel element and it supplied a needed corrective. Declaring that there is no 'pure intellect' and that all logic is 'logic of the will', he sought to bring purpose and intention into the picture. The individual – the ultimate aim of philosophy and religion – is to be seen not merely as the determinate object of a completed knowledge, but rather as the fulfilment of a purpose, the expression of a Will that wills *this* universe and no other, and *these* individuals and no others. Each of us, in short, was 'meant' to be as a fulfilment of the divine purpose. This idea is the substance of Royce's 'voluntarism' and its presence should have been taken more seriously by critics who charged him with the 'intellectualism' typical of Absolute Idealism. We shall return to this point later on.

Ever adept at dialectic and thoroughly convinced of the power of logic in metaphysics,[27] Royce set forth in *The Religious Aspect of Philosophy* an ingenious argument for the existence of an Absolute knower to whom all truth is known. The argument is too extensive to be presented in detail but the basic point can be elucidated. Royce frequently employed the dialectical device of starting with a position diametrically opposed to the position he aimed to establish in order to show that the opposed view cannot be coherently maintained and, properly understood, even implies Royce's own view! He sought to show, for example, that a world of doubt itself implies the existence of some knowledge, that the reality of error implies an absolute truth and that the one who passionately embraces pessimism by recognizing the force of the evil which the optimist denies shows deep concern for the truth and is thus open to the possibility of an insight which overcomes pessimism.

In this case he started with the fact of error and the principle that an idea or judgment can be true or false only in relation to the object or reality which it intends. Royce sought to show that no real error is possible without an appeal to an infinite knower who possesses the truth about all reality. To be in error an idea must be false in relation to its object; but, Royce argued, the finite idea or isolated judgment apart from the whole of experience has no object about which it could be true or false. An error is an incomplete thought which is known by a higher thought, including both it and its intended object, to have failed in its purpose. Without the infinite thought, an assertion has no external object about which it could be in error. If error is real, the argument runs, and it is, then the Absolute thought is also real. Although the setting of the argument determines that the emphasis must fall on the Absolute as a *knower*, it is important to notice that Royce, believing in the intimate connection between intellect and will or purpose, came later to describe the divine life as a Will expressing itself in the universe which is its realized intention.

Royce regarded his conception of the One Infinite Thought as having religious significance to a high degree. Comparing the view with that held by Augustine, Royce declared that we are all within and part of this thought, that we are known and judged through it in our truth, and that our destiny is to reach fulfilment by losing our finite selves in the divine life through loyal devotion to the moral ideal. In the course of developing this doctrine, however, Royce found himself caught up in a tension which is never entirely resolved even in later works. The more he contrasted the Absolute thinker with finite individuals, the more the finite reality became endangered. What is only ideal for us is already realized in the Infinite, the errors which deceive us are dispelled for the Absolute knower, and the moral goodness for which we struggle is already embodied in the divine life. Whereas we know in part, the one thought is now in possession of the whole, and individuals, in Royce's language are 'drops in the ocean of absolute truth'.[28] What room, critics asked, does such a view allow for novelty, creativity, finite freedom, and especially for the struggle to overcome evil? What is left to be done when all has even now been accomplished? Postponing the general question for the moment and concentrating on the question of evil, it is only fair to say that Royce was more tough-minded than many idealists have been in dealing with this problem. He rejected any suggestion that evil is 'mere appearance' or that it is necessary merely in order to form a contrast with the good. His contention is that goodness in the form of moral experience *is* the overcoming of evil so that the evil impulse is a conquered element *in* the good will. When we work for the extension of the moral ideal in the world, we do so in the knowledge that we are not alone, since our action and devotion are part of the Absolute thought which approves of us.

In later writings such as *The Spirit of Modern Philosophy* (1892), *The Conception of God* (1897),[29] and works written after 1900 Royce abandoned the language of the Absolute in favour of the language of the Self, referring at times to a 'World-Self' and not hesitating to interchange this term with the term 'God'. The change is not unimportant because it freed Royce from the onus attached to the term 'Absolute' with its connotation of what James called the 'block universe' which excluded freedom and individuality. The term, moreover, had long been associated with the name of Hegel and this enabled Royce's critics to describe his thought as 'warmed-over Hegelianism' without appreciating the genuine originality of many of his ideas.

In developing the idea of the World-Self, Royce set forth what I regard as a valid and important distinction between a 'world of description' which forms the basis of science, and a 'world of appreciation' which has to do with the concerns of morality, religion and philosophy.[30] Experience, according to Royce, has two faces. An experience can be *described* when it is reproducible at will by the one who describes it with the use of general types or categories such as spatial and temporal determinations, size, shape, density, etc. What can be described, in short, forms the domain of natural science and it is a public world to which all who understand the abstractions involved have access. This world of law, atoms and energy is, nevertheless, a human world since in it everyone can communicate with everyone else through the medium of abstract concepts.

The world of description, however, as Royce was well aware, does not exhaust the real world since it is an account of but one sort of reality which all accept and seek to understand. What, asked Royce, is the status of my friend and neighbour; in what way is he real to me? I can, to be sure, describe him as being just so tall, as having certain habits and as occupying a certain place among the things that make up the world. But if I pursue his reality in the world of description, I never come upon his intelligence, his private and inner life, his will and his ideals, and yet these are all facts to be accounted for. They are not products of my imagination, but *neither do they* appear in the world where the universal features of things form the links of communication. Royce's conclusion is that the facts about the inner life of human beings, though real and subject to error, are not describable but are to be found only in a 'world of appreciation' which is essentially a communion of spirits. Our relations with the world are all social, on Royce's view, and even the world of description manifests a spiritual intercourse because in communicating through abstract concepts we must assume that each individual is able to identify in his own experience the same description as his neighbour. Therefore, the togetherness of selves in one Spirit is a fact which is not describable in physical terms but is nevertheless something upon which *all* communication depends. Royce called the world of appreciation one of 'reflective' interconnectedness, the presupposition of all exchanges of meaning. If we were unable to communicate with each other, there could be no truth in our descriptions.

The world of science is now seen to depend on a world of spiritual oneness, or the unity of Self. This Self is the deeper reality and, indeed the world of description, though perfectly real, is essentially only the world of a finite knower, or, more boldly stated, the world of description is the way in which the world of the true Self appears to a finite knower. The world of appreciation with its categories of self-consciousness is the real world of personality and the inner life; it is a manifestation of a world Logos or Self providing the necessary basis for all communication. That infinite Self knows the spatio-temporal order and all the selves in a time-transcending fashion of which we have a hint in our own experience when we grasp the meaning of a sentence as a whole or apprehend a tune in a moment over and above the awareness of the succession of words or notes. As finite selves, we stand to the infinite Self as parts of a time-transcending appreciation.

Much of the tension in Royce's thought, but also a source of its creative originality, has to do with his attempts to show how the finite selves are related to the World-Self and how they can be preserved in their individual integrity and yet be 'parts' of that Self. As may be imagined, this problem was a focal point for Royce's critics. I do not believe that he ever overcame all the difficulties, largely because of his insistence on the completed World-Self being in some sense 'all there at once'. But the most successful of his attempts is to be found in his later philosophy of the community where the doctrine of the Absolute is left behind. As evidence, however, of his refusal to set aside vexing questions or to answer them with a facile 'idealism', let us consider his treatment of the problem of evil at a time when he still adhered to the doctrine of the World-Self.

We often speak uncritically of 'the' problem of evil as if it were a single dilemma, eternally formulated and well-known to all, whereas in fact we are confronted with a cluster of problems which may concern either the origin, the justification or the overcoming of evil. Royce focused on the issue of justification and stated the problem in terms of what he called the 'great antinomy' of the spiritual world – the opposition between the evil which necessarily attaches to a finite will striving in a temporal order, and the doctrine that God, the true *Logos*, has chosen this world as the expression of an ultimate perfection. Royce envisaged human life as fraught with endless cares in which there is no lasting satisfaction, no joyous moment in which we can remain content, and, from a mundane standpoint, no sense that God is present to unravel the mystery. On the other hand, Royce agreed with Leibniz that this is the best of all possible worlds and hence his task was to show how this claim is compatible with the essential evil accompanying finite existence.

Royce's realistic approach to this antinomy manifests itself in his rejection of two solutions popular at the time. According to an optimistic religious 'idealism', love is all-triumphant and there is no intractable evil in the world, only ignorance, imperfect social institutions, inequalities stemming from the existence of private property, etc. At the other end of the spectrum were the sceptics and agnostics who, as Royce put it, take facts and the results of science seriously but do not find any spiritual significance in the world and therefore must reject the problem of evil entirely or dissolve it in advance.

Royce could accept neither view; against the former, he held that evil is not a dream but a bitter truth, and that we encounter its spiritual significance only in conquering it. Against the latter he contended that confining attention to the facts and regularities of nature to the neglect of the experience of the self and its 'world of appreciation' provides a totally inadequate basis for any philosophy whatever. The optimists degrade religion in their refusal to confront the actual world in its reality, and the agnostics set religion aside as outmoded, the product of a pre-scientific day. Mistaken as these views may be, their rejection does not solve the basic problem which is to understand how the world of the Self can be at once a world of moral issue and one of moral completeness, a world of goodness and a world where evil is a genuine fact.

The key to Royce's solution here is found in the idea that the life we seek, if it is to be serious and worthwhile, will always have the tinge of bitterness, of sorrow, of restless longing. To will a perfect goodness, the infinite Self must express itself in a world of finite persons who are limited and subject to sin and failure in the human conflict. Through an analogy focusing on the individual's experience of temptation wherein an evil impulse is resisted and overcome, Royce sought to express the attitude of the divine Self to the moral evil in the world. In resisting the evil impulse, the finite self makes it a part of its more encompassing moral goodness; the justification of that impulse comes just at the point when it is hated and condemned. Each individual in

God is part of a good will, and God has the same relation to human sinfulness as the good will of the virtuous man to the evil impulse within him. In a conclusion that would have delighted the heart of Jonathan Edwards, Royce declared, '*the hatred and condemnation of just your life and character makes God holy*'.[31]

In the Gifford Lectures, *The World and the Individual*, Royce continued his quest for a true understanding of the individual self and its relation both to a moral order and to God. This work is of special importance because there Royce defined the proper philosophical approach to religion as the need to connect religious insight with a metaphysics or a theory of what it means *to be*. With remarkable dialectical skill, he set forth and criticized a version of modern realism, ancient mysticism and Kant's transcendental philosophy with the aim of showing, first, that neither realism nor mysticism can account for truth and hence that they fail to reach what is truly individual, and, second, that although Kant's philosophy does allow for truth (at least in the sense of *validity*), he also could not reach the individual – 'the only ultimate form of Being' – because the understanding is confined to an order of universals, the conditions for all experience. Royce was quite right in his claim that modern rationalist philosophies have not done justice to the individual self and he sought to overcome that deficiency with a new theory of Being, called simply 'Idealism' which established will and purpose at the centre of reality.

On his view, to be is to be *individual* and thus to be a unique being for which no other could be substituted. The ground of uniqueness, for Royce, is to be found only in the fulfilment of a purpose. Individuality becomes a category of the 'satisfied will', and in two dimensions; first, the world as a whole is seen as the purposeful expression of the one Will which *meant* this world and no other, and, second, every individual in it stands as this being and no other adequate to the cosmic purpose. Focusing as sharply as possible on the ensuing problem of relating God to the plurality of individuals, we may view the matter thus: I, as the individual I am, was, from the time-spanning consciousness of God, the one that was 'meant to be' and my uniqueness consists in that alone. On the other hand, in accordance with Royce's understanding of the self in terms of purpose and will, one cannot think of the individual as existing 'ready made', so to speak. I am, in the end, 'what I will or mean to be', as Royce repeatedly insisted in his account of the self and its place in the scheme of things. But how is this possible? How are we to adjust what I *was meant* to be and what *I mean* to be?

The human self is to a degree a product of nature and thus subject to fortune and the contingencies of historical life. The self is also to a degree insubstantial, transient and uncertain, subject to failure and error. It was Royce's contention, however, that man is able to know all this about himself precisely because of his ontological relation to God from whom his *individuality* comes. In short, there are many finite selves because there is a One, and each of us as individual persons enjoys both the presence and the freedom of God. For Royce, to be a person is to be an ethical individual and the supreme such Individual is God. God's perfection is attained *through* the evolution of the finite selves who remain *partial*, though in a sense infinite, persons in the divine life. The reference to evolution and time makes it necessary to appeal to Royce's conception of the eternal consciousness. Such a consciousness is *not* a result or the end of a process but a time-spanning unity in the sense in which a melody or a symphony exists as a unity or whole and does not come into being only with the final note or chord. Every instant of time, like every note in the melody, stands related to the *whole* of God's purpose. The question is, how does the development of finite individuals in time stand related to this purpose?

Unlike many thinkers who have thought of God in terms of completion and perfection, and who consequently have had difficulty explaining how a real historical order of the sort insisted upon by the Judeo-Christian tradition can make any difference to God, Royce did indeed attempt to allow for creativity and novelty. He emphasized the fact that new ethical individuals continually appear and they 'add to the significance of the world'. In this sense there is progress, but there is also decay in the form of what passes away, the loss of values inherent in each stage of a process which must perish in order to make way for the next stage and the disappearance of great men and nations. No progress is unmixed. Even the coming of new individuals, described by Royce as 'the most creative feature' of the world's order, is not unalloyed good because these creatures are themselves problems, being the source of strife and contention as well as servants of the moral ideal. Nevertheless, despite Royce's refusal to equate the realization of the divine purpose with some forms of progress, and his recognition of the reality of waste and perishing, he insisted on the importance of another perspective which he persistently described as a knowledge which is eternal and *not* properly understood as 'fore-knowledge'. From this perspective, all the finite selves are understood and understood as performing *service to the divine life*. Since to be a person is to have a life with a meaning, and each person is to find this meaning in a life plan which is unique because it is his and no other, each self comes to see that the pursuit of that plan contributes to the realization of God's purpose. In seizing upon what I was meant to be – this self who does what no other can do – I come to a realization that my uniqueness, my own way of expressing God's will, *is* my very self. The ethical task for me is to mean to be, as far as it is within my power and determination, the self who realizes just that part of the divine plan which no other can realize. In the world our moral task is endless; the essential individuality we have is not fully known to us until we see it in union with God. In God, all selves are infinite, though *partial*, and all preserve their uniqueness precisely because each is needed for the complete expression of the divine life. For the many selves to blend into an undifferentiated unity would violate Royce's fundamental principle of finite individuality which is that each self requires for its being, *contrast* with other finite selves. This principle will have its final application in Royce's doctrine of the Beloved Community which is both a One and a many wherein the many, though distinct, are united through the bond of love and their mutual devotion to each other as well as to the cause for which that community lives.

Royce's idea that being a person means having a dominant purpose or life-plan to be carried out as an ethical task, clearly anticipates a theme basic to the thought of the existential philosophers. Unlike them, however, Royce would not have agreed that the self *is* freedom in a sense that would have endangered the existence of a social, moral order and would have led in the end to the 'death of God'. Royce acknowledged our inheritance of a world and of some place in it, dependent, not upon man's freedom alone, but upon a reality transcending both man and the world. It is within this framework that the individual attempts to realize the life-plan which is its own unique being. My being is neither brought forth from nothing by my will alone, nor is it merely the unfolding in time of a previously given essence unconnected with the life-plan I envisage. There is, on Royce's view, a coming together of my will and the divine will of which this world is the expression. Royce repeatedly described self-hood as a *task* to be accomplished which means that every self has to combine some insight into what he or she was meant to be with the ingenuity and effort to express that purpose in his or her own unique way. Although all individuals are unique and distinct, no individual stands alone in the quest for self-hood; we are all related in various ways to each other and to the communities in which we participate. A belief in the basically *cooperative* feature of all human endeavour led Royce to a study of *loyalty*[32] which, in turn, formed the basis for his philosophy of community and his thoroughly justified attack upon an individual*ism* which has always contributed to the fragmentation of American life.

All human activities, he said, are rooted in the basically social character of life; science, religion, politics, commerce, etc., represent cooperative enterprises involving many individuals and they can be carried on successfully, in

Royce's view, only insofar as these individuals are *loyal* and devoted servants of the goals which define these enterprises. The legal community, for example, exists to perform a mediating function *vis-à-vis* conflicting interests and claims before the law. One of the conditions for sustaining that community is a loyalty to confidentiality in relation to clients. An individual lawyer who ignores that loyalty and breaks a confidence is guilty of a double-barrelled failure. On the one hand, he has done a disservice to a particular client, and on the other, he has struck a blow against one of the foundations on which the whole legal community rests. Royce came to see loyalty to the cause of extending the loyal spirit in all human endeavour as the highest virtue and he invoked it in reinterpreting the ancient religious insight that 'he who loses his life for my sake, shall find it'. According to Royce, the isolated individual pursuing his own little interest is lost; only he who loses his life in loyal devotion to a cause uniting many individuals in its service, shall find fulfilment. Although a person may be dedicated to numerous causes, they are not all on the same level of importance. The religious community for Royce, is the ultimate one because it is concerned with the being of the person and with the sort of meaning which, if it should fail, all else loses its value.

In *The Sources of Religious Insight* (1912),[33] Royce came to define a 'religion of loyalty' which he saw as overcoming the tension between morality and religion. Unlike those who confuse the two under the vague heading of 'values' or who suppose that one can be reduced to the other, Royce insisted that the moral and religious demands are distinct even if closely enough related to contend with each other. Morality bids us to search for a principle of conduct and thus to determine what we are to do. Religion for Royce has a different focus. On the one hand it says that there is some one highest end of existence, a goal or chief good for man, and, on the other, it insists that man, by nature is in danger of failing to attain this good and that the meaning of salvation is precisely to be saved from this danger. The tension between the two develops from both sides. Those for whom morality is enough may try to substitute it for religion, firm in the belief that no religious need exists or, if it does, that it can be overcome by moral striving. The religious man, on the other hand, regards this outlook as 'mere moralism' and may even come to feel so secure in his faith that he sees himself as standing beyond the moral demand. The issue is, as Royce well understood, whether we stand in need of help from a power beyond ourselves or whether our own moral activity will suffice. Royce sought for a form of spiritual life in which this issue might be resolved, and he began by asking whether there exists a kind of morality which is essentially religious in that the conflict between duty and faith is overcome.

The concern of morality is with what I am to do and the principle determining my will. Recognizing that neither from myself nor from social experience can I find a formula which dictates my action, Royce offered a revised version of Kant's principle: '*So act as never to have reason to regret the principle of your action.*'[34] In short, the individual should act so as never to have ground for saying that the choice he made thwarted his own will. The problem is, where is such a principle to be found and how is the natural man able to abide by such a counsel of perfection? Royce found the answers in what he called the life of loyalty and devotion to a cause. Whether it be an obscure lighthouse keeper dedicated to the saving of lives, a mother sacrificing her own comfort for the good of her offspring, a martyr, or a life of devotion to science, it was Royce's contention that one and the same spirit of loyalty to our common good is manifested in all these lives. The loyal have strength of character and a will of their own; they also have a strong sense of the social value of what they do. Most important, however, in Royce's view, is the constancy of their motive, their love, and their sense that they have a peculiar grace, a talent which seems not to belong to them as one possession among others. This grace Royce identified with the *cause* they serve, whether it be called 'science', 'the truth', 'God's will' or 'mankind'. For Royce, a cause is a singular sort of reality in the sense that it is a 'real spiritual unity' which binds many distinct lives into one and is essentially superhuman in character. Loyalty to this unity is no mere sentiment because it is a *practical* devotion requiring service. Royce's central idea is that the one who loves the cause will never regard his or her loyalty as mere morality; it will also be essentially a religion since the cause is the finding of an object that comes from without, like a source of grace. It is more accurate to say not that one finds the cause, but that one is found by the cause; the cause is a religious object and on this account Royce could claim that true loyalty is 'a complete synthesis of the moral and religious interests'.[35] This concept of loyalty was to serve as a foundation for Royce's reinterpretation of Christianity in his last comprehensive work, *The Problem of Christianity* (1913).[36]

This work contains some new ideas, notably the theory of interpretation for which Royce acknowledged his indebtedness to C. S. Peirce, and a fully explicit doctrine of community as the ultimate form of life. Near the end of his career, Royce claimed that the community theme had been central for his thought from the outset, but this contention has given interpreters some pause. It is true that Royce had written much earlier about the inescapably social character of self-consciousness and about the spirit of loyalty which is at the root of the community doctrine. The continuity, nevertheless, is not so evident as Royce would have it. To begin with, the process of interpretation so central to the theory of community was not introduced prior to the

Problem and, in addition, there is now an emphasis on time and history not noticeable before, plus a focusing on specific Christian ideas as compared with the previous treatment of religion in a generic sense. In fact, what constitutes the 'problem' of Christianity is precisely the difficulty it encounters in making intelligible to the modern man certain articles of faith which can neither be surrendered nor dissolved into some moral or aesthetic form. Religion, for Royce, includes insight and consequently he insisted on the question: 'How can the modern man be "in creed" a Christian?' On this head, Royce chided James by saying that while James was interested mainly in the usefulness of religion, he was left to deal with the problem of its truth!

The outline of the *Problem* is as clear as its development. Royce assumed the role of interpreter as illustrated by a person who can understand both French and English and therefore can effect communication between two other persons each of whom can understand only one of these languages. Royce defined himself as neither an apologist for the religious cause nor a hostile critic. Instead he saw himself as a mediator in a quite specific sense. On the one side there is the Christian tradition as represented by what Royce called its three essential ideas – the religious community or church, sin and atonement – and on the other is the critical modern mind which either no longer understands these ideas or regards them as outmoded in a scientific era. Royce's task, then, was to create a community of understanding between the religious tradition and the modern man, first, by reinterpreting the essential ideas in an experiential and philosophical mode, and, second, by relating them to a theory of the real world.[37]

Important as the teachings attributed to Jesus are (and Royce depended heavily on his preaching about the Kingdom of God), Christianity, as Royce rightly pointed out, has never appeared simply as the religion taught by the Master, and for at least two reasons. First, it was necessary for those who accepted Jesus to interpret his life, death and transcendence of death in terms of some doctrine concerning his mission, and second, the full cycle of his life and being could be known only to those who, like St Paul, came afterward and were thus in a position to fathom the divine meaning of that life taken as a whole. With this justification of the Pauline theology as a background, Royce set out to develop the three essential theological ideas upon which his interpretation rests.

Jesus, to begin with, had singled out the two supreme objects of love – God and the neighbour. Love to God in purity of heart forms the religious substance, and love to the neighbour the moral substance. To these two, Royce claimed, St Paul added a third object, namely, the Christian community itself as the living spiritual unity of all the devoted selves. The neighbour is now seen as the one beloved of God and as a member of the same community of love which binds together all the members. If love to the neighbour is to pass beyond feeling, sentiment, and 'good intentions', an individual must know his neighbour with a measure of the insight through which God knows him. And, Royce believed, this insight is possible only within the relations existing in the Beloved Community. The religious or redeeming function of this Community can be understood only in relation to the other two ideas, sin, or what Royce called 'the moral burden of the individual', and the doctrine of atonement.

His treatment of the moral burden is one of Royce's most original contributions to the philosophy of religion. Starting with the Christian conviction that the natural man, man in existence, carries within him a flaw from which he needs to be delivered, Royce sought to approach the problem of transcending the sterile polemics of the 'humanists' for whom any doctrine of corruption is a slander against man, and of orthodox theologians who not only insisted on such a doctrine, but claimed that its very rejection is itself an evidence of its truth! Royce avoided the dispute based on generalizations about human conduct and cited St Paul's statement from Romans 7, 'Howbeit, I had not known sin, but for the law?' which raises the problem to a new level. It is our *consciousness* of our conduct which is the main concern and Royce set out to show how this comes about. Relying on his social theory of the self – that we come to our self-consciousness only through being related to other selves – and his studies in social psychology, Royce held that the principle result of the individual's participation in highly integrated communities is the attainment of a high degree of self-consciousness and power of self-assertiveness. Social existence leads men to say, 'Not thy will, but mine be done', so that the law in the individual collides with the social will. In order to sustain itself in the face of this rebelliousness, the social will asserts itself with authority, and the consequent restraint leads the individual to see his fellows, not as neighbours and brothers, but as enemies. The individual, though forced to submit, does so against his will and while he may have respect for the law that restrains him, he has no *love* for it. The outcome is a divided consciousness which Royce identified as the state St Paul found himself in when he cried, 'O, wretched man that I am.' This situation is, said Royce, 'no mishap of my private fortune', but belongs to the structure of human existence and defines the plight of the natural man, a predicament from which there is no escape with purely human resources.

The problem here presented is to find its resolution in the form of love that pervades the Beloved Community, but how this triumph is brought about cannot be understood apart from the notions of guilt and atonement. By extending the idea of sin to cover overt and wilful acts which a person knows contradict his own perception of what is right, Royce was able to introduce the crucial factor of guilt. What is a man to say to himself when confronted with the deed done which ought not to have been done? The only escape from the predicament as it appeared to Royce from the Gospel record is to accept and follow the 'road to repentance'. Repentance, however, is not sufficient; as Royce noted, another factor is required and it is one which Jesus' contemporaries regarded as quite mysterious, namely the power to *forgive* sin. Repentance together with the resolve to do better in the future make their own contribution, but of themselves they do not deal with the sin itself which is not undone. Forgiveness in some form becomes essential. To retain his status as a moral agent in this situation, Royce argued, a person must somehow *participate* in the divine judgment passed upon man's sin and not find that it comes merely in the form of an alien condemnation by a divine despot. In this regard Royce was anticipating the fine point made later by Paul Tillich when he declared that 'we cannot be obedient to the commands of a stranger, even if he is called God'. Royce's solution to the problem is to have the agent acknowledge the need to judge himself consistently; in recognizing responsibility for the deed for which we cannot forgive ourselves, we at the same time condemn ourselves to what Royce called 'the hell of the irrevocable'. The disloyalty or disobedience to the law is a fact and, although our consciousness may come to alter, the disloyalty remains. As Royce rightly saw, the doctrine of Atonement is addressed to man at this point.

According to Royce, two transformations are necessary; the disloyalty itself which cannot be undone must receive a new meaning, and the consciousness of the sinner must be changed. Eschewing both the traditional penal theory of atonement which concentrated exclusively on the act of disloyalty, and the so-called moral theories which focused solely on the consciousness of the sinner, Royce sought to recover the Pauline theology at this point in the belief that it does justice to both sides at once. Through the wilful deed the sinner has alienated himself from the Kingdom of God. The question is, can this Kingdom or Community be re-established in such a way that the sinner is again brought within it, being at once reconciled with himself and with the spirit of the Community he has broken? The answer is yes; the work of the Suffering Servant accomplishes the deed by having the power to found the Beloved Community on the far side of man's disloyalty. The wilful act is forgiven from beyond man's consciousness and thus is no longer existent as a brute fact; man sees the condemnation as just because it is precisely the judgment he has already made upon himself. Both of the necessary transformations are effected. We have here yet another version of the ancient *felix culpa* doctrine; the Community of love which Christ alone can bring into being is a new reality which the act of treason has made both possible and necessary. The world is now better than it would have been had the treasonable act never taken place.

Royce's analysis of the nature of community is one of his original contributions to philosophy; he applied it most effectively for an understanding of the religious community in particular. The central religious idea is that God's redeeming power becomes manifest in and through the spiritual Community which Christ founded; it is a mirror in human history of the vision of the Kingdom of God wherein the divine love triumphs over individual wilfulness. To show the true nature of that Community, Royce availed himself of much that C. S. Peirce had written about the nature of signs and the process of interpretation, and also of his own theory of the self as a purposeful life wherein the present self is continually interpreting the past self to the future self. According to that theory, the self is never an object of perception, nor is it ever as such a datum; instead it is an interpretative unity extending over time and governed by a dominant purpose or life-plan – what the person *means* to be. Through memory and anticipation, the self has the ability to extend and identify itself with traditions stemming from the past and with causes which define a hoped-for future. The ability to extend our selves and our capacity for interpreting signs which makes possible a community of understanding between persons otherwise distinct in space and time, lie at the root of what Royce called communities of interpretation – a spiritual unity of many members. A community is thus a well-ordered togetherness of distinct individuals who have come to regard as belonging to their own lives and history a *common* memory and a *common* hope. Binding all together is the faith that every other member is related to the same *third* reality to which he or she is related, and the members are related to each other in turn because of this common faith. The third reality is that of the Spirit, the living power uniting the many into a one, while the members as such remain individually distinct. There is to be, Royce insisted, no mystical blending of selves precisely because the unity of their life is rooted in the *relations* of faith in which they stand. There can be no community without distinct individuals. On the other hand, Royce was correct in his insistence that it makes no sense to speak of a community as the 'sum' of these individuals; it is even doubtful whether a crowd or a mob, neither of which is a genuine community, can be described in this way. Community is a distinct level of being which exists in the *relations* – the actual, meaningful and purposive links – binding the many selves into a spiritual unity. It is indeed ironic that philosophers like Russell, thinking under the shadow of Hegel and Bradley, should have declared that for 'idealists' relations are regarded as 'unreal', whereas for Royce they are as real as the individuals they connect.

In the case of the Beloved Community, the mediating reality is complex. There is first the memory of the teachings, the life, death and resurrection of Christ and each individual makes that past a part of his or her own life; secondly, there is the anticipation of the cause of salvation, being reconciled with God, or the cause for which that Community was brought into being. The anticipation or hope is incorporated by faith into the life of each member and thus all members have in common, regardless of other differences between them, their devotion to the same past tradition and the same future hope. In this Community the tragic circle of sin is broken by the power of the Redeeming Person who alone was able to establish the reconciliation of God and man.

Whatever view one may take of this attempt to reinterpret an ancient theological tradition, it should be clear that Santayana, Royce's illustrious student, was wide of the mark when he criticized his mentor for offering to his generation a kind of idealist substitute for a religion they could no longer in a scientific age accept. As Reinhold Niebuhr pointed out some decades ago, no one who is trying to make religion 'palatable' to the self-assured, technological man would be well advised to start out by insisting on the concept of sin! Royce was somewhat unique, at least among the philosophers of his time, first, in his refusal to reduce the religious to the moral, and, secondly, in his unwillingness to follow the lead of the so-called 'liberal' theology which subordinated the insights of Paul to the 'religion of Jesus' understood almost exclusively in terms of the Old Testament prophetic tradition.

The thought of James and Royce on the subject of religion can be most profitably and succinctly compared on three heads – the role to be played by conceptual thought, the relations between the individual and social factors, and the idea of God. It is clear that Royce was committed not only to the elucidation of basic theological doctrines but to reinterpreting them with the resources of an idealist metaphysics. James, on the other hand, repeatedly insisted on 'feeling' as the deeper source of religion with the consequence that articulation was invariably turned by him into something secondary and derivative. This result was dependent partly on James' uncertainty about assigning to the conceptual order a definite cognitive role of its own, but perhaps more decisively on his belief that religious and metaphysical doctrines are basically living *options* proposed to the believing will of the individual so that their validity can never be independent of their consequences in integrating and sustaining a significant life for the one who adopts and embodies them. By contrast, Royce found, for all of his emphasis on the will, essentially 'practical' solutions inadequate and demanded that religious insight be related to a metaphysical theory of reality. Royce could not accept, in the phrase used by W. E. Hocking to describe James' approach, 'the retirement of the intellect'.

The contrast between the two is equally sharp when one considers the relation between the individual and the social in the religious situation. James focused exclusively on the individual; for him religion is found in the depths of the self or what he called the 'unique pinch of destiny' felt by every person. The sort of religious phenomena cited in the *Varieties* and derived from diaries, autobiographies, confessions, meditations and the like, serve to underline the point. Whenever James mentioned the social expression of religion he had in mind so-called 'organized religion' with the implication that it is necessarily a falling away from the genuine article, a dissolution of religion into something 'second-hand'. Royce stood poles apart from such a view. Not only did he hold that individual self-consciousness is dependent on social contrasts, but that community and the working togetherness of many selves is the deepest and richest form of life. For him the existence of a religious community of some sort is the most pervasive fact disclosed by the history of religion. But it is important to notice that by community Royce did not mean the institution and its organization no matter how necessary they may be. He meant the bond of unifying love and the cause to which the members are committed, the 'city out of sight'. Royce frequently referred to the isolated individual as the 'lost' individual and repeatedly pointed to the biblical emphasis on bringing such an individual back into a community of love.

As regards the concept of God, the comparison between James and Royce is more complex. James made a break with the classical Theistic position, whereas Royce sought to maintain it on a new metaphysical basis. We have seen that James rejected the God represented by the attributes of traditional metaphysical theology; his aim was to arrive at a new conception of the divine based on experiences of a religious sort and consistent with his vision of a developing cosmos in which there is always 'more to come'.

James' universe was, in the end, a pluralistic one, filled with contingencies and open ends, a mixture of good and evil. The God he envisaged is a 'finite' reality, a Power seeking to improve the world but still limited by the existence of evil. According to what James called his 'piecemeal supernaturalism', God's power must be manifest at particular points in human life and the world's history, notably in the actual transformation of divided selves. For James, God is not to be thought of as a cosmic spectator who knows all but whose reality makes no 'difference' in the world's life and simply leaves everything where it was before. By contrast, Royce leaned most definitely in the direction of monism, even if his latest writings placed a new emphasis on time and history and less on the Absolute as an 'ocean of Being'. Royce could accept no 'finite' God, as his attempts to resolve the problem of evil show. He saw God as the Absolute Self who, like the God of Augustine, knows us in our truth and has a conspectus on our lives as a whole which is the consistent outcome of our being the unique expression of the divine will. This view, of course, raises problems about the reality of finite freedom which James, with his unfinished universe, did not have to face. Royce's conception of God can be seen as an original construing of a theological tradition that goes back to classical Augustinianism; James' view, on the other hand, has no such roots, but is rather the expression of his own reflection and his experience of life on the American scene. For James, to believe in God is the ultimate risk, whereas for Royce it is the acknowledgment of a reality which cannot *not* be.

Notes

1 *The Principles of Psychology* (2 vols., New York, 1890).
2 In *The Will to Believe and Other Essays in Popular Philosophy* (New York & London, 1897), pp. 63–110. This is a composite essay; the first third consists of extracts from an article which was published in *Mind* (July, 1879) and the remainder is an address published in the *Princeton Review* (July, 1882).
3 'Sentiment', p. 70.
4 'Sentiment', p. 72.
5 'Sentiment', p. 77.
6 'Sentiment', p. 82.
7 'Sentiment', p. 96.
8 'Sentiment', p. 97.
9 In *The Will to Believe*, pp. 111–44.
10 First printed in the *University Chronicle*, 1 (September, 1898), pp. 287–310, Berkeley, California. Reprinted in *Pragmatism*, Works of William James, vol. 1 (Cambridge Mass. & London, 1975), pp. 257–70.
11 'Reflex Action', pp. 115–16.
12 'The Will to Believe', in *The Will to Believe*, pp. 1–31.
13 *The Varieties of Religious Experience* (New York & London, 1902); references are to the Modern Library Edition.
14 *Varieties*, p. 493.
15 *Varieties*, p. 476.
16 *Varieties*, p. 492.
17 *Varieties*, p. 494.
18 *Varieties*, p. 500.
19 *Ibid.*, n. 1.
20 *Varieties*, p. 502.

21 *Varieties*, p. 503.

22 *Varieties*, p. 505.

23 *The Religious Aspect of Philosophy* (Boston, 1885); references are to the sixth edition of 1895.

24 *Religious Aspect*, p. 3.

25 *Religious Aspect*, p. 4.

26 *The World and the Individual* (New York & London, vol. 1, 1899; vol. 2, 1901).

27 *The Spirit of Modern Philosophy* (Boston & New York, 1892); references are to the ninth edition, 1897. Royce was an advocate of proof in philosophy and he repudiated idealisms based on 'moral enthusiasm' as compared with his own position which he regarded as the result of a 'rigid logical analysis'. A good illustration is found in his use of the logic of interpretation for defining the structure of the religious community.

28 *Religious Aspect*, p. 441.

29 *The Conception of God* (New York & London, 1897).

30 It is somewhat unclear as to whether he still held to this distinction in his last sustained work, *The Problem of Christianity*. One could argue that the theory of 'interpretation' introduced in that work is a more precise form of appreciation because interpretation, as distinct from the perceiving and conceiving most appropriate for the description and knowledge of objects, is peculiarly adapted to the way in which selves know and communicate with each other.

31 *Spirit*, p. 460; italics in original.

32 See *The Philosophy of Loyalty* (New York, 1908).

33 *The Sources of Religious Insight* (New York, 1912); this book represents the Bross Lectures for 1911.

34 *Sources*, p. 189; italics in original.

35 *Sources*, p. 206.

36 *The Problem of Christianity* (New York, 1913, 2 vols.; reprinted in one volume with Introduction by John E. Smith, Chicago & London, 1968).

37 It needs to be pointed out that Royce was much criticized for neglecting the Founder of Christianity, by which was meant that he failed to give what in classical theology was called a doctrine of the Person of Christ. I do not agree entirely with these critics, especially in view of the role assigned to Christ as the only possible founder of the Beloved Community, but the issue is complicated and cannot be resolved here. Two points, however, should be stressed; first, Royce had a greater acquaintance with theology than most philosophers of his time, and, second, he never made what is now commonly regarded as the mistake of opposing some simple conception of the 'religion of Jesus' based on biblical sayings to the 'theology of Paul' as if the latter were merely a secondary accretion of little significance as compared with parables and beatitudes.

Bibliographical essay

These bibliographical notes are meant to furnish the reader with three distinct sets of information. First, there is a list of those original works of James and Royce quoted or referred to in the essay and a standard citation for each, following the edition or printing I have used. The reader is reminded that publishers do not always distinguish between an 'edition' and a 'reprint'; I have followed the publishers' designations on the title page, e.g., 'Ninth Edition' even if, in fact the volume is a reprinting of the original without alterations. Second, I direct the reader to bibliographies containing a complete listing of the writings of these two thinkers, insofar as any such list can be called complete. Third, there is a selection of books about James and Royce with annotation and critical commentary.

JOHN E. SMITH

I. Works cited

William James
The Principles of Psychology (2 vols., New York, 1890; reprinted New York, 1950), two
   volumes bound as one.
   'The Sentiment of Rationality' in *The Will to Believe and Other Essays in Popular
   Philosophy* (New York & London, 1897); reprinted in *The Works of William James*, vol.
   6, *The Will to Believe*, Frederick H. Burkhardt, general editor (Cambridge, Mass. &
   London, 1979), pp. 32–64.
   'The Will to Believe' in *The Will to Believe*; reprinted in *The Works of William James*, vol. 6,
   pp. 13–33.
   'Reflex Action and Theism' in *The Will to Believe*; reprinted in *The Works of William
   James*, vol. 6, pp. 90–113.
   The Varieties of Religious Experience (Gifford Lectures) (New York & London, 1902);
   references are to the modern Library Edition, n.d.
   Pragmatism (New York, 1907); reprinted in *The Works of William James*, vol. 1, 1975.
Josiah Royce
The Religious Aspect of Philosophy (Boston, 1885); references are to the sixth edition, 1895.
   The Spirit of Modern Philosophy (Boston & New York, 1892); references are to the ninth
   edition, 1897.
   The Conception of God (New York & London, 1897); this edition is an expanded version of
   the original published in 1895 by the Philosophical Union of the University of California
   as 'Bulletin no. 15'.
   The World and the Individual (Gifford Lectures) (New York & London, vol. 1, 1899; vol. 2,
   1901); reprinted with an Introduction by John E. Smith (New York, 1959).
   The Philosophy of Loyalty (New York, 1908).
   The Sources of Religious Insight (New York, 1912).
   The Problem of Christianity (2 vols., New York, 1913); reprinted in one volume with an
   Introduction by John E. Smith (Chicago & London, 1968).

II. Bibliographies of primary works

William James
The most complete single bibliography of the writings of William James is to be found in *The
Writings of William James*, edited, with an Introduction by John J. McDermott (New York,
1967), pp. 811–58. This bibliography is based on a list of James' writings as prepared by
Henry James, Jr. and Edwin B. Holt published in 1911 and which was brought up to 1920 by
Ralph Barton Perry. Addenda provided by Ralph Barton Perry, III brought the list up to
1950, and McDermott writes in a Prefatory Note, 'Some slight further corrections and
additional material to 1967 have been integrated by the present editor' (p. 812). The
bibliography in McDermott includes those works of James published after his death in 1910.
A definitive edition, *The Works of William James* is currently being prepared under the
general editorship of Frederick H. Burkhardt in collaboration with Fredson Bowers and Ignas
Skrupskelis. To date ten volumes have been published: *Pragmatism; The Meaning of Truth;
Essays in Radical Empiricism; A Pluralistic Universe; Essays in Philosophy; The Will to Believe;
Some Problems of Philosophy; Principles of Psychology* (3 vols.).
Josiah Royce
The reader is advised to consult 'An Annotated Bibliography of the Publications of Josiah
Royce', prepared by Ignas Skrupskelis and to be found in *The Basic Writings of Josiah Royce*,
edited with an Introduction by John J. McDermott (Chicago & London, 1969), vol. 2, pp.
1167–1226. I entirely agree with the judgment of McDermott that this work is 'outstanding'

346

and that it 'comes as close to being definitive as is humanly possible'. Skrupskelis also calls attention to the bibliographies of Benjamin Rand, James Harry Cotton, Karl-Theo. Humbach, Frank M. Oppenheim and Andre A. Devaux; his comments on the special features of these bibliographies are very helpful; see pp. 1168–9. *The Letters of Josiah Royce*, edited with an Introduction by John Clendenning, (Chicago & London, 1970). This large collection of substantial letters spanning the period from 1875 to 1916 is enormously valuable and throws some light upon just about every aspect of Royce's life and thought. The editor has provided an excellent Introduction as well as annotations that are indispensable. In addition, there is an Appendix in which those to whom Royce wrote are identified and another containing a list of other letters (and their locations) which the editor inspected but did not include in the edition.

III. Works about the philosophies of James and Royce

William James

Ralph Barton Perry, *The Thought and Character of William James* (2 vols., Boston, 1935). This Pulitzer Prize-winning classic is indispensable for the student of James. In addition to being a storehouse of information about James' life and career, especially through his letters, the book offers an intellectual portrait of the man and the development of – including the many reactions to – his thought. Perry, being a philosopher in his own right, was firmly wedded to the views of the 'New Realists' in America, a fact that left him less free to interpret the several aspects of James' thought than he realized. He underestimated the extent to which James' conception of experience was in fact a critique of classical British empiricism. The edge of this critique is found in James' claim that the older empiricism gave primacy to the atomic fact in experience while ignoring the connections and transitions equally present.

Ralph Barton Perry, *In the Spirit of William James* (New Haven, Conn., 1938); reprinted Bloomington, 1967. While the bulk of this book is devoted to concise accounts of James' theory of knowledge, metaphysics of experience, moral outlook and conception of faith, the opening chapter, 'Two American Philosophers' is a brilliant set of comparisons, based on personal acquaintance as well as reading, between the thought and character of James and Royce. Perry shows in a convincing way how each 'idealized his opposite'. Royce, born on the Western frontier where individuals had to make their own way, placed the community and social experience in the centre of his conception of reality. James who inherited the best traditions of American and European society and was thoroughly at home in both, never ceased to praise individual initiative, freedom and uniqueness. A similar inverse relation appears with regard to their background as Americans. Royce had the experience of pioneer America, but his philosophy was deeply rooted in European thought. James' intellectual inheritance was all British and Continental, but, along with Charles Peirce, he succeeded in developing an indigenous American philosophy in the shape of Pragmatism. Perry, in my view, went astray in his assumption that Royce believed that any cause is admissible as long as it evokes devotion.

John Wild, *The Radical Empiricism of William James* (Garden City, N.Y., 1969). A unique, well-documented, critical and zestfully written book. It is unique in that, as the author tells us, after his becoming interested in phenomenology and existential thinking through study with Heidegger, and after discovering that Husserl was deeply engaged in reading James' *Principles*, he himself was led to an intensive study of that work. As a result he ceased to think of phenomenology as an exclusively European movement and saw in James' approach through the analysis of lived experience an American counterpart to the new European mode of thinking. Drawing on the *Principles*, James' other major works and especially the *Essays in Radical Empiricism*, Wild presents, or, better, allows James to present himself as a master of conveying to a reader the patterns inherent in the phenomena of personal life and the life-

347

world in which it unfolds. The bibliography (pp. 418–20) contains items on Continental philosophy relevant to James not to be found in other bibliographies.

Josiah Royce, *William James and Other Essays on the Philosophy of Life* (New York, 1912). The title essay is an illuminating treatment, by his long-time colleague and friend, of James as a 'representative thinker' on the American scene where Royce has him join company with Jonathan Edwards and Ralph Waldo Emerson as his predecessors in the role of interpreting American life and experience. Royce emphasized the originality of James and the centrality of his concern for morality and human destiny.

George Santayana, *Character and Opinion in the United States* (New York, 1921). Although somewhat informal in approach and focused on the personalities involved, this account by another of James' colleagues at Harvard serves to underline the role played by James' vision of the 'strenuous life' in contrast to Santayana's decidedly esthetic perception of the shape of things.

J. S. Bixler, *Religion in the Philosophy of William James* (Boston, 1926). Despite its age, this study continues to be among the best that has been written on a topic of the greatest interest to James throughout his life and thought.

Andrew J. Reck, *Introduction to William James* (Bloomington, Ill., 1967). Very useful as an initial approach to James and supplemented by several texts expressing his basic ideas.

Gay Wilson Allen, *William James, a Biography* (New York, 1967). This is an excellent biography, imaginative, well-documented and engaging in its style. I believe the author correctly perceives the differences between his work and that of Perry. In addition to having more information at his disposal, especially concerning the important role played by Mrs James, Allen aims at showing the interconnections between James as a developing person and his intellectual life. By contrast, Perry's study was not meant, as Allen points out, to be a biography, but an analysis of James' ideas in which his personal life was subordinated to his professional career. Allen's biography redresses the balance by painting an integrated portrait in which we see the connection between temperament and philosophy in James' own case.

Josiah Royce

John E. Smith, *Royce's Social Infinite* (New York, 1950); reprinted Hamden, 1969. Primarily focused on the theory of interpretation and community, this book seeks to show the bearing of that theory on Royce's later philosophy of religion. Royce's acknowledged dependence on Peirce's theory of triadic relations and interpretation is discussed along with the original use Royce made of these ideas in his reinterpretation of the three central Christian ideas – the Church or Beloved Community, the moral burden of the individual and the idea of atonement. It is interesting to note that prior to this study very little attention had been paid to the topics it treats and in addition Royce's thought as a whole was overshadowed both by the development of Pragmatism and the new versions of positivism stemming from both England and the Continent. In the intervening decades the balance has been redressed and Royce has since become the object of extensive study.

Bruce Kuklick, *Josiah Royce, An Intellectual Portrait* (Indianapolis & New York, 1972). An important book for understanding Royce's thought since no other study offers so extensive an account of his excursions into logic and the foundations of mathematics together with his attempts to use these ideas in the articulation of his metaphysical system. The author calls the book an 'exercise in the logic of the history of ideas'. He presents Royce as a serious and logical thinker in a philosophical climate not particularly hospitable to either religion or metaphysics. For all that is to be learned from this book, and there is much, its aim seems to me misguided. It makes no sense to suggest, as Kuklick does, that religion was for Royce no more than an area for the display of logical ingenuity, as indeed it is for some philosophers at present. Royce's concern for the religious dimension of life was both genuine and profound; his philosophy cannot be understood without taking it into account. The problem is that Kuklick is on very unfamiliar ground when it comes to the religious and theological notions Royce was discussing. In the final chapter, 'The Absolute and the Community', dealing with Royce's analysis of the basic Christian ideas, Kuklick's logical interests far outdistance his theological knowledge so that, to take but one example, he seems never to have heard of the traditional *felix culpa* doctrine of which Royce's interpretation is a modern example.

Frank M. Oppenheim, *Royce's Voyage Down Under* (Lexington, 1980). An extremely interesting and thought-provoking account of Royce's thinking during a voyage he took around the world in 1888 in order to recover his health. Oppenheim seeks to relate complex insights concerning community and loyalty attained by Royce during his trip to the overall growth of his thought. Upon encountering the civilization of Australia, Royce became engaged in social and political issues and, as the author rightly says, '. . . only in his Australasian writings did Royce allow himself any major expression of his socio-political views'. The truth is that, although Royce had a philosophically sophisticated theory of human community, he cannot be regarded as having a social and political philosophy of any great significance.

James Harry Cotton, *Royce on the Human Self* (Cambridge, Mass., 1954). An illuminating attempt to construe the unity of Royce's thought in terms of his conception of the self. The author makes use of numerous unpublished papers and lectures, a partial listing of which is contained in the Bibliography. The latter also includes a number of important periodical articles by and about Royce.

Peter Fuss, *The Moral Philosophy of Josiah Royce* (Cambridge, Mass., 1965). A careful and insightful treatment of this important topic, with attention to the growth of Royce's position and especially to some psychological and epistemological ideas that helped to shape his ethics.

INDEX

Index

influence on Newman, 91–2, 99–101; radical, 255, 256, 260, 316
'Encounter', theologies of, 244
encyclicals relating to Modernist movement, 147–8, 172; *Pascendi dominici gregis*, 141–2, 144, 148, 149, 156, 159, 160, 170, 171
Engert, Thaddäus, 171
Enlightenment, 31, 39, 114
Erigena, John Scotus, 2, 113
Essays and Reviews, 14, 83, 232, 235, 244
Eucken, Rudolf, 160
evangelicalism, 7, 72, 88, 92, 94, 97; in U.S.A., 56
evidence-theology, 1, 13, 15, 16, 83, 95, 256–7
evil, problem of: British idealists and, 294, 296, 299, 304, 310; Coleridge and, 2, 17–18; Dostoevsky and, 189–90, 204; Royce and, 329–30, 331–2; Solovyov and, 216–17
evolutionism, 231, 245, 246, 255, 282; *see also* development; progress
Ewing, A. C., 271, 294, 298
existentialism, 102, 255
experience: agnostics' restrictive account of, 257; British idealists and ideas of, 293, 295, 298; 'given' element of, 284–5; linguistic philosophy and notions of, 258, 259, 260; Royce's account of, 330

Faber, Frederick William, 78
faith, 255, 302, 306; in Russian religious thought, 182–3, 199–200; *see also under* Coleridge; James
Fall, doctrine of, 183, 211, 212
Fathers, Church, patristic period, 43, 76, 77, 83, 96, 135, 212
feeling, religious, 7, 24, 95, 151, 152, 324, 342
Feidelson, Charles N., 64
feminism, 59
Fenallosa, Ernest, 63
Fénelon, François, 88, 124
Ferrier, James Frederick, 274–5
Feuerbach, Ludwig, 23
Fichte, J. G., 2, 4, 46, 47, 56, 114, 125, 179, 328
filioque, 181
Findlay, J. N., 272
finite individuality, distinctness of persons, 285, 290, 295, 296, 297, 298, 299, 307; Royce's theory of relation of finite selves to World-Self, 331–5
First World War, effect on course of philosophy, 272–3, 283, 291
Fitzpatrick, John Bernard, 56
Flew, Antony, 232, 243, 261
Florovsky, Georges, 206, 207, 208
Fogazzaro, Antonio, 169
Forsyth, P. T., 1
France, French, 2, 86, 113, 167, 169, 180, 218

freedom, human: British idealists' thinking on, 289–91, 295–6, 297–8; Dostoevsky's philosophy of tragic, 188–91, 196; Emerson and, 44, 45; Royce and, 330, 335; William James and, 316, 330
Frothingham, Octavius Brooks, 52, 57
Froude, Hurrell, 78, 81, 83, 85
Froude, James Anthony, 70, 88
Fruitlands communal experiment, U.S.A., 56, 61
Fuller, Margaret, 51, 58–60, 63; *Women in the Nineteenth Century*, 59
future-orientation, 187, 188–9, 190, 193, 194, 195, 203, 204, 205, 206, 207
Fyodorov, Nikolai Fyodorovich (1828–1903), 180, 204–8, 216, 218; attack on future-orientation and Western ideas of progress, 205, 207; concept of life, 207; ethical position, 206; and Nietzsche, 205–6, 207; obsession with task of vanquishing death, 204, 205, 206–7; project of 'spiritualization' of the cosmos, 207–8, 217

Gallarati-Scotti, Tommaso, 169
Galton, Francis, 237
Gandhi, M. K. ('Mahatma'), 54
Geach, Peter, 310
Germany, 290; influence of philosophy of, 4, 7, 35, 182; biblical scholarship, 147, 159, 171; Roman Catholic Modernism in, 144–5, 170–1; Romanticism, 59, 180, 183; *see also* Tübingen
Gibson, A. Boyce, 187
Gioberti, Vicenzo, 56
Gladstone, William Ewart, 84
gnosticism, 57, 62, 64; Gnostics, 122
Goethe, Johann W. von, 22, 43, 45, 46, 59
Goetz, Frederick, 214–15
Gore, Charles, 232
Gorky, Maxim, 198, 199
Görres, J. J. von, 114
Gratry, Alphonse, 146, 167
Greek philosophy, 37, 167, 284
Green, Thomas Hill (1836–1882), 232, 281–91, 296, 300–3; account of 'given' element in experience, 284–5; attitude to religion, 257, 300–3; and Eternal Spiritual Principle, 282–3, 284, 285, 303; idea of history and progress, 282–4; importance for idealist philosophy, 275, 286, 291; influence of Kant and Hegel on, 276, 280, 281–2, 286, 287; *Prolegomena to Ethics*, 273, 276; social and political theory, 289, 290–1; stand on moral questions, 286–9; and theory of relations, 285, 291; view of self as centre of unification, and distinctness of persons, 282, 285, 286, 290

Hamilton, Sir William, 233, 234, 235, 245; philosophy of the Unconditioned, 238–40

Index

Hare, Julius, 1
Harnack, Adolf, 153, 154
Harris, Errol, 271
Harrison, Frederic, 233, 246, 247
Hazlitt, William, 274
Hecker, Isaac, 44, 56
Hedge, Frederic Henry, 31, 51, 63
Hefele, Karl Joseph, 112, 113, 114, 136
Hegel, G. W. F., Hegelianism, 2, 22, 111, 114,
179, 181, 317, 342; British Hegelians, 155,
239; and British idealism, 272, 275, 276, 281,
282, 287, 297, 298–9, 307; Coleridge and, 5,
13; Emerson and, 38, 47–8; Royce and, 330;
and Russian thought, 181–2, 189, 203, 210,
212
Hepburn, Ronald, 242, 261
Herbst, Johann Georg, 112, 114, 136
Herder, J. F., 46
Hinduism, 75, 324; and idealist philosophy,
274, 297
Hirscher, Johann Baptist von, 112, 113, 114,
136
historical science, historical criticism: attack on
orthodox Christian belief, 235–6, 247, 249,
250; challenge to traditional Catholic
teaching, 141, 146–7, 149–50, 151, 153, 156–
8, 159, 169, 171–2
history: Emerson's conception of, 45, 48;
Green's view of, 282–4; Leontyev's theory of,
195; Slavophile philosophy of, 181–2; see also
historical science
Hobbes, Thomas, 289
Hobhouse, L. T., 291
Hochfield, George, 63
Hocking, W. E., 343
Hodgson, W. E., 252
Holland, Bernard, 158
Holtzmann, H. J., 159
Hook, W. F., 74, 81
Hooker, J. D., 247
Hooker, Richard, 86, 87, 88, 97
Hort, F. J. A., 1, 14, 242
Hügel, Friedrich von (1852–1925), 145, 148,
158–60; dislike of immanentism, 143–4, 159;
influence on Tyrrell, 160, 161; and
reconciliation of historical criticism and
traditional faith, 158, 159; role in Modernist
movement, 158
humanism, 339; Christian, 180, 188, 196
Hume, David, 1, 3, 4, 276; influence on British
agnosticism, 234, 235, 242, 247, 248, 249,
250, 254; and Newman, 91, 95, 99, 100
Hutton, R. H., 252, 256
Huxley, Thomas Henry (1825–1895), 232, 242,
246, 247, 248, 249–52, 262; attack on
ecclesiastical establishment, 237–8; biblical
criticism, 249–50; critique of, 252, 253;

Evolution and Ethics, 255–6; influence of
Hamilton on, 234, 239; invention and
definition of term 'agnosticism', 233–5;
morality of knowledge, 251–2; as precursor of
twentieth-century analytical critics of
religion, 250

idealism, 23, 294, 296, 299, 315; Coleridge and,
4, 7, 18, 274; Emerson and, 33, 39, 46–8;
Royce and, 315, 327; see also British idealism
imagination: Coleridge's view of role of, 7, 9,
11, 35; Newman and, 95, 256
immanentism, 159, 165–7, 199, 303;
Modernism and, 142, 143, 149, 159, 165–7,
169–70, 171
immortality, 200, 307, 309
incarnation, divine-human unity, 97, 212, 242,
302, 307, 308
Index Librorum Prohibitorum, Modernist works
placed on, 144, 145, 148, 167
individualism, individuality: Coleridge's
principle of individuation, 5; Dostoevsky and,
185–7; individual freedom and accountability,
289–91, 295–6, 297–8; religion as individual
experience, 151, 152; Tolstoy and, 203; see
also finite individuality *and under* James;
Royce
Ireland: Catholics in, 71; Church of, 71
Irvine, William, 250, 257
Irving, Edward, 1
Islam, 128, 202
Italy: Margaret Fuller's visit to, 59–60;
Modernism in, 144, 168–70, 171
Ivanov, Vyacheslav, 191
Ives, Charles, 63

Jacobi, F. H., 4, 8, 125
James, William (1842–1910), 179, 248, 255,
315–27; argument for superiority of theism
over materialism, 319–20, 321; compared
with Royce, 315, 327, 342–4; concept of
God, and 'piece-meal supernaturalism', 316,
319, 320–1, 326–7, 343–4; conception of
rationality, 316–17, 319, 320; emphasis on
individuality and rejection of monism, 315,
316, 317, 324, 343; importance of element of
faith in thought of, 318–19, 322–3; influence
of psychology, 315–16, 319, 325, 326;
intellectual career, 315–16; interpretation of
religion and working of unseen world
through the subconscious, 316, 323–7;
pragmatism, 316, 317, 321, 325, 327;
psychology of belief and 'the will to believe',
13, 25, 257, 316, 318–19, 321–3; radical
empiricism, 260, 316; 'Reflex Action and
Theism', 319–20; and subordination of
intellect and theory to feeling and experience,

355

Index

Index